In the Kingdom of the Thunder Dragon

In the Kingdom of the Thunder Dragon

HAPPINESS, HISTORY, AND ENVIRONMENT IN A CHANGING BHUTAN

Betsy Bolton

ASIANetwork Books

Series Editors:
Erin McCarthy (St. Lawrence University)
Lisa Trivedi (Hamilton College)

ASIANetwork Books strives to publish high-quality, original monographs, edited collections, and translations that embody a rigorous liberal arts approach to Asian Studies. A collaboration with ASIANetwork, a consortium of Asian Studies faculty at 160 colleges, the series seeks to fill a space between works that address the critical pedagogical strategies of the Asian Studies classroom and works of specialized scholarship that engage a broad readership outside higher education. Manuscripts published in the ASIANetwork Books series, no matter how narrowly focused, are expected to raise broad questions of interest for the public and demonstrate classroom utility for Asian Studies.

Titles in the Series

Katherine Ngo, *Unlocking the Treasury: Elementary Learning for Boys in Qing China*

Kelly Ngo, *Ordering Tang China: Cultural Memory, Emperor Taizong, and the Essentials*

Vikash Yadav and Jason Kirk, *The Politics of India under Modi: An Introduction to India's Democracy, Economy, and Foreign Policy*

A complete list of titles in the series can be found at www.leverpress.org

Lever Press (leverpress.org) is a publisher of pathbreaking scholarship. Supported by a consortium of higher education institutions focused on, and renowned for, excellence in both research and teaching, our press is grounded on three essential commitments: to be a digitally native press, to be a peer-reviewed, open access press that charges no fees to either authors or their institutions, and to be a press aligned with the liberal arts ethos.

The complete manuscript of this work was subjected to a partly closed ("single blind") review process. For more information, please see our Peer Review Commitments and Guidelines at https://www.leverpress.org/peerreview

DOI: https://doi.org/10.3998/mpub.12970479
Print ISBN: 978-1-64315-082-6
Open access ISBN: 978-1-64315-083-3

Library of Congress Control Number: 2024950297

Published in the United States of America by Lever Press, in partnership with Michigan Publishing.

Table of Contents

Member Institution Acknowledgments

Lever Press is a collective effort. This work was made possible by the generous support of Lever Press member libraries from the following institutions:

Amherst College
Atlanta University Center Consortium
Berea College
Bowdoin College
Carleton College
Central Washington University
Claremont Colleges
Claremont Graduate University
Claremont McKenna College
Clark Atlanta University
College of Saint Benedict & Saint John's University
The College of Wooster
Davidson College
Denison University
DePauw University
Grinnell College
Hamilton College
Hampshire College
Harvey Mudd College
Hollins University
Iowa State University
Keck Graduate Institute
Knox College
Lafayette College
Macalester College
Middlebury College
Morehouse College
Morehouse School of Medicine
Norwich University
Occidental College
Penn State University
Pitzer College
Pomona College
Randolph-Macon College

Rollins College
Santa Clara University
Scripps College
Skidmore College
Smith College
Spelman College
Susquehanna University
Swarthmore College
Trinity University
UCLA Library
Union College
University of Delaware
University of Idaho
University of Northern Colorado
University of Puget Sound
University of Rhode Island
University of San Francisco
University of Sheffield
University of Vermont
Vassar College
Washington and Lee University
Whitman College
Whittier College
Willamette University
Williams College

List of Tables

List of Maps

List of Figures

NB: color versions of the Figures can be found in the ebook of this volume, available at: https://doi.org/10.3998/mpub.12970479.

Glossary of Bhutanese Terms

Arra	Local alcohol, fermented and/or distilled from maize (sometimes spelled ara)
Atsara	Jester, master-of-ceremonies in masked dances
Beyul	Hidden valley, a place where enlightenment is more easily obtained
Bokhari	Small wood-burning stove (pine cones are also burned), heats very quickly
Bumpa	Ritual vase with a spout, often holding holy water in temples
Chibdrel	Ceremonial procession
Chilip	Foreigner ("grey hairs")
Chimi	Representative in Bhutan's Tshogdu or National Assembly
Chhoe-sid-nyi	The "dual system" of government established by Zhabdrung
Cholwa	Wild or uncontainable

Chorten	Buddhist monument, usually round, holding offerings and prayers, symbolizing the Buddha's mind
Chuko miko dum	Closed hearth/closed water restrictions; villagers ban a household from using the village spring and refuse to enter the "exiled" household
Chuu	River
Dakini	Female embodiment of liberating energy (sometimes outstanding female Tantric practitioners, sometimes consorts of great masters). Khandro in Tibetan/Chokey
Dasho	"Excellent one"—officials who have received this honorific and a red scarf from the Druk Gyalpo, King of Bhutan
Dharma	Buddhist truth, sometimes used in the sense of faith, sometimes in the sense of reality
Doma	Betelnut, wrapped with lime paste and leaf, chewed as a stimulant; turns mouth red
Driglam	Traditional Bhutanese etiquette; a "system of harmony" including wearing Namza national dress
Drubchen	Ten-day communal meditation retreat working to counter obstructions and promote world peace
Druk	Dragon; Bhutan is Druk Yul, dragon country; the king is Druk Gyalpo
Dzong	Bhutanese fortress, now administrative buildings
Dzongdag	Royal appointees who are the chief executive officer of each dzongkhag, like a governor
Dzongka	Language of the dzongs; Bhutan's official national language

Dzongkhag	District; Bhutan is composed of twenty dzongkhags
Dzongpön	Ruler of a dzong: part of the royal cabinet under Zhabdrung's dual system of government
Dungchen	Great trumpet or Tibetan horn, sounded to accompany the chanting of religious texts
Ema datse	Hot chilis and cheese—the national dish
Ezay	Relish of chilis, tomato, onion, garlic, ginger, cilantro, and spices
Garps	Famously speedy trail runners who carried messages and mail from one dzong to the next
Garuda	A mythological bird believed to have all its wing feathers fully developed inside the egg. Sometimes seen as "enemy of snakes" (or lu/naga). Represents fearlessness, power, wisdom
Gedinche	Thanks
Geog/gewog	Block; group of villages headed by a gep
Gep	Leader, ranging from king through governor to local ruler; the four geps of Bhutan are the four kings associated with the cardinal directions, with different colors, powers, animals, etc.
Geshe	Advanced degree within Vajrayana monastic tradition, similar to a Ph.D.
Gho	Traditional men's dress in Bhutan, folded and tightly belted at the waist to create a large "pocket" at the front
Goemba	Monastery (also spelled goenba)
Goenkhang	Inner sanctum of temples, lhakhangs, from which women have traditionally been excluded
Gomchen	Lay monk (not celibate)

Gson'dre	Malevolent spirit of the living—an evil (ambitious, envious, competitive) spirit housed in the body of a living being
Gyaling	"Chinese flute"—double-reeded oboe-like instrument played during monastery rituals, associated with peaceful deities; played with circular breathing
Guru	Teacher (Guru Rinpoche: Precious Teacher, a common title for Padmasambhava, who brought Buddhism to the Himalayas, where he is revered as a second Buddha)
Heruka	Wrathful meditation deity
Kabney	Man's raw silk scarf, to be worn from left shoulder to right hip, for formal occasions or at a dzong. Colors denote different status: saffron for the King and chief abbot; orange for ministers, red for dashos (male members of royal family and high officials, or in recognition of service to nation), green for judges, blue for members of parliament, red stripes for geps (headmen of Bhutan's 205 gewogs), blue stripes for head of municipalities, white for civilians
Kasho	Royal command
Kata	White silk scarf for ritual uses
Khandro	"Sky-goer" or "sky dancer"—a female form of energy. May refer to a meditational deity (yidam) or a woman with special capacities or a woman serving as consort to a male Vajrayana adept in sexual tantric practices. Dakini in Sanskrit.
Kidu	Bhutanese welfare system, tied to the King's personal beneficence. Reformed by the fifth King to provide clearer procedures and guidelines for means-tested social assistance.

Kira	Traditional women's dress, created by wrapping a woven cloth around the body, with belt and brooches to hold it together; half-kira modifies the kira into a kind of wrap-around skirt using Velcro and hooks
Klesha	Harmful mental attitudes, sometimes called poisons (aggression, desire, ignorance; also pride and jealousy)
Kuensel	The national newspaper, associated with the government: it began as a government circular and gradually achieved independence, though it is still often seen as presenting government views
Kurjey	Body print: marks in stone of Padmasambhava's meditation and/or cliff landings
Kuzozangpola	Hello
La	Used to show respect; also, a word to mark a mountain pass (as in Yonphula)
Lhakhang	Temple
Lhotshampa	Southern Bhutanese; most speak Nepali, may practice Hinduism, Christianity, Buddhism
Lopon	Literally, teacher. The officials directly below the chief abbot or Je Khenpo in Bhutan's monastic establishment.
Lozey	Oral compositions in verse, lines four to twelve syllables long, filled with metaphors, figures of speech, and analogies
Lu	Water spirit, sometimes demon; see naga (Sanskrit)
Lungta	Windhorse, a cultural concept and sometimes a practice associated with good good fortune and success

Lyonpo	Government minister
Mani	Wish-fulfilling jewel
Mani wall	Mani dangrim: structures designed for circumambulation; about a meter in width, a dozen meters in length, and two meters high, lined with stone slabs on which mantras and/or Buddhist figures have been carved
Manidhar	Long white prayer flags mounted to a tall pole to commemorate a person's death
Marchang	Ceremonial offering of alcohol, representing the five spiritual nectars
Momo	Dumpling
Naga	Water spirit and/or demon; the word naga is Sanskrit; Tibetan/Bhutanese term is "lu"
Name same	Beyond earth and sky (part of traditional phrase: name same gedinche la—beyond earth and sky, thank you)
Ney	Place of spiritual power
Ngalops	People of Tibetan origin who migrated to Bhutan as early as the ninth century
Ngolops	Anti-nationals (Tib. ngo.log.pa "rebel," "mutineer")
Padmasambhava	Guru Rinpoche, a precious teacher who spread Buddhist dharma throughout the Himalayas; considered a second Buddha
Phurba	Three-sided dagger (also called a peg, stake, knife, or nail-like ritual implement)
Pönlop	Regional ruler, like a governor. Most important were the Paro pönlops and the Trongsa pönlops. Also spelled penlops.

Puja	Ceremony
Rgyal po	A haughty spirit, one of the malevolent spirits in the Tang valley discussed by Kunzang Choden
Rinpoche	"Precious one"—a spiritual master who has chosen rebirth to help others
Sangha	Buddhist community, including "holy and ordinary beings"
Sharchop	Easterner; informal word for language spoken in the east (officially Tshangla)
Shedra	Dharma school, often attached to a monastery
Shi'dre	Malevolent spirit of the dead—might be produced if officiant conducting death rites failed to help person's conscious principle make the transition to the next bardo
Soelra	Gifts or grant
Taktsang	Tiger's nest: the name for 13 meditation caves used by Padmasambhava across the Himalayas; most commonly used to name a monastery on the cliffs near Paro
Tashi tagye	Eight lucky signs (parasol, two fish, vase, lotus, conch shell, eternal knot, victory banner, wheel of dharma)
Tegu	Bhutanese women's jacket, to be worn over wanju and kira and pinned
Tercham	Name of a masked dance performed every third year in Sakteng
Terma	Scriptural treasure. Padmasambhava and Yeshe Tsogyel are said to have hidden treasures across the Himalayas, to be discovered by later tertöns (treasure revealers) when needed

Tertön	Treasure revealer, such as Pema Lingpa of Bumthang
Thangka	Vajrayana painting, usually depicting a meditational deity (yidam), traditional scene, or mandala (Sanskrit: ashtamangala)
Thangkha	Religious painting, usually of a Buddhist deity (Buddha, bodhisattva, dakini, protector deity, etc.)
Thongdrel	Huge tapestry promising "enlightenment through sight," often displaying multiple figures from a particular Vajrayana lineage
Trulku	Reborn adepts: highly accomplished Buddhist masters who choose rebirth in order to ensure the preservation and transmission of a particular lineage (also tulku)
Thrung	Black-necked crane
Tsangmo	Poems in quatrains, six syllables per line, conveying one main point; in a tsangmo exchange, people may sing tsangmo to one another in a friendly, romantic, or more combative exchange
Tsawasum	Three main elements (in Vajrayana, three roots). In a political sense, usually taken to mean the king, country, and people of Bhutan
Tsechu	Literally, tenth day: a religious festival of dances celebrating the life and activities of Padmasambhava
Tshogdu	Bhutan's National Assembly
Wanju	Bhutanese women's blouse—no buttons or integrated means of closure
Yeshe cholwa	Crazy wisdom, chaos of primordial wisdom; yeshe = pre-existing wisdom

Yidam	Meditation deity (often figured on thangkhas, shaped as sculptures, etc.)
Zangtopelri	The paradise of Padmasambhava; often used as a synonym for lhakang, temple
Zhabdrung	Tibetan abbot who fled sectarian conflict and unified Bhutan's isolated river-valley communities into a nation in the seventeenth century; title means "he at whose feet we submit"
Zomdu	Village meeting (the same term can be used for meetings at various levels of local government)
Zorig Chusum	Traditional arts

Timeline of Key Events in Bhutanese History

627–649 Aum Jomo inspires Brokpa people to rebel against a tyrannical king, then leads them into exile from Tibet to Sakteng and Merak. (Some accounts give a much later date for these events, in the fourteenth century.)[1]

659 Tibetan King Songtsen Goenpo builds temples in Bumthang and Paro as part of a larger project of pinning down a demoness interfering with the construction of a temple in Lhasa.

747/810 Padmasambhava battles local deity Shelging Kharpo and wins, forcing the deity to release ruler Sindhu Raja and binding the spirit to defend Buddhist dharma (in Bumthang). Translating different calendar systems into modern terms can give rise to very different dates for the same event. The *Kuensel* has used the later (810) date.

755–797 Reign of Trisong Detsen, the second of Tibet's "Dharma kings." In one of the foundation tories of Sakteng, Trisong Detsen is the emperor responsible for the scapegoating and exile of young men who end up settling in Sakteng and surrounding villages. This story is the basis of the tercham dance performed every third year in Sakteng.

822	Padmasambhava's second visit to Bhutan, with Yeshe Tshogyel (he meditates at Gomphu Kora to defeat a demon, blesses Aja Ney as a beyul, flies from Singye Dzong to Taktsang [Tiger's Nest] on the back of Yeshe Tshogyel in tiger form, blesses other sites in Paro valley, Gasa, Haa, Jomolhari).
876	Padmasambhava's third and final visit to Bhutan.
1075	Roughly the time Machig Labdrön (1055–1153) has the vision underlying her teaching of Chöd (severance, sometimes called feeding demons); later, she will meditate and teach near Taktsang in Paro, Bhutan.
1180	Tibetan lama Tsangpa Gyare (1161–1211) founds Ralung Monastery and the Drukpa Kagyu school of Vajrayana, the latter named after the thunder dragons (druk) he witnessed near the site.
1347	Alternate date for Aum Jomo's arrival in Merak-Sakteng area.
1455	Drukpa Kinley ("the divine madman") born at Ralung, part of the Gya family; visits Bhutan frequently, deploying his "magic thunderbolt of wisdom" (aka his penis) to defeat demons and demonesses (including at Chimi Lhakang). Phallic imagery in Bhutan often attributed to influence of Drukpa Kinley though at least some of it predates him.
1475	Pema Lingpa, a Bhutanese religious figure and tertön (treasure revealer) from Bumthang, discovered his first terma (scriptural treasure) from Membartsho (Burning Lake) near Bumthang.
1594	Ngawang Namgyel born in Ralung, Tibet, with family connections to Drukpa Kinley, Pema Lingpa, and other Tibetan monastics who established themselves earlier in Bhutan.
1616	After sectarian conflict with the local Tsangpa ruler in Tibet, Zhabdrung Ngawang Namgyel leaves Ralung for Bhutan, though armed conflict follows him.

1623 Zhabdrung undertakes a three-year retreat.

1627 Zhabdrung sends out his poetic seal along with edicts of his dominion over Bhutan, to be placed at mountain passes, rivers, cliffs, monuments, etc. Visiting Portuguese Jesuits provide an eyewitness account of Zhabdrung's rule.

1629 Zhabdrung builds Semtokha dzong at head of Thimphu valley, establishing control over traffic between Paro and Trongsa.

1634 Zhabdrung defeats Tibetans and their Bhutanese allies in the Battle of the Five Lamas, thereby unifying Bhutan into a single nation; Semtokha dzong destroyed.

1637 Foundation of Punakha dzong laid.

1638 Foundation of Wangdiphodrang dzong laid.

Additional waves of Tibetan invasion defeated by Bhutanese forces in 1639, 1644, 1648.

1651 Zhabdrung enters his final meditation. Battles to bring the east of Bhutan under the rule of the Zhabdrung's administration are carried out ostensibly under the Zhabdrung's guidance.

Additional waves of Tibetan invasion defeated by Bhutanese forces in 1656–57, 1668, 1675–76, 1714, 1729 and 1732.

1667 Bhutan ruled by Migyur Tenpa, Third Desi, who pursued warfare with Tibetans within and beyond Bhutan's borders (especially area near Darjeeling, now Sikkim).

1681 Tenzin Rabgay (descended from Drukpa Kinley line, possibly illegitimate son of Zhabdrung) installed as Gyaltshab, prince regent; acts as patron of the arts, codifies zorig chusum.

1694 Gedun Chöpel takes throne as Fifth Desi, installs Zhabdrung's grand-daughter Tshokye Dorji as Gyaltshab.

1708 Zhabdrung's death revealed.

1729	First written legal code based on Zhabdrung's "dual system" of government. Code includes this assertion: "if the government cannot create happiness (dekidk) for its people, there is no purpose for the government to exist."
1730	After years of partial engagement, Cooch Behar requests Bhutanese assistance against Mughal Empire; becomes a Bhutanese dependency.
1772	A rival to the throne in Cooch Behar invites British troops to support his bid; Cooch Behar becomes British dependency.
1774	Under treaty between Bhutan and Britain, Bhutan returns to pre-1730 borders; Britain permitted to harvest timber in Bhutan.
1784	Britain cedes Bengal Duars to Bhutan.
1864	Duar War (Bhutan/Britain): lasts five months, ends with Bhutan's defeat and the Treaty of Sinchula, under which Bhutan cedes territories in Assam Duars and Bengal Duars as well as Dewangiri to Britain in exchange for annual subsidy.
Late 1800s	Nepalis settling in southern Bhutan, partially at urging of British.
1907	Coronation of the first King Ugyen Wangchuk.
1910	Treaty of Punakha with Britain doubles the annual subsidy to Bhutan, clarifies Bhutan's internal independence within acceptance of Britain's guidance in external affairs.
1926	Death of first King Ugyen Wangchuk; start of second King Jigme Wangchuk's reign.
1931	Death of Jigme Dorji, the last officially recognized mind emanation of the Zhabdrung; official accounts claim he died in his sleep; popular accounts claim he was strangled by king's men.

1949	Treaty of Peace and Friendship between Bhutan and India: India will guide Bhutan's foreign affairs without influencing internal affairs.
1952	Death of second King Jigme Wangchuk; start of third King Jigme Dorji Wangchuk's reign.
1951	Jigme Dorji Wangchuk marries Kesang Choeden Dorji.
1952	Kesang Choeden's brother Jigme Palden Dorji becomes Gongzim or Chamberlain, a role inherited from his father.
1958	State visit to Bhutan by Jawaharlal Nehru and his daughter Indira Gandhi, traveling by pony and by yak over high passes from Sikkim. Slavery abolished; first Nationality Act enacted. Jigme Palden Dorji's role of chamberlain modernized into position of prime minister.
1959	Dalai Lama flees occupied Tibet, taking refuge eventually in Dharmsala India.
1961	Bhutan's first Five-Year Plan, with development activities fully funded by India.
1962	First motorized road to Thimphu from Phuentsholing, on border with India, completed.
1964	Assassination of Prime Minister Jigme Palden Dorji, brother-in-law to the third King; the King's uncle is among those executed for the assassination; the King's Tibetan mistress Yangki is unofficially blamed for Palden Dorji's death (said to have provided the pistol used to kill him). Lhendup Dorji becomes prime minister briefly before the Dorji family as a whole go into exile in India, under suspicion of conspiring against the King.
1965	Unsuccessful assassination attempt against the third King.
1969?	First census estimates population at 1,034,774. Figures are revised downward after mathematical error of 100,000 discovered.

1971 Bhutan joins the United Nations.

1972 Death of third King Jigme Dorji Wangchuk, age 42, as he was undergoing medical treatment in Kenya; start of fourth King Jigme Singye Wangchuk's reign (age 16).

1973 India takes military control of Sikkim after the Chogyal (ruler of Sikkim) requests assistance with mass protests in front of the royal palace. National Assembly passes a bill compelling Tibetan refugees living in Bhutan to cut their hair to match Bhutanese norms, attend Bhutanese schools, assimilate into Bhutanese communities.

1974 March–April: Dorji and Wangchuk families reconciled with return of Dorjis from India, after assassination plot against fourth King Jigme Singye Wangchuk uncovered. Twenty-eight Tibetans arrested and charged, including the Dalai Lama's representative in Thimphu. The third King's Tibetan mistress Yangki and her children go into exile in India.

June 2: Coronation day of King Jigme Singye Wangchuk, celebrated annually with a day of public service.

1975 Sikkim Parliament announces the Chogyal has been deposed and Sikkim has joined India via a referendum (later revealed to have been manipulated by Indian agents). Sikkim becomes an Indian state.

1979 Private marriage between the fourth King and four sisters, great-nieces of Jigme Dorji, the assassinated Zhabdrung emanation.

Tibetan refugees required to become Bhutanese citizens, return to China, or accept refuge in a third country (India agrees to take 1,500 Tibetan refugees).

1980 First mention of Gross National Happiness (GNH) in the print record (*New York Times*).

Marriage Act—The Marriage Act of 1980 discouraged marriage between Bhutanese citizens and non-Bhutanese, by restricting valuable government benefits, employment and promotion for any Bhutanese citizen who married a non-Bhutanese.

1985 Citizenship Act—The Citizenship Act reduced transmission of citizenship to people who had documented Bhutanese citizens for both mother and father; citizens had previously been able to access Bhutanese citizenship from a Bhutanese father alone.

1987 Broader discussion of Gross National Happiness in *Financial Times.*

1988 Census begins, conducted only in southern Bhutan; southern Bhutanese object to anti-Lhotshampa bias in execution of census.

1988 State marriage between fourth King and the four queens, recognizing all offspring as members of the royal family.

1989 Kasho issued requiring national dress at government offices, dzongs, temples, schools.

Tek Nath Rizal arrested for creating trouble in southern Bhutan; flees to Nepal where he publishes pamphlet advocating revolution; forcibly returned to Bhutan where he is held shackled in solitary confinement for over two years.

1990 June. Two government officials beheaded by anti-government forces.

September–October. Mass protests in the south: up to 50,000 marching.

Annual meeting of National Assembly canceled.

Government closes southern shops, schools, health centers; reports of state violence and anti-state violence with Lhotshampa villagers caught in between.

1991 High-level civil servants join villagers leaving Bhutan for Nepal; refugees report army and police officers committing murder, rape, torture.

National Assembly meets and proposes many harsh legislative responses to unrest in the south, including repurposing development funds for security purposes; the King threatens to abdicate if National Assembly does not leave him to resolve the Lhotshampa crisis in his own way (including royal pardons, development funding for the south, etc.).

1992 National Security law passed by the Tshogdu.

1993 Ongoing flight of Lhotshampa refugees to Nepal with ongoing reports of rape and violence.

1994 Flight of Lhotshampa to Nepali refugee camps starts to slow.

1997 First reference to Gross National Happiness in National Budget 1996–97.

1998 The fourth King devolves royal power to a royal cabinet.

1999 Planning Commission (with support from UN Development Programme) publishes *Bhutan 2020*, explicitly linking national sovereignty and national cultural identity.

2001 The fourth King issues a kasho calling for a written Constitution to be drafted for Bhutan.

2003 Joint Verification Exercise: Nepalese and Bhutanese officials investigate refugee claims of residents in Khunabari camp, finding 2.5 percent are Bhutanese citizens, 70 percent are "voluntary emigrants," 24 percent are non-Bhutanese, 3 percent are criminals. None are repatriated to Bhutan.

2005 Draft Constitution announced; public discussions held. Many people express concerns over the introduction of democracy.

2006 Early abdication of fourth King Jigme Singye Wangchuk; start of fifth King Jigme Khesar Namgyel Wangchuk's reign.

2007 Practice elections with four color parties: Druk Yellow, Druk Red, Druk Blue, Druk Green. First nonpartisan elections for Bhutan's National Council (upper house of Parliament).

2008 Jigmi Thinley becomes first elected prime minister of Bhutan as head of Bhutan Peace and Prosperity Party winning 45 of 47 seats in the National Assembly (lower house of Parliament); the opposition party PDP (People's Democratic Party) holds only two seats.

Constitution signed into law by the fifth King, Je Khenpo, Parliamentarians.

2013 Tshering Tobgay becomes second elected prime minister as head of the PDP.

2018 Lotay Tshering becomes third elected prime minister as head of Druk Nyamrup Tshogpa (DNT; Bhutan United Party).

2024 Tshering Tobgay elected to a second term as prime minister; PDP wins 30 of 47 National Assembly seats; Pema Chewang is head of the opposition Bhutan Tendrel Party with 17 seats. (Tendrel is the word for the Buddhist doctrine of dependent arising or the interdependence of all phenomena.)

Prologue

Bhutan is a tiny, mountainous, landlocked country in the eastern Himalayas, sandwiched between China's Tibetan Autonomous Region in the north and India in the south. Until 2023, it was officially a "least developed nation" (according to the United Nations)—and yet Bhutan was also the first officially designated "carbon neutral" nation in the world, while also leading efforts to redefine prosperity away from the world's materialist focus on GDP. Bhutan's particular combination of climate and environmental leadership and its promotion of "gross national happiness" even amid conditions of relatively constrained resources has made it an intriguing model for those interested in alternatives to "business as usual" in the midst of climate catastrophe.

Yet few Americans have the opportunity to spend much time in Bhutan, especially given the country's remote location, its challenging mountain passes and variable road conditions, as well as its emphasis on "low volume, high value tourism." A daily charge of $250 for most foreign tourists has meant that most visitors remain no more than six days in the country, mostly in the west, accompanied by a personal guide. (Recently the governmental fee portion of that daily charge rose from $65 to $200—though that $200 was then cut to $100 as a "time-limited incentive" to encourage longer stays.) Beyond the capital region of Thimphu and Paro, Bhutan remains "closed" to foreigners: even those legally employed in Bhutan need travel permission to move beyond the district in which they work. As a result, many people have only a superficial understanding of Bhutan as "the land of happiness," an orientalist image of an impossible Shangri-la.

As a Fulbright scholar based in the underdeveloped east of Bhutan, I had an unusual opportunity to take a closer, longer look at Bhutan's complex history and culture, as well as some of its environmental and social challenges. This book offers an introductory overview of that history and culture, conveyed through my experiences with my family as we arrived in Bhutan, traveled across the country, settled into the college town of Kanglung, observed Vajrayana rituals, and traveled with my graduate students on field trips to explore environmental challenges and strategies. To set the stage for chapters to come, let me begin by describing Yonphula, the mountain on which I taught, on the local holiday of Blessed Rainy Day: September 23, 2017.

BLESSED RAINY DAY

I sat cross-legged on a woven rug in the middle of a grassy field on a mountaintop. We were gathered, a group of almost twenty people, just below the peak of Yonphula, a mountain pass in the east of Bhutan, roughly 9,000 feet above sea level. The mountain is some 300 miles by road from Thimphu, the capital of Bhutan, but when we first arrived, the monsoon-drenched roads were so difficult and ongoing construction so pervasive that the journey took us three days to complete. Here, Yonphula mountain plunged from its peak behind us to the Drangme Chhu, the longest river in Bhutan, only 318 feet above sea level at its lowest point. Another mountain rose steeply on the far side of the river, the buildings of the famous Drametse monastery visible on a promontory jutting out into space. Dark clouds sweeping by overhead sharpened the light and cast shadows across the meadow. Cows grazed nearby. A Bhutanese family had invited me and my family to join them for a picnic to celebrate Blessed Rainy Day—the one uniquely Bhutanese holiday, we had been told, and the gateway to Bhutan's autumn festival season. Our friends Sonam and Dechen and their extended family had laid out woven rugs and bamboo mats in a large circle for us all to sit on. The women of the family were pouring hot drinks. The sun shining through those dark clouds offered an almost tangible relief after months of monsoon rain and drizzle.

Dechen's sister handed me a paper cup and then filled it from a large insulated thermos. The liquid was laced with semi-solid white strands; I could feel its warmth through the wall of the cup. Dechen, her sister, and her husband Sonam all watched closely as I took a sip—and then laughed at the look on my face.

"Arra," Sonam confirmed, as I blinked at the liquor still stinging my tongue and the roof of my mouth. Arra is the local liquor, homebrewed in Bhutan from a base of corn.

"But . . . " I sputtered. This was not your standard arra.

"This is special," Sonam agreed. "My sister-in-law could explain better, but the basic process is to half-scramble an egg over heat, and then pour in the arra." Sonam spoke fluent, barely accented English, and as a result, he tended to speak for the family as a whole.

"Stronger than usual," I said, still feeling the zing of the alcohol and the strangeness of the half-cooked egg. Dechen and her sister laughed and nodded. Her sister topped up my cup, despite my laughing attempt to pull it away.

"You must accept seconds," Sonam explained, "or we will be enemies. This is our tradition."

Each of the women wore a plaid kira, a dress made from a length of woven cloth wrapped around the body and secured with brooches at the shoulders and a tight woven belt at the waist. Two members of this extended family were nuns: they wore maroon robes over saffron-orange tops. As the sun dropped toward the horizon, the nuns would wrap a section of their robes around their shaved heads for warmth. Sonam, his uncle, and his brother-in-law were all wearing the traditional male gho, a knee-length plaid robe, again wrapped around the body and tightly belted to produce "the world's biggest pocket" in the folds of fabric over the chest. Even the colors of the men's ghos were mostly the traditional red with contrasting stripes of green alternating with blue and white.

When his sister-in-law tried to hand him a paper cup, Sonam reached into the front of his gho and pulled out a small wooden cup of richly patterned wood, lined with silver. He held it up for her to pour him a drink. Then he dipped the tip of his fourth finger into the drink, turned his hand palm-side up, and used his thumb to flick a drop of liquor into the air—a kind of libation to the gods. He smiled at me and downed the cupful of arra before holding it up again for a refill. As he held it out, the swirls of the wood grain caught the light, and the cup seemed to glow. Sonam saw me looking at the cup and, after draining it a second time, held it out to me for a closer look (Figure P.1).

"I inherited this from my aunt," he said. "I like to keep the old things. With a Bhutanese pocket, you can always be prepared. No need for plastic and paper." He gestured at the disposable cup, now perched in the grass in front of me. Beside us, my ten-year-old son Jeremy and Sonam's youngest children were playing an upright tic-tac-toe style game we had brought from home, with its plastic frame and plastic disks. I felt embarrassed about the plastic but also relieved that the game gave the kids

Figure P.1. Sonam holding his silver-lined traditional cup, full of warm arra, at the Blessed Rainy Day picnic.

a way to connect. Still, I was aware that in contrast to our plastic, the silver inside of Sonam's cup was both beautiful and practical: silver has antimicrobial properties, capable of killing off bacteria, fungi and some viruses. Drinking from a silver vessel was not just elegant, it was also self-protective. Then Sonam's teenagers brought out a set of battery-powered speakers and started blasting Bhutanese popular music as a soundtrack to the cinematic scenery—a reminder that Bhutan was above all a rapidly developing country, intent on maintaining its national sovereignty while also expanding economic opportunities.

APPROACHING BHUTAN'S COMPLICATIONS

Outsiders writing about Bhutan tend to be split between supporters making positive claims (about Buddhist environmentalism and/or the holistic development model of gross national happiness—GNH) and critics attacking an authoritarian government (for discrimination, denaturalization, and expulsion of minority citizens).[2] Developing a coherent image of the country from these different perspectives remains challenging at best. If Bhutan were more like Western countries, a proliferation of analyses might lead to a general consensus with some outlying views, but Bhutan defends its borders and its reputation vigorously. I had been startled to discover that Bhutan was one of only three countries in the world that have no diplomatic relations with the United States: Iran, North Korea . . . and Bhutan.[3] People seen as critics are mostly not allowed into the country.

As an academic, I wanted to understand how Bhutan worked, not just on a superficial level, but as deeply as I could grasp its social, political, and spiritual logic—without the language skills or background I desperately wanted but didn't have time to acquire. I was working flat out as an English literature professor at Bhutan's new Yonphula Centenary College just a hundred meters down the mountain to the east of our picnic site. Personal challenges deepened the already substantial professional challenge of trying to work within a radically different academic system. Housing in the area was very limited: we were staying, a family of four, in a one-bedroom apartment in the Sherubtse College guesthouse, 2,500 feet down the mountain in the town of Kanglung. Privacy was a thing of the past: we slept all together in a bedroom just large enough to hold four beds. Because of the monsoon rains, our other space (a tiny shower and toilet room next to a larger space with sink and two burners against a wall, a table with a bench and three chairs, a refrigerator) was always draped with clothing that never quite dried. These material constraints made it harder to romanticize our surroundings—especially since we knew we were still better off than many of our neighbors. On my way to work, I often hiked past rural houses where I could see blue (or, more often, rainy) sky through gaps in the stones: these houses would be better ventilated, less likely to grow mold, but miserably cold in the coming winter.

Our family was struggling with culture shock as well. I came up the mountain to teach almost every day and James had a shared office in the Sherubtse College math department, but Jeremy and Zoë struggled at the local elementary school—Jeremy bullied by a fifth-grade classmate, Zoë as an awkwardly under-utilized English language teaching assistant—and they barely left the apartment otherwise. We had been in Bhutan almost two months and had seen only one other Westerner in Kanglung. Jeremy and Zoë found this particularly hard. College students and personnel from the nearby Indian military base all wanted selfies with Jeremy and tried to touch his tight blond curls even as he ducked away from their reaching hands. When Zoë, already prone to self-consciousness, went out in public, her long, curly strawberry-blond hair was so unusual that people would stop what they were doing and stare at her until she had passed out of sight. We had thought Bhutan would feel exotic to us; we hadn't expected our everyday selves to appear quite so exotic to our Bhutanese neighbors. Over the course of ten months in Kanglung, we would see no more than ten other Westerners, though Indian professors, military personnel, and laborers were all around us, mingling with Bhutanese citizens.

So what could I learn, within the limits of my time and energy and my family's resilience? The first step, it seemed to me, was to make my questions more specific:

- What did it mean—politically, culturally, ethically—to call Bhutan the "last Vajrayana state"?

- Was Bhutan's constitutional democratic monarchy more authoritarian or more democratic? Was the country's governance constrained by its history? By its identity as a tiny country between two giants (China and India)? What lessons might Bhutan have for Western democracies grappling with populism?
- What led to the expulsion of tens of thousands of ethnic Nepalis from southern Bhutan and why was Bhutan still struggling to resolve its ethnic divisions? Why was it so hard to talk about these issues?
- Was Bhutan's framing of GNH just ideological cover for ethnic discrimination? How robust a resistance to global capital could GNH offer?
- Were Bhutan's traditional arts valuable only as a form of nostalgia, to support a ruling clique clinging to power? Or did Bhutan's traditions have practical implications, some potential for increasing human resilience in catastrophic times?
- What models of human mobility and naturalization did Bhutan's pre-national history offer?
- What lessons if any could I bring back to share with my communities at home?

These questions, among others, will structure the chapters to come. But for the moment, let's stick with what we can see from the top of Yonphula.

NATIONAL BORDERS, AIRPLANES, AND SPIRITS ON THE MOUNTAINTOP

On a clear day, the snowy peaks of the Indian Himalayas fill out the horizon across from Yonphula. The Indian town of Tawang, some 80 kilometers northeast, retains close ties with minority communities in Trashi Yangtse, the neighboring district in Bhutan. The border with China is only a little further due north. Because of that nearby border, Bhutan has allowed India to maintain a small military base at Yonphula. In June 2017, just a few months before our September picnic, Chinese and Indian troops had faced off on Bhutanese territory, in Doklam, western Bhutan, after China had attempted to extend a road in territory claimed by both China and Bhutan.[4] The Bhutanese eye China's expansionist tendencies with some concern, but despite substantial aid and 50 years of diplomatic "friendship" from India, many Bhutanese, at least in the east, seemed a little uneasy with Indian influence as well. Indeed, some people in Bhutan described the country as an orange between two boulders: soft, juicy Bhutan in danger of being squashed between its giant neighbors.[5] In 2017, roughly half of Bhutan's national budget came in the form of loans and aid from India, with those monies particularly focused on road construction and maintenance and hydropower projects where India has been involved in construction and then purchases much of the electricity produced.[6] When it comes to road construction, "they give us the money and then they take it back again," one of our neighbors complained. Other neighbors worried that Bhutanese children learned Hindi from watching Indian television but lacked fluency in Bhutan's national language, Dzongkha, taught only one hour a day in school where the medium of instruction is English. When the Indian Border Regions Organization (BRO) put up a road sign in Kanglung in Hindi and English (without Dzongkha), it was removed after local objections.

The meadow where we sat that Blessed Rainy Day was located just above the Indian military base. In the 1960s, India built a rough emergency airstrip as part of its military base, and Bhutan had recently renovated the airstrip to make it suitable for commercial use. The renovations included removing a significant bump in the middle of the airstrip, minimizing its slope, and grinding down two hills, one on either side of the airstrip, that threatened to take off the wings of a less-than-perfectly positioned plane. The Yonphula airport was finally scheduled to open in just a couple of weeks, and the local community had been invited to come and celebrate Blessed Rainy Day on the mountain, before the newly functioning airport closed the area to pedestrian traffic. Still, it was hard to imagine a functioning airport here. On this afternoon—like most afternoons—the airstrip was lost in the clouds which swathed the mountaintop, less than a hundred meters above us.

Earlier that day, we had driven up to the paved surface of the airport and then carefully swerved through clusters of people picnicking right on the macadam in thick fog. Sonam had parked his truck near the edge of the runway and we had all piled out into the clouds and the sharp wind whipping our hair past our eyes and our clothes around our bodies.

Walking to the edge of the cliff at the side of the runway, we looked down the other side of the mountain. The clouds parted briefly in the wind, and a few hundred feet below us we saw a small lake, half muddy brown, half brilliant turquoise (Figure P.2).

"Once there were two lakes here," Sonam told us. "Magical lakes: jewels of the mountain, a beautiful deep blue in color. But now: look. This is the result of the construction." He waved a hand at the airstrip and the small terminal in the distance. Below our feet, one lake had apparently vanished; the other was half-clogged with construction run-off. "We believe the lake is inhabited by a mermaid," Sonam went on, looking at me sideways to see how this idea would land. Mermaid, I thought, was one translation for "naga" (Sanskrit) or "lu" (Dzongkha)—a part-human, part-serpent figure from Hindu and Buddhist mythology. I wondered what it meant for Sonam to believe in the mermaid.

But Jeremy, standing beside us, had no such questions. He had a very positive view of mermaids, having recently given a popular performance

Figure P.2. The lake at Yonphula, muddied by run-off from the airstrip construction.

as Chef Louis in *The Little Mermaid* back home. "Cool!" he exclaimed, letting go of my hand and scampering down the scree slope toward the lake. When I tried to call him back, the wind pulled the words away from my mouth. Sonam laughed at me and followed Jeremy; I trailed them both down the slippery mountainside. In the meadow below the scree slope, the wind died and the sun played peek-a-boo between the clouds. Jeremy tried to edge even closer to the lake, but Sonam stopped him. "It is very deep!" he said. "Don't go any nearer." By the time we turned to climb back up the hill, Dechen and her children were on their way down, along with James and Zoë. Jigme, their six-year-old, started sliding past us to join Jeremy near the shore of the lake—until Dechen stopped him sharply.

"We believe if you go in the lake, she will not let you go again," she called to me and Jeremy, articulating each word carefully. Later, I heard a local story about a boy who had drowned in the lake, his death attributed to the mermaid. No one on this picnic day referred to this boy's death (though people recounted the story to me multiple times afterwards), but the idea of being caught and not released captured Jeremy's attention much more firmly than any worries about depth. He edged back up the slope toward me and took my hand.

Sacred sites—like sacred groves in India—are often seen as places of ecological refuge where species under threat from external pressures can retreat, to re-emerge and repopulate larger regions once the threat has passed. Fear of supernatural forces like the mermaid help create that refuge.[7] But the fate of Yonphula's sacred lakes suggests that faith-based protections may be faltering under the development pressures. People may keep their children far from the edge of a naga- or lu-inhabited lake, but when a naga faces off against a newly built airport, who wins?

VAJRAYANA BUDDHISM, ETHNIC TENSIONS, AND GROSS NATIONAL HAPPINESS

As evening shadows lengthened around our picnic site, the young people broke out a karaoke mic and passed it around our little circle. The elders (including me) sang traditional songs that didn't translate terribly well across our language barriers. Meanwhile, other trucks packed with picnickers rumbled down the dirt track from the airstrip at the top of the mountain. One truck-bed held a mass of young monks, all standing, holding each other on board as the truck jolted down the rough road. In the bed of another pick-up, grandparents balanced young children over the bumps as the children smiled and waved at us. Schoolchildren called out to Jeremy by name. Everyone we knew seemed to be on the mountain-top that afternoon: my dean and his family, neighbors from the Sherubtse faculty, Jeremy's classmates. I didn't see my Yonphula College graduate students, however: I might have missed seeing them in the mists at the top of the mountain, or perhaps they had decided to give the airport a miss, having already had more than their fair share of cloud and fog, living amid overcast skies day in and day out. In any case, thinking about who wasn't present on the mountain as well as who was made me think of my Lhotshampa students and the larger Lhotshampa community in Kanglung and Yonphula.

Blessed Rainy Day is a Vajrayana holiday, based on esoteric accounts of astrological concurrences at Mount Meru, the mythical mountain at the center of the Buddhist universe. The crossing of a planet and a giant statue of the cosmic Buddha Vairocana produces rain which is then blessed by all the Buddhas and the Bodhisattvas, resulting in a rainfall so cleansing that bathing in it will remove all negativity and defilement in a person's life. The local astrologer is supposed to tell you when to put out your bucket and in which direction, but we never managed to find the local astrologer. I asked at a local shop about this magic time and direction, and the shopkeeper told me to look it up online. When I stared at him, befuddled, he consulted an app on his phone and showed me the directions in Dzongkha, which he then kindly translated: "the time" was 3:30 a.m. "Any time after that, you can bathe." He also clarified that blessings would shower down with or without actual rain. The water in the bucket would hold the blessings, whether it rained or not. I thought it might have made more sense to call it the "night when blessings rain down," but of course this wasn't my national holiday. My neighbors on the mountain didn't seem to be behaving in particularly pure ways, nor did my own splash bath in freezing rain water seem to have had any significant spiritual effects, but Blessed Rainy Day was definitely a good opportunity to gather with family and friends.

When Americans talk about "Tibetan Buddhism," we are referring to Vajrayana: a form of Buddhism practiced across the Himalayas, in Mongolia, and to a lesser extent in parts of southeast Asia. I knew a little something about Vajrayana Buddhism because of a young Tibetan refugee monk named Lobsang who had come to live with my family decades earlier and who had remained an informally adopted family member. In fact, I had applied for this Fulbright posting after Lobsang's premature death from stomach cancer a year and a half earlier, hoping that learning more about Bhutan as a Vajrayana state would help fill the gap he had left in our lives.

Vajrayana is sometimes maligned as "lamaist" (first by European scholars, more recently by China's Communist Party) for its reverence toward the teachers shaping different lineages within the larger tradition. Padmasambhava, also known as Guru Rinpoche (c. 8th–9th centuries CE), was the founding teacher of Vajrayana in the Himalayas, where he is considered a second Buddha. His teachings, and those of the practitioners and teachers who followed him, include elite practices that demand extensive training and discipline. In Bhutan and across the Himalayas, these practices were preserved in monasteries and hermitages, supported by royal patronage along with many small donations from a largely illiterate population of self-sustaining pastoral communities and farm families. In the implied social contract here, Vajrayana practitioners pray and perform rituals for members of the community, while the community supports local monasteries and practitioners.[8]

Given this context, I wondered how it felt to be Lhotshampa—literally, "southern Bhutanese," ethnically Nepali, probably Hindu—on a Buddhist national holiday. Was it like being Jewish or Muslim on Christmas Day in the United States? Or was the experience more pointed than that?

State discrimination against Bhutan's largest ethnic minority, the Lhotshampa, has been criticized by parts of the international community for decades—even as other international organizations have celebrated Bhutan's enlightened model of gross national happiness. The roots of the Lhotshampa conflict date back to the era of British colonialism. Nepali-speaking people began migrating into Bhutan in sizeable numbers in the mid-nineteenth century, after the conclusion of the Duar war, when Britain seized Bhutanese territories in Assam and Bengal as well as dismantling the Bhutanese fort at Deothang in the east. Nepali-speakers settled in the largely uninhabited malaria-ridden southern jungle areas of Bhutan, clearing land for tropical crops. While northern Bhutanese subjects (Ngalong or Drukpa in the west, Sharchops in the east) paid taxes in kind (bolts of handwoven cloth, bushels of grain, and so on), Lhotshampa communities were required to pay in cash. As a result, they were the first communities in Bhutan to produce cash crops and engage with larger market forces. By the mid-twentieth century, Lhotshampa constituted roughly a third of the Bhutanese population, though census figures were often fudged and thus unreliable.[9]

Bhutanese anxieties about immigration and borders rose after China's annexation of Tibet in the 1950s. They rose even higher after Sikkim's 1973 national referendum deposing its Chogyal, or hereditary king, and the 1975 referendum requesting annexation by India, especially since the deposed Sikkim Chogyal was related to Bhutan's own young king.[10] Over the course of the 1980s, apparently trying to fend off Sikkim's fate, Bhutan passed various government policies tightening citizenship requirements. A census in 1989 intensified xenophobic fears of northern Bhutan being overrun by "illegal immigrants" from Nepal—even as many Lhotshampa who had previously held Bhutanese citizenship cards were denied citizenship on the basis of not speaking Dzongkha (a new citizenship requirement), or failing to present decades-old tax receipts to prove residency. Between 1990 and 1993, tens of thousands of southern Bhutanese left their homes and country; by mid-1993, some 85,000 Lhotshampa were housed in refugee camps on the borders of Nepal. By the end of the century, there were over 100,000 residents in the camps, a major point of dispute between Nepal and Bhutan. Eventually, a majority of the refugees were settled in third party countries, over 90,000 in the United States alone. In the decades following the crisis, ethnic tensions within Bhutan became quieter but were never fully resolved.[11]

Bhutan is perhaps best known on the international stage for its framing and promotion of Gross National Happiness or GNH. Bhutanese and non-Bhutanese promoters of GNH stress the importance of a broader approach to human well-being than a single measure of economic productivity (GDP): they also underscore the importance of protecting cultural diversity against the largely mono-cultural pressures of development. But critics argue that Bhutan's promotion of Gross National Happiness provides ideological cover for discrimination against the southern Bhutanese, in part because its focus on "cultural preservation" is aligned with regulations that require Bhutanese citizens to abide by a code of official etiquette (driglam namzha) when engaging with state services and officials. Driglam namzha is sometimes (mis)translated as "the way of harmony," which seems ironic, given the conflicts created by its legal imposition, and the code of etiquette includes a requirement that "national dress," or the northern Bhutanese dress of gho for men and kira for women, along with scarves that define different kinds of public status (commoner, judge, minister, royal, etc.), be worn in schools and government offices.[12] Lhotshampa refugees often cite the imposition of national dress as one form of discrimination they faced within Bhutan.

SIMILARITIES AND DIFFERENCES BETWEEN BHUTAN AND THE UNITED STATES

Amid my ongoing discomfort over anti-Lhotshampa discrimination in Bhutan, including everything I didn't know and didn't feel comfortable asking about, it seemed important to remember and acknowledge racial discrimination and anti-immigrant feeling in the United States. On that Blessed Rainy Day—September 23, 2017—we were less than six weeks out from the "Unite the Right" rally in Charlottesville, VA, and I was all too aware that with rising inequality and increasingly contentious politics, the ever-elusive American dream was seriously frayed. In November 2017, news broke that immigrant children were being separated from their parents at the southern border of the United States. By June 2018, we had learned that thousands of children had been separated from their families, traumatized, kept in cages. Surging anxieties over national cultural coherence seemed to be be-deviling both countries.

Environmental stresses and strains were visible in both countries as well. The United States was just beginning to confront its history of environmental racism as recently evidenced in the Flint, Michigan water crisis (2014–15), Louisiana's "cancer alley" (1988 on), and its larger failure to protect the public from industrial pollution such as "forever chemicals." Bhutan's "traditional" material culture—locally woven fabric, wooden implements, food and drink—could be produced largely within the environmental constraints of this mountainous land; "modern" or "Western" material culture like Apple computers, Toyota trucks, airplanes and airports required a much more disruptive exploitation of natural resources. How long would Bhutan's environmental resources—protected by its people's past co-existence with other ecological forces—remain intact if it embraced the West's consumption-driven models of development?

Our presence here—my Fulbright posting at the not-yet-inaugurated Yonphula Centenary College—was part of this particular cultural moment, part of Bhutan's balancing between local traditions and broader global norms, including expectations for material resources.[13] Some aspects of material culture such as national dress, Sonam's beautifully turned wooden cup, and home-distilled arra all had a long history, in some cases (such as national dress) backed by the government and the force of law. But this family, one of the wealthiest in Kanglung, also had access to Western material culture—the gleaming truck that had brought us up the mountain, the speakers providing the cinematic soundtrack to the amazing view, the karaoke mic the teenagers were now tossing back and forth, along with more emphatic song requests. Sitting on the mountaintop, I was surrounded by material evidence of decisions Bhutan was in the midst of making, even as I watched, nervously, my home country wrestling with some of its own fundamental values.

Surface differences between the two nations were also self-evident. In its 2008 Constitution, Bhutan had committed to maintaining at least 60 percent forest cover forever; in 2009, it promised to remain carbon neutral in perpetuity. By contrast, the United States had recently withdrawn from the Paris climate accord. In Bhutan, discrimination against the Lhotshampa had diminished though not vanished; along the southern US border, meanwhile, President Trump was still trying to build a wall and get Mexico to pay for it. (Government shut-downs and declaration of a national emergency were still a year or more in the future.) The United States under Bush and Obama had moved toward a more autocratic model of "imperial presidency"; under Trump, authoritarian populism seemed the order of the day.[14] Bhutan, meanwhile, was still adjusting to the new democracy that had been more or less foisted upon it by the fourth King.

Other differences seemed still more innate. If, as some historians argue, geography is destiny, Bhutan's strikingly mountainous geography points toward a very different destiny than that of the Great Plains of the US heartland. So too Bhutan's small size means that small policy changes can have dramatic effects. I had to keep reminding myself that Bhutan's national population was only about half that of Philadelphia, and only two-and-a-half times the global population of the Amish, who have maintained their own distinct decisions about material culture in small communities in the United States, Canada, and beyond. Still, I wondered whether it would be possible to pull apart some of the cultural decisions Bhutan was making in order to see their careful negotiation of tensions, as well as some of our own often-unacknowledged decisions in sharper relief.

My adopted brother Lobsang had come to the United States to learn strategies that could help his Tibetan community face the crisis of exile and poverty in India. I thought perhaps I could reverse his trajectory, that I might learn from Bhutan a set of strategies that could help American communities cope more gracefully with climate catastrophe, broader environmental crises, and our social calamities of loneliness and despair. I hoped Bhutan's commitment to zero carbon and its careful parsing of "gross national happiness" through attention to fair and equitable socioeconomic development, cultural preservation, environmental conservation, and good governance would provide some guidance—and that living among people putting these principles into practice would help us understand how gross national happiness might function back home. This book attempts to summarize what I learned over the course of the ten months we spent in Bhutan, including some of the history that helps explain Bhutan's cultural, environmental, and policy decisions.

CHAPTER SUMMARIES

"Between Earth and Sky," the first part of this book, invokes a Bhutanese expression of gratitude—name same gedinche la, or "beyond the sky and the earth, many thanks"—only to invert it, to reposition Bhutan firmly between earth and sky (Figure P.3). The one chapter in this section, entitled "The 'Real' Bhutan," takes Bhutan less as a utopian model for the

Figure P.3. Between Earth and Sky: View from the edge of the Yonphula airstrip, Blessed Rainy Day, 2017. The post on the right side of the image supports a windsock.

world and more as a small mountainous country struggling to improve the lives of its citizens while defending its (narrowly defined) culture from international development pressures. The chapter tracks some signs of development and development pressures as well as the assumptions creating an infinite regression in which the "real" Bhutan is always just out of reach.

The second part of the book, "The Last Vajrayana State," looks at the costs and benefits of Bhutan's ongoing investment in maintaining cultural continuity with a moment of past grandeur. The second chapter, "Vajrayana Nation-building," explores two very different historical figures whose influence defines Bhutan as a "Vajrayana state": Padmasambhava, the founder of Vajrayana Buddhism, and Zhabdrung Ngawang Namgyel, the Tibetan warrior-monk who unified Bhutan as a nation in the early seventeenth century. Padmasambhava's particular mode of "crazy wisdom" both produced and disrupted multiple offers of kingship, but the

Zhabdrung committed himself from an early age to constructing a dual system of spiritual and secular rule. The third chapter, "King of Destiny—and Democracy," traces the process by which Bhutan moved from rule by religious figures—reincarnations of the Zhabdrung—to rule by a hereditary monarchy to the establishment of a constitutional democratic monarchy. Focusing on the widely respected figure of Bhutan's fourth King, Jigme Singye Wangchuk, the chapter explores both the stability and the fragility of the monarchy, along with the paradox of the fourth King pushing for representative democracy against the expressed will of a significant portion of the population—as well as the possibility that this new representative approach to democracy might do less to represent and respond to people's needs than previous models of local government.

The book's third section, "National Trauma, National Happiness," balances the crisis of the Lhotshampa expulsion against Bhutan's greatest "soft-power export," its promotion of Gross National Happiness. Chapter 4, "The Lhotshampa Expulsion," looks at some underlying causes as well as the progress of the conflict, from a change in citizenship law, a disputed census, government imposition of (northern Bhutanese-styled) national dress and courtly etiquette, Lhotshampa protests, and finally a mix of terrorist and state violence, from which tens of thousands of Bhutanese citizens fled to refugee camps on the border of Nepal. The aftermath of the crisis includes the resettlement of the vast majority of refugees in third-party nations and an unofficial ban on discussion of the crisis within Bhutan.

The fifth chapter "The Rise and Fall of Gross National Happiness" traces the rise of GNH from the fourth King's early play on words, through the first elected prime minister's policy promotion to a public intellectual's careful definition and economic modeling of the concept. But the promotion of GNH became more challenging after Bhutan signed onto the UN Sustainable Development Goals—and the third prime minister's focus on GDP growth was sufficiently at odds with GNH that in 2023, he announced the de-commissioning of the GNH Commission. The return of a more pro-GNH prime minister (Tobgay) in 2024 has led to greater engagement of policy with GNH principles, but Bhutan's current Five-Year Plan still maintains the previously established goal of 10 percent GDP growth. This chapter argues that GNH constitutes a missed opportunity on multiple levels: Bhutanese policy makers could have explicitly involved minority communities in shaping GNH as a force for national unity and international policy makers could have taken cultural diversity and preservation more seriously as a key component of resisting GDP growth as a dominant and unsustainable political ideology.

The book's fourth section, "Learning from Bhutan," explores some aspects of "traditional" Bhutanese culture that support official formulations of GNH and other aspects that challenge official accounts of national identity. Chapter 6, "'Only Poor People Can Do This Work,'" examines the ways Bhutan's zorig chusum or traditional arts keep practitioners and consumers connected to local environments and to one another. Chapter 7, "Demons and Existential Anxiety," explores a range of practices by which Buddhists in Bhutan respond to demons, ranging from protector deities to malevolent spirits to foreigners, focusing in particular on a specifically Vajrayana model of responding with radical generosity to territorial conflict and aggression. Chapter 8, "Aum Jomo—Immigrant to Local Deity," engages some of the stories associated with remote minority communities to understand how earlier immigrant communities became naturalized in their new communities. The book's Epilogue revisits questions of ecological relationship, national identity, and ontological security through the experience of the annual Yonphula tshechu, a three-day religious festival full of masked dances and community connections, and a simple teaching known as "Ten precious breaths."

CONCLUDING

As Blessed Rainy Day drew to a close, dusk fell over the Indian military base and the cows grazing nearby, and we began to pack up all the detritus of the picnic: thermoses, mats, games, and music. Behind us, the airstrip and the now-polluted sacred lake; below us, the military base and the temple (and the new college beyond); among us, a visible shift in norms from the older generation's national dress to the jeans and t-shirts of the young. "It is our tradition," said Sonam, "to close with thanksgiving." He herded us into a circle, and with the help of his aunt and uncle, launched out into the traditional song and its accompanying steps and gestures. My family stumbled along, trying to follow the moves and the song's shifting pitches in the gathering dark. But the dance quickly broke down into giggles. "We can't remember quite how it goes!" Sonam said, laughing along with his children. But then he spotted a group of students leaping down the hill from the airstrip. "The students will help us," he said. I couldn't see why these students would remember a traditional dance more clearly than their elders—until I remembered that the official curriculum at Sherubtse included training in driglam namzha or Bhutanese etiquette, and driglam namzha includes dances such as this ritual of thanksgiving. The students joined our circle and led us through the dance. My family still struggled with the shifting maneuvers—graceful turns of wrist and hand, a hop on one foot, a kick, a turn from one direction to the other—but our companions seemed steady, balanced, reassured. The song once finished, the students waved and continued on their way, walking ten kilometers along the dark road down the mountain to Sherubtse's campus. We carried the mats and thermoses back to Sonam's truck, then piled in for our own much quicker drive down the mountain, still feeling surrounded by the music and motion of giving thanks.

PART I

BETWEEN THE SKY AND THE EARTH

CHAPTER ONE

THE "REAL" BHUTAN

As we first flew through the mountains into Paro airport, one of the world's most dangerous flight paths, I looked out the plane window and saw a cowherder glance up from his cows on the side of the mountain. I wasn't looking down: he and I were at roughly the same elevation, the mountain summit stretching up behind him. I had expected to feel scared, swerving among the mountaintops, but I felt instead an uncanny pleasure, as if the plane was dancing us through the steep sloping peaks—as if this year would indeed help me see things from a brand-new vantage point. But would it? Cowherders and planes: the contrast was suggestive, but perhaps too predictable.

My family and I were the last passengers to walk down the airplane steps onto the tarmac outside the airport. The terminal was decorated in traditional Bhutanese fashion: large brightly painted columns supported cantilevered balconies and windows as well as rooftops. The mountains rose up close behind the building. We stood and stared. Most passengers had already vanished, quick to go about their business. Inside the terminal, though, we found a few men dressed in ghos, the tightly belted robes worn by Bhutanese men: they were standing around a single luggage carousel, which clanked loudly in the cavernous hall.

The luggage took its time. "BST," one of the men said to us. When we looked blank, he explained: "Not British standard time—Bhutanese *stretch* time." We smiled belatedly, and he traveled from our ignorance to the obvious conclusion: "You are tourists? Where are you going?"

"I am a Fulbright Scholar," I said, "going to teach at the new College in Yonphula. Do you know it?"

"Ah, Yonphula!" our fellow passenger replied, nodding wisely. "It is being run from Sherubtse College in Kanglung. I know Kanglung. Everyone will know you there. How long will you stay?"

"Ten months," I said.

Our new acquaintance shook his head, marveling. "Ten months!" he repeated. "In Kanglung. Well, in Kanglung you will see the real Bhutan."

The clunking of the carousel intensified over an alarming mechanical whine. Before I could ask what he meant, we were all reaching for our bags, and the moment was gone.

The drive from Paro airport to Thimphu took a little over an hour, and it felt like driving through a three-dimensional tourism advertisement: a glacial river, bright green rice fields filling the floodplain, colorful buildings dotted along the valley's edge, just at the point where the floodplain meets the steeply rising mountain slopes. These buildings too were of traditional Bhutanese construction: white-washed walls of rammed earth, the arched windows, the upper stories wood-framed, painted in stylized patterns evoking lotus blossoms and other auspicious Buddhist symbols. Brightly colored prayer flags flapped briskly over the river, especially along suspension bridges for pedestrians or the occasional steel bridge for vehicular traffic. Chortens—rounded monuments evoking the Buddha's mind—gleamed white and gold amid shifting sun and clouds. On the far side of the river, a tall pole of vertical prayer flags adorned a collection of buildings: a famous monastery. Painted metal signs along the road ranged from the kind of punning comic slogans associated with Indian road builders ("If you are married, divorce speed"), to the earnestness of Bhutanese government public service announcements: "A Healthy Nation must have a Healthy Society! Let us build a Healthy Nation! Without Drugs, Alcohol and Tobacco!" A large grey langur monkey sat on a pillar by a bridge, holding a bit of greenery as if mid-snack, and giving us a long, assessing stare as we paused, waiting for our turn to cross.

Norzin Lam, the main street in Thimphu, 7,656 feet above sea level, runs for about a mile east to west and is full of shops and restaurants.

At the western edge of the street, mountains rise steeply: indeed, mountains loom over the capital, visible from all angles. Here too the buildings feature traditional Bhutanese architecture, their walls whitewashed or painted a pale yellow or apricot. The cantilevered upper stories protrude slightly over the lower stories, making the buildings seem top-heavy. Up on some of the rooftops, multicolored prayer flags flutter on vertical flag-posts topped with a knife to represent the cutting through of delusion. Signs with the names of hotels and restaurants sprout from the sides of buildings in a kind of multicolored jumble—blue, green, white, red—though there seems to be a size limit for the signs. Government regulation of Bhutanese architecture has required inclusion of traditional Drukpa or northern Bhutanese features since at least 1993. Some traditional features are permissible only for dzongs, royal buildings, and monasteries; others are permissible for "less important buildings"; still others "only for store, godown, toilets, and warehouses."[1] For the moment, the result is a capital city that keeps the look of a small town.

By the time we had found a place to stay for the night, we were almost too tired to speak. But when we said we were traveling to Kanglung, the hotel's night manager smiled. "In the east," he said, "you will see the real Bhutan." In the dining room half an hour later, as we scoured the menu for something that might feel like comfort food, a young waitress asked where we would be going next. "Kanglung?" she repeated. "You are fortunate. In the east, you will see the real Bhutan."

The next day, after some altitude-disrupted sleep, we met Bhutanese friends in Thimphu for shopping and lunch. Jigme had just graduated from Swarthmore College, where I teach in the United States. His older sister had recently completed a Master's degree in the UK. We were sitting with them and their family around a picnic table outside a hamburger place on Chang lam, the lower of Thimphu's two main streets. As I swirled a momo, a Bhutanese dumpling, in ezay, a local relish, someone remarked, "Ah, Kanglung! There in the east, you will see the real Bhutan!"

"People keep saying that to us," I said, abandoning my momo. "What does it mean? What is the real Bhutan?"

"Well, it's not Thimphu," Jigme replied. His family were all wearing Western clothes, though they had been helping us buy traditional clothing they told us we would need in the east. "People won't dress this way," he said, gesturing at his family.

"No hamburgers," added one of his sisters. "No NGOs. No Westerners in the streets."

"No clubs," said the other. "No football stadiums. No movie theaters."

The list of items missing in eastern Bhutan went on for quite a while. "What does the east have?" I asked. "What does 'real Bhutan' feature?"

It turned out that only Jigme's dad had been to the east. "It's beautiful," he said briefly. "Very traditional." Then he swept us off to buy a SIM card for my mobile phone.

If the East represents traditional Bhutan, Thimphu in the West seems to be the meeting place between tradition and modernity. The Bhutanese people we met in Thimphu pointed to many signs of Bhutan's rapid modernization: communications (television, the internet, cell phones), transportation (roads and private vehicles), finance (visible in new construction, shops, NGOs, and more), democracy (new as of 2008). We were as charmed as any other tourists with the beautifully uniformed police officers conducting traffic: their job involved standing in or just outside a wooden gazebo-like structure in the middle of the main intersection, stopping and waving traffic on with white-gloved, balletic gestures. Thimphu is the world's only capital city without a traffic light: a unique choice underscored by the fact that a traffic light was once installed, but then removed on the grounds that the people didn't like it. Traffic jams seemed both surprising and predictable in a town with few streets but many cars.

We were taken to cafés and bookstores apparently designed to appeal to Westerners—and to the post office, which invites tourists to have Bhutanese stamps made from their own photographs while they wait. We watched a gleaming white garbage truck trundle down the busy street of Norzin Lam playing a cheery melody like an ice cream truck in the United States, calling people to bring their trash and pour it into the compaction container themselves. The textile museum was also gleaming, sophisticated in its ethnographies of Bhutanese textile cultures. The Jigme Dorji Wangchuk National Referral Hospital stood out as the apex of a free health care system throughout the country: doctors there can send patients abroad to hospitals in Thailand or elsewhere at public expense if the patient needs care the national hospital cannot provide.

Still, we were bemused to find ourselves spending most of a day on the front steps of the Jigme Dorji Wangchuk National Referral Hospital, waiting while Ugyen tried to help us get mandatory medical certificates before the nearby Immigration office closed for the day. As the hours stretched on, the kids played riddle games and cat's cradle, and we all watched a field fill up across the street, just above the Memorial Chorten built to honor the third King. People arrived alone or in small groups: they sat on the ground, gradually unfurling brightly colored umbrellas for protection from the midday sun. By noon, the field seemed full of massive, unearthly flowers (Figure I.1). About 1 p.m., a Rinpoche, a reincarnated lama, appeared and began giving a spiritual teaching: the umbrellas vanished to reveal a field still more densely packed with bodies clothed in colorful national dress: men in ghos and women in kiras.

Ugyen brought a nurse to meet us, in the hopes she might be willing to give us the medical certificates early. But when she heard that we were

Figure I.1. Umbrellas providing shade as people wait to receive a religious teaching from a high lama across the street from the Jigme Dorji Wangchuck National Referral Hospital in Thimphu.

staying for ten months, and had arrived from low altitudes, she balked. "If you were to develop altitude sickness, we would not be prepared to admit you without proper intake procedure," she explained.

Across the street, the teaching ended. The Rinpoche and his retinue moved through the crowd, bestowing blessings. Four of the attendant monks wore yellow hats with a stiff central rim; two of them handed out some indiscernible object (probably some pills of traditional medicine plus a blessing thread) from a large bag into people's outstretched hands, while the other two played the gyaling—a kind of double-reed woodwind instrument, like a very loud oboe. Other monks remained on the teaching platform playing the long horns known as dungchen. All the while, traffic continued down the road between the hospital and Memorial Chorten. The scene seemed at once traditional and modern, ceremonial and quotidian.

Ugyen came to fetch us thirty minutes before the offices opened: lines had formed to pay fees at one window, collect forms at another, wait to see the doctor behind yet another door. Finally we made it to the front of the queue and sat before the doctor. "Do you have blood pressure, madam?" he asked.

"Err. Yes?" I replied. "It's usually normal."

The doctor smiled at me, ruffled Jeremy's hair, thumped a stamp onto an ink pad, then onto the form, and then signed the form across the stamp. Intake completed.

TRADITION, MODERNITY, AND DEVELOPMENT

Bhutan is famous for sharp contrasts between tradition and modernity—and some blurry in-between areas like the intake procedure—but where a person locates the dividing line between tradition and modernity may shape their understanding of the country. That division could be temporal or spatial, it seemed to me. The people we were meeting in western Bhutan, many of whom had never been to the east of the country, seemed to imagine we might find there a version of Bhutan that pre-dated the influx of tourists, cell phones, movies, and more. Western Bhutanese citizens seemed to imagine the East of their country much the same way Western tourists imagine Bhutan as a whole: as an underdeveloped, simpler version of their own hybrid complexity. I wondered whether the "real Bhutan" functioned as a mirage: always elsewhere, just out of reach.

Of course, the contrast between tradition and modernity is itself a modern invention, one we can trace back to social theorists such as Karl Marx, Émile Durkheim, and Max Weber on the one hand, and to Cold War politics on the other. Marx equated modernity with an industrialized capitalist society powered by the labor of the proletariat: he saw modernization as a necessary step on the path to overthrowing capitalism and establishing a communist society. For Émile Durkheim, primitive (or what we might now call "traditional") society is marked by little division of labor: people are connected through "mechanical solidarity," or the similarity of their work and lives. Modern society, by contrast, is characterized by highly specialized, differentiated forms of labor, and people are connected through "organic solidarity," or interdependence on one another's labor. Max Weber characterized the divide between traditional and modern society in terms of a shift from traditional authority based on religious belief and superstition to modern authority based on rationality and bureaucratic legal structures.

Bhutan's longer history disturbs some of the expectations built into these models, mingling elements of the modern and the traditional over extended periods of time. By unifying Bhutan as a nation in early seventeenth century, Ngawang Namgyel, known as the Zhabdrung (or "he at whose feet one prostrates") could be said to have brought this land of distinct river-valley societies into what European historians describe as the "early modern period," marked by the development of the nation-state. In relation to Durkheim's model, the Zhabdrung's administration worked to distinguish spiritual and temporal rule, and to codify a set of crafts, now known as traditional arts, based on differentiated labor. In Weberian terms, the Zhabdrung and the heirs to his rule also launched the development of a bureaucratic state with a legal code based on Padmasambhava's earlier distinction between the spiritual laws as a gradually tightening silken knot and temporal laws like a golden yoke that grows gradually heavier as crimes become more serious.[2] My experience of obtaining a work permit suggested a highly developed though not always rational bureaucracy. In economic terms, however, earlier capital accumulation, instead of being invested in development of heavy industry, was used to maintain monastic (and eventually monarchical) institutions. Agriculture remains a core element of the economy to this day.

One might also consider modernity as a policy structure rather than a social descriptor. While Marx, Durkheim, and Weber all contributed to the notion of a radical split between (agricultural, undifferentiated, religious) tradition and (industrial, specialized, rational) modernity, perhaps the most influential account of modernity versus tradition comes from a very particular discourse of international development that emerged in the United States and allied western European nations during the Cold War. In this account, mass consumerism and social mobility represent an ideal toward which every society should strive—a model which has been especially influential in determining how intergovernmental agencies like the World Bank and the International Monetary Fund (IMF) distribute international aid dollars. In 1962, just after Bhutan began implementing its first Five-Year Plan with development activities funded by Indian aid, American economist Walt Whitman Rostow published a book entitled *The Stages of Economic Growth: A Non-Communist Manifesto*, laying out five stages of "development" toward the goal of "modernization." The title acknowledges the extent to which Rostow was intentionally framing international aid as an economic front, another arena of struggle in the Cold War. Indeed, the language of "First World" (modern, Western, industrialized economies), "Second World" (Communist less-industrialized economies), and "Third World" (poorer countries the West should woo away from communism with development aid) comes out of Rostow's work.

Within Rostow's modernization model, traditional society was the first stage of development, characterized by subsistence agriculture, limited technology, and cultural preferences for stability over change. Rostow described modernization, the final goal, in terms of full industrialization, widespread consumption of high-value goods (such as cars), and disposable income beyond basic needs.[3] Under normal conditions, Rostow suggested, a nation might pass through three intermediate stages in moving from tradition to modernity: stages he named "Preconditions to take-off," "Take off," and "Drive to Maturity." The preconditions stage is characterized by a shift from subsistence agriculture toward cash crops and commercial farming, by a transformation of physical environments to increase production, by the spread of technology, changing social structure and increased social mobility, and the development of a national identity with shared economic interests. The take-off stage is marked by a few leading industries, often textiles and apparel, beginning to produce at scale (as in Great Britain's Industrial Revolution). The drive to maturity shows industries diversifying and expanding, shifting from capital goods toward consumer durables, alongside a rapid development of transportation infrastructure and social infrastructure.

But Rostow established a linear narrative of development only to call for its disruption, insisting that the West should help developing nations leap more rapidly to higher levels of development in order to bypass any temptation to turn to communism and thus fall into the Soviet Union's sphere of influence. Still, leapfrogging may not be the best metaphor for imagining the situation of a country like Bhutan. In relation to Rostow's model, for instance, Bhutan seems to feature aspects of both modernity and tradition, challenging any sense of linearity. Again, a significant portion of Bhutan's population remains involved in subsistence agriculture, and the country exhibits strong cultural preferences for stability over change, in keeping with Rostow's sense of traditional societies—yet Bhutan's citizens are also clearly purchasing high-value consumer durables such as cars and computers. The country's landscape resists industrial diversification, but the spread of technology—especially cell phones and the internet (unknown to Rostow in 1960)—has altered social structures, shifting patterns of social mobility and perhaps intensifying a sense of national identity. The country's geography—its steeply sloping mountains, lack of level ground, and unstable geology—makes industrial development especially challenging. Conversely, however, much of Bhutan's GDP is tied to its hydroelectric plants, enabled by that same challenging geography, built with funding from India and selling surplus electricity to that country.

In global terms, decades of development aid did little to produce the results Rostow had projected: in fact, "underdeveloped" countries found themselves paying more and more in raw material exports for the same amount of manufactured goods from developed countries.[4] "Dependency theory" analyzed the failures of Western-led international development: scholars such as the Guyanese historian Walter Rodney suggested that European imperialism (the center) had exploited Africa and Latin America (the periphery) through control of technology and technological innovation, as well as through policies of surplus extraction and capital accumulation.[5]

After 1980, neoliberal policies implemented by organizations like the International Monetary Fund (IMF) and the World Bank, under what came to be known as "the Washington consensus," focused on "structural adjustment programs," in which countries could acquire loans to build sewers, roads, hospitals, and so on, only if they agreed to deregulation (removing restrictions on businesses and employers engaged in world trade), privatization (selling off state-owned industries to private interests), and tax reductions (aimed at reducing government size). Deregulation also meant governments removing prior protections for workers and the environment. Trade "protectionism" became a dirty word. But the neoliberal answer to the shortfalls of modernization did not solve the problems of global inequality. According to a broad-based review of global economic and government data from 1980 to 2000, "rates of economic growth were, on average, about half those prevalent at midcentury, and in much of the third world growth has stagnated."[6]

More recently, "post-development" thinkers have argued that Western-led models of modernization not only assert dubious values (such as mass consumption linked to runaway carbon emissions): those models also threaten to exterminate Indigenous cultures and values that seem better able to foster human thriving in balance with the environments that sustain them.[7] For post-development scholars, the failure of Western development models to help poor nations achieve prosperity is no accident. Instead, Eurocentric colonial dominance produces and maintains global inequality and creates a sense of neediness or poverty in nations of the periphery, which Rostow called the "Third World" and which are now known collectively as the Global South. To counter Eurocentric and US-centric organizations such as the World Bank and the IMF, proponents of post-development strategies look to local cultures and traditional knowledge.[8]

Traditional knowledge: the formulation both maintains and inverts the binary opposition structuring many views of development as modernization. Sociologist Anthony Giddens, writing about "post-traditional societies" in 1994, argued both that we are all part of post-traditional societies, and that the traditions of any given society provided community members with a form of "ontological security," a sense of meaning and place that was maintained by the guardians of the tradition.[9] Giddens' formulation of the "post-traditional" highlights a lingering sense of longing for traditions left behind. And while most of the thinkers surveyed above (Marx, Weber, Durkheim, Rostow) emphasize temporality in their discussions of modernization and development, Giddens focuses attention on some of the spatial dimensions of globalization.

According to Giddens, modernization replaces tradition's guardians with experts, but expertise "is disembedding; in contrast to tradition it is in a fundamental sense non-local and decentred."[10] Note the negative prefixes proliferating here: *dis*embedding, *non*-local, *de*centred. While urban designers, architects, and planners are busy theorizing practices of "place-making," Giddens seems to suggest that modern reliance on expertise produces an unmaking of place.[11] The process of development "evacuat[es . . .] the traditional or customary content of local contexts of action" and then "reorganiz[es . . .] social relations across broad time-space bands." This reorganization is integral to the process of becoming post-traditional: "Expert systems decontextualize as an intrinsic consequence of the impersonal and contingent character of their rules of knowledge-acquisition; as decentred systems, 'open' to whosoever has the time, resources and talent to grasp them, they can be located anywhere."[12] But Bhutan, a tiny country sandwiched between two giants, fiercely maintains traditional content, and local places and contexts, even as it promotes the impersonal rules of bureaucratic systems.

In fact, Bhutan has famously contributed to discussions of post-development or alternative development by insisting on the importance of Gross National Happiness (GNH) over Gross Domestic Product (GDP) as a measure of national success. At this point, the country is so strongly identified with ideas of happiness that many Westerners mistake Bhutan for "the happiest country in the world," despite the country's status as a least-developed nation—from which it graduated only in 2023, thanks to impressive GDP growth over the preceding decades. An early framing of GNH in terms of "four pillars" balanced "fair and equitable socio-economic development" with the goals of "environmental conservation," "cultural preservation," and "good governance." Jigmi Thinley, first elected prime minister of Bhutan and sometime Bhutanese ambassador to the United

Nations, effectively promoted this model of Gross National Happiness in international circles while also establishing a "happiness" brand for Bhutan's national tourism bureau.[13] Later, under the direction of Karma Ura, the Centre for Bhutan Studies developed nine domains as part of the GNH Survey and Index. The nine domains include living standards, education, health, psychological well-being, time use, community vitality, cultural resilience, ecological resilience, and good governance.[14] After the development of the GNH Index, however, the fifth King and the GNH Commission more loosely defined GNH as "development with values."[15] Which values, exactly? one might ask. Marking the divide between tradition (values) and modernity (development) is one way of responding to that question—but the boundary between Bhutanese tradition and modernity seems difficult to establish with any certainty, as a quick survey of modern markers such as democracy, infrastructure, and communications demonstrates.

DEMOCRACY, MONARCHY, ECCLESIOCRACY

On our third day in Bhutan—a Saturday, so the immigration office was closed—the place where we were staying in the hills above Thimphu hosted the inauguration of the new Jigme Singye Wangchuk School of Law, temporarily housed next door. Once the road was open, after all the royals and dignitaries had arrived, we went out for the day, but when we returned, we discovered that the somewhat elusive fourth King was talking with the first batch of Bhutanese law students, not far from the balcony of our hotel room. Of course we crowded out onto the balcony to listen quietly. The former King was speaking to the students in a mix of English and Dzongkha. In English, he urged them to work hard for the sake of the nation. "You must do your best," he said. "The country needs you to do your best." The students nodded, their eyes lowered in respect. Later, after the King had left, the students built a bonfire and sang late into the night. Most of the songs I couldn't recognize or understand, but the last song I heard consisted of a single word, repeated on a range of pitches: gedinche, gedinche, gedinche la. Gedinche is the word for thanks, and la a word used for emphasis and respect.

Bhutan's transition to democracy—or more precisely, to a "democratic constitutional monarchy"—is frequently cited as a mark of its modernity.

That transition made international headlines in 2007 and 2008, for instance, though the development of democratic structures in Bhutan took many decades. The third King established a National Assembly in 1953 and abolished serfhood or slavery in Bhutan in 1958. In 1965, the third King created a Royal Advisory Council; in 1969, he renounced his own veto power over the National Assembly and instituted a triennial vote of confidence in the monarch. When the fourth King took office in 1972 at the age of 16, the conservative National Assembly insisted that he reclaim veto power and get rid of the triennial vote of confidence. But the fourth King later decentralized power by creating regional development committees. He also relinquished his own executive authority by establishing an executive branch of government headed by a prime minister, separate from the monarch who remained the head of state, in 1998. When one of the royal advisors criticized this diminishing of monarchical power, the King insisted on the value of democracy for Bhutan, asserting that

> . . . the principles and goals of democracy are inherently good, and a democratic system is desirable for Bhutan. If the lessons of some democracies are not encouraging, it is not because the concept of democracy is flawed: it is because of mismanagement or susceptibility to corruption by those who participate in the democratic political systems in some of the countries.[16]

Popular resistance to democracy was, as this response of the fourth King suggests, not without its reasons. The Bhutanese looked at unrest in nearby India and Nepal and were underwhelmed by democracy's ability to deliver social and economic benefits. By contrast, the fourth King and his hand-picked ministers, while urging the international community to consider "gross national happiness" rather than just gross domestic product, had also overseen unusually high GDP growth across multiple decades. A set of hydropower deals with India—whereby India funded construction of large hydropower plants with 60 percent grants and 40 percent loans, and agreed to buy surplus electricity thus produced—seemed to be serving Bhutan well (though the loans have become a significant burden in recent years). Under the rule of the fourth King, Bhutan could apparently have its GNH and feast on GDP at the same time.

Still, the King pressed forward toward democracy, issuing a royal decree in 2001 that created a 39-person committee charged with drafting a written constitution. Once that constitution had been drafted, the King launched a process of nationwide consultation in October 2005. During his annual National Day address in December 2005, the fourth King acknowledged that "the main concern of the people is that it is too early to introduce parliamentary democracy in Bhutan." But the King publicly disagreed with this view. He reminded the Bhutanese people of the decentralized development committees already begun in 1981 and 1991. He announced that in 2006 and 2007, the Election Commission would undertake to educate the public in the procedures of parliamentary democracy and that he would pass the throne to his son in 2008. Then in early December 2006, the fourth King announced he would be abdicating in favor of the Crown Prince two years earlier than previously planned, as if to clear the way for the democratic transition.[17] Bhutanese commentators often frame this as a royal sacrifice on the altar of democracy.[18] And while the Constitution was originally to have been approved through a national referendum, that referendum was never held, perhaps for fear that the Constitution and the democratic structures it defined would not be approved.[19]

Western news accounts of Bhutan's move toward partisan elections emphasized the paradox of a monarch insisting on democracy, apparently against the will of his people. *The New York Times*, for instance, quoted different Bhutanese voters all asserting that they were participating in representative democracy primarily to please their King. In 2007, reporting on the "practice elections" Bhutan was holding to prepare for their first partisan elections the following year, the *New York Times* began the article with a somewhat facetious question, "Can 'Desperate Housewives,' free trade and multiparty elections deliver happiness?" and went on to quote reluctant Bhutanese practice voters:

> Kesang Dorji, 36, said he was puzzled by the royal order to vote, but intended to obey.
>
> "We have to stand fast to the wisdom of our monarch," Dorji said. "He knows what's best for us. Any normal person would think, 'Why this, when everything is okay?'"[20]

Western news outlets did not, however, canvass the thoughts of Lhotshampa activists who had pushed for an earlier expansion of Bhutanese democracy. Reporting on the first partisan elections of 2008, the *New York Times* again spoke only with northern Bhutanese voters reluctantly following the lead of their King:

> "There was much resistance when His Majesty told us that we must decide our future if Bhutan was to prosper," said Karma Dorji, a 55-year-old civil servant who was waiting to vote.
>
> That was in late 2006, and since then "we have come to see that this is an opportunity he has given us because he is farsighted and wise."
>
> Still, he said: "We prefer our King."[21]

Rather than marking a firm division between a former monarchy and modern democracy, Bhutan's transition to a democratic constitutional monarchy blurs the boundary between traditional allegiance to the King and a more ostensibly modern participation in representative democracy.

MODERNITY AND ROADS

Infrastructure might provide a clearer mark of modernity than politics. Consider 1961, when Bhutan's first Five-Year Plan, funded by India, began producing the first paved roads and more broadly available secular schools. Before 1961, travel occurred largely by foot over mountain trails, with mules carrying goods. Garps or trail runners carried messages between dzongs, those combined monastery-fort-municipal administration buildings, along the trail.[22] When Indian Prime Minister Jawaharlal Nehru visited Thimphu in 1958, the trip from the Indian border to Thimphu took six days on horseback.[23] Once the road was completed, the trip could be accomplished in six hours by car. Roads and schools brought many other changes in their wake. In 1961, transhumant pastoralism—seasonal migration of humans and their livestock from winter lowlands to summer uplands—still shaped a significant portion of land use and social organization in the north. Bhutanese life expectancy was less than 35 years in 1961, as compared with over 72 years in 2023.[24] If modernism is impossible to separate from Western development and its emphasis on material goods, Bhutanese modernism might well be seen to begin in 1961.

But roads in Bhutan are not a fixed accomplishment. By 1989, roads stretched over 2,280 kilometers, but only 1,761 kilometers of those roads were paved.[25] Even the paved roads, connecting principal towns, were only the width of a single lane (2.5 meters wide), limiting traffic speed to an average of 15–20 kilometers per hour as drivers attempted to avoid head-on collisions. In an attempt to overcome these constraints, the lateral road, also known as the east–west national highway, was again under construction from 2014 to 2023. (The road widening was originally scheduled for completion by 2017, but that three-year work plan dragged on over nine years, blocked by intense monsoon storms, unstable geography, and pandemic border closures.) When we arrived, in 2017, the fastest, most reliable route from Thimphu to my posting in the east was to take the "India road"—driving due south from Thimphu to the Indian border at Phuentsholing, then east through Assam, India before striking due north at the border town of Samdrup Jongkhar. But this route involved some anxiety over border crossings, the use of extra visa entries, potentially violent strikes in Assam, and uncertainty about the status of the north–south roads. We chose to go the Bumthang road, though without fully understanding what that would entail.

The day before our proposed departure, Ugyen insisted that we visit Dechenphu Lhakhang, a temple dating back to the thirteenth and fourteenth centuries, to make prayers and offerings for a safe voyage (Figure 1.2).[26] We were happy to visit the temple—Ugyen asked for and received special permission for us to enter the grounds, though not the fourteenth-century goenkhang, the fortified tower. Still struggling with jet-lag, we didn't fully grasp the importance of the site, and Ugyen's insistence on making offerings for a safe voyage struck us as merely quaint. But by the time we reached Kanglung, after almost three days' driving through slippery muddy mountain passes, we understood more clearly the rationale behind prayers and offerings before trusting one's life to the unstable road.

The roads around Thimphu and Paro were broad and well-paved. But perhaps ninety minutes into the drive, after the city of Wangdue Phodrang, the roadworks began, and the paved road vanished (Figures 1.3 and 1.4).

Figure 1.2. Dechenphu Lhakhang, outside of Thimphu, where Ugyen took us to make offerings and request safe travel.

Over the summer, I had read Kunzang Choden's novel *The Circle of Karma*, in which the protagonist Tsomo toils on the road from Thimphu to Phuentsholing—then the only (unfinished) road in Bhutan—with a group of mixed Bhutanese and Indian workers. The description matched what we began to see on the east-west national highway—at least when

Figure 1.3. Sample road conditions during our three-day drive from Thimphu to Kanglung along "the Bumthang road." I sometimes felt the road was just a pause in an ongoing landslide.

it was clear and dry enough to work. Women and children sat or crouched on the sides of the road, near stones that they were responsible for breaking up. In Choden's words,

> They held the circular clasps with their left hands around the piece of stone which they were breaking into gravel. They hit the stones with the hammers, tack, tack, and the circular clasps prevented the broken stones from scattering. Sprays of fine pieces flew into their faces, which were already covered with dust from the crumbling stones. Their eyes watered with the dust and the wind. Their hands were rough and cracked and often bled. Their arms ached from the constant hammering. The men chopped down trees and fed entire logs into the fire to melt the tar cooking in shallow containers. The fine gravel was mixed into the tar and poured on the road. Men and women with spades spread out the mixture manually before the rollers came and pressed it into place. [. . .] While their

Figure 1.4. Sample road conditions amid more characteristic monsoon fog and rain. If you look closely, you can see large stones packed to try to solidify the road over a recent slide.

> insides were being coated with tar fumes, the noise of blasting rocks rang in their ears, partially deafening them.
>
> Yet these women lived. They chatted, laughed, sang, and dared to dream of better things to come.[27]

Out the window of the Sherubtse College Hilux, I watched some older children help their mothers break stone, sitting and crouching on the roadside, while others herded toddlers away from the center of the road as vehicles came through. Men were shoveling the broken stone to distribute it along the road. Engineers were setting dynamite to blow out part of a cliff or drilling large blocks of stone to clear a path or add to the road-building materials. The cooking tar, which was heated over open flames when a road surface was ready to cover, made us cough and choke as we drove slowly by—and of course the roadworkers could not get away from the toxic fumes.

We noticed clever metal boxes, like giant card-houses, that people had made by flattening the barrels of bitumen used to build the road. These metal huts were located sporadically along the road, right at its margins: they were covered with dust and mud from the large trucks traveling through. We had imagined that those low, ad hoc shapes were used to protect equipment from the elements. But then, during a pause in the rains, we saw people moving in and out of them. (See Figure 1.5 for similar construction, though more clearly housing.)

"Ugyen, what are people doing in those boxes?" I asked.

"They live there, madam."

"Those are their homes?"

"Yes, the Indian workers making the road live by the road. They make their houses from the barrels." Ugyen, and most Bhutanese people we spoke with about this later, thought these Indian roadworkers were lucky to be living in Bhutan, able to take advantage of free health care and free education. Some older Bhutanese people lived in shelters not much more substantial than these houses, though usually farther from the road and the tar.

Figure 1.5. A post-monsoon photo of housing built from flattened bitumen barrels, October 2017.

Figure 1.6. Road workers breaking and shoveling stone on the road from Trashigang to Rangjung, October 2017.

Focusing on the first paved roads as a marker of modernization draws attention to the presence of "outsiders" within the Kingdom, from lowly paid roadworkers to high-paying tourists (Figure 1.6). In the early years of Bhutan's "modernization," Indian aid money helped pay over 30,000 Indian and Nepali laborers to work on the roads alongside Bhutanese laborers: a significant influx in a country of (then) less than 600,000 inhabitants. In 1980 and 1982, expat workers constituted roughly 58 percent of public sector workers, 47 percent of private sector workers, and 96 percent of casual labor.[28] According to KM Dixit, 15,000 of these workers were made to leave Bhutan in the late 1980s as part of efforts to reduce the size of the non-Bhutanese work force and control immigration pressures.[29]

Meanwhile, with the inauguration of the fourth King in 1974, Bhutan opened its borders and its roughly 1,500 kilometers of road to foreign tourists, though the slow expansion of the road system kept Bhutan distinct from the "developed" or "modern" world outside its borders. Bhutan consciously pursued a "low volume, high value" approach to tourism. Before the pandemic, most tourists paid $250 per day, which included a

$65 Sustainable Development Fee (abbreviated SDF, paid directly to the government to help fund Bhutanese education and healthcare).

The per diem cost covered most expenses, including a guide, hotel, food, and transportation. (Citizens of India, Bangladesh, and the Maldives didn't need a visa, which significantly lowered their travel costs.) Reopening to tourism after the pandemic, Bhutan shifted its policies: Indians, Bangladeshis, and Maldivians now pay roughly $15 SDF per day, and all other tourists pay $200 SDF per day—but that fee no longer includes hotel, food, transportation, or guide.

Ironically, while Bhutan's reputation as an "untouched" wilderness and unique cultural destination appeals to travelers eager to step off the beaten path, the cost of tourist visas means that most Western tourists remain in western Bhutan, where the roads are good. Bhutan's high per diem cost means that the average tourist stays only five or six days: waiting five hours for a landslide to be cleared so they can finish a ten-hour drive as part of a six-day tour seldom seems like a good idea. Hence part of the reaction we kept hearing in Thimphu: the "real Bhutan" was a place largely free of Western tourists, even though that "real Bhutan" was the place tourists most wanted to reach.

As if to underscore the impact of road construction on Bhutanese culture, a recent approach to tourism attempts to turn the clock back before the construction of the road system. During the pandemic, some 900 workers, furloughed from their ordinary jobs, rebuilt 18 bridges and thousands of steps that had fallen into disrepair after the roads became Bhutan's main thoroughfare. Offering yet another version of "the real Bhutan," the country opened the Trans-Bhutan Trail in October 2022: a restored, recreated version of the trail network that existed before Bhutan's first roads. To complete the entire trail is said to require 36 days, but the travel writers exploring this hot new destination are again limiting their treks to six or seven days, no doubt because there are limits to the expense accounts even of Condé Nast Traveller.[30]

In many ways, roads seemed synonymous with development during our months in the east. Bhutanese roads represented both the promise of ease and market access and the stubborn materiality of Bhutan. Engaging with Bhutanese roads means confronting the prevalence of landslides, the necessity of frequent repairs, as well as reckoning with the still-porous border visible in the bodies of Indian roadworkers maintaining the roads. In March 2018, a presenter with the Lhomon Society (a civil society organization founded by Buddhist teacher Dzongsar Khyentse Rinpoche) told my students that the greatest benefit one could offer people from remote villages was connection to a road: more than anything else, a road would enable villagers to thrive. In April 2018, we made a class field trip to Sakteng, one of the more remote villages in Bhutan, where the acting head of school told us that the villagers had opposed the construction of a road to the village, but that government officials had insisted on constructing one nonetheless. Both the strengths and costs of development were frequently invoked as roads continued to be built, and debated, across Bhutan.

COMMUNICATIONS AND SOCIAL MEDIA

Communications and social media are often described as another key inflection point in the country's modernization process—in part because Bhutan is the only country in the world to have banned television until 1999. Television, internet, and mobile phones brought the outside world to Bhutan. The first television broadcast occurred on June 2, 1999, during the celebration of the fourth King's silver jubilee, the 25th year of his rule. In that same year, internet access became available for the first time within Bhutan; mobile phone networks first appeared in 2003. In 1999, less than 25 percent of the country had electricity available at home, but in 2016, Bhutan achieved 100 percent electrification, four years ahead of its 2020 target date—and electricity subsequently increased access to computer-based internet. The internet, cellular networks, and the social media platforms they enabled brought a host of new cultural forms and trends to far-flung Bhutanese communities. Where roads emphasize material elements of Bhutan's national infrastructure and communal identity, communications and social media engage virtual networks and cultural identities.

Communications and social media in Bhutan have grown at a breathtaking rate over the past two decades. In 2003, mobile phone networks were available only in five towns, and so only about two thousand people subscribed to mobile phone services. By 2006, however, mobile networks became available nationwide, and by 2008, those mobile networks had 230,000 subscribers. In 2013, the Bhutan Information and Media Impact Study reported that 560,000 out of 730,000 Bhutanese citizens owned a mobile phone. More recent figures vary by source, but all seem to track ever deeper penetration of mobile technology. The World Bank asserted in 2021, for instance, that mobile phones had reached 100 percent of the Bhutanese population.[31]

Both the internet and mobile phone networks host social media, which have transformed Bhutanese communications and communities. YouTube became available in Bhutan in 2005; Facebook arrived in 2006, and the Chinese social media platform WeChat launched in 2011. By 2021, an assessment of the "Social Media Landscape in Bhutan" reported that the Bhutanese exceeded the global average of daily time spent on social media: the global average being 145 minutes per day, while the average person in Bhutan spends 163 minutes, more than two-and-a-half hours, on social media each day. Still more strikingly, urban people spend 217 minutes, over three hours, per day on social media, while rural people spend a mere 136 minutes each day. Older and less-educated Bhutanese prefer WeChat, which makes it easy to send voice messages, while people aged 13–44 prefer Facebook.[32] YouTube, like television, gives people access to Indian and other international films. The incursion of other national cultures into Bhutanese media habits has had other, knock-on effects: the popularity of Bollywood movies, for instance, has made Hindi an appealing language for young people to pick up—and even my more middle-aged students had a pronounced Bollywood aesthetic in their creative writing.

Facebook accounts in Bhutan can also be used to deliver anonymous critique of established figures or institutions, both locally and nationally. Students criticizing Sherubtse College, for instance, often did so through anonymous Facebook posts. Disputes over Bhutan's harsh anti-tobacco laws were similarly conducted in part over Facebook. In 2011, after a monk was sentenced to three years of jail for possessing less than three dollars' worth of chewing tobacco, opponents of the law created a Facebook campaign to protest this draconian implementation of the tobacco ban. This campaign constituted the first digital protest against the Bhutanese government.[33] Social media began to be seen as a new platform through which citizens could communicate more frankly with their government, though the growing prevalence of anonymous comments and fake accounts would soon be criticized for degrading the quality of public discourse.

Bhutanese politics have been strongly influenced by social media platforms, particularly Facebook and WeChat. Tshering Tobgay, Bhutan's second elected prime minister (2013–18), came to public attention in part through his digital fluency: his use of Facebook, a blog, Twitter, and more. And while his party, the People's Democratic Party (PDP) was defeated in the primary elections of 2018, that defeat was far from a negative judgment on social media usage. The two parties who won the primary and thus contested the general election both relied on Facebook to reach potential supporters—but the party eventually elected, Druk Nyamrup Tshogpa (DNT, Bhutan United Party, formerly the Social Democratic Party), had a more sophisticated Facebook operation, including Livestreams, the use of a Facebook page (rather than a profile), and more positive posting techniques. Druk Phuensum Tshogpa (DPT, Bhutan Peace and Prosperity Party), the party of the first prime minister, Jigme Thinley, by contrast, relied on a Facebook profile (not designed for large numbers of followers), and got caught up in combating anonymous accounts posting attacks and "fake news."[34]

The intensity of Bhutanese social media usage seems a striking sign of modernity—and yet tradition also hums along those cellular networks. WeChat's voice messaging in particular plays to the orality of Bhutan's traditional cultures while erasing the effects of distance. While the average person in Bhutan uses Facebook more than YouTube or WeChat, monks use WeChat almost twice as much as they use Facebook. Our friend Sonam occasionally shared with me snippets of dharma teachings that were delivered to him (and other followers of his teacher) over WeChat. In this way and others, WeChat seemed to extend Bhutan's existing cultural norms. Our acquaintance at the airport had been correct, that many people in Kanglung knew who we were, long before we met them. But WeChat broadened those circles of intimacy and knowledge as well as enabling faster circulation of information. When I visited the local temple in Kanglung, for instance, someone snapped a picture of me with their mobile phone, and by class time the next day, all my students had seen the image. And when, after attending a conference in Thimphu, my return to work was delayed by a landslide, my dean knew about the road blockage before I did—and even people on the bus with me seemed to be getting their information about the blockage ahead via WeChat messages from people on the far side of the landslide.

THE "REAL" KANGLUNG?

The western Bhutanese people who had told us we would find "the real Bhutan" in Kanglung were of course connoisseurs of their country's norms and customs in ways that we, as foreigners, would never be. For us in Kanglung, the "real Bhutan" was whatever struck us as unfamiliar—and much of what seemed different centered on social and familial networks. Picking Jeremy up from school at lunchtime, for instance, meant that I encountered a network of mothers (and the occasional father) who brought picnic lunches to the school grounds. A small gaggle of women and younger children would gather shortly before 12:30, waiting for the primary school to release children for lunch. Some women brought tiffin tins full of rice and curry; some brought mats of woven bamboo to lay out and sit on; some brought foam pads. Everyone sat around the prayer wheel near the entrance to the school. One old woman sat on a rackety school chair and kept the prayer wheel spinning without stop. Children came pelting down the hill, throwing themselves upon their mothers and/or chasing their younger siblings around the prayer wheel. One day, I met a young professor of Media Studies named Chencho waiting for her children. When I said I was charmed by the picnic lunch tradition, Chencho smiled and nodded. "Here in Bhutan," she said, "we may not make as much money, but we can spend more time with our families."

A few weeks later, Chencho and her husband Chimi Dorji invited our family over for dinner. We had been warned that Bhutanese norms involved hosts leaving guests alone in a room while preparing supper, but our modern hosts had food mostly ready and waiting for us. Over a delicious meal, we talked about our different food norms. When we said we had struggled to find green vegetables in the shops, Chencho looked startled. "Just buy them from the farm children," she said.

"What farm children?" I asked. It turned out that children of local farmers would make the rounds of Sherubtse faculty housing, bringing bunches of turnip greens, green beans, and other vegetables to sell door-to-door. The Sherubtse guest house, occupied by foreigners, was not one of their stops, and we hadn't known that this farm-to-table network existed. Chencho said she would send the children our way. But we had other food queries as well, mostly focused on dairy products.

"Of course we have fresh milk," said Chencho, when she heard we had been buying long-life milk from the shops. "Just buy it off the cart."

"What cart?"

"The milk cart. Drawn by the mule. The man sells the milk off the back. It comes mid-morning." But our family was all dispersed, at the primary school or one of the two colleges, by mid-morning. "No problem: my sister can get it for you. She gets it for many people." Chencho's "sister" was something like an au pair: while Chencho's biological siblings lived in Paro, near their mother and grandfather, this honorary sister hailed from nearby Mongar and helped with cooking and childcare. The milk off the cart was raw and would have to be boiled at home to be safe to drink.

"What about butter?" we asked, tired of the plasticky margarine available in the shops.

"Oh, you just get it from the librarian!" said Chimi Dorji. "She has a small dairy and she will sell you butter." But it was hard for us to get a fix on which librarian we should approach and whether her English would make it easy for us to complete this transaction. Chimi kindly went to negotiate on our behalf and brought us an enormous half-ball of butter—perhaps a kilo of butter—a few days later. Unfortunately the butter tasted—or perhaps just smelled—strongly of wet cow, which seemed reasonable but not enticing.

Cheese was yet another point of cultural difference. In Kanglung, there seemed to be two options: dried cheese cubes hanging on pieces of string in the roadside shops, or slightly larger blocks of highly processed white cheese, wrapped in aluminum foil and then boxed in plastic. People would stick a dried cheese cube in their cheek and chew on it, slow time—or cubes could be added to stews, soups, rice porridge. The processed cheese was used in curries and in some cases on pizza.

A few weeks after our shared dinner, Chimi and Chencho took us to a more industrial dairy, run through a Japanese-Bhutan partnership, an hour's drive away, where we could purchase blander butter and a massive wheel of Gouda-style cheese to complement our otherwise vegan fare. Another friend, giving us a ride down to the Indian border later in the year, stopped at a nearby town to try to find some specialty cheese for his mother: this cheese, part of the cultural heritage of the Brokpa minority community, is finished by being sewn up inside a sheep's stomach and left to cure for several months. But the shops had none in stock—once again, to acquire this food, one needed to be in touch with local networks. This kind of tight connection between food acquisition and social networks underscored the larger importance of social bonds in the east of Bhutan.

TRANSITIONAL GENERATIONS

My students, and the larger group of civil service teachers of whom they were a part, seemed to consider themselves as something like a new class within Bhutanese society. Becoming a teacher in Bhutan means becoming a member of the civil service, with a guaranteed government job for life.

But that higher-class status carries pricy social responsibilities as well as privileges. Both my students and the local primary school teachers, for instance, formed themselves into small self-insuring groups, similar to what was known in eighteenth-century England and America as "Friendly Societies." Each member of the group contributed a certain amount of money to a general pool. Anyone whose parent or parent-in-law died during the period of the MA program (or perhaps a year at the school) would receive a sizeable amount from that shared pool to help them cover the costs of funeral rituals. "For people in our class, these are some of our heaviest expenses," one of my students explained to me. Rituals must be performed in the days immediately following a death, then again during the seven weeks that followed, on the seventh, fourteenth, twenty-first, and forty-ninth days after death, with particularly important rituals completed on the twenty-first day. All of this requires funds: gifts for astrologers and lamas, food for community members coming to join in the rituals, butter lamps, and more.

Such rituals were far from the only expenses this new class and generation faced. One of my students, Yangchen Lham, spelled out some of the other financial burdens in a digital story full of nostalgia for the simplicity of village life. Yangchen tells her viewers:

> I was born and brought up in a small rural village of around twenty to thirty Bhutanese houses. When I was young, people used to say that life in the city was easier, healthier, more comfortable and peaceful than life in the country. Like many people, I longed to have that attractive city life.

But life in Thimphu was full of unexpected financial stressors: "I had to compete with others even though I was poor. I had to carry fancy gadgets and wear expensive clothes though I had little food to eat at home. I had to drive expensive and updated cars which I could only afford by taking on huge debts." Yangchen describes the hedonic treadmill of many Western societies, in which competing with others in status-based consumption can feel like a trap. In village life, Yangchen noted, she would wear her best kira and other new clothes "only during festivals" and she would "save food especially for the different celebrations. But now my rural special food became my daily meal." So too, "in the city, gathering became part of my daily schedule, whereas in the village, we gather only during the festivals. Those gatherings have more charm because they are so much less frequent." Yangchen ended with a warning: "let me tell you, before it is too late: treasure the life of the village. Hold onto its rhythms, its smoked food, its charming celebrations before they vanish."

While Yangchen celebrated the consolations of Bhutanese traditions, another digital story, by Sherubtse College English Professor Choki Beda, suggests how firmly-entrenched traditions, such as tales of ancestors' heroic actions, might exclude some Bhutanese citizens from full participation in the nation and the culture. "Stories are the mirror of our lives and define who we are," Choki Beda asserted. People are defined by the stories they inherit:

> I begin with the great stories of my ancestors: a grandfather who fought a wild beast and rode on its back into the depths of a ravine. Or the grandparent who hunted bears and jackals with just a bow and arrow.

> The stories of their bravery and courage, while riding the sharp edge of death, I tell and retell around dancing fires.

Choki Beda celebrated these stories, while also noting the way their machismo made it difficult for a woman, a mother, an everyday citizen, to enter into that tradition. "Nations rise, or stumble, without me [. . .]. Men fill the larger dimensions of life and call out. Not for me." Glorification of the past can block movement toward a different future. "And yet, just yet. I am a person, so extraordinary: a daughter, wife, and a mother. Such ordinary roles, people say. Breathing and measuring my life in tea cups and handwashes. How tedious, they say." But Choki Beda is unwilling to let that judgment stand unchallenged: "Born to parents so small and low, raised with siblings no better, no less. How common a story, people say. And yet, just yet, I am extraordinary." Choki Beda's digital story, dedicated to her small daughter, highlights the way social expectations and definitions of heroism can change in a shifting world.

My students and colleagues in Kanglung were keenly aware of the larger transitions of which they were a part. On the plus side, the physical, material demands of Bhutanese life seemed significantly easier than they had been in earlier days. Rising life expectancy figures registered not just longer lives, but easier ones. Family photos highlighted the contrast between the smooth faces of these teachers and the weather-beaten faces of their parents, most of whom were or had been subsistence-level farmers. Medical interventions had saved a significant number of people even in this small community: people who once would have died of tuberculosis, congenital heart disease, or other conditions. Some of the students had cars, which made travel much easier than it would have been for earlier generations. But living conditions up at Yonphula were still cold, damp, and cramped. And even as they articulated commitment to family as a traditional Bhutanese value, many people traveled far from their homes and loved ones for professional advancement. One colleague, for instance, told of abruptly weaning her still-nursing baby so she could leave the child with her mother while she pursued a Master's degree in Australia: despite desperately missing her infant daughter, she couldn't turn down the professional advancement and career stability promised by the graduate degree. Most of my students, undertaking this 18-month degree in a remote location within Bhutan, had similarly left their children with their spouses or parents for the duration of the program, despite or perhaps because of their deep love for those children and a desire to give them all possible opportunities.

This ongoing disruption of family life, along with other shifting social norms, was creating new problems, particularly with mental health issues among Bhutanese youth. In 2014, for instance, *The Bhutanese*, an online news source reported that suicide was the second-highest cause of death in Bhutan, after road accidents, and that suicide rates were unusually high in youth aged 18–25.[35] The previous year, an editorial in the national newspaper the *Kuensel* had put the blame for Bhutan's rising suicide rates on development: "Development brings more opportunities, opportunities beget competition, competition triggers pressure to perform and do more, in some that causes depression, and depression makes people highly suicidal."[36] Other Bhutanese sources similarly connected Bhutan's rising suicide rates with "development." Sonam Pelden's 2016 Ph.D. thesis at the School of Occupational Therapy and Social Work from Curtin University, for instance, argued that

> Bhutan like any society is seeking a place in the world. The desire for materialistic gains, the changing structures of families and communities are changing some values that the Bhutanese cherished for generations. [. . .] Participants [. . .] argued that individualist views and thoughts about individual rights are becoming prominent in an increasingly competitive Bhutanese society. These comments perhaps reflect Durkheim's thoughts that anomie was the result of a society which was disturbed by a crisis, causing disequilibrium as human aspirations were no longer regulated by social norms or rules.[37]

Does modernity, still largely associated with material gains and Western models of development, bring an increase in well-being—or anomie? Decades on from the fourth King's early suggestion that gross national happiness might be more important than gross national product, Bhutanese debates about modernity and the human costs of development were still ongoing. In Bhutan in the mid twenty-teens, development still looked like a major, even existential risk: a threat to the survival of the individual and the nation alike. One government strategy for combating individual and national anomie was to force a communal embrace of the country's cultural and spiritual identity as the last Vajrayana state: this strategy, implemented in the late 1980s, would be both controversial and definitive for Bhutan.

PART II

THE LAST VAJRAYANA STATE

CHAPTER TWO

VAJRAYANA NATION-BUILDING

Figure 2.1. The inside of the lhakang (temple) at the (Nyingma) Rangjung Woesel Choeling Monastery in Rangjung, Trashigang, showing the brilliant colors and vivid imagery used to guide prayers and meditation. Our guide, the monk Karma, encouraged us to take photographs and share them. (In Drukpa Kagyu temples, by contrast, photographs are officially banned, though our Bhutanese neighbors did not seem to abide by this prohibition.)

In retrospect, I had been foolish to imagine that living in Bhutan would teach me about my brother Lobsang's Tibetan culture. Of course the two countries were very different. Bhutan's unique history and diverse cultures would already be more than I could manage to grasp in the brief time we would spend in the country. And yet, I thought stubbornly, a few weeks after our arrival in Kanglung, there must also be lessons here for me about Vajrayana Buddhism, given its development among these mountains.

Lobsang had been a wonderful translator of cultural practices: very matter-of-fact about the usefulness of Buddhism, and amusing about Vajrayana's more esoteric practices. After taking a nap, for instance, he would claim he had been practicing "sleeping meditation" (which is indeed a practice, but not one he had been engaged in). I tried to follow some of Lobsang's ideas and practices, but I wanted to relate to him as a family member, not as a trendy Tibetan meditation teacher. When I drove Lobsang to hear the Dalai Lama speak in New Jersey, I went mostly as a chauffeur, and I struggled with the teaching on emptiness, though some of the ideas and phrases echoed in my mind for years afterward: "For those to whom nothingness is possible, all things are possible." When I tagged along with my brother Jim to attend the Dalai Lama's Kalachakra initiation in Madison Square Garden, I went as the American version of a Himalayan peasant: with no expectation of grasping the deep meaning of the ritual, but with hopes of advancing a tiny step or two along the path to enlightenment. Lobsang sat up on the stage in the rows of monks. "Don't worry about all the arms and legs," he said, when I told him I was having a hard time keeping the meditation deities straight. "Just practice being a good person."

But now that he was gone, I wished I had worried more about all the arms and legs. I wanted to understand how Vajrayana Buddhism had made sense to him: so much sense that he had devoted his life to its practices.

Bhutan as a nation is similarly devoted to Vajrayana Buddhism, staking its survival on its Vajrayana culture and traditions, both implicitly and explicitly underscoring its status as "the last Vajrayana state."[1] Addressing both internal and international audiences, Bhutanese policy-makers have argued that

> Bhutan's survival as an independent nation rests on its unique cultural identity. [. . .] [I]n the absence of military might or economic power, Bhutan's sovereignty hinges on its unique cultural heritage, which makes Bhutan distinct among other nations in the frenzy of a globalised meld.[2]

Bhutan lacks the military and economic power other nations rely on for self-defense, which means that it relies on other, more powerful nations to defend Bhutanese sovereignty in case of need. What would bring others to Bhutan's defense? The country has chosen to frame its value to the larger world in terms of cultural uniqueness, a uniqueness shaped by Vajrayana Buddhism.

But describing Bhutan as "the last Vajrayana state" does more than emphasize Bhutan's unique culture: it highlights the prior existence (and disappearance) of numerous Himalayan kingdoms or princely states which promoted the monastic institutions and elite practices associated with Vajrayana. Most of those princely states have now been subsumed into other modern nations, the pre-existing partnership between rulers and religion dissolved. As Jessica Locke notes, "Sikkim, Spiti, Lahul and Ladakh have been absorbed by India; Dolpo, Mustang, Solu-Khumbu and Walung are now Nepalese districts, and of course, Tibet has been colonized and systematically Sinicized by China." Locke also notes that the loss of political patronage in these newly secular, "non-Buddhist-majority nations" has weakened the strength of Buddhist institutions there.[3] To frame the nation's identity as "the last Vajrayana state" is thus on one level to fear cultural extinction.

And yet, Bhutan is not exactly a "Vajrayana state." The Constitution defines Buddhism as the country's "spiritual heritage," but not explicitly as the state religion. Instead, it specifies that the King, as a Buddhist, embodies the "dual system" of spiritual and secular government, and it commits the government to continue providing funding for the "central monk body." Overall, however,

> [. . .] it shall be the responsibility of religious institutions and personalities to promote the spiritual heritage of the country while also ensuring that religion remains separate from politics in Bhutan. Religious institutions and personalities shall remain above politics.[4]

How do we recognize a space "above politics"? And what does it mean for Bhutan to be recognizably but not technically a Vajrayana state? How do ideas of Vajrayana Buddhism connect with the model of the nation-state, anyway?

VAJRAYANA AND PADMASAMBHAVA

Vajrayana is a tantric form of Buddhism developed and practiced across the Himalayan region, as well as in Mongolia and some other parts of the world. Tantra is a Sanskrit word meaning "loom," "warp," or "weave." One etymology points to "tan" as meaning to elaborate (an extension of weaving) and "tra" as liberation, leading to an understanding of tantra as a system of liberation.[5] Meanwhile, "yana" means "vehicle" in Sanskrit, and Vajrayana is one of three main "vehicles" for pursuing enlightenment within Buddhist traditions (see Table 2.1):

- Sravakayana or "the vehicle of listeners" is a vehicle of individual liberation, often called Theravada (the doctrine [vada] of the elders [thera]): a mode of Buddhism practiced in southern India, Sri Lanka, Thailand, Myanmar, Laos, and Cambodia, based on the Buddha's teachings as preserved in the Pali canon.
- Mahayana, or the "great vehicle," recognizes the teachings of the Pali canon but expands further into philosophical exploration of the nature of reality, while also delineating the path of a bodhisattva, a person who strives to reach enlightenment not for their own benefit but for the sake of all sentient beings. Mahayana developed in India and spread through the east: Tibet, China, Korea, Mongolia, Taiwan, Japan.
- Vajrayana is sometimes described as a path within Mahayana, but it is also considered a third vehicle to enlightenment. "Vajra" can be translated both as "diamond" and as "thunderbolt" and so Vajrayana is sometimes translated as the "diamond vehicle" and sometimes as the "thunderbolt vehicle." Vajrayana traditions spread throughout the Himalayas (Tibet, Bhutan, northern India, Nepal) and Mongolia; some Vajrayana schools also exist in Japan.

Table 2.1. Three Vehicles of Buddhism: Sravakayana, Mahayana, Vajrayana

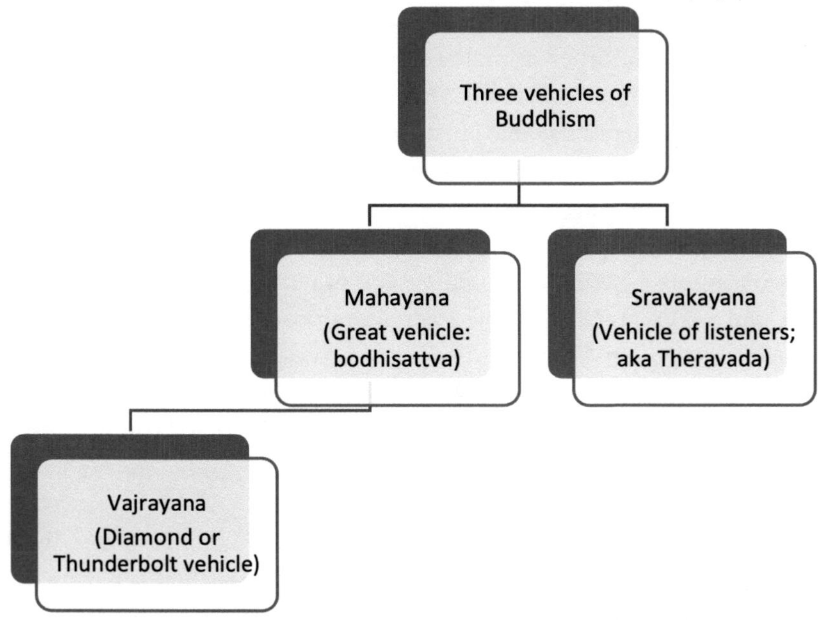

Aiming to achieve enlightenment for the sake of all sentient beings but within a single lifetime, Vajrayana practices, developed from roughly 700–900 CE, combined Mahayana philosophy with rituals developed by mahasiddhis or wandering yogis: practices designed to turn poisons (harmful mental states) into wisdom. These techniques metaphorically or literally engaged in taboo substances such as alcohol, meat, urine, as well as other taboo elements, such as forbidden sexual practices: practitioners use the power of the taboo to defeat dualistic thinking and grasp the nature of reality. Wrathful deities—fierce, forceful, frightening manifestations of enlightened Buddhas—are often invoked to destroy obstacles to enlightenment such as passion, aggression, and ignorance (or delusion). But from the outside, those wrathful deities can look demonic and the taboo-busting practices can seem like witchcraft. Westerners have oscillated between condemning Vajrayana's demonic rites and idealizing and exoticizing its teachers and practices.[7] In either case, Vajrayana's association with radical and counter-intuitive practices makes it an odd partner for state-building—and the heritage of Padmasambhava, the first major Vajrayana figure associated with Bhutan, underscores the unsettling effects of taking Vajrayana as a state religion.

Before its unification as a nation, Bhutan was often considered merely the "southern lands" below the high Tibetan plateau, and Tibetan policies and trends had a sizeable impact on those southern lands. Buddhism played an important role in Tibetan politics and culture from the moment Trisong Detsen (742–97) made Buddhism Tibet's state religion and undertook a series of monumental building and translation projects. In these projects, he relied on guidance and supervision from Indian teachers and adepts, including one Padmasambhava—a figure often called Guru Rinpoche or "Precious Teacher"—who is credited with founding Nyingma, or the oldest school of Vajrayana Buddhism. Padmasambhava evidently gathered so much local support in Tibet that Trisong Detsen asked him to leave, whereupon Guru Rinpoche began his travels across the greater Himalayan region.[8]

A few centuries after the life of the historical Padmasambhava, writers began associating a range of extraordinary stories with that figure. These stories matter because they highlight core components of the Guru's character and legacy: crazy wisdom, acceptance of impermanence as seen in dramatic shifts of fate, and supernatural powers. The stories are often encapsulated in iconography as the "Eight Manifestations of Guru Rinpoche." As Pema Gyelpo, or "Lotus King," Padmasambhava emerges at the heart of a lotus flower as a self-born four-year-old child. According to the stories, King Indrabhuti of Oddiyana, seeking for a wish-fulfilling jewel, finds Padmasambhava in the lotus, and adopts him to be the next King of Oddiyana. But then Padmasambhava kills a minister by dropping his staff off a rooftop, and he is exiled—giving him the chance to live as a wandering mahasiddha, practicing tantric rituals in charnel grounds: a life encapsulated in the form of Nyima Ozer (Ray of Sun). As Loden Choki (Super Knowledge Holder), he departs Oddiyana to gather all wisdom in India. Then, in Himachal Pradesh, as Guru Padmasambhava, he teaches tantric rituals to Mandareva, a king's daughter: when the king finds out, believing his daughter to be dishonored, he tries to burn both the guru and the daughter alive, but Padmasambhava turns the fire into a lake on which he and Mandareva float upon a lotus. The king, astonished, gives Padmasambhava his kingdom: Padmasambhava and Mandareva convert the kingdom to Vajrayana

Buddhism, but then move on. In Bodhgaya, India, as Shakya Senge (Lion of the Shakyas), the Guru brings the great King Ashoka to Buddhist dharma; as Senge Dradog (Lion's Roar), he "utterly destroys" non-Buddhist debaters. Pema Jungne (Born from a Lotus) matches the form in which he would have been seen in Tibet, Bhutan, and Nepal: he wears Tibetan shoes and a Nepalese hat. Dorje Drolo (Potbellied Vajra) is Padmasambhava's wrathful form, in which he subdues the obstacles of degenerate times—and the form in which he bids farewell to the Himalayas, departing from multiple Taktsangs (Tiger's Nests) simultaneously.

Bhutan's most famous and photogenic temple is named Taktsang or Tiger's Nest, based on the story that Padmasambhava arrived at the cliff on the back of his student and consort Yeshe Tshogyel, who had turned herself into a tiger in order to carry him there. Some say Padmasambhava first came to Bhutan at the Paro Taktsang site; others say he first arrived in Bumthang. But all agree on the pervasiveness of his presence throughout the country: the Guru apparently claimed that he had left not a horse's hoof of Bhutanese territory untraversed. Traces of Padmasambhava's presence can be found all across Bhutan. Many massive trees are described as Guru Rinpoche's walking stick: he seems to have thrust many staffs into the ground, only to have them take root and climb toward the sky for centuries.[9] Many stones and boulders similarly bear the imprint of Padmasambhava's meditations or his struggles with demons. The Guru's kurjey or "body prints" appear more or less plausibly in temples great and small across the country. I especially enjoyed the more implausible prints, like those that suggest Guru Rinpoche landing on a cliff from mid-air, leaving the impact of two handholds and a foothold (or vice versa) before he entered a nearby cave to meditate. The massive triangular boulder that nearly blocks the main road from Trashigang to Trashi Yangtse is seen as Padmasambhava's weapon against a demon he chased south from Samye, Tibet. After his success against the demon, the Guru placed the boulder as a protective marker—or perhaps his consorts left the boulder as a fertility site, where their own followers could access the fertility of the "sky-goers" (khandroma, sometimes translated "sky dancers" or "travelers through space").[10]

Along with his Tibetan consort Yeshe Tsogyel, Padmasambhava is also understood to have hidden spiritual treasures across the landscape for future "tertons" or treasure-revealers to discover: these hidden spiritual treasures offer a way to update the tradition while maintaining the Nyingma connection to Padmasambhava. In central Bhutan, for instance, at the end of the fifteenth century, a young blacksmith named Pema Lingpa became a major treasure-revealer, and (on the authority of his received visions) a founder of monasteries and creator of sacred dances. Ugyen Wangchuk, first King of Bhutan, with family ties back to Pema Lingpa, attempted to end the ongoing internal conflicts within Bhutan by building a temple to honor Padmasambhava at Kurjey Lhakhang, the site of the Guru's first spiritual battle in Bhutan.

Everyone in Bhutan knows the story of Padmasambhava's battle with the local deity. Sometime in the eighth century, the son of a local king named Sindhu Raj had been killed in battle by a ruler to the south, and Sindhu Raj blamed the local deity (known as Shelging Karpo) for failing to protect his son and heir. In his anger, Sindhu Raj not only withheld the normal offerings—he also caused Shelging Karpo's sacred places to be defiled with excrement. (Ten-year old Jeremy found the poop reference hysterically funny.) In response, all the local deities gathered together and agreed Sindhu Raj must be punished. Shelging Karpo snatched the king's life force, and Sindhu Raj lay very close to death. One of Sindhu Raj's secretaries thought the situation was sufficiently dire to call for external help. He wrote to Padmasambhava, asking him to come to Bumthang to rescue the king. In some versions of the story, this secretary also sent seven vessels filled with gold dust as an enticement to the Guru. When Guru Rinpoche also demanded a tantric partner, an established khandro or sky-dancer, he was offered one of the king's four daughters, the one recognized as a khandro. But even with all these preliminaries, once he arrived in Bumthang, Padmasambhava took three months to meditate in preparation for his battle with Shelging Karpo, that local deity—and his meditation left a body print on the rock of the cave.

The battle between Vajrayana adept and local deity took the form of a dance. Shelging Karpo was apparently lured out of hiding by light glinting on the vase carried by the king's khandro-daughter. Once he emerged, in the form of a snake or a snow lion (accounts vary), Guru Rinpoche was waiting for him as a garuda, a mythical horned bird. In garuda form, Guru Rinpoche grasped Shelging Karpo, lifted him into the air, and persuaded him not only to hand over the king's life force but also to become a protector of Buddhism in Bhutan—a protector of the dharma, in which dharma is understood to offer a grasp of ultimate reality. Dangling from Guru Rinpoche's garuda claws, Shelging Karpo agreed. In America, I think we'd call this a deal you can't refuse.

Strikingly, Guru Rinpoche's first major action in Bhutan was specifically a *dance* for and with a demon, performed in order to heal a rift, resolve a conflict, help a community recover from a death. Extending the Buddha's philosophical teachings to a new audience, Padmasambhava also reshaped them into art. Followers of Padmasambhava, such as Pema Lingpa in the fifteenth and sixteenth centuries, also emphasized the teaching power of sacred dance and other art forms. And Bhutanese tshechus, held on the tenth day of various months in the Bhutanese calendar, explicitly honor and invoke the presence and aid of Guru Rinpoche through the performance of similar ritual dances, making Padmasambhava central to Bhutan's intangible cultural heritage. Some of these dances perform ritual work (such as clearing the ground of obstructive energies), others represent aspects of Vajrayana teaching, others represent Padmasambhava's own Buddhist "victories" over demonic forces. One of the traditional dances is known as the "Eight Manifestations of Padmasambhava," in which eight or more masked forms dance together, bringing together those loosely linked stories about the great teacher and his "crazy wisdom" practices (Figure 2.2).

Notably, while Padmasambhava is central to the story of Vajrayana in Bhutan, he is at least as much a disruptor of social structures as he is a nation-builder. Indeed, the stories told about him demonstrate an ongoing ambivalence about governance and Vajrayana practice: Guru Rinpoche becomes a king and ceases to be a king not once but twice. The stories also suggest that Padmasambhava's curiosity about the nature of reality and his development of spiritual powers could be dangerous to those around him: an Oddiyana minister dies (accidentally) at his hands, debaters are crushed (in some stories literally, by a landslide) by his superior powers. Yet though he himself was not a nation-builder, Padmasambhava is said to have prophesied that a ruler would someday ride over the mountains from Tibet to Bhutan—and in the seventeenth century, a young monk did indeed ride over the mountains, apparently in fulfillment of that prophecy.

Figure 2.2. Yonphula dancers in The Eight Manifestations of Guru Rinpoche. My students from western Bhutan pointed out that the monastery seemed to be missing some of the relevant masks and filled in with other wrathful masks. People sitting near me told me that the yellow robe and mask represented Padmasambhava who taught Mandareva and saved them both from an early honor killing. The red form, they said, was Pema Gyelpo, lotus-born King (of Oddiyana). The white form was Loden Choki, the "proclaimer of wisdom," who mastered all the secret practices of Vajrayana. The blue form was Tshoki Dorji, Vajra born from a lake, signaling Guru Rinpoche's status as successor to the Buddha. The blue forms on the left might be Senge Dradog, the Lion's Roar, who eliminates wrong view. The purple forms on the right were probably Dorje Drolo, conqueror of demons. Missing: Shakya Senge (Lion of the Shakya, who renounced the kingdom of Oddiyana to study dharma) and Nyima Wozer (Ray of Sun, who lived and taught in charnel grounds). Of course my neighbors wanted me to check these identifications with a monk; I tried to check them with books instead.[6]

"OUR NATIONAL DRESS: OUR IDENTITY!"

On my first day of teaching at Yonphula Centenary College, I struggled into Bhutanese national dress. I wrapped a blue, silver, and gold half-kira around my waist, securing the modern plaid with velcro at my left hip before bringing the remaining fabric behind my back and using a hook-and-bar closure at the right hip to close the long woolen wrap-around skirt. Was Bhutanese national dress really a good idea? I wondered. I knew my students were required to wear it: schools and universities counted as government offices, where national dress was mandatory for all Bhutanese citizens. I had also been told that I would need to wear national dress sometimes, but foreigners didn't have to wear it all the time. But how would I know what was appropriate when? It seemed safer to stick with the local norms—if only I could work out how to get dressed!

Back in Thimphu, some hotel staff had helped us all put on national dress one day, but it all seemed more complicated now that I had to face the clothes alone. At least I had the benefit of the half-kira: a recent innovation, meaning I didn't have to work out how to wrap a rectangle of cloth into a dress secured by two brooches and an excessively tight belt. When women in southern Bhutan objected to taking on national dress back in the late 1980s, they were grappling with the full kira, usually woven of wool: not a great match for the southern climate. I shrugged into a blue wanju—a blouse without any button or integrated means of closure—and then a gold-colored tegu or satin jacket, and pinned them both shut in several places down the front. My sleeves—both wanju and tegu—still hung a foot below my hands when I let my arms drop to my sides. On each arm, I rolled the two sleeves together to form a four-to-five inch cuff, then tried to pin the cuffs so they wouldn't fall down in the midst of my teaching. When the College truck arrived outside to drive me up to Yonphula, I ran with tiny constrained steps into the kitchen, grabbed my backpack, shoved my feet into my clogs, knowing that my female students would probably be wearing strappy sandals instead. How did Bhutanese women climb mountains in these clothes? Hiking up my kira to climb into the Toyota Hilux, I felt like a Jane Austen heroine, two hundred years and thousands of miles out of place.

Twenty minutes later and 2,500 feet higher, I climbed down out of the Hilux, deeply grateful that neither skirt nor cuffs had yet unraveled. I walked up the steps and into the academic building I had cased over the weekend; I tried to settle my nerves. When the time came to teach, I opened the door of the classroom and walked into an explosion of color. Rows of tables stretched to the back of the long narrow room, compressing 32 middle-aged Master's students into too small a space. The women, mostly clustered in the first few rows, wore jackets of patterned satin in gold, royal blue, sky blue, pink, green, and scarlet; the tables blocked their kiras from view. The room held twice as many men as women: perhaps a quarter of the men wore traditional red plaid ghos; another set wore varying stripes of yellow, maroon, and brown; a few wore the plain grey gho the driver Ugyen had favored. The women had intricately worked gold brooches holding the neckline of their tegus and wanjus closed. A few of the men wore pins with an image of the fifth King and his queen on the left side of their ghos. Their gleaming white cuffs covered most of their forearms. From the walls, portraits of Bhutan's four Kings looked down on us: the fifth King's portrait hung over the entry to the room. Stunned by the mass of colors and the neat dark heads close together, I felt relieved to be in national dress, fitting in as best I could, despite my frizzy hair. Still, as I introduced myself and launched into a description of the syllabus, I wondered how I would live up to my students' elegance over the course of the semester. I had exactly one kira, wanju, and tegu. It seemed unlikely that the fashionistas in front of me would be wearing the same outfit every day of the week (see Figure 2.3).

When I announced a five-minute break in the middle of class, two women students rushed up to me from different sections of the room, looking distressed, apparently on my behalf. "Who dressed you this morning?" the first one demanded, reaching out for the neck of my outfit.

"What do you mean? I dressed myself!" I said, pulling back.

Figure 2.3. Some of Yonphula Centenary College students in national dress at the inauguration of the College.

"Never mind," she answered. "It's not a problem." But clearly it was a problem. Together, the two of them unpinned my blouse and jacket—in the middle of the classroom!—in order to put me back together in the way they felt I should be dressed. Back in Thimphu I had heard about a (male) Fulbrighter being undressed down to his underwear in a parking lot. "The ritual undressing of the chilip," a friend had called it, chilip ("grey hair") being the local word for foreigners. I had laughed then, but now I felt deeply uncomfortable, undressed in my own classroom—not that anyone else seemed fazed.

That morning, I had learned that the College needed me to teach part of a class on South Asian literature—not a field in which I had any background—starting the next day. At least my students would have the cultural context I lacked, I thought: I could ask them to summarize the history and culture of Pakistan, India, Afghanistan and Bhutan as a backdrop to our literary studies. The next day, I let the Bhutan group present first, and as one student stood and spoke for his group, I found myself anxiously worrying about time. Of course, they all knew too much about Bhutan! I should made that group go last. After a lengthy summary of Bhutan's early history, the speaker finally arrived at the moment of national unification:

> "The Zhabdrung gave us our national dress: our identity!"

"Zhabdrung" is a Tibetan title of respect for great Buddhist teachers, but in Bhutan, there is only one Zhabdrung, often referred to by this title alone: a Tibetan warrior-monk named Ngawang Namgyal who unified Bhutan in the seventeenth century. I winced a little at my student's praise of national dress, thinking of ethnic disputes over clothing from the early 1990s, but the Lhotshampa students in the class seemed unperturbed. I was also struck by the student's eager embrace of dress as identity—an equation at odds with my own sense of identity as something interior as opposed to the exterior markers of dress.

In fact, as the Bhutan group went on to point out (in a little too much depth for my class plan), the Zhabdrung was responsible for structuring many elements of Bhutanese culture, far beyond the national dress. Most of the classic features of Bhutanese culture look back to these forms often attributed to the Zhabdrung, the father of the nation: the warrior-monk who unified the nation, in no small part through the construction and maintenance of social and religious ritual.[11]

To understand Bhutan, my students seemed to be telling me, I had to understand the Zhabdrung and his legacy.

THE ZHABDRUNG AND THE MAKING OF A VAJRAYANA STATE

Images of the Zhabdrung appear all over Bhutan: in almost all of them, he wears a long, pointed gray beard. This is Zhabdrung as law-giver, founder of a nation, greatly matured from the brash 22-year-old who rode over the Himalayas from Tibet with only thirty monks and some mules loaded with the treasures of his monastery. In some ways, that combative young man was a figure of crazy wisdom not unlike Padmasambhava. When he was only eight years old, the head of another Vajrayana line—the Sakya hierarch—gave him the title of Zhabdrung, or "he at whose feet we submit," and Zhabdrung seems to have taken such submission as his due. Unlike Guru Rinpoche, however, Zhabdrung understood state-building as central to the promulgation of his spiritual lineage.

Political and spiritual challenges in Tibet drove Zhabdrung to embark on this southern adventure: the man who would unify Bhutan against waves of Tibetan invasion was, after all, a Tibetan lama himself. After the days of Padmasambhava, Vajrayana practitioners gradually split into four separate schools, with some of those schools branching out in further subdivisions (see Table 2.2).

Table 2.2. Vajrayana Schools: Nyingma, Kagyu, Sakya, Gelug

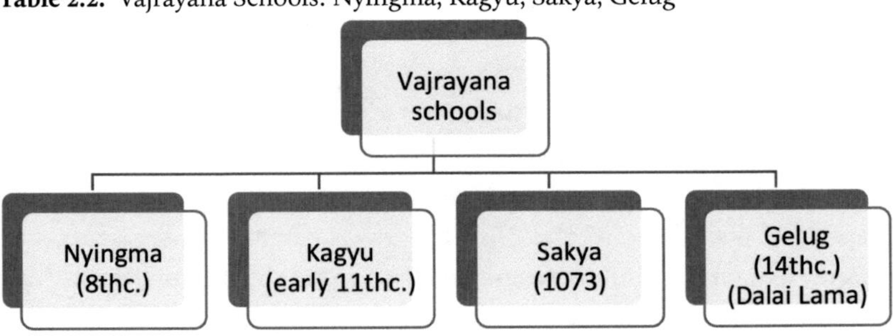

The Nyingma school (Nyingma meaning "ancient") is considered closest to the original eighth-century teachings of Padmasambhava. The Kagyu school (kagyu meaning "whispered transmission" or "oral lineage") was founded in the early eleventh century: it emphasizes meditational practice techniques and takes pride in an unbroken line of oral transmission back to Indian teachers such as Tilopa and Naropa. The Sakya school, founded in 1073, blends Vajrayana teachings with a claim to divinity: "family records and Tibetan histories state that the noble family is descended from celestial beings from the Realm of Heavenly Clear Light." To maintain that family link, at least one male member of the Sakya family in each generation must be not a monk but a married lineage holder, responsible for producing heirs to the tradition.[12] The Gelug school, youngest of the four Vajrayana lineages, is based on the work of Tsongkhapa, an influential fourteenth-century teacher: Gelugs are best known in the West as the school headed by the Dalai Lama, whose new reincarnation is chosen or discovered by signs and portents after the death of the previous Dalai Lama. Among Vajrayana practitioners, the Gelug school is known for its scholarship and strict maintenance of monastic practices. Of these four schools, the Sakya lineage is the smallest in terms of followers, while the Kagyu school has produced the greatest number of subsidiary lines. Within Bhutan, most Buddhists are either Kagyu or Nyingma, while Gelugs are few, since Tibetan Gelugs with their Mongol allies repeatedly invaded the newly unified Bhutan in both the seventeenth and eighteenth centuries.

Zhabdrung's arrival in Bhutan was the result of a power struggle over monastic power back in Tibet. By the eleventh century, powerful Tibetan families and clans had built monasteries and endowed monastic communities with important economic resources, and those families had a vested interest in maintaining control over the monastery's assets and spiritual affairs. One strategy for control was to retain the position of abbot (the head of the monastery) within the family. In some cases, the position of abbot might pass from uncle to nephew or from father to son (with a high-placed male fathering children before taking monastic vows). But the vicissitudes of human reproduction, including reasonably high levels of infant and childhood mortality, made continuity of family leadership an ongoing problem.[13] And, as powerful families and clans struggled to keep control of resources, monastic leaders chafed at their interference. Eventually, the monastics drew on the doctrine of reincarnation to put forward their own model of succession and continuity, a model based on "finding the *trulku* or reincarnation of the deceased person and passing down the monastic establishment and all associated entitlements and assets through [. . .] successive incarnations."[14] The trulku institution enabled the monastery rather than the family to maintain control over its resources: a reincarnation, once discovered, would be brought to the monastery and trained by older teachers who would rule the monastery until the reincarnation had attained his majority. Again, this apparently mystical practice worked to solve very practical and worldly tensions: in the case of the Dalai Lama, the practice also distributed influence as different reincarnations were "discovered" in different regions of Tibet.

But the inheritance-by-reincarnation model created its own set of troubles. Unfortunately, the procedures for identifying the child reincarnation were "highly unclear and flexible" and thus "prone to abuse and manipulation."[15] Karma Phuntsho quotes from the "great fifth" Dalai Lama's memoir to stress the various misunderstandings and misrepresentations marring the process from its early days. These issues had major political implications: a dispute over rival claims to trulku status drove Zhabdrung Ngawang Namgyel from Tibet to Bhutan, while later disputes over who was or was not a valid reincarnation of the Zhabdrung himself would eventually destabilize the country he had shaped.

Ngawang Namgyel, the future unifier of Bhutan, was born into the Gya family of abbots, larely co-extensive with a Vajrayana school known as Drukpa Kagyu (Dragon Kagyu), which had been founded by a teacher named Tsangpa Gyare (1161–1211) at the end of the twelfth century. When Tsangpa Gyare was building a monastery at Ralung, a violent storm raged overhead: the founder took the rolling thunder, understood as the voice of the clouds or the voice of a thunder-dragon, as an omen, and added Brug (pronounced Druk, meaning thunder dragon) to the name of the monastery and the sect he was founding. The name would eventually accrue to the country unified as Druk Yul, land of the thunder dragon, by Zhabdrung Ngawang Namgyel.

The first recognized reincarnation of Tsangpa Gyare appeared only some two hundred years after the founder's death, which meant that the assets of this Drukpa Kagyu school had mostly passed down through the

Gya family line. But if recognized reincarnations of Tsangpa Gyare had been few, they had also been powerful: in particular, the fourth reincarnation was the impressive Pema Karpo, known as "the omniscient" for the breadth of his learning and mastery. Ngawang Namgyel, already installed at age 13 as the abbot of Ralung monastery through his family line, was one of the young protégés aspiring to be recognized as Pema Karpo's reincarnation. Unfortunately, the regional Tsangpa ruler had already chosen to back Zhabdrung's major rival as the reincarnation instead. Tensions over the competing claims led to threats and curses on both sides, until, in 1616, when Zhabdrung was 22, he learned that the Tsangpa ruler was about to attack him at Ralung.

Zhabdrung at first planned to seek Mongolian help against his opponents (the Mongols were not yet closely allied with the Gelugs), but a visiting Bhutanese patron suggested that Zhabdrung go south instead—and a vision persuaded the young abbot to take this advice. His party left under cover of darkness and took two days to reach a border made impassable by heavy snow. For days, the travelers sheltered from the blizzard in a cave, eventually finding their way through the mountain pass by following a fox. Having received advance warning of Zhabdrung's coming from his Bhutanese patron, lamas and chieftains from Gasa in northern Bhutan met the party on the other side of the pass. From Gasa, Zhabdrung traveled to Thimphu, where he visited a temple founded by one of his ancestors, then continued on to Paro. His arrival came to be seen as the fulfillment of Padmasambhava's prophecy.

In seventeenth-century Bhutan, Zhabdrung was a figure of spiritual, magical, and military power—categories that overlapped and blended throughout the Himalayas—and on all these fronts, Zhabdrung's quarrel with the Tsangpa ruler followed him to Bhutan. Early on, for instance, the Tsangpa ruler's Bhutanese allies forced Zhabdrung into an undignified withdrawal from Paro, but later, after Zhabdrung undertook a retreat to strengthen his occult powers, his magic was credited with causing the death of the Tsangpa ruler by smallpox. In Tibet, people started saying, "Do not compete with the Drukpa in magical power." In Bhutan, Zhabdrung celebrated his power by composing a poetic seal or emblem known as the "16 I's," identifying himself through a series of claims that seem a little like a medieval Buddhist version of a hip-hop throwdown. The most combative and magical assertions include claims like "10. Who is the rival that does not tremble before me?" and "11. I am the hero who destroys hosts of demons," or even "12. Who is the powerful one that can repulse my power?" Later, after completing a three-year retreat from which he emerged with the long grey beard he wears in Bhutanese iconography, Zhabdrung sent out an edict to be placed at mountain passes, monuments, cliffs, rivers, and other strategic locations in Bhutan, announcing that "all gods, humans, and spirits of the Lhomonkhazi from this day fall under the dominion of great magician Ngawang Namgyal and all must heed to his words." Zhabdrung's magic and the force of his protector deity could also be seen at work in accidents, as when a second Tibetan invasion managed to take over the dzong Zhabdrung had been building (Semtokha), but ammunition stored in the dzong then exploded and the dzong collapsed on the invaders. In multiple ways, Zhabdrung's claim to occult powers contributed to his success in shaping Bhutan into a recognized nation.[16]

Above all, Zhabdrung became Bhutan's pre-eminent law-giver, builder of dzongs, architect of governance structures. As Richard Whitecross points out, Zhabdrung's Ngachudrukma, his poetic emblem of the 16 I's, not only emphasizes his power and willingness to take on any comers, it also stresses the importance of the "dual system" of governance in his thinking. The first three I's are particularly important in this regard:

1. I turn the wheel of the dual systems (secular and spiritual).
2. I am a good refuge for all.
3. I hold the teachings of the glorious Drukpa.

After achieving enlightenment, the Buddha is described as returning to earth to "turn the wheel of dharma for sentient beings," but Zhabdrung turns a slightly different wheel: that of the dual system of secular and spiritual rule. And where Buddhist prayers usually begin with taking refuge in 1) the Buddha, 2) the dharma (Buddhist teachings), and 3) the sangha (the community of believers), Zhabdrung's claim to offer good refuge comes not as a first step but as a follow-on to his model of rule. Finally, the dual system is linked to his own role as a Drukpa lineage holder. The dual systems (secular and spiritual) will come to define Zhabdrung's approach to state-building in Bhutan: for him to define himself first and foremost in terms of that dual system even before he had put it into action underscores its importance in his mind and his heritage.[17]

What exactly is the "dual system"? The phrase evokes the combination of spiritual and secular rule in a way that looks back to the figure of Padmasambhava even as it comes to be closely associated with the figure of Zhabdrung. Tibetan king Trisong Detsen (742–97) asked the scholar Padmasambhava (the historical figure around whom the mythological stories grew) to compose a legal code for Tibet, a legal code appropriate to Tibet's relatively new status as a Buddhist nation. In developing this code, Guru Rinpoche distinguished spiritual from temporal laws by describing spiritual laws as "a Silken Knot (*dargye duephue*) that is easy and light at first but gradually tightens, while temporal laws were compared to a Golden Yoke (*sergyi nyashing*) that grows heavier and heavier with the degree of the crimes."[18]

In the seventeenth century, Zhabdrung put himself at the head of this dual system, and the sixteen dzongs he built embodied the connections he forged between the secular and spiritual systems. Dzongs are massive, fortified structures, housing both monastics and state administrators, and capable of withstanding attack (see Figures 2.4 and 2.5).

Just as the dzongs house both monastics and state administrators, so the dual system branched out from the Zhabdrung to include the

Figure 2.4. Punakha dzong, seen from across Ma Chhu, the mother river.

Figure 2.5. Paro dzong, seen from below in winter, emphasizing its defensive strengths

Je Khenpo, the top authority on the monastic side, and the Druk Desi, or the chief ruler on the administrative side.[19] Under the Druk Desi came an executive cabinet comprised of three governors (chila or pönlops) representing the West (Paro), South (Dagana), and East (Trongsa), along with three Dzongpöns (rulers of the dzongs) at Thimphu, Wangdiphodrung, and Punakha, as well as a state leader of protocol (zhung drönyer). Map 2.1 shows the locations of these various centers of power.

Central to Zhabdrung's vision of Bhutan was the idea of a religious state. As Karma Phuntsho describes it, "The whole enterprise of state-building was [. . .] a religious project at the heart of which was the sacrosanct figure of Zhabdrung and his Gya family line. The state existed for the line and vice versa."[21] Unfortunately for this vision of the nation, Zhabdrung's line would end with him, after his offspring, including a granddaughter, died within his lifetime. On April 30th, 1651, Zhabdrung entered a "retreat" at Punakha from which he never emerged; that day is

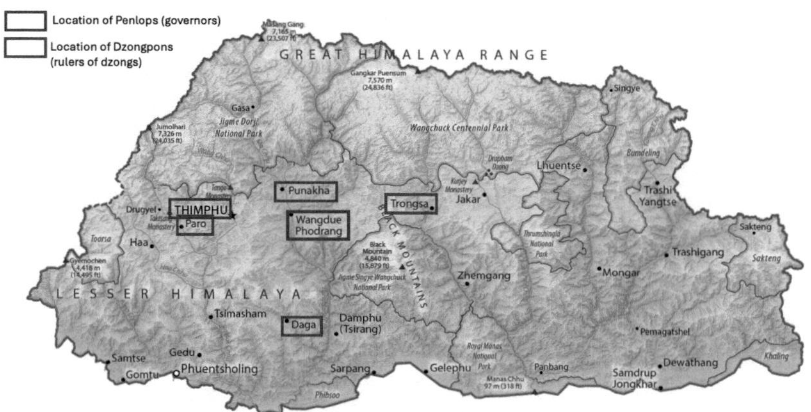

Map 2.1. Political Map of Bhutan with Dzongpöns, Penlöps, and mountain passes marked; adapted from Nations Online Project[20]

now celebrated as the anniversary of his death, though his death was not acknowledged for decades.

During those years of what we might call the Zhabdrung's un-death, military campaigns conducted in his name (under public belief that Zhabdrung was alive and guiding the campaigns) expanded the power of his government across central and eastern Bhutan.[22] Many features of Bhutanese culture that are attributed directly to Zhabdrung were codified in writing only after his death: this includes Bhutan's zorig chusum, or 13 traditional arts, codified by Tenzin Rabgye, the fourth Druk Desi, who ruled Bhutan 1681–94, and the legal code, formalized in 1729. Despite the uncertainty over his death, Zhabdrung's heroic stature within Bhutan is hard to overstate. Zhabdrung appears in most Bhutanese shrines as one of the "Three Gems of Bhutan," given equal standing with the Buddha Sakyamuni and Padmasambhava.[23] A sense of mystical or magical power still adheres to his figure as the founder of the nation—and the power of Drukpa Kagyu as a state religion can be viscerally felt in community rituals like this moment, when the monks of the Kanglung Drukpa Kagyu monastery emerged from a 45-day retreat (Figure 2.6). Both the country's strengths and its fragility extend forward from the time of Zhabdrung and the fault-lines left from his early nation-building.

Figure 2.6. Kanglung monks and community members process up the national highway to celebrate the completion of Yarney, a 45-day monastic retreat. Kanglung residents line the side of the road, putting candy, pins, matches and other small items into the monks' ceremonial begging bowls. Drukpa Kagyu monks receive a stipend from the government, which makes the begging symbolic rather than necessary.

LINGERING GEOGRAPHIC AND POLITICAL DIVISIONS

In the early years of the eighteenth century, once Zhabdrung's death was officially acknowledged, Zhabdrung's regents, those responsible for sustaining the nation-state he had created, officially recognized four separate lines of reincarnation—including mind, body, and speech reincarnations of the Zhabdrung, as well as a separate reincarnation line for his son. Historians suggest that the recognition of four separate reincarnations worked, and perhaps was designed, to blunt the power that might otherwise be held by a single incarnate ruler. This splintering of recognized authority led to chaotic periods of rivalry and instability, intensified by regional rivalries.

Sonam Kinga's brief history of the period of ecclesiocracy, or rule by religious figures, underscores the extent to which the existence of multiple lines of Zhabdrung reincarnations encouraged internecine strife and political turnover: "Between 1680 and 1907, Bhutan had 16 heads of states known as gyaltshab (rgyal tsbab). [. . .] Most of them were enthroned at very young ages"—as young as three years old—"by factions who stood to profit from the offices associated with having one's protégé as head of state. Although their average reign was 17 years, most spent these years growing up and getting educated." Civil governance was in still worse shape: while there were 16 heads of state between 1680 and 1907, there were 59 civil rulers (with the title of Desi) of whom "15 served for less than a year and 24 served between two and four years."[24]

Karma Phuntsho, meanwhile, notes how power moved from one regional center to another, with the fifth, sixth, and "probably" the seventh Desi all coming from Kabji, the eighth and ninth from Wang, the tenth and eleventh from Bönbji, and then the twelfth through the sixteenth from Wang.[25] Holding power was a bloody business, as Kinga notes, quoting further research by Sangay Dorji (2017): "Thirteen of the civil rulers were assassinated. Eleven were forced to abdicate at the risk of assassination. Seven abdicated on their own, fearing for their lives if they continued in office."[26] Lack of continuity and clarity drastically limited government power and authority. By the end of the nineteenth century, different political forces were backing separate reincarnations and maintaining two distinct seats of government: one in Thimphu, the other in Punakha.

Even beyond the struggles among these ruling powers, larger regional divisions shaped the country. The mountain ranges separating distinct river valley societies had given rise to different language groups across the country, and Zhabdrung's arrival underscored some of these geographical differences. When Zhabdrung began his project of national unification under a Drukpa Kagyu banner, many of the groups he encountered were already Vajrayana Buddhists, and not all of them were happy to welcome him. The histories tell of "five lamaist factions" who opposed him, though the listing of his opponents lacks consistency. In the West (Thimphu, Punakha, and the Paro and Shar valleys), Zhabdrung's forces allied with some groups and conquered or exiled others, with the result that the areas most fully under Zhabdrung's control were also most extensively Drukpa Kagyu by 1639.[27] In the center and east of the country, however, Drukpa military forces struggled not with religious figures but with secular chieftains, many of whom were perpetually at war with one another and/or with nearby Tibetan forces. In extending their range of governance, Drukpa administrators were able to separate religious differences from political arrangements—especially because Zhabdrung had maintained close connections with various Nyingma practitioners in Tibet, and many religious leaders in the center and the east were Nyingma lamas. As a result, while Zhabdrung's Drukpa Kagyu school of Buddhism dominates the west of Bhutan, Nyingma temples and practitioners still predominate in the east.

Along with the Drukpa Kagyu religious community, Zhabdrung's government remained more strongly established in western territories than in the east. Dzongkha (the language of the dzongs) was used predominantly in the west; the center of the country featured multiple different languages, and easterners (Sharchops) tended to speak Tshangla or Sharchop—the latter term meaning literally the language of the east. George van Driem's work on the linguistic diversity of Bhutan in 1993, represented in Map 2.2, shows both later historical developments with the presence of Nepali-speakers in the south and the persistence of distinct linguistic communities in different regions of the country.

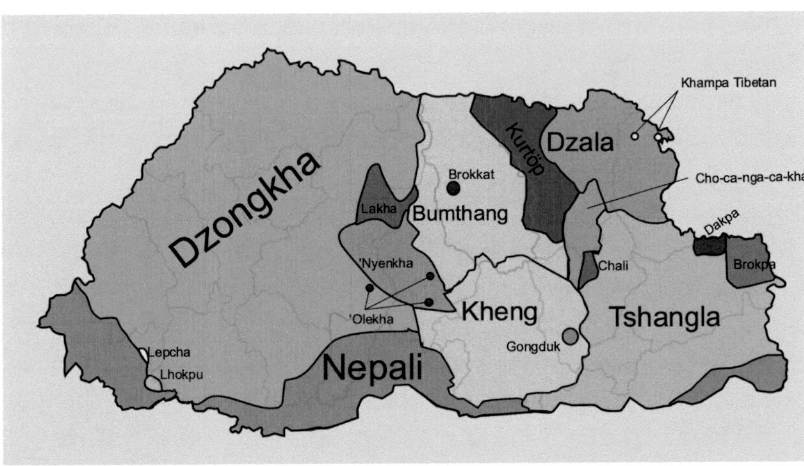

Map 2.2. Map of language groups in Bhutan, after Van Driem 1993[28]

Differences in government structure can be loosely mapped onto this kind of linguistic differentiation, as suggested by Map 2.3. Eastern territories such as Tashigang were only roughly integrated into tax and control structures in 1659, and boundaries remained "unclear and variable" for "several centuries."[29] The cabinet of executive leaders ruling the country during and after Zhabdrung's "retreat" and death leaned heavily to the west: the Pönlops of "the east," for instance, was based in Trongsa, firmly in the center of the country. In the actual east, local chieftains continued to operate with significant degrees of independence—and after the installation of the monarchy, it was in the east that disruptive Zhabdrung reincarnations continued to emerge, as discussed in chapter three.

While the figure of Zhabdrung emblematizes Bhutan's national identity to this day, the history of his arrival, his early campaigns, his premature death, and the geographic features of the country all contribute to ongoing regional differences within the country. Bhutan's kings inherited these regional divisions and resolving those (often unacknowledged) rifts remains a work in progress.

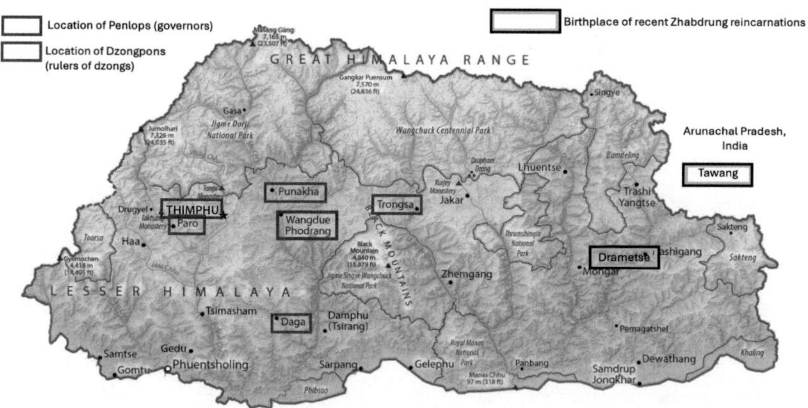

Map 2.3. Political Map of Bhutan with Dzongpöns, Penlöps, mountain passes, and locations associated with recent Zhabdrung reincarnations marked; adapted from Nations Online Project[30]

THE SPIRITUAL HERITAGE OF BHUTAN

This chapter has focused on Bhutan's earlier history, highlighting the influential figures of Padmasambhava and Zhabdrung Ngawang Namgyal, but Bhutan's understanding of itself as "the last Vajrayana state" brings with it important consequences for the country's recent history as well. It bears repeating that, despite Bhutanese reverence for Zhabdrung as the ruler who shaped the nation as an explicitly religious project, the 2008 Constitution does not define the nation itself as a religious state. Instead, the role of maintaining Zhabdrung's dual system of sacred and secular rule is explicitly but somewhat elliptically assigned to the monarch in Article 2, The Institution of Monarchy, which proclaims,

1 His Majesty the Druk Gyalpo is the Head of State and the symbol of unity of the Kingdom and of the people of Bhutan.
2 The Chhoe-sid-nyi of Bhutan shall be unified in the person of the Druk Gyalpo who, as a Buddhist, shall be the upholder of the Chhoe-sid.

The Constitution was published in both Dzongkha and English, but the English-language version resists translation of certain key words and concepts such as Druk Gyalpo (the King) and Chhoe-sid-nyi (the dual system). Non-Dzongkha readers might not fully grasp the element of sacred rule this point assigns to the King: the sentence at once seems to take the King's Buddhist identity for granted and require that Buddhist identity as a core component of the monarch's own identity. Nothing in the subsequent discussion of lineal monarchical descent requires the monarch to hold Buddhist beliefs or engage in Buddhist practices, though marriage to a non-Bhutanese person explicitly disqualifies a person otherwise entitled to succeed to the throne.[31]

Having established the monarch as upholder of the dual system as well as the country's symbol of unity, the Constitution then takes a step back. Rather than proclaiming Bhutan a Vajrayana State, the Constitution-Drafting Committee asserted in Article 3, Spiritual Heritage, that

1. Buddhism is the spiritual heritage of Bhutan, which promotes the principles and values of peace, non-violence, compassion and tolerance.

2. The Druk Gyalpo is the protector of all religions in Bhutan.
3. It shall be the responsibility of religious institutions and personalities to promote the spiritual heritage of the country while also ensuring that religion remains separate from politics in Bhutan. Religious institutions and personalities shall remain above politics.

Effectively blurring conceptual boundaries among culture, heritage, and religion, Article 3 offers an aspirational statement of religious tolerance and political inclusion. But while "spiritual heritage" may seem more inclusive than a "state religion" would be, Bhutan's ongoing struggle (pre- and post-Constitution) to define and maintain a common cultural heritage has not always been especially inclusive or peaceful.

In his essay, "The Zhabdrung's Legacy: Buddhism and Constitutional Transformation in Bhutan," Richard Whitecross quotes from a provocative set of notes on the constitutional drafting process: notes briefly available online that have since been removed. When it came to the official status of Buddhism within Bhutan, one delegate, Dasho Ugen Dorji, then Speaker of the National Assembly, remarked that "ethnic and religious differences are the main causes of problems in this world." He recalled "the problems caused by vying religious factions when the Zhabdrung, Ngawang Namgyal, arrived in the seventeenth century," and then referenced similar conflicts "in recent years in Dramitse," as well as Tibet's loss of independence as a result of "politicization of religion." Whitecross glosses the reference to Dramitse as "a brief challenge to the central government that had arisen in the 1990s in eastern Bhutan," but that challenge is difficult to find in the public record.[32]

The United Nations High Commission on Refugee maintains a "Chronology for Lhotshampas in Bhutan," which includes another fleeting reference to discontent in eastern Bhutan: a summary in the *Japan Economic Review* of a 1994 article in a Nepali newspaper *The Independent*, claiming that eastern Sharchops had organized anti-government demonstrations in eastern and southern Bhutan, and that those demonstrations were crushed by Bhutanese government security forces when police fired on the demonstrators and killed eight. The Nepali newspaper claimed that "The Sarchokpas [*sic*] are angry with the King for the false promises made by him during the last three years, when he managed to raise over 10,000 militiamen from among them to crush the southern Bhutanese movement."[33] Bhutan's National Assembly (Tshogdu) was canceled in 1994 (as it had been in 1990 due to concerns over Lhotshampa protests). In 1995, the National Assembly Speaker's Report for 1995 made several references to troubles in the east. Apparently, the Home Ministry had distributed a brief to the Chimis, the "People's Representatives," identifying six Sharchops or easterners who were "involved in ngolop ["anti-national"] activity." One of the Mongar representatives corrected that figure, expressing "his regret that about 20 individuals from the east are said to be involved in ngolop activities although only six names had been given in the brief." This confession of unrest in the east emerged in the midst of multiple pledges of loyalty to the King and the Tsa Wa Sum (the "three core elements," usually the King, the government, and the people of Bhutan), and so the Mongar representative went on to assert that "that the claims made by these ngolops that they have the support of the people of eastern Bhutan are blatant lies. Leave alone any material or physical support, as everyone knows, not even a single word of support will these ngolops receive from the people." The speaker then reiterated the total loyalty and support of the people of Mongar for the Tsa-Wa-Sum.[34]

The Speaker's Report also included an earlier extended discussion of the National Assembly's desire to extradite and execute a man known as Rongthong Kinley Dorji, who had gone to Nepal, "established a subversive party called Druk National Congress with himself as president" and then began

> [. . .] spreading baseless allegations of human rights violations in Bhutan. He has been attempting to create misunderstanding between the government and the people by falsely claiming that the people of eastern and western Bhutan support his subversive activities. However, nobody believes a single word of the malicious lies spread by him in an attempt to erode the pure bond that exists between the government and the people.

Western Chimis emphasized Kinley Dorji's failure to repay business loans; eastern Chimis rejected his claim to be from Rongthong in Trashigang district.[35] The Home Minister spoke up to identify Kinley Dorji as a man born in Zhemgang (southeast of Trongsa) and to suggest that he was not worth the Assembly's attention—but it took several speakers to move the discussion as a whole past the Chimis' fury with this "two-faced" false Tashigang man. Even when it was acknowledged that Bhutan had no extradition treaty with Nepal, Chimis demanded that the government attempt to extradite him in order to execute him. The idea of rebel activities in the East of Bhutan seems to have been so outrageous as to be unspeakable, and, over time, perhaps unthinkable.

Attempting to sidestep religious conflict by defining Vajrayana as Bhutan's spiritual heritage rather than state religion, the Constitutional Drafting Commission drew on earlier debates linking national identity to a broad sense of cultural heritage and practice. Those debates had themselves developed out of the government's insistence on cultural uniformity as a means of overcoming challenges to national sovereignty. Unfortunately, uniformity came at a high cost, as Chapter 4 will show. Before we look in detail at Bhutan's cultural conflicts, however, we need to understand the figure of the monarch as a bridge between the seventeenth-century nation shaped by Zhabdrung and his dual system and twenty-first century Bhutan, newly democratic and developing fast. The next chapter, Chapter 3, "King of Destiny—and Democracy," looks into the ways in which Bhutan's monarchy has picked up Zhabdrung's mantle, and how the country's turn to constitutional democratic monarchy relates to the dual system of rule on the one hand and to key features of Bhutanese monarchy on the other.

CHAPTER THREE

THE KING OF DESTINY—AND DEMOCRACY

For the most part, issues of cultural uniformity, like the Zhabdrung's power and mystique, seemed far distant from my graduate students' struggles with timed writing and close analysis of literary texts. Near the middle of the semester, however, larger national forces started to command local attention. Yonphula Centenary College was being officially inaugurated in early October 2017, with Prime Minister Tshering Tobgay confirmed as the official "guest of honor" just a few days ahead of the event. The inauguration followed an elaborate program beginning with the chibdrel, modeled on the ceremony performed by the Zhabdrung when he launched the construction of the Punakha dzong as his official seat. This ceremony began with a procession including costumed dancers, ritual chanting, a marchang (alcohol offering), prayers, and the serving of some 15 fruits and special foods (Figure 3.1).

Shortly before the inauguration, my students had gently confirmed that my everyday clothes were not adequate for the event. My neighbor Chencho offered to loan me something nice to wear, and she suggested I look through the clothing cupboard in her bedroom. As I walked into the room, the first thing I saw was the standard portrait of the fourth King, in a traditional gilt frame, draped with a kata, hanging on the bedroom wall. I paused, struggling to imagine hanging a portrait of any US president on my bedroom wall back in the United States.

Figure 3.1. Yonphula Centenary College Inauguration. Students, faculty, and dean pictured with the Prime Minister of Bhutan (in orange), the President of Sherubtse College (to my left), and the Vice-Chancellor of the Royal University of Bhutan (on the other side of the Prime Minister, next to my colleague Chitra, Director of the MA program). The Dean of Yonphula Centenary College is on the far right, standing; to his right, Ugyen Tshering, linguistics instructor.

Chencho saw me looking at the portrait. "We don't talk about favorites," she said,

> [. . .] but really, he is our favorite King. We call him the King of destiny. When he became King in 1972 at the age of 16, he was the youngest King in the world. He had to rise to the challenges of a nation in the midst of modernization and transition. And then he gave us democracy! We didn't even ask for it!

Something in her voice suggested that democracy had come too soon. Back in the United States, I had read Western newspapers quoting Bhutanese citizens to this effect, but this was the first time I had heard it myself. "You think Bhutan was not ready for democracy?" I asked, a little skeptically. Media portrayals of happy Bhutanese people clinging to their King had seemed condescending, even orientalist to me.

"Oh, all these ministers!" my friend exclaimed. "It used to be that you only had to respect the King—but now you have to respect all of these ministers too. We are not a large country! Soon we will have to respect everyone!"

I laughed, thinking she was joking, since respecting everyone didn't seem a bad thing, but then I realized Chencho meant the more elaborate Bhutanese etiquette of respect, or driglam namzha: bending one's body down, visibly deferring, both physically and verbally. Bhutanese citizens are not supposed to look their King in the eye, for instance, though the many photographs of the royal family smiling into the camera lens seemed to counter that prohibition. Did that deep demonstration of respect now apply to ministers too? At the inauguration the next day, I was relieved to learn that my family and I could speak upright and informally with Prime Minister Tshering Tobgay, who made us all laugh with his swift repartee even as he cracked open a walnut for young Jeremy to eat.

Still, my conversation with Chencho had upended my prior understanding of Bhutan's transition to democracy. Was Bhutan being democratized? Or was democracy being transformed by its adoption within the Dragon Kingdom? Or both? And what exactly was the role of Bhutan's Kings in this transition to democracy? In order to understand the way democracy functions within Bhutan, I realized, I would need to have a clearer understanding of democracy more generally, as well as an understanding of the intersection of democracy with the monarchy, given the King's central role and power within the country.

The first section of this chapter looks at Bhutan's transition from ecclesiocracy (rule legitimated by association with Zhabdrung incarnations) to monarchy, as well as the vulnerabilities created through this transition. The second section surveys key roles and functions associated with the King, from symbolically embodying national unity, to upholding the dual system of spiritual and secular government through the power of appointments, to the combination of kasho (royal command) and kidu (royal grant) or soelra (gift), used to steer and implement national policy. The third section considers different forms of democracy operating in Bhutan, from participatory democracy occurring at the village level to partisan forms of representative democracy first introduced and explicitly practiced in 2007 in the lead up to Bhutan's first official party-based elections in 2008. The fourth section follows Winnie Bothe in arguing that while the fourth King used kasho (royal command) to try to maintain and increase broad citizen participation in Bhutan's new representative democracy, political elites framed this new democratic government as the King's gift (soelra), as a way of maintaining existing power hierarchies, with the result that the new democracy could be seen, paradoxically, as expanding rather than sharing the King's power.

COMPLEXITIES OF A LATE HEREDITARY MONARCHY

I had read Karma Phuntsho's lengthy *History of Bhutan* before arriving, but I found it hard to process all the names and dates, which left my recall of key events a little cloudy.

"Where did the Kings come from, anyway?" I asked Ugyen as he drove us across Bhutan. "I thought the country was ruled by reincarnations of the Zhabdrung. Where did the reincarnations go?"

Ugyen glanced at me in the rearview mirror, then looked away. He gave a slightly nervous chuckle. "I am not sure, madam."

I hadn't meant to make him uncomfortable. I dropped the subject.

Months later, I tried again, asking one of my students about politics at the end of a writing conference. We'd been talking about a political reference in a Shakespearean sonnet, so it seemed reasonable to extend the conversation. "What happened to Bhutan's older form of government, anyway?" I asked. "How did Bhutan shift from Zhabdrung reincarnations to the five Kings?"

My student's eyes slid away, reminding me of Ugyen's earlier reaction. "The reincarnations stopped, madam. No more reincarnations." I had asked my students to call me Betsy rather than madam. Some students could not accept the informality of using my given name; others oscillated. In this case, the formal address seemed like another sign of discomfort.

In my experience, Bhutan's emphasis on consensus and public accord meant that instances of conflict and dispute tended to be glossed over and drop out of public awareness. Bhutanese journalists were not allowed to write about the royal family (except in a vein of celebration and praise) and ordinary people I spoke with tended to be similarly long on commendations and short on details. Still, I found the discomfort on the subject of the Zhabdrungs puzzling, especially when I went back to written histories, which seemed to deal with the topic quite directly. Of the Zhabdrung's four separate reincarnation lines, two had apparently fizzled out by the end of the nineteenth century (though "fizzling out" probably occurred under some pressure I didn't see described). The first King, Ugyen Wangchuk, was crowned at a time when the Zhabdrung's mind reincarnation, the most influential of the lines, was between the fifth and sixth incarnations. The King had been on good terms with the fifth incarnation and welcomed the sixth incarnation, who was enthroned in 1912. (The King was emphatically not on good terms with the Zhabdrung's speech reincarnation, sometimes called the Chogley incarnation, to the point that he banned official recognition of further incarnations after Yeshe Ngödrup, the fifth incarnation, unilaterally undertook work to "restore" Bhutan's two most sacred relics: the Zhabdrung's body and the Rangjung Kharsapani, a vertebra from the cremation of Tsangpa Gyare marked with an image of Chenrezing.[1]) After 1917, the monarchy recognized only one incarnation line—and that recognition would not last long.

The problem was that in the first half of the twentieth century, the Zhabdrung's influential mind incarnation retained enough power to pose a threat to the monarchy. When the sixth mind incarnation encroached on the (second) King's authority by giving away grazing rights that belonged to the throne, the dispute soon rose to an armed conflict in which the young lama's uncle was killed. Amid rumors that the young lama was practicing black magic against the King came the news that he had sent his brothers to ask Mahatma Gandhi for help, and that he was planning to flee to somewhere outside of Bhutan, escalating the public relations threat to the monarchy. Eventually, armed soldiers surrounded the young spiritual leader in his official residence. When high-level monastics failed to intervene, the sixth incarnation was assassinated by the King's men, though the King told the British political officer that the young lama's death was a mystery, "his passing not even noticed by the monks who were sleeping in the same room."[2] What could have been a major threat to the newly established monarchy had been summarily removed.

This was not quite the end of the story, however: even though the third King is best known for his modernization efforts, his rule was still insecure enough to be threatened by the institution of the Zhabdrung's incarnations. At the outset of the third King's reign, another mind incarnation, clandestinely recognized in eastern Bhutan, was killed by men supposedly in the King's service. In 1962, Indian diplomat Nari Rustomji took a seven-year-old boy recognized as the Zhabdrung's ninth mind incarnation to live in Manali, northern India, under the protection of the Government of India; this incarnation died in 2003 after an extended struggle with cancer. In the twenty-first century, social media pages still online in 2023 celebrate the "tenth mind incarnation of the Zhabdrung," born in Trashi Yangtse in 2003.[3] But despite the persistence of the reincarnation lines (a new speech reincarnation has also been recognized), Bhutan's monarchy now seems too well established for clandestine incarnations to challenge its rule. Still, I could see that the story of one of Bhutan's wise Kings ordering the assassination of a Zhabdrung incarnation was precisely the kind of thing that might drop out of most official histories and public recollection. And while Karma Phuntsho reports that the Je Khenpo, Bhutan's chief abbot, had proclaimed the fourth King, Jigme Singye Wangchuk, as the Zhabdrung mind incarnation, that proclamation doesn't seem to have been widely accepted.[4]

It seemed odd to think of religious-political assassinations occurring in the generation just preceding the fourth King: the man we had heard urging new law students to dedicate themselves to their country. It was even more unsettling to remember that the Zhabdrung incarnations weren't Bhutan's only high-level assassinations in the twentieth century: in 1964, the third King's brother-in-law and prime minister, Jigme Palden Dorji, was also assassinated, allegedly at the instigation of the King's mistress, a Tibetan woman named Yangki. This assassination too seemed to reveal some vulnerability in the monarchy and in the government more generally—a vulnerability dating back to the role of the Dorji family in the original installation of the Wangchuk dynasty.

Jigme Palden Dorji was the grandson of Ugyen Dorji, an influential Bhutanese leader and diplomat, the man who officially proposed that Ugyen Wangchuk be raised to the role of Druk Gyalpo or hereditary King.[5] With a power base both in Haa (in northwestern Bhutan) and in Kalimpong (West Bengal), Ugyen Dorji was a successful trader and businessman who was comfortable communicating in English and Tibetan as well as Dzongkha. The British appointed him as their "Bhutan agent," and some say that British officials suggested to Dorji that he appoint himself King of Bhutan. (Ugyen Dorji supposedly replied that he had no interest in being King, though he was willing to play kingmaker.) Dorji wrote to Bhutan's council of state laying out the case for installing Ugyen Wangchuk as hereditary monarch; the rationale included the need for a head of state to manage foreign relations, especially with Britain, then the major power in the Himalayan region, which had already honored Wangchuk with a knighthood.[6] Since most of the members of the council of state had been appointed by Ugyen Wangchuk, Dorji's "bold proposal" was soon accepted. Along with the hereditary monarchy granted the Wangchuk family, the arrangement seems to have established a hereditary role of Gongzim, or Chamberlain, for Ugyen Dorji and his heirs.

The sons of the first King and his Chamberlain had an even warmer, closer working relationship than their fathers had, and by the third generation, the two families were joined by marriage: Jigme Dorji Wangchuk, soon to be Bhutan's third King, married Kesang Choeden, the daughter of Sonam Tobgay Dorji, Bhutan's Lord Chamberlain, and the granddaughter of Ugyen Dorji. Soon Jigme Palden Dorji, brother to Kesang Choeden, became Bhutan's lord chamberlain, a post converted to that of prime minister after Jawaharlal Nehru's influential state visit in 1958. In this period, the Dorjis remained a powerful family in their own right, able to draw on their British connections and wealth derived from their oversight of Nepali settlements in southwestern Bhutan.

The Wangchuk-Dorji alliance was soon under strain, however. Prime Minister Jigme Palden Dorji evidently raised military hackles both by establishing new policies and appointing non-elites to high positions. The third King suffered his first heart attack at age 20 and struggled with ill health for much of his life. He also began a long-running affair with a Tibetan woman named Yangki, with whom he had four children (two sons and two daughters). While the second King had maintained two sister-queens with separate households and the fourth King would one day formally marry four sisters, the third King never officially married Yangki, nor did he legitimate any of their offspring. Yet despite her lack of official status, Yangki accompanied the King to many official events and held a great deal of unofficial power. On at least one occasion, Yangki had army vehicles and personnel transport her personal luggage. When the prime minister (the brother of Bhutan's Queen) found out about this, he had the luggage returned and forbade Yangki's personal use of state vehicles.

In 1964, when the King was receiving medical care in Switzerland, an army corporal shot and killed Jigme Palden Dorji during a family card game, allegedly with a gun the third King had given to Yangki. Soon, news emerged that the corporal was under orders from the King's uncle, who was also the head of the Royal Army. The army quartermaster was said to have come up with the plot. In the aftermath of the assassination, the quartermaster died of wounds from a suicide attempt; five men, including the King's uncle, were executed by firing squad.[7] Jigme Palden's brother Lhendup was briefly appointed as the new prime minister, but he eventually fled to Nepal under suspicion of participating in a new attempt to overthrow the King—a suspicion denounced by his sister, now the Queen Grandmother, when it re-emerged in an Indian diplomat's memoir in 2016.[8] The position of prime minister was not just left vacant—it was effectively abolished for decades, until being re-instated as a part of Bhutan's more gradual shift toward democracy.

The assassination of Jigme Palden Dorji emphasized the challenges posed by rapid social transitions: not just the transition from ecclesiocracy to monarchy, but also the transition to a modernizing, democratizing state. Within a year, the third King would narrowly escape a grenade thrown at him in Paro, though some onlookers accused the King himself of orchestrating the apparent assassination attempt in order to gain public sympathy. The third King died in 1972 after extended health problems. In the aftermath of his premature death, Ashi Kesang Choeden, the Queen Mother and sister of the assassinated prime minister, effectively held off Tibetan efforts to establish Yangki's son on the throne in the place of Jigme Singye Wangchuk, the Queen's own son and legitimate heir to the throne. But the power of the Dorji family, the Queen's family of origin, never recovered after the assassination of her eldest brother.

The fourth King himself allegedly survived an assassination attempt on the eve of his coronation. Jigme Singye Wangchuk was only 16 years old at the time of his father's death; his coronation ceremony was held in 1974, after he had reached the age of majority (18). The assassination plot announced by the government again involved the third King's Tibetan consort Yangki; Tibet's government in exile was believed to have supported the attempted coup.[9] Yangki, her supporters, and her children all took refuge in India. Five years later, in 1979, Jigme Singye Wangchuk privately married four sisters, great-nieces of Jigme Dorji, the Zhabdrung mind reincarnation who had been assassinated by his grandfather's men.

"Why did the fourth King marry *four* sisters?" I asked one of my students. "Wouldn't one have been enough?"

"There was a prophecy, madam, that the marriages would increase the longevity of both families."

One of the four Queen Mothers, Ashi Dorji Wangmo Wangchuk, told the story of the Zhabdrung's assassination in print, in 1999, twenty years after she and her sisters privately married the fourth King and eleven years after those private marriages were publicly formalized.[10] The story she tells—as told to her by her father—is vivid indeed: in the middle of the night, the young lama on his sleeping mat is woken by a circle of assassins who first kick him in the scrotum and then suffocate him by stuffing a prayer scarf, a kata, down his throat. The monks who were said not to have noticed his passing were in hiding, terrified of the assassins; they promised to say nothing official of what they had seen. I was bemused: what did it mean to have this visceral story of murder and betrayal authored by one of the four queen mothers of Bhutan? This was a murder attributed to her grandfather-in-law. How did the book affect marital relations among the King and four Queens? Reading Dorji Wangmo, I thought of William Faulkner, writing of the American South: "The past is never dead. It isn't even past."

The royal weddings solidified the Wangchuk dynasty with a new Crown Prince (now the fifth King) and many other offspring, thus substantiating the prophecy's promise of familial longevity; they also may have played an important role in shifting government personnel and policy at a critical juncture (Table 3.1). In the midst of the Lhotshampa expulsion crisis, dissident economist D. N. S. Dhakal and journalist K. M. Dixit noted that "five of the most powerful members of the administration" were related to the four sisters who had been formally raised to the status of queens only three years earlier, in 1989. Those powerful administrators included

> Home Minister Dago Tshering, Foreign Minister Dawa Tshering, Social Services Minister Tashi Tobgyel, and Bhutan Army chief Gongloen Lam Dorji. Further, the Joint Secretary in the Planning Commission is Their Majesties the Queens' elder brother; the final authority in deciding Bhutanese citizenship is the youngest brother.

Table 3.1. Dynastic Marriages and Assassination Attempts Affecting the Wangchuk Monarchy

Dorji family	**Complications within Wangchuk dynasty**	**Wangchuk dynasty**	**Zhabdrung and sister's family**
Ugyen Dorji (nominates Ugyen Wangchuk for king)		Ugyen Wangchuk (first King)	
Sonam Pelden Dorji (Lord Chamberlain)		Jigme Wangchuk (second King)	Zhabdrung assassinated by men of second King
Jigme Pelden Dorji Lord Chamberlain; assassinated in plot attributed to Yangki; brother appointed, then flees the country	Tibetan mistress Yangki presents challenge to Queen Kesang Choeden, sister to Jigme Pelden Dorji	Jigme Dorji Wangchuk (third King; heart trouble)	
	Yangki attempts assassination of fourth King	Jigme Singye Wangchuk (fourth King)	Fourth King marries four sisters, great-nieces of assassinated Zhabdrung

Meanwhile, "the King's three sisters and his paternal uncle Namgyal Wangchuk, all of whom once had charge of key ministries, have been sidelined."[11] Given the discreet media coverage of the royal family in Bhutan, outsiders may never fully understand the logic that led to this dramatic shift in Cabinet-level ministries. But immediately after these political changes, the Lhotshampa crisis, already underway, rapidly intensified, with Foreign Minister Dawa Tshering promoting the idea that Bhutan's cultural identity was under threat, and Home Minister Dago Tshering implementing draconian policies, discussed below in Chapter 4.

The fact of high-level assassinations in Bhutan's twentieth-century history underscored for me the vulnerability of the monarchy and the government. But of course US history had also suffered high-level assassinations at a similar period: President John F Kennedy in 1963, then Malcolm X in 1965, and Martin Luther King Jr. and Robert F. Kennedy in 1968. And just as the prospect of a high-level assassination in the United States seemed remote in 2017, so too the likelihood of an attack on the monarchy in Bhutan seemed unlikely. Still, in both cases, it is worth remembering the threat of violence in the not-too-distant past, as the 2024 attempted assassination of Donald Trump perhaps confirms.

BHUTANESE KINGSHIP: SYMBOLISM, AUTHORITY, KASHO, AND KIDU

One day in spring, the fifth King, biking through eastern Bhutan, decided to stop in and visit Sherubtse College. With less than two hours' notice, the entire college community (over two thousand students, faculty, and staff) put on their finest clothes and lined up to welcome him. James and Zoë found a place in the long reception line stretching from the College gate off the main road to the assembly hall. The College's president introduced James to the King and the King stopped to chat with him for a few minutes.

"What did you talk about?" Jeremy and I asked later.

"The challenges of fatherhood, among other things," James said, with a smile at Jeremy.

"But how did you talk to him?" I asked. "Did you talk to his feet?"

"No," said Zoë. "He cheated! I didn't dare."

James kept his face down but peered up at the King sideways, making eye contact, which seemed to work for them both. The King, who was on an "incognito" mountain-biking trip, talked about the pleasure he found in talking with people as a fellow Bhutanese citizen, without the weight of his royal identity having to be maintained. Only when the King masks his identity can people look him in the eye, speak to him face to face. The King's pleasure in these biking trips is well known: they may offer some escape from the formality of courtly life.

What does it mean to be King in Bhutan? Monarchy differs from one nation to another: kings in the Muslim world (Morocco, Jordan, and Saudi Arabia, for instance) tend to have fewer limits on their powers than European monarchs whose powers are limited by a written document, even one as vague and ancient as England's Magna Carta. In Asia, Bhutan, Cambodia, Thailand, and Japan all have constitutional monarchies with variable powers assigned to the monarch. In many cases, temporal power is associated with spiritual stature, as in the European doctrine of the divine right of kings, or the King of Morocco's title of Commander of the Faithful, or the Saudi Arabian title, "Protector of the Holy Places."

As mentioned in the previous chapter, the Bhutanese Constitution identifies the King, the Druk Gyalpo, first as "the Head of State and the symbol of unity of the Kingdom and of the people of Bhutan," and second as the Buddhist "upholder of the Chhoe-sid-nyi" or the dual system of spiritual and secular government. Bhutan's monarchs are also understood to be carrying the country's spiritual heritage in particular ways. In the words of Karma Ura:

> The Raven Crown is a symbol of responsibility to create peace and happiness for the people in the Kingdom. The leader, who wears the Crown, makes a commitment like a Bodhisattva to alleviate the suffering of the people. The throne has not been, and is not, a seat for respite and enjoyment.[12]

The Bhutanese monarchy is framed above all as a spiritual call to service: Kings, like Bodhisattvas, labor for the enlightenment of all. Jessica Locke, looking at Bhutan's recent history in light of broader Buddhist political theory, notes that in Buddhist theory more generally, "the [. . .]

measure of monarchical legitimacy is the overall flourishing of the realm [. . .]. To the extent that a monarch can use public resources and policies to facilitate that [collective spiritual advancement or] liberation for their subjects, they are a successful ruler."[13] Sonam Kinga adds a slightly different perspective: rather than or in addition to contributing to the enlightenment of his subjects, those subjects also constitute the King on a spiritual plane: "the Bhutanese King is seen as the fruition of collective merit of all the people."[14] Calling all to enlightenment and embodying collective progress toward enlightenment, the King holds a central place in Bhutan's political and spiritual imaginary. The King's symbolic importance and resonance within Bhutan would be hard to overstate—and most likely hard to uphold.

The King's constitutional role as upholder of the "dual system" of spiritual and secular rule leans heavily toward the secular in the 2008 Constitution. Under Article 2, which lays out the parameters of the monarchy, the King has the power to appoint 17 different kinds of government officials, including Supreme Court Justices, High Court Justices, Election Commissioners, Royal Civil Service Commissioners, Heads of the Defense Forces, the Attorney General, Secretaries of the Houses of Parliament and of different Ministries, Ambassadors, District Governors (Dzongdag) and more. Against the expansiveness of these appointed secular positions, the King makes only a handful of spiritual appointments, each based on the recommendation of leading monastics: the Je Khenpo (upon retirement of the previous Je Khenpo) and, when necessary, each of the five Lopons (literally "Teachers," the title for the monastic leaders immediately under the Chief Abbot or Je Khenpo).[15] These monastic appointments cover the top level of monastic authority, while secular appointments penetrate down through several layers: not just the Supreme Court but the High Court, not just Royal Civil Service Commissioners but also the secretaries of various ministries and so on. Beyond the Constitution, however, the King's power and importance within Bhutan carries spiritual overtones.

While upholding the "dual system" of governance links the Kings of Bhutan directly to the Zhabdrung, the King's leadership and authority are most often seen through his use of kasho and kidu: kasho meaning royal command, and kidu meaning royal grant. The King's kashos cover many aspects of Bhutanese life. A 1981 kasho, for instance, created District Development Committees as a means of devolving power to more regional governmental structures. A 1989 kasho more controversially established the obligation for Bhutanese citizens to wear national dress to government offices and services (including dzongs, schools, etc.). Kidu, a grant from the throne, can take multiple forms, including land grants, relief from taxes or interest, and outright grants of money. Sometimes relief funds are characterized as kidu in the government newspaper the *Kuensel*; other times, the word "soelra" or gift is used instead.

Both kasho and kidu underscore the ongoing centrality of the King in Bhutanese understandings of government functions. In the midst of the pandemic, for instance, the *Kuensel* noted that

> [. . .] the simplest lay interpretation of *kidu* is that, in the Bhutanese system, the King personally takes care of the well-being of the people. It is a unique and humane social security system to ensure basic necessities and livelihood as well as any other aspect of a Bhutanese citizen's life when necessary.[16]

During the pandemic, one kidu—royal financing for a national service youth program—was converted into another: the Druk Gyalpo's Relief Kidu (DGRK), providing immediate financial relief for those suffering from Bhutan's tight pandemic shut-down. The DGRK "waive[d] interests on loans and defer[ed] loan repayment for individuals and businesses." The *Kuensel*, noting public complaints of inequality, since businesses reaped greater benefit than individuals, stressed the shared responsibility of King and citizen in the relationship shaped by kidu. The *Kuensel* notably did not discuss the government's potential responsibility for preventing or prosecuting pandemic relief fraud. Kidu binds the people directly to the King; the government seems to stand outside that close relationship.

Kidu and kasho also evoke underlying associations of family relations within Bhutan, as Sonam Kinga argues:

> Bhutanese society [. . .] identifies the King as the source of justice and welfare. In popular parlance, he is referred to as a benevolent parent

> *drinchen gi pham* (*drin can gyi pham*) or parent of welfare, *kidu gi pham* (*skyid sdug gyi pham*). We find the echo of such concept even in the King's own public pronouncement. In his coronation speech on 1 November 2008, the present King said, 'Throughout my reign I will never rule you as a King. I will protect you as a Parent, care for you as a brother and serve you as a son.' This is suggestive of a national community conceived in the image of a larger family with the King at the centre.[17]

As we have seen, familial imagery and even familial relations have not precluded violent struggle in the history of Bhutan's monarchy. Still, an understanding of Kingship based on powerful commands and benevolent concern for welfare might extend the reach of Bhutan's monarchy beyond what outsiders might expect.

For instance, one of my female students seemed to suggest that the King himself might have some direct oversight of the work she had been called on to perform during the previous election. Teachers in Bhutan are civil servants, paid by the government and blocked from campaigning in any way. As an extension of this principle, teachers were also called upon to serve in the polling process. My student described being transported to a distant polling place in the back of an unroofed high-sided truck. The drive took hours through the rain. She rode with dozens of other teachers, all of whom were wet and frozen. They had nowhere to sit; some were throwing up from motion sickness on the rough roads. At the end of the journey, they faced hours of work helping with the polls before being trucked back home again, arriving past midnight.

"That sounds terrible!" I exclaimed. "Couldn't you have said that you couldn't serve in this way? Cited some health concerns?" This particular student was not physically robust: I was surprised she hadn't come down with bronchitis or pneumonia.

"Oh, madam, I would have been too frightened. To be released from this duty, we had to write a letter asking for an exception. And the King might have seen that letter."

"But what would the King do? Surely he's too busy with affairs of state to worry about a single teacher's health needs."

"Madam, it's the King." End of conversation.

MODES OF DEMOCRACY IN BHUTAN

Like monarchy, democracy carries different meanings in different times and places. Direct democracy as practiced in ancient Greece meant that all citizens (a category including only those who had completed military training) participated in the making of political decisions. Switzerland today practices direct democracy, with Swiss citizens aged 18 or older being called "approximately four times a year to vote on an average of fifteen issues," with voter turnout slightly "over 40% on average."[18] Deliberative or participatory democracy (particularly as practiced in some Indigenous communities) similarly involves all members of the community participating in the deliberations and debates that lead to political decisions. In a representative democracy, by contrast, a specific number of representatives are elected by the people and entrusted to carry out the business of governance. In constitutional democracies, a written Constitution often specifies how representatives will be chosen, and what actions they will take to represent their constituents. These different forms of governance bear one name—democracy—but they may overlap and/or operate in radically different ways. Bhutan's Constitution, signed into law in 2008, established a national government as summarized in Table 3.2. But the common Western framing of Bhutanese politics—suggesting that Bhutan moved from an absolute monarchy to a democracy in 2008—oversimplifies events and consequences by equating democracy only with its representative form.

Table 3.2. Components of Bhutanese Government Based on the Constitution of 2008

<table>
<tr><td colspan="2">The King</td></tr>
<tr><td colspan="2">Prime Minister
(leader of party that won majority of National Assembly seats);
Ministers are appointed by King on the advice of the Prime Minister</td></tr>
<tr><td>National Assembly (47 members)
1 from each of 47 constituencies</td><td>National Council (25 members)
1 from each Dzongkhag;
5 appointed by King</td></tr>
<tr><td colspan="2">Election Board</td></tr>
<tr><td colspan="2">The Constitution</td></tr>
</table>

The oversimplification appeals in part because of Bhutan's careful stage-managing of the transition to partisan elections. Faced with widespread public skepticism about party-based politics, the fourth King announced in his 2005 National Day speech—the King's traditional speech at the annual celebration of Bhutan's turn to monarchy in 1907—that the Electoral Commission would hold practice elections in 2006 so that people could develop greater understanding of and facility with the mechanisms of voting. People were invited to vote for nominal parties, which were defined by their color and a cursory platform: in the 2006 practice elections, Druk Yellow won the most votes, because yellow is the color associated with the monarchy; Druk Red, the color associated with monks, came in second. Druk Blue, with a pro-business platform, came in third, and Druk Green, with an environmental policy focus, came in last. (So much for the notion that all Bhutanese were passionate defenders of the environment.) This colorful dry run of electoral politics worked as intended, and the first national elections in 2008 went relatively smoothly, except for the fact that the results underscored Bhutan's preference for consensus agreement rather than the forced choice of voting. The Druk Phuensum Tshogpa (Bhutan Peace and Prosperity Party) won all but two seats in the election, making for a very strong ruling party and an apparently weak opposition (People's Democratic Party), though that opposition party would win a majority in the 2013 election before being replaced by yet a third party in the 2018 election.

Still, the story of democracy in Bhutan is more complicated and influenced by Bhutanese traditions than this story of colorful practice elections would suggest. First, Bhutan's villages seem to have operated as a kind of limited direct democracy long before democratic developments at the national level. Early democratizing moves seem to have built on these older Bhutanese traditions, as summarized in Table 3.3. In 1953, the third King's installation of an early National Assembly (the Tshogdu) moved national politics closer to Western norms of representational self-governance, but the published summary of debates in the Assembly seems very similar to descriptions of the rhetoric used in the zomdu or village meeting. In 1981, the fourth King began devolving power to the dzongkhags or districts of Bhutan by creating Dzongkhag Yargye Tshogchungs (DYTs or District Development Commissions), that were empowered to

Table 3.3. Graduated Steps in Bhutan's Development of Representative Democracy

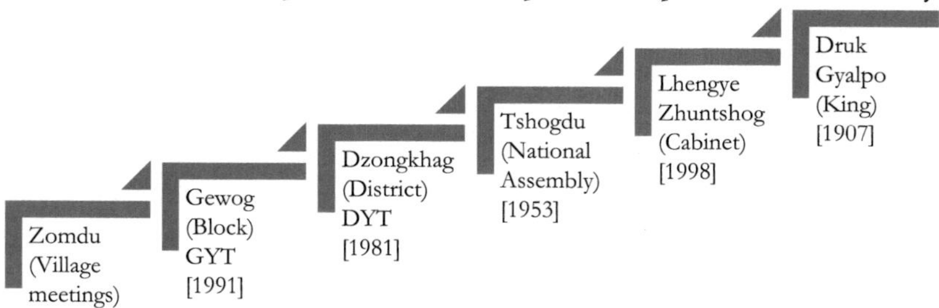

create and put forward proposals for development projects. In 1991, power was further devolved to Gewog Yargye Tshogchungs (GYTs). The King also handed over executive power to a Council of Ministers in 1998, and in 2001 he called for the creation of a Constitution defining procedures for party-based elections. The draft Constitution was discussed in each of the districts of Bhutan in 2005; the first party-based elections were held in 2008 and the Parliament thus elected affirmed the Constitution. Each of these components of democratic functioning are influenced by Bhutan's particular history and the results can seem paradoxical.

On a college field trip to a remote area, I found myself chatting with a student while on a winding trail within a mini-woodland of rhododendron bushes and other small trees. Sound carried less well through the leaves, creating a sense of solitude, which may have helped shape our conversation. I said something positive about the central schools (public boarding schools) based on a conversation I had had that morning with our host. My student responded with a noise expressing disagreement (from an American, I would have called it a snort).

"You disagree," I said, knowing better than to ask a question that could not be answered politely in the affirmative. "Tell me why." The student replied at length:

"Central schools were instituted after only a single year of study, long before we had enough information to know what kind of effect they would have. That is what happens with a short-term government. Major decisions are rushed. Students in central schools are given everything, down to toothbrushes and clothes. Now parents are unwilling to give anything toward their children's education. Meanwhile, day schools lack resources. And the central schools are intensifying inequities. Remote areas go begging. The places that need more attention do not receive that attention."

"That doesn't sound good," I said.

"This government instituted a one-month summer break so that students could help with the transplanting season, but the majority of students live in urban areas, so for them, this break is irrelevant. The change was not consultative. Democracy has undercut the process of consultation."

"Hang on," I said. "Isn't democracy itself a consultative process?"

"Oh, democracy." My student's tone was dismissive and pitying all at once. "Democracy has only helped to centralize power. In the past, requests would come from the community and be raised up through the dzongkhags. Now, ministers send directives from the King down to the communities."

"You're saying that democracy has strengthened the monarchy?" I asked, befuddled by this unexpected turn.

"Yes," the student said, nodding emphatically. "Democracy serves the King."

To understand what my student was trying to say, it might help to take a step back and look at each stage of democratic governance in Bhutan.

Zomdu (Village Meetings)

The case for considering Bhutan's villages as embodying direct democracy was made perhaps most strongly by Tashi Wangchuk, head of the Bhutan Museum of Natural History, in 2004. Sketching Bhutan's autonomous villages and their traditional strategies of self-governance, Wangchuk argued that "village society is fundamentally democratic" in contrast to the larger institutions of the state.[19] Wangchuk implicitly defined democracy in terms of participation in deliberative debate: he quoted Leo Rose's view of village administration as "semidemocratic" and broadly "autonomous," in contrast to the "decision-making process within the Royal Government [which] continues to be a very narrow one, involving only a small number of officials."[20] By contrast, the village meeting includes one representative from each family, in a meeting that might include anywhere from twenty to two hundred family representatives. For Wangchuk, furthermore, village-level deliberations drew on oratory as a "weapon of the weak," as described by James Scott.[21] In a Bhutanese zomdu:

> Decisions are made once a consensus is reached, and all differing viewpoints are debated. Vociferous debaters wielding well-honed oratory can sway decisions in their favor. Because most Bhutanese villagers are illiterate, oratorical skills (*kha*) are highly valued in their own right and persuasive debaters are respected.[22]

Wangchuk's description implies that equal numbers of men and women participate as family representatives, but Bhutan's ongoing difficulties achieving gender equity in national government make it seem likely that most zomdu participants would traditionally have been men.[23]

Noting that debating eloquence is not all-powerful, Wangchuk stressed the larger networks also shaping village democracy: what Robert Dahl called "the totality of community life," and Robert Putnam describes as "norms of reciprocity and networks of civic engagement."[24] As Wangchuk pointed out, Bhutanese villagers depend on one another for "sharing farm labor," or contributions to "building a house." Such interdependence was in the past maintained by ostracizing any family that sinned against the community. The form of ostracism was officially defined as "closed hearth/closed water restrictions (*chuko miko dum*) [. . .] under which villagers agreed not to enter an 'exiled' household and the household itself was banned from using the common village spring." The Royal Government banned such severe social ostracism, but evidently the threat was still being evoked in the early twenty-first century.[25] Wangchuk offered both negative and positive examples of the zomdu in action: when villagers require shared labor to build a house or harvest their crops, arrangements could be made smoothly and efficiently. When a particular village decided to build a new temple and fill it with statues funded according to villagers' relative wealth, by contrast, conflict over the implementation of the plan led to multiple fruitless meetings and a threat of closed hearth/water restrictions; the situation was resolved only through an appeal to the local gup or headman. Wangchuk's vision of democracy at village level includes much more than individual votes on particular issues; rather, this view of democracy encompasses the broader health and functioning of the village as a communal entity.

1953: National Assembly (Tshogdu)

Institutions like the zomdu (and enforcement mechanisms like chuko miko dum) seem to have been established for centuries, but the National Assembly or Tshogdu, created in 1953 by the third King, marked the first substantive democratic innovation within Bhutan's traditional modes of governance. The Tshogdu included representatives of the government, representatives of the (Drukpa) monastic establishment, and representatives of the people. The people's representatives, known as Chimis, had to be at least 25 years old, with no criminal record; from 1995 on, they also had to speak Dzongkha. Before 2008, Chimis were selected in ways that tended to privilege the "traditional ethnic chiefs or village headmen from the hills" and the "pliable, loyal, and faithful subjects of the [*sic*] southern Bhutan."[26] In the south, district officials held public meetings in each village and each head of household had one vote (for the household as a whole). In the north, district officials summoned members of each village (the headman and some heads of households) to a constituency meeting "where they attempted to reach a consensus upon one candidate." When consensus was elusive, other strategies such as casting dice, might be used in addition.[27] Like A. C. Sinha, Leo Rose noted that this electoral system was "only minimally disruptive of Bhutan's pre-1953 polity."[28] The National Assembly met either once or twice a year, for a limited period. Its role was mostly to discuss national policy priorities and to advise the King and his ministers. In many ways, the Tshogdu simply functioned as a super-zomdu, with debates deploying traditional sayings and stories to frame a response to policy proposals, as seen in debates (discussed below) over the King's 1998 kasho calling for National Assembly members to elect the Council of Ministers.

Om Dhungel, a civil servant from the south of Bhutan who fled the country in the midst of the Lhotshampa expulsion (described in Chapter 4), was even more blunt than Sinha and Rose about the relationship between the National Assembly and the nation's administrators in the late 1980s:

> After the King and his ministers, leading civil servants pretty much ran the country, and had much more power than members of parliament, who were often uneducated and had been plucked out of their villages to ensure the National Assembly looked representative. Ministers also sat in the National Assembly, but were hand-picked by the King. One home minister, Tamji Jagar, had previously looked after the third King's horses, and was illiterate. In those days, even a low-level civil servant could boss MPs around.[29]

Was the Tshogdu a well-meaning attempt at representation, or a more cynical performance? Or perhaps something in between these two extremes? Issues of performativity aside, some tensions between the monarch and the Tshogdu existed from a fairly early period. While the third King had tried to increase the power of the National Assembly—renouncing veto power over legislation and insisting on a triennial vote of confidence on his rule—the conservative Assembly members insisted that these measures be repealed when the young Jigme Singye Wangchuk became Bhutan's fourth King. Tensions among the King, forward-looking Western-educated civil servants, and less-formally educated Chimis who remained invested in traditional modes of governance, complicated Bhutan's engagement with democratic structures.

1981/1991: District and Block Development Committees

Bhutan's path to democracy became still more complex as later, more significant delegations of royal power became entangled in a larger national crisis over citizenship. While the tale of Bhutan's transition to democracy is often told separately from accounts of the Lhotshampa expulsion, the stories are in many ways inseparable. This is how the narrative of democratization had been framed: in the 1980s and 1990s, the fourth King created development committees as a means of decentralizing some of his royal authority. District Development Committees (Dzongkhag Yargye Tshogchung or DYTs) were established in 1981 and smaller Block Development Committees (Gewog Yargye Tshogchung or GYTs) began in 1991. These committees expanded the number of voices included in development goal-setting and funding decisions; they built institutional connective tissue, linking far-flung Bhutanese communities with the central government.[30] Our friends and colleagues described local communities submitting requests and proposals for development projects to the DYTs and later to the GYTs; the most worthy of these proposals were promoted up the line of discussion for eventual funding. In the face of public concerns that the transition to representative democracy was happening too quickly, the fourth King pointed to the DYTs and GYTs as examples of his successful decentralization of power.[31]

Still, the timing of the GYT, created in 1991, highlights the intersection of development dollars, democracy, and ethnic conflict. In the 70th National Assembly meeting, held in October 1991 (after a year in which the annual meeting of the National Assembly was canceled out of fear of unrest arising from the Lhotshampa protests), both Cabinet ministers and people's representatives urged the government to take money that had been earmarked for development activities in the south and repurpose that money for security needs instead. Chimis and ministers alike pointed out that infrastructure had been destroyed in many southern districts and that development workers did not feel safe working in the region. Refugees and their supporters argued that the Royal Army was responsible for the destruction that was blamed on the refugees, but no one in the National Assembly dared or chose to speak on behalf of the refugees. Anti-southern views were hotly expressed, and the King stood almost alone in his insistence that development across the country would strengthen the country as a whole. In the end, as discussed in greater detail in the next chapter, he threatened to abdicate if the National Assembly refused to agree to ongoing development activities across the country. In retrospect, however, the founding of Block Development Committees is consistently represented dispassionately, as a neutral extension of the District Development Committees—as another, almost inevitable step on the path to democracy.

Despite the careful appearance of neutrality, politics around the Lhotshampa crisis generated a new degree of religious nationalism, largely centered on the figure of the King as the symbol of the nation. In 2004, Karma Phuntsho, tracing the "frequency and ubiquity [that] have rendered [. . .] weighty concepts [such as Tsawasum and driglam namzha] meaningless catchphrases," simultaneously charts the rise of Bhutan's new religious nationalism, though he is careful to note that his essay "is not to be construed as a calculated critique of either the social norms or the state policies and practices in vogue but a systematic scrutiny of the religious, ethical and political dimensions of the themes in question."[32] On the most practical level, Phuntsho defines driglam namzha as a "a system of ordered and cultured behaviour, and by extension, the standards and rules to this effect."[33] This system of order, often seen as developing out of the monastic rules established by the Zhabdrung, ranges from physical dress and deportment (including eating, walking, sitting, bowing in relation to superiors), through verbal behavior, to mental discipline. Phuntsho traces Bhutan's pre-1989 concern with driglam namzha not to the Lhotshampa crisis, but rather to "the onslaught of modernization and the insidious invasion of western culture, particularly among the youth, in the 1980s." Regardless of its earlier intended usage, driglam namzha was increasingly "linked with national identity," and "acquired a new political significance," culminating in "the royal decree of 16 January 1989, [. . .] the beginning of a systematic promotion of driglam namzha, particularly with the enforcement of the national dress."[34] That enforcement of national dress soon fed into the Lhotshampa crisis, as southern Bhutanese experienced the enforced dress code as an attack on their broader culture and identity, and the government and its most patriotic supporters doubled down on the importance of national homogeneity of dress and culture.

Winnie Bothe draws on the work of both Karma Phuntsho and Yeshe Dargey in tracing the rise of what I am calling religious nationalism in Bhutan. Bothe presents Dargey as "an academic spokesperson for the conservative sections of society," in contrast to Phuntsho, who "represents a liberal group whose members have pursued academic studies outside Bhutan."[35] Bothe follows Phuntsho in suggesting that earlier understandings of driglam changed "with the semantic addition of namzha, connoting 'system.'"[36] Bothe focuses on the moment in which driglam (+ namzha)

> [. . .] became systematised and made obligatory for the entire population, whose members were tutored on how to follow 'their' traditional culture in correct ways. In the process this diffuse set of practices was ritualised, standardised and homogenised and came to epitomise a Buddhist national identity.[37]

While driglam namzha is not exactly an "invented tradition" of the kind described by Eric Hobsbawm, Terence Ranger, and others, this codification and homogenization significantly altered the physical and psychological impact of monastic/courtly etiquette in ways that Norbert Elias and Pierre Bourdieu might find interesting.[38] Bothe also cites Dargey in order to emphasize relations of subordination embedded within the broader understanding of driglam namzha: "in its traditionalised version, the 'taming' of body, speech and mind came to signify the right way of behaving in the hierarchical relationship between the governors and the governed."[39] For Bothe, Dargey's framing of driglam namzha shows the extent to which "subordinates (the citizens)" are expected to "treat their superiors (the state officials) with the utmost respect, whilst the latter in return govern with benevolence."[40] This emphasis on subordination would be quite emphatically on display when Bothe observed the public presentation of the Constitution in a remote dzong.

In contrast to the materiality of driglam namzha (encompassing clothing and physical gestures in addition to internalized respect), the rhetorical usage of Tsawasum around the time of the Lhotshampa crisis remained powerful precisely through its spiritual abstraction. Karma Phuntsho explains that "the tantric Buddhist *Tsawasum* refer to the triad of *guru* or *bla ma* [lama], *devatā* or *yi dam* [yidam] and *ḍākinī* or *mkha' 'gro* [khandro]. They are roots because they serve as sources of blessings, attainments and activities respectively." A lama is a teacher, a yidam is a meditation deity with whom a practitioner identifies through a very precisely specified meditation practice, and a khandro (aka dakini or skydancer) is a feminized figure of energy. Phuntsho notes that the triad Tsawasum was first applied to national identity in the 1950s, with the legal code specifying "Country, King and Government" as Tsawasum, though the original intent may have been "to enumerate the Government, Country and People as Tsawasum." Dargey presents Tsawasum as

> [. . .] the three basic foundations of the country—the King, the Government and the People, which means His Majesty as the most benevolent of benefactors, the Royal government as the most considerate and beneficient of governments, and the subjects as the devoted and faithful citizens.[41]

But in the eyes of Phuntsho and Bothe, the primary effect of Tsawasum discourse seems to have been the religious intensification of patriotic feeling:

> Probably the first officially documented reoccurrence of Tsawasum was in the 65th session of the National Assembly in 1989, when the 'anti-national' conspiracy through distribution of pamphlets and booklets was discussed and officially defined as an act of treason against the Tsawasum. [. . .] [A]ll persons who went against the Tsawasum were branded as ngolops or 'anti-nationals' and Tsawasum were hailed as the trinity of Bhutanese nationhood.[42]

As the Lhotshampa crisis intensified with a war of words—literally, a pamphlet war—words and concepts shaping Bhutanese understandings of the King and government were retroactively sanctified, even though that process involved twisting key religious terms out of their original context and meaning.

While Padmasambhava's shifting relationship to monarchical power, discussed in Chapter 2, suggests that Buddhism and nationalism are not natural allies,[43] the campaign against "anti-nationals" helped define and in large part create Bhutan's new religiously inflected nationalism, especially after armed conflicts in the south:

> Tsawasum became an iconic political category which people cited so profusely as the cause to fight for. Loyalty and service to Tsawasum became the mantra to excite patriotism and nationalism in order to combat the threats posed by the crisis. It served as a buzzword which encapsulated everything that is Bhutanese and that Bhutan stood for.[44]

Despite this new passion for Tsawasum, however, precise understanding of the term remained elusive, as Karma Phuntsho's essay demonstrates: a would-be soldier defined the Tsawasum as the army, bodyguards, and police force, while some trainee-teachers, asked to identify the Tsawasum on an examination, listed the names of their three best friends.[45] Lack of a clear definition or understanding of Tsawasum meant that the term could be used to encapsulate whatever an individual found precious, while also connecting that sense of value to Bhutan as a nation.

By the 1991 National Assembly session, the Speaker was defining "TSA-WA-SUM" (original all-caps) as "King, People and Country," thereby elevating the importance of the King.[46] Devotion to the Tsawasum was presented both as an example of democracy and a defense against the Lhotshampa exiles' demands for greater democracy, as suggested by the sequence of events at the close of the Assembly. When the Home Minister read out the demands of the dissident Bhutan's People's Party—demands that prioritized establishing a constitutional monarchy and proportional representation in the Cabinet and National Assembly—these demands were perhaps predictably dismissed as an attempt to take over Bhutan and turn it into another Nepali-majority state. Against this vision, Assembly members asserted "that although democracy in Bhutan might not be institutionalised in form it was enjoyed by the people in spirit as well as in practice. The people had a decisive say in all issues that directly concerned them as well as in affairs of national importance."[47] Having "a decisive say in all issues" swiftly led to appreciation of "the nation's beloved sovereigns," and from there to an articulation of the King's centrality to the nation. In fact, the Chimis expressed themselves

> [. . .] greatly shocked and disturbed by the very mention of the word abdication by His Majesty the King. They requested His Majesty, for the sake of the TSA-WA-SUM, not to entertain even the slightest thought on such a drastic step under any circumstances. There could be no TSA-WA-SUM without the King. They strongly requested that His Majesty's statement about abdication should be deleted from the proceedings of the National Assembly.[48]

"There could be no TSA-WA-SUM without the King": the growth of religiously inflected nationalism in Bhutan elevated the King as a defining feature of the Tsawasum, even as the Assembly strove in practice to erase the King's more troubling actions, such as his threat to abdicate. The Chimis' attempts to delete the threat of abdication from the historical record lasted for some time on the final day of the Assembly. Only after "the King's insistence" that the record reflect the actual debates within the Tshogdu did the people's representatives "relent" and come to terms with the historical record.[49]

1998: Council of Ministers

Bhutan's next move toward representative democracy—the fourth King's 1998 devolution of royal power to a Council of Ministers—is often cited by Western sources as Bhutan's first step toward its current form as a constitutional democratic monarchy. Ironically, from a Western perspective, when the fourth King announced by kasho or royal command that the National Assembly (Tshogdu) would henceforth elect a Council of Ministers by secret ballot, he preemptively demanded unanimous agreement—and the people's representatives then spent most of the 1998 legislative session praising the King while arguing against his plan.

These Tshogdu debates offer evidence of ambivalence on both sides: from one perspective, the King was the one insisting on democratic elections, with Assembly members resisting; from a different angle, the King could be seen as insisting unilaterally on the prompt implementation of his kasho. From either perspective, what stands out in these debates is the King's central role in Bhutanese government. At the same time, the language used in the debates harks back to the oratory that presumably held sway in village meetings—claims made vivid through reference to traditional sayings or stories—even as the concerns put forward sometimes reflected sophisticated understandings of regional politics.

The fourth King's 1998 kasho is reproduced in full at the beginning of the "Translation of the Proceedings and Resolutions of the 76th National Assembly." The kasho begins by informing the Speaker of the National Assembly of a "matter of great importance" to be discussed and decided in the 76th session. The next two paragraphs attest to the King's commitment, over the 26 years of his reign, to "put the interest and well-being of the country and people first," and to "encourage and prepare our people to participate actively and fully in the decision making process of our country."[50] District and Block Development Committees are cited as examples of how "the people are also playing an increasingly active role

[. . .] in the formulation and implementation of development programmes and in bringing forward issues of national concern for discussion in the Tshogdu Chhenmo." The kasho then announces that

> The time has now come to promote even greater people's participation in the decision making process. Our country must be ensured to always have a system of government which enjoys the mandate of the people, provides clean and efficient governance, and also has an inbuilt mechanism of checks and balance to safeguard our national interest and security. As an important step towards achieving this goal, the Lhengyel Shungtshog (Royal Advisory Council) should now be restructured into an elected Council of Ministers that is vested with full executive powers to provide efficient and effective governance of our country.

Oddly, however, the restructuring proposed does not appear to have been forwarded to the National Assembly by any of the District or Block Development Committees. Instead, the King himself is calling for this restructuring without clearly identifying how it either "enjoys the mandate of the people," or provides the desired "mechanism of checks and balances."[51] Furthermore, after identifying three issues for debate and decision (1. The National Assembly's secret ballot election of Council of Ministers, 2. The role and responsibilities of the new Council of Ministers, and 3. Mechanism for a vote of confidence on the King), the kasho calls for a "fruitful" discussion and unanimous decision. The King seems to assume—against the norms of any mechanism of checks and balances—that the Tshogdu's agreement is a foregone conclusion.

The National Assembly eventually provided the "unanimous decision" the King demanded, but not before extended protests and an eventual modification of the King's plan (accepted as a "clarification" rather than a revision). Those arguing against a Council of Ministers elected by secret ballot saw the King's "wise leadership" as responsible for "peace and happiness along with the benefits of unprecedented socioeconomic development."[52] Bhutan's GDP growth rate in the 1990s was higher than the regional average, largely because of the success of hydropower projects financed by India. In order to maintain these national benefits, what was called for was "unity, loyalty, and dedication" in response to threats from "ngolops" ("antinational" rebels from southern Bhutan) and Assamese militants who had established camps in Bhutan's southern jungles. According to the Dzongda or governor of Lhuentse, "the introduction of a system of electing cabinet ministers will lead to divisive politics based on regionalism and communalism and the promotion of individual interests." Lack of Bhutanese expertise with party politics could be seen as making the country especially vulnerable to such individual ambitions:

> As the vast majority of the people who live in the rural areas will be in no position to know the qualities and capabilities of the ministers and government officials or their thinkings, the ambitions of a few individuals bent upon gaining personal influence and power can create divisions and problems among the people.

Finally, the Lhuentse governor articulated a larger concern that distributing the King's power could lead to divisions within the national community, which would in turn create opportunities for outsiders to purchase influence:

> When the power which has been vested in one person is divided among different persons, the loyalty and thinking of the people will also be divided. This can lead to internal conflicts and problems. It will also enable outsiders and vested interests to use financial power to buy influence in the country, thereby endangering its very sovereignty and security.[53]

One change in procedures could bring on other changes threatening the trust underlying Bhutan's social fabric. These points, repeated in various ways during the debate, seemed to prefigure what people would also see at stake in larger shifts from absolute monarchy to democratic constitutional monarchy.

The rhetoric of the debate used traditional sayings mostly to affirm tradition, but occasionally to counter the power of the King. One major innovation implied by the King's kasho was that deputy ministers could now be elected to the Council, and a number of deputy ministers expressed some concerns about this new state of affairs. A series of proverbs were invoked to express this anxiety; the deputy finance minister, for instance, warned all members of the Assembly that they must shoulder this new responsibility with all due seriousness: "We must not become irresponsible and behave like a person over-burdened by an unbearable load." The deputy minister for health and education also felt that "the contents of His Majesty's Kasho [. . .] seems like imposing a heavy responsibility on a mere child." Yet another member complained that "this also seems like asking a physically weak person to carry a very heavy load which is beyond his capacity." Or in the words of another speaker, the kasho's devolution of power "like asking a child to carry a spear before he can even carry an arrow."[54] While the King may traditionally be seen as a benevolent parent, the debaters here explicitly called into question his parenting skills—even though the King's benevolent intentions and sacrifice for the nation were never in doubt. One deputy minister presented the fourth King as the hero of the "fable of the Golden Moon" in which God in the form of a golden moon agrees to fulfill the King's wishes for the well-being of his subjects in exchange for some body part to balance each wish: "Eventually, the King, having parted with his eyes and limbs, even sacrifices his own life for the peace and security of his country."[55] The dark moral of this tale was that members of the National Assembly, forced to shoulder the King's burdens and sacrifices, would come to recognize the King's virtue all the more deeply. Ironically, broad recognition of the King's virtuous stewardship of Bhutan itself could present a barrier to integrated participation in national development.

Some sayings emphasizing the King's power were nonetheless used to introduce the speaker's disagreement with the King's command for innovation:

- Although the command of His Majesty the King is heavier than the mountains and more precious than gold, I cannot help feeling that it may be too early to introduce such changes in our country at this juncture.[56]
- The command of a King is like the waters of a river flowing down the mountains, and the waters of a river cannot be made to flow upstream. However, as submitted by many other members, introducing a system of electing cabinet ministers could unleash the divisive forces of communalism and regionalism.[57]

In both of these cases, the speaker begins by acknowledging the King's absolute power as a way of clearing space for their disagreement with the King's command.[58] While the sayings insist on the King's power, however, the debates concluded with what appeared to be a compromise proposed by the dzongda or governor of Chhukha and repeated by the governor of Pemagatshel—that the King should nominate candidates for the ministry and forward their names, portfolios, and biodata to the National Assembly for a secret ballot of affirmation or rejection.[59] This solution was approved by the King as a "clarification" of the kasho, despite the fact that it left the selection of Ministers largely in the King's hands.

2001–08: Constitutional Drafting, Consultation, and Installation

This Council of Ministers, ostensibly holding the executive power of the government, had been in existence for several years when the fourth King delivered yet another kasho calling for a Constitutional Drafting Committee to be convened in order to produce a written Constitution sketching the terms of a constitutional democratic monarchy for Bhutan. Presumably, movement toward a constitutional monarchy seemed too big a step for the Council of Ministers to propose, but the fact that it took a kasho to convene the Constitutional Drafting Committee makes it clear that not all executive power had actually been vested in the Council of Ministers.

Again, the fourth King consistently framed Bhutan's movement toward decentralization and representative democracy as a means of increasing public participation in the nation's work of development. When the King first met with the Constitutional Drafting Committee in 2001, he told them that "During the past years of my reign, I have made constant efforts to empower the people by delegating authority, resources and responsibility to them."[60] In this address, the King went on to refer specifically to the DYTs and GYTs, as well as the devolution of executive power to the Council of Ministers in 1998. In a National Day speech the following year (2002), the King emphasized that "the extent of progress and development achieved in the villages, geogs (blocks) and dzongkhags (districts) of Bhutan will depend upon the role and participation of the people."[61] In 2004, he stressed that "under the policy of greater decentralization and empowerment of the people," the District and Block Development Committees "have been given full administrative, policy making and financial powers in their respective Dzongkhags."[62] In the King's view, empowerment was also clearly responsibility. He proclaimed in his 2004 National Day Speech that

> I have every confidence that our people will shoulder their responsibility well and that the administrative, policy making and financial powers given to them by the government will be utilized properly to ensure the progress and development of the Dzongkhags, especially in the rural sector.

This expression of confidence is also an articulation of expectations: "our people" need to step up and shoulder their responsibilities.

Public perception of democracy, by contrast, framed the constitution and the installation of representative democratic elections as a gift from the King. Soelra, the term used to capture the idea of the gift, is both similar to and different from kidu, a royal grant, often of land. The King provides soelra in a sign of his care for his people: soelra may include medicine, disaster relief, development support, and more.[63] Of course democracy was not a gift that had been requested, nor was it welcomed by all, or even by most. In 2012, Winnie Bothe noted that the "gift" framing was introduced not by the King but by some of the elites in power under the King—and that the framing may have disrupted the King's intention of increasing citizen participation in government.

My friend Chencho's concern that representative democracy would expand the degree of submission owed to public figures was also shared by Winnie Bothe, who argued that "the process of 'gifting' the constitution [. . .] runs the risk of promoting processes of subjugation rather than deliberation," because of the way that discourse reproduces "earlier understandings of authority" and emphasizes "the relationship between the citizens and the state as one that is characterised by loyalty, divinity and unequal worth."[64] Bothe describes her experience of seeing the Constitution being delivered to a remote western Bhutanese community:

> As Dasho Dzongdag (the district governor) proceeded past the line of attendants, they, in turn, respectfully stepped backward in prostration, whilst stretching their *kabneys* and *rachus* (sashes) forward and displaying their palms. Following the code of Driglam Namzha, they were paying tribute to his high rank. His position was symbolised in the way he enjoyed the privilege of wearing a *patang* (sword) as well as his fully red coloured scarf, which went with his title of *dasho*, equivalent to the designation of nobility. The procession proceeded into the main temple, where the monks performed a series of prayers and religious rituals. [65]

Driglam namzha, the code of courtly etiquette, was used here to frame the Constitution in highly ceremonial ways, making it operate as something of a sacred object. The speeches that followed the monks' prayers and rituals underscored the power of the King through reference to his "kindness," his "visionary leadership," and his "royal command" to read out the Constitution. After the speeches were finished, the governor "held the constitution high above his head, before handing it over to the local representatives, who received it with their heads bowed and palms turned upward, according to the codex of Driglam Namzha."[66]

The framing of democracy in Bhutan as a royal gift—something both precious and undesired except as a sign of favor from an enlightened ruler—captures the ambivalence of Bhutanese elites toward shifting political norms within the country. Bothe suggests that the fourth King's presentation of democracy as shared responsibility was hijacked by the way Bhutanese elites presented the Constitution and democracy as soelra: a gift which should be received with reverence. Table 3.4 shows Bhutan's gradual movement toward democracy being accomplished by often contentious royal commands rather than gifts. Sonam Kinga, both politician and scholar, engages Bothe's critique somewhat glancingly in arguing that the "gift" of the Constitution had to be "de-sanctified" through Parliamentary debates in order to function effectively during the first democratically elected Parliament.[67] But how far did this de-sanctifying process go, in a country where citizens still speak to the King's feet rather than to his face except when he travels incognito?

Ironically, the ongoing power of kasho and kidu may complicate constitutional limits on royal power (limits originally produced by kasho and

Table 3.4. Monarchy and Democracy in Bhutan

Democratic institution	Produced by kasho (royal command)	Described as soelra (royal gift)
National Assembly (Tshogdu) 1953	Third King	
District development councils (1981)	Fourth King	
Block development councils (1991)	Fourth King; King threatens to abdicate if Tshogdu bans development activities in the south	
Council of Ministers (Cabinet) 1998	Fourth King, *not* Tshogdu or development councils	
Constitution, establishing partisan elections (2001–08)	Fourth King, *not* Council of Ministers	yes

kidu). Just as the fourth King's kasho creating the Constitutional Drafting Committee seems to have over-ridden the executive power he had previously given to the Council of Ministers, so too government programs can be seen as an extension of the King's personal gifts (kidu, soelra) to his people. The finances of the Kingdom, with centralized revenues coming from both hydropower and Indian aid, might contribute to the sense of the government serving as an extension of the King's traditional provision of social welfare. Tight connections between the figure of the King, the government, socioeconomic development, and social security may contribute to popular understanding of the government as centralized power, embodied in the figure of the King, despite the efforts of specific rulers to decentralize their power.

Bhutan's political culture continues to change and adapt to changing circumstances, which makes it impossible to assess the state of politics from afar. In 2017 and 2018, however, it seemed clear to me that

Bhutanese democracy had been changed by the specific history of its adoption within Bhutan at least as much as Bhutan had been changed by the adoption of representative democracy. Democracy "with Bhutan characteristics" and Bhutan's "constitutional democratic monarchy" operated in ways both similar to and quite distinct from representative democracy in the West. I could see why at least one of my students believed that democracy served the King, even if I wasn't entirely sure of the balance of power myself. Shifting politics at the level of District Development Councils, for instance, had created troubling confusions over relative power (and over questions of how grassroots initiatives could access funding), while representative democracies in the West were famous for the kind of short-term thinking my student had identified in the policy shift to central schools.[68] My friend Chencho's concern over "respecting everybody" supported Winnie Bothe's view that political elites were using the "gift" of democracy to accrue greater power for themselves. Finally, my student who had been unwilling to request an exemption from the rigors of serving as a poll worker in remote locations reminded me of how small Bhutan is and thus how intimately connected even a teacher and a monarch could be. That small size and intimacy would make the troubled years of the Lhotshampa crisis all the more painful, as the next chapter describes.

PART III

NATIONAL TRAUMA, NATIONAL HAPPINESS

CHAPTER FOUR

THE LHOTSHAMPA EXPULSION

Even before we arrived in Bhutan, people warned us not to talk about the Lhotshampa crisis. The issue was "delicate." A Fulbright Scholar teaching at Sherubtse the semester before my arrival told me that a German student visiting at Sherubtse College had wanted to write about the Citizenship Act (1985) or the Immigration Act (2007) for a politics class, but his professor told him the topic was out of bounds: she could lose her job if she let him write such a paper. The story left me with a free-floating sense of anxiety about what could and could not be said in relation to ethnic issues in Bhutan. I had read Jamie Zeppa's book about her time in Bhutan, including student protests over the imposition of national dress and rising national tensions in the early 1990s.[1] More than 25 years later, it seemed that some of those tensions remained.

IMMIGRATION FEARS

The Lhotshampa crisis grew out of immigration fears. The government argued that over the course of three decades, southern Bhutan had been overrun by illegal ethnic Nepali immigrants, invited in by ethnic Nepali Bhutanese citizens:

> Unlike the entry of Nepalis in the first half of the century when they came as contractual forest labourers, this [more recent] influx was a case of

> outright illegal immigration over a porous and open border. Pre-occupied with the implementation of development programmes and with only a skeletal administrative set-up in the south headed by civil officials who were mostly ethnic Nepalis, the government remained ignorant about the scale of this silent invasion by economic migrants.[2]

Ethnic Nepali civil officials are presented as a fifth column, intentionally leaving the government (of which they were a part) in ignorance about a "silent invasion" on the part of their ethnic fellows. As a result, government officials argued, "almost three decades passed before the Royal Government became aware of the presence of illegal immigrants. By then substantial numbers of them had already mingled and merged with the local population in southern Bhutan."[3] By implication, differences between ethnic Nepali citizens and illegal immigrants had become impossible to discern—because of disloyal actions by ethnic Nepali civil servants. As this report shows, immigration conflicts are never just about immigration: disputes over immigration turn into disputes over loyalty and belonging and identity.

Similarly, while we often think of civil conflicts arising out of hate speech, Susan Benesch, founder of the Dangerous Speech Project, notes that dangerous speech (speech most likely to incite violence against others) often evokes fear before hatred. That distinction seems to hold true for Bhutan: the Lhotshampa crisis was fueled by claims that ethnic Nepali immigrants threatened Bhutan's independence and national sovereignty.[4] China had annexed Tibet (on Bhutan's northern border) in the 1950s, and India had annexed Sikkim (to Bhutan's west) in 1975, after an ethnic Nepali majority forced political reforms and voted for annexation. Other Himalayan princely states had been swallowed up as well.[5] In the 1980s, Bhutanese public figures claimed the country's freedom and independence were at risk from ethnic Nepali immigrants: people the third King had called "Lhotshampas," or southern Bhutanese.

Sikkim in particular was seen as a frightening example of what could happen to Bhutan. In the nineteenth century, British administrators had encouraged Nepali workers to come to Sikkim, especially to Darjeeling, to work the British-run tea plantations for which Darjeeling became known. By the beginning of the twentieth century, Sikkim's population was 75 percent ethnically Nepali, but Nepali citizens had only minority representation in the government, even after a new Constitution was adopted in 1953. Rising political tensions led to riots in front of the palace in 1973, during which the Chogyal, hereditary Buddhist ruler of Sikkim, reluctantly requested India's military assistance. For the next two years, Indian administrators effectively ran the princely state, with the Chogyal remaining as a figurehead. In 1975, a (rigged) referendum in Sikkim requested annexation by India.[6] The Chogyal was deposed, and India duly made Sikkim first an "associate state," and then a full Indian state.[7]

At the height of the Lhotshampa crisis, Bhutan's foreign minister repeatedly invoked the specter of Sikkim's loss of sovereignty as a sign of what could happen to Bhutan. In January 1992, for instance, he told the *Calcutta Statesman* that if the "influx" of "illegal immigration" continued, in another two decades Bhutan would be "another Sikkim and Darjeeling."[8] The next month, the fourth King echoed this framing, telling Reuters that at the current rate "it is only a matter of time—in the next 10, 15 or 20 years—before Bhutan will no longer be a Bhutanese nation. It will be a Nepali state [. . .] just like Sikkim."[9] Twenty-five years later, a northern Bhutanese colleague would tell me to read a book entitled *Sikkim: Requiem for a Himalayan Kingdom* as a means of understanding challenges faced by Bhutan as well as Sikkim.

GEOGRAPHY AND RESOURCES

Unlike Sikkim, where Nepali immigrants blended into the overall population, ethnic Nepalis in southern Bhutan remained largely separate from the Ngalong population in the west and the Sharchops in the east, both of whom had historically avoided the malaria-ridden jungles of the south. Until China's annexation of Tibet, Bhutan's culture and economy had been oriented toward the north, but that orientation changed rapidly in the 1950s and '60s. Once trade with Tibet was blocked by closed borders and Bhutanese citizens went to India for education, bringing back demands for "economic and political development," the King and his government needed to develop new sources of employment and production. In short, "until the 1950s, the south had been a hinterland; after the 1950s it became a frontier [. . .] the region [. . .] with the greatest potential for [. . .] planned economic growth."[10] Indeed, as Bhutan slowly came out of geopolitical isolation, with its northern border closed, the economic importance of its southern lands could hardly be overstated. In contrast with the northern pine forests, southern forests were primarily hardwood, a much more profitable source of timber. Lhotshampa communities had cleared southern jungles to plant cardamom and orange plantations, producing cash crops unlike the more subsistence-level smallholdings of the north.[11]

The 1964 assassination of Jigme Palden Dorji discussed in Chapter 3 unsettled broader relations between the south and north—and money remained central to these newly unsettled relations. The Dorji family had remained close with and sympathetic to the Nepali settlers they oversaw, while also maintaining a well-administered system of tax collection.[12] A retired Drukpa official told journalist Kanak Mani Dixit that "in the old days when Bhutan was poor and needed cash, we invited the Nepalis in. The money collected from Sachi was taken to the Paro penlop. From Sarbhang, Chirang, Phuntsholing, Tala, Kali Khola, Dagana, too, money flowed into Bhutan's coffers." The list of locations covers most of Bhutan's southwest. The same official noted that originally "there were strict rules prohibiting new settlements, and the system was tight because you needed data to collect taxes." After Jigme Palden Dorji's assassination, the Royal Government of Bhutan "assumed direct control" over taxation in the south. But the bulk of the Dorji family went into exile after the prime minister's assassination, leaving behind a regional power vacuum. This disruption would have made it difficult for the royal government to access previous tax records. As a result, "slack entered the system," and previously tight record-keeping was lost. Looser oversight by the national government might well have resulted in some irregular immigration.[13]

As development activities advanced in Bhutan, the south grew ever more economically important. Mining resources were particularly valuable there, and hydropower projects facilitated with Indian funding were also based in southern Bhutan. Bhutan's first major hydropower project, Chukha Hydropower Corporation, went online in 1988 and "suddenly started injecting huge amounts into the national exchequer."[14] On the one hand, then, Lhotshampa families were profiting from ownership of productive southern lands; on the other hand, with the growth of profits from mining, cement, and hydropower, the central government had new reasons to want to control properties in the south.

NARROWING DEFINITIONS OF CITIZENSHIP AND IDENTITY

Over the course of the 1980s, the Royal Government of Bhutan began tightening both its borders and its definition of citizenship, increasingly insisting on (Ngalong) Bhutanese cultural identity and norms:

- The Marriage Act of 1980 discouraged marriage between Bhutanese citizens and non-Bhutanese people by restricting valuable government benefits, employment, and promotion for any Bhutanese citizen who married a non-Bhutanese. While "non-Bhutanese" could be citizens of any other country, the Act was seen as targeting ethnic Nepalis thought to be entering Bhutan through marriage.
- The Citizenship Act of 1985 reduced transmission of citizenship to people who had documented Bhutanese citizens for both mother and father: citizens had previously been able to access Bhutanese citizenship from a Bhutanese father alone. Like the Marriage Act, the Citizenship Act seemed to target Lhotshampa families who were thought to be bringing ethnic Nepali women to Bhutan to marry their sons: the offspring of such marriages would now be considered (retroactively) illegal immigrants.
- In 1988, a census was conducted only in the south (rather than throughout the country). Those claiming citizenship were asked to present tax receipts showing proof of residence back to 1958 and demonstrate proficiency in Dzongkha. Some people who had previously held citizenship cards had their cards taken away, their claims to citizenship rejected.
- In January 1989, the fourth King put out a kasho, or a royal decree, proclaiming that all Bhutanese people should wear national dress (gho and kira) at dzongs and official occasions. National dress had to be worn at all government offices, including schools. Before issuing

his kasho in 1989, the fourth King had consulted with southern communities about the form that national dress might take, but no one in those communities had felt able to raise concerns about the idea of making Ngalong-style clothing the national dress. Furthermore, implementation of the King's kasho was uneven and excessive: people on the streets not wearing national dress were fined a week's wages, with the police keeping half the money; others were assaulted or imprisoned.[15] A policy apparently intended to create unity became intensely divisive in practice.

- At roughly the same time, Bhutanese schools stopped providing instruction in Nepali. Dzongkha (meaning "the language of the dzongs," simplified from classical Tibetan or Chokey) was taught as the national language, with English used as the language of instruction.[16] Removing Nepali-language instruction was seen by some as a way of closing an achievement gap by reducing the variety of subjects southern students had to learn—but many Lhotshampas saw it as an attack on their culture and their inclusion in the nation.

The government's expressed goal was to defend national sovereignty by maintaining a recognizable, unified culture, but the absence of Lhotshampa elements in that unified culture, combined with a tightening of citizenship requirements and a census that stripped citizenship from members of Lhotshampa communities made Bhutanese unity seem dependent on erasing ethnic Nepali identity.

Implementation of the new Citizenship Act via the 1988 Census—and later censuses held each year in the south—created multiple forms of non-citizenship: in addition to the F1 listing of "genuine Bhutanese citizens," residents might now be considered as F2 through F7 (see Table 4.1).[17] In October 1990, the home minister of Bhutan, Dago Tshering, said:

> We were not planning to throw out anybody. We wanted to issue identity cards — red ones to the genuine residents, who were here before 1958, and green ones to later immigrants. The green ID, modeled on the Green Card of the US, gives all rights to the residents, except the right to vote and the right to apply for foreign scholarship.[18]

Table 4.1. Citizenship Categories Laid Out in the 1985 Citizenship Act.[19]

F1	Genuine Bhutanese citizens
F2	Returned migrants (people who had left Bhutan and then returned)
F3	"Drop-out" cases—i.e., people who were not around at the time of the census
F4	A non-national woman married to a Bhutanese man
F5	A non-national man married to a Bhutanese woman
F6	Adoption cases (children who have been legally adopted)
F7	Non-nationals, i.e., migrants and illegal settlers

But the home minister's claim understates the extent to which the government was both rejecting the idea of birthright citizenship and effectively de-naturalizing groups of existing citizens. A United States State Department report of 1994 summarized the conflict over the census and citizenship in this way:

> Exile political groups complain that the law makes unfair demands for documentation on largely illiterate people in a country that has only recently adopted basic administrative procedures. They claim that many ethnic Nepalese whose families have been in Bhutan for generations were expelled because they were unable to document their claims to residence. The Government denies this and asserts, for example, that the word of village leaders is an acceptable substitute for written documentation. Refugee groups dispute this statement and report that village elders are not present when citizenship interviews are carried out.[20]

This kind of conflict over basic facts persisted throughout the crisis and its aftermath.

DISPUTED DATA

Indeed, as ethnic tensions rose, there was little agreement over actual population numbers, though both sides agreed that the Lhotshampa population was growing. In the twenty-odd years between the country's earliest official census and the Lhotshampa crisis, growth of the Lhotshampa population had led to a dwindling population percentage for both the Ngalong and the Sharchop populations, as shown in Table 4.2. Did Lhotshampas already outnumber Ngalongs and Sharchops put together? Dissident groups in exile claimed they did.

As Table 4.2 demonstrates, even official Bhutanese demographic data were highly variable. In 1969, for instance, Bhutan had conducted a nationwide census as part of its application to join the United Nations.[21] The 1969 Census report recorded a total population of 1,034,774—but population totals were later adjusted by roughly 10 percent, down to 930,614, after a district-by-district recount exposed an arithmetic error.[22] And in 1992, in the middle of the crisis, the fourth King told a Kolkata magazine

Table 4.2. Population Percentage Estimates for Linguistic Groups and Geographical Regions.[23]

Language Groups by Geographic Region	**1969 Royal Govt of Bhutan (RGB) Census: Geographical Regions**	**1988–92 Royal Govt of Bhutan (RGB) Census: Language Groups**	**1992 Bhutan's People's Party (dissidents): Language Groups**
Ngalongs (Drukpa) / West	28% West	20%	16%
Sharchops / East	57% East	37%	31%
Lhotshampa / South	15% South	30%	53%
Total population estimate	930,614 (revised down from 1,034,774)	600,000 (revised down from 1,400,000)	700,000–800,000

that Bhutan's population, then estimated at 1.4 million, was actually only 600,000: roughly 42 percent of the prior estimate.[24] Refugee leaders agreed that population estimates had been inflated, but they insisted that 600,000 was an underestimate, arguing that Bhutan's total population was somewhere in the range of 700,000–800,000. Still, refugee leaders used the 600,000 figure "to accuse the Government of attempting to depopulate a sixth of the country's population"—using the lower number for Bhutan's overall population and a higher one for the number of refugees produced a more dramatic statistic.[25] The difference in figures no longer registered just an error in arithmetic: instead, the disputed 100,000 represented, depending on one's perspective, either the number of illegal immigrants occupying the southern borderlands, or the number of Lhotshampas displaced by the crisis.[26]

ESCALATION: PROTEST, VIOLENCE, AND BUREAUCRACY

Back in 1988, Tek Nath Rizal, a southern member of the Royal Advisory Council, protested the new Citizenship Act and the Census, first in a private conversation with the King and then, at the King's request, in an official petition, drafted with the aid of multiple southern Bhutanese civil servants. Upon receipt of the petition, the King traveled to the south to speak directly with other Lhotshampa citizens—who felt unable to complain directly to the King about the Census. The King decided Rizal was "spreading false allegations and inciting southern Bhutanese against the government."[27] Rizal's petition was declared seditious; he was expelled from the Council and jailed for three days. Once released, Rizal fled first to India, and then to Nepal, where he founded a resistance party and published pamphlets full of inflammatory language. He was later returned to Bhutan by the Nepali police, despite the absence of any extradition treaty between the two countries. According to Amnesty International, the Royal Government of Bhutan arrested 45 people in autumn 1989 for writing "seditious pamphlets," but while others charged with sedition were pardoned or released early, Rizal was held in solitary confinement for three years without trial, in shackles for 20 months of that time, under threat of a death sentence that would eventually be changed to life imprisonment.[28] The severity of his treatment shocked many Lhotshampa civil servants: if a Royal Councilor could be treated with such severity, what would happen to less exalted community members?

In June 1990, the Bhutanese People's Party (BPP) was launched to represent southern interests, despite a national ban on party politics. Then, on June 2, two Lhotshampas associated with the Royal Government were beheaded, purportedly by Lhotshampa dissidents and anti-nationals or ngolops. The Royal Government reported that the heads carried a "warning letter in red ink," stating that "all those who supported the Royal Government would meet the same fate."[29] Some argued that the perpetrators were not actually Lhotshampas, or were individuals acting alone to take revenge for abuses suffered by their families, but soon the government was publishing booklets full of gory color photographs of Lhotshampas allegedly killed and maimed by ngolops.

The conflict escalated quickly. In a circular notification dated August 17th, 1990, the Bhutanese Home Ministry advised that "any Bhutanese national leaving the country to assist and help the antinationals shall no longer be considered as a Bhutanese citizen [. . .] Such people's family members living under the same household will also be held fully responsible and forfeit their citizenship." The 1985 Citizenship Act allowed for this assertion of guilt by association, since under Article 6c, citizenship could be revoked for any naturalized citizens who have "shown [themselves] by act or speech to be disloyal in any manner whatsoever to the King, country, and people of Bhutan."[30] Familial relationships including cohabitation could now be taken as evidence of disloyalty to the King, country and people of Bhutan.[31]

In September 1990, Bhutan was shaken by mass protests, organized by a combination of the BPP, the People's Forum for Human Rights (PFHR, founded in Nepal by Tek Nath Rizal), and others. Bhutan had never before seen such large-scale demonstrations. As many as 50,000 people took part in marches held throughout the southern districts between September 19 and 25, with an additional march in Chirang on October 4.[32] These marches were particularly stunning in a country unused to political protest. Some people were apparently coerced into participating—in threatening reference to the June beheadings, agitators told some villagers they too could "lose six inches" if they did not participate[33]—but coercion alone could not have produced crowds of such large numbers.

The marchers presented political demands as shocking as the size of their crowds. They demanded the unconditional release of political prisoners; a change from absolute monarchy to constitutional monarchy; judicial reform; amendments to the Citizenship Act of 1985; rights to culture, dress, language, script, religion, education; freedom of speech, press, and expression; freedom of union and political party formation; equal access to public employment; equitable distribution of wealth and funds, and more. In 1990s Bhutan, these were blockbuster demands. Political party flags, banned in Bhutan, were hoisted in some town centers; some ghos and kiras were burned. The government announced that police constables had been injured and one killed after being abducted by a mob.[34] The National Assembly was canceled for the year, and public life in the south was largely shut down.

Om Dhungel, a former Bhutanese civil servant who eventually resettled in Australia, summarized the government's response to the protests as an

> economic embargo on southern Bhutan. All shops, including my parents' grocery, were ordered to shut. The flow of salt, sugar, cooking oil and other essential items was restricted. The government stopped paying for cash crops and instead confiscated them, a clear attempt to starve people. Then it sent in the army, and the violence began.

Dhungel described four people killed above his family home after soldiers fired on a crowd trying to stop the troops from closing the local health unit and removing the medical supplies. Schools were turned into prisons.[35] Dhungel's retrospective summary largely matches the "confidential report of a Western bilateral development agency" from 1992, which asserted that ethnic Nepalis' "participation in public life has been made extremely difficult. There were no schools, no health facilities [. . .] sale of produce was difficult, trade licenses were withdrawn, and employment opportunities were minimalized."[36]

The reduction of opportunities for Lhotshampa citizens came partly through the mechanism of "No Objection Certificates" (stating that the police had no objection to a given person, no knowledge of anti-national actions or connections), which were required for employment, admission to schools (outside of the south, where schools remained closed), or work-related travel outside of Bhutan. The bilateral agency report noted that "If one then adds the fear of physical violence, it is no wonder that many families see no future in this country and decide to leave." Reports of state violence were denied by the Bhutanese government but recognized by independent agencies, the UNHCR, and the US State Department. According to the US State Department report, "most alleged incidents of torture in southern Bhutan took place in 1990 and 1991. [. . .] [R]eported rapes continued at a high rate into 1992; however, there were few reported cases of rape and torture in 1993. The Government flatly denied such abuse ever occurred."[37] Given government denials of wrongdoing, no clarity over responsibility for state violence ever clearly emerged.

One of the perversities of the expulsion process was that Lhotshampas, even or especially those threatened with state violence, were legally required to request formal permission to emigrate from Bhutan. "Voluntary leaving certificates" legalized the process by which the state seized Lhotshampa lands: families who had been "declared 'illegal'" or threatened with violence would be called to the district office and told to sign a form and receive compensation for their house and land. Rosalind Evans, for instance, interviewed a refugee woman who said the Mandal (a local official) "told my father that he had to fill in a form to leave the country or he would be arrested. Many people were leaving the country and it was risky for my older sisters because of the army's activities. After my father filled in the form in Dzongkha, we were taken for photos. They told us to stand in a line and show our teeth [smile]." In other words, the family, fearful that their daughters would be raped, decided to leave Bhutan, but they were warned that unless they went through state procedures for departure, they could be arrested—and, by extension, presumably tortured and raped. Only belatedly did the family of this Lhotshampa woman understand the point of the procedure: "Later we realised the statement said [my father] was happy to leave the country and was going willingly."[38] As the crisis progressed, compensation was reported to have fallen by 90 percent in Samchi, from Nu 40,000 per acre of paddy field to 4,000 per acre.[39] Families were leaving the only country they had ever known, with only 10 percent of their lifetime assets in hand. If a family member had been jailed during the protests, a sum of 2000 ngultrum per month of imprisonment was subtracted from the compensation. These Voluntary Leaving Certificates were later used to deny refugees the right of return to Bhutan. Their land had already been re-distributed to those seen as loyal citizens from the east and west of the country.

DESTABILIZING NATIONAL IDENTITY

Two stories, both involving the King, epitomize the destabilizing nature of the Lhotshampa crisis. First, in a stand-off with the National Assembly and his Cabinet, the King threatened to abdicate if he could not find an effective resolution to the crisis on his own terms. Then, faced with a mass exodus from a southern district, the King begged his southern subjects not to abandon their country. Years later, people quoted both speeches to me as evidence of the King's desperate desire to resolve the crisis—but neither speech stopped the violence at the time, raising questions about who exactly was in control of the government.

The King's threat to abdicate in 1991 was something of a "nuclear option" that only partially succeeded in blocking retribution against the Lhotshampa community as a whole. The National Assembly of 1990 had been canceled after the protest marches, and when the Assembly next convened, in October 1991, the legislators (Chimis) were unrestrained in their expressions of outrage and betrayal. According to the Assembly report, "most members" wanted to evict "all Southern Bhutanese," including those married to "original" Bhutanese and those working in the government.[40] Assembly members also objected to the King's unilateral pardoning of some 1,500 people arrested as ngolops, and suggested that all southerners be required to take a pledge of loyalty to the Tsawasum (understood as the King, country, and people of Bhutan)—a suggestion the King promptly shot down.[41] The Assembly and a group of Cabinet members together further proposed that southern development funds be re-purposed for security needs, but the King refused to abandon existing plans to build ten more schools and eight health centers in the south, along with a new 65-kilometer road. He made a point of saying that he was acting "not out of compassion" but rather "keeping in mind the larger interest and the long term security and well-being of the nation and the national goal of achieving a uniform and balanced development throughout the country."[42] Still, the Tshogdu pushed back: "The Representatives of the Government and the People submitted that although the wishes and commands of His Majesty the King were sacred and inviolate, they begged to submit their sincere and heartfelt" and almost unanimous view that Bhutan should stop all development activities in the southern Dzongkhags.[43] In response, the King reminded the Assembly that they had already agreed to leave him to resolve the ngolop problem and he had promised to give it his best efforts. Now, "His Majesty gave the Assembly his pledge to abdicate if he did not succeed in finding a lasting solution to the ngolop problem." That pledge—"If I, as the King, cannot protect the sovereignty and integrity of our country and ensure a secure future for our people, then it will be my duty to accept full responsibility and abdicate"—was widely quoted in the aftermath of the discussion, although various Chimis, shocked and traumatized by the very idea of abdication, tried to have any mention of it struck from the Tshogdu's official record.[44]

The King's threat to abdicate brought the day's discussion to a hasty conclusion, but the following day started with Home Minister Dago Tshering attacking at length what he framed as the ngolops' commitment to regime change in Bhutan. The home minister began by reading out the demands of the Bhutan People's Party, most of which he dismissed as propaganda. He claimed that

> the ngolops openly boasted that there were 18 million Nepalis in Nepal and 10 million Nepalis in India, most of them living across Bhutan's immediate borders in Kalimpong, Darjeeling, Sikkim and the Duars region. It was the ultimate aim of the anti-nationals to turn Bhutan into a Nepali dominated State and include it among the Nepali dominated areas in the Himalayan region. Although, fortunately, they were not yet the majority, the repeated claims of the anti-nationals that Nepalese in southern Bhutan comprised 60% of the country's total population clearly reflected their intention of dramatically changing the demographic balance in Bhutan.[45]

In fact, the home minister claimed, "the antinationals in southern Bhutan would never be satisfied until they had taken over the country and turned it into a Nepali dominated state."[46] He ended his speech with the required gesture of confidence in the King's ability to resolve the ngolop problem—but the speech as a whole deepened the sense of an ethnic divide between people the northern Chimis tended to call "true" or "original" Bhutanese and those he encouraged the Assembly to consider alien Nepalis. This speech and other speeches from this 1991 Assembly fit the definition of "dangerous speech," that is, speech that increases "the risk its audience will condone or participate in violence against members of another group."[47] The King's threat of abdication seems to have lived on in popular Bhutanese memory, but it failed to turn the tide of dangerous speech or the resulting violence.

The contrast between the ongoing violence and the King's apparent defense of Lhotshampa communities was baffling in a nation so dedicated to its monarchs. In grappling with this puzzle in 1992, Nepali journalist Kanak Mani Dixit suggested a kind of palace capture, in which "the King's three sisters and his paternal uncle Namgyal Wangchuk, all of whom once had charge of key ministries, have been sidelined," with important positions given instead to family members of the four queens, including "Home Minister Dago Tshering, Foreign Minister Dawa Tshering, Social Services Minister Tashi Tobgyel, and Bhutan Army chief Gongloen Lam Dorji. Further, the Joint Secretary in the Planning Commission is Their Majesties the Queens' elder brother; the final authority in deciding Bhutanese citizenship is the youngest brother."[48] Years later, I still heard mutterings about corruption associated with the Queens' family, though no Bhutanese ever made the kind of argument implied by Dixit here.

The King's other famous speech amid the crisis was an address to villagers near Gelephu: some four hundred families who had all signaled their intention of emigrating out of Bhutan. The King sent a high-level delegation down to meet with them and ask them to remain. When the families refused to linger, the King instructed the team to pay the families to remain long enough for him to come and meet with them. On July 14, he met with the families, giving the following speech as reported in the *Kuensel*:

> All of you are bonafide citizens who have been issued with Bhutanese Citizenship Cards. It is very important that I understand your problems and know the reason why you want to leave your country. [. . .]
>
> Short of literally going down on my knees with folded hands, I have tried everything possible to resolve the serious problem we have today in southern Bhutan. I am therefore deeply pained that all of you here today who are genuine citizens have not only applied to leave your country but even declared that you would not wait for more than two days to have your applications processed. I have come here from Thimphu to ask you all not to migrate and leave your country. I have every hope that you will reconsider your decision and not abandon your country when it is going through a very difficult time.
>
> I have done everything I could think of to make you responsible citizens. I can now only hope and pray that you will stay back so that we can all live together like members of one household and make our country strong.[49]

The King's speech was especially striking in the context of Bhutan's absolute monarchy: 25 years later, Drukpa friends referenced the speech in explaining the crisis to me. "The King begged them to stay, but they refused!"

The background for this speech, however, provides a striking context for the King's words. On May 23, 1992, the *Kuensel* reported that Chimi Dorji, a popular Dungpa or subdistrict officer of Gelephu, had been killed. On June 4, his replacement, Tobgay Tshering, called a meeting for villagers in the Gelephu region. According to Dixit's reconstruction of that meeting, based on accounts of refugees who had been present, Tshering asked people to raise their hands if they thought families of persons identified as ngolops should be told to leave Bhutan. When only one man raised his hand, Tshering responded with a dehumanizing and inflammatory diatribe. The first line ("Do you still have the dead Dungpa's meat sticking to your teeth, you murderers?") defined the audience as cannibals. The middle of the speech rehearsed a set of anti-Lhotshampa tropes. First, guilt by association: "So you want to keep the ngolops. That makes all of you ngolops." Second, a narrow definition of national identity: "We Drukpas fought the British, we fought the Tibetans. We spilt blood for this country, not you. This country is ours', and the Government is ours. You all were only guests, so now go back to your country." Third, a threat: "You definitely cannot stay here. You cannot pretend to be a citizen by just wearing the bakhhu [national dress]. Better to go while there is still time, or you will suffer. You have three days to depart. It does not matter if you are F-1 or F-7. Better that weeds grow here than you plough your fields." Fourth, a bureaucratic command: "Do not run away, fill the form of voluntary departure, take your compensation and go." Fifth, a straightforward lie about the condition of those who have left already: "The people of Samchi who went before you have got citizenship in Nepal and have come back and thanked us for suggesting that they go. Go to Nepal, there the Koirala Sarkar [the prime minister] will keep you in comfortable buildings and feed you." The "people of Samchi" or residents of a different part of southern Bhutan may have been distinct enough from the community around Gelephu that such a lie about Nepal would be marginally credible, but it seems likely that many Lhotshampas already knew the truth: Nepali citizenship was not available to Bhutanese refugees, nor were comfortable buildings on offer. The last two sentences equated the villagers with monkeys to be hunted: "When you all are gone, we will come down here to hunt. Let it not be that we get some monkeys when we aim for the wild game."

The contrast between the King's speech and the words attributed to the Dungpa underscores the cognitive dissonance created by the crisis: how could the government address the same people in such radically different ways? Were the Lhotshampa officially seen as cannibalistic monkeys or family members of a single national household? Was the King gaslighting the villagers? Was he ignorant of the actions of his officials?

The villagers' understanding of their situation was reported at the time but disbelieved. The *Kuensel* asked Dungpa Tobgay Tshering why the migrants blamed him for their departure and he gave a flat denial: he could not have said all of those things when he had just taken office. The home minister appointed a team to enquire into villagers' complaints against Tshering—but as noted above, the home minister was largely responsible for the policies contributing to the Lhotshampa expulsion. The team, without ever contacting the refugees interviewed by Dixit, dismissed the allegations against the Dungpa, though Kinley Dorji asserted (without specifics) that "government officials and security personnel responsible for excesses against the people have been dismissed and tried in court."[50] On August 8, 1992, three weeks after the King's visit, *Kuensel* reported that the emigrants had inflicted millions of ngultrum of damage on public facilities before leaving: primary schools, basic health units, government and agricultural support offices had been destroyed, along with irrigation and rural water supply systems, revealing "that the people of Geylegphug had been Ngolops all along, with no intention of remaining in Bhutan." The refugees claimed innocence, suggesting that the army committed the damage in order to blame the refugees. Again, disagreement over basic facts blocked any resolution of the conflict.

IRRESOLUTION: THE JOINT VERIFICATION EXERCISE AND ITS AFTERMATH

Numbers of Bhutanese refugees arriving at the camps in Nepal slowed significantly in 1993 and 1994. But the question of their future was deeply fraught, and the refugees made various attempts to return to Bhutan—attempts complicated by the fact that India was working at the same time to deport ethnic Nepalis from its own territories. Over the course of 1996, for instance, an organization called the Appeal Movement Coordinating Council (AMCC) organized an extended protest march from Nepali refugee camps to Bhutan with the goal of pressuring the King to permit their repatriation. India, however, refused to permit protestors to cross Indian territory. More than a thousand of the marchers were arrested in India over the course of the year, though they were eventually released after the courts declared the arrests illegal. At the end of 1996, thousands of Lhotshampas staged a sit-in on the India-Nepal border, protesting India's additional deportation of ethnic Nepalis from West Bengal. In March 1997, the AMCC organized a hunger strike by some 15,000 refugees to press the United Nations to secure their return to Bhutan. The hunger strike lasted almost a month.[51]

Bhutan, while acknowledging that residents of the refugee camps exceeded 100,000 by the end of 1993, still insisted that the number of genuine refugees was far lower. Karma Phuntsho, for instance, asserts that "the UNHRC camps in eastern Nepal received about 6000 refugees from Bhutan at the height of the conflict."[52] Phuntsho's explanation for the striking discrepancy in numbers was that "many stateless and landless people in the area joined the refugee bandwagon" in order to take advantage of the "generous daily allowance" and "poor process of verification."[53] Bhutanese officials suggested that people in the camps were coming from the larger pool of ethnic Nepalis expelled from various northern Indian communities, particularly Assam, Meghalaya, and Mizoram.

In 2003, pressed by the United States among other parties, the governments of Nepal and Bhutan established a "Joint Verification Team" to assess the claims of refugees. The team began in March 2001 with a small, late-established camp (Khudunabari) of 12,173 residents. Michael Hutt argues that this particular camp was not especially representative: since it held mostly late arrivals to the camps, its residents were less likely to have strong citizenship claims.[54] In June 2003, after two years of slow work, the Joint Verification Team announced its findings:

- Two and a half percent of the refugees (only 293 people) in Category I: bona fide Bhutanese citizens who would be eligible for repatriation to Bhutan;
- Seventy percent (8,585 people) in Category II: refugees who "voluntarily emigrated" from Bhutan and would be required to reapply for Bhutanese citizenship.
- Twenty-four percent (2,948 people) in Category III: non-Bhutanese people whose claims to citizenship were rejected and would be returned to their respective countries;
- Three percent (347 people) in Category IV: so-called "criminals" who would be liable to be tried in the Bhutanese courts.[55]

These results pleased no one, and the statistics were read in opposing directions.[56] For Karma Phuntsho, the most relevant fact was that almost 25 percent of the purported refugees "were said to have no link to Bhutan"; for Michael Hutt, "having consistently denied [. . .] that the camps contained any significant number of its own people, [. . .] the Bhutanese government had now accepted that around 75% of the population of this first camp either were, or had once been, Bhutanese citizens."[57] Were the camps one-quarter empty or three-quarters full? Despite presenting effectively the same data, these accounts supported very different political arguments.

The Joint Verification Exercise did little to resolve the conflict or mediate claims over the right of return. Seventy percent of the refugees were classed as voluntary "emigrants" (suggesting that the Joint Verification Team had not seriously grappled with the problems inherent in the "Voluntary Leaving Certificates"): these refugees could apply for Bhutanese citizenship, but they would have to submit their applications from within Bhutan, where they would have to wait at least two years for a decision. They would be given employment but not housing; they could not have any record of "anti-national" activity; they would have to be able to speak Dzongkha, and display a "good knowledge" of the culture and history of Bhutan. These were stiff requirements for many refugees, especially those who knew their land had been given to Ngalong and Sharchop settlers from other parts of Bhutan—or had been occupied by Assamese militants setting up camps in the jungle. When the results were read out in the camp, residents rioted in protest. Back in Bhutan, the National Assembly protested the repatriation of any individuals from the refugee camps—even the 293 people in the first category, whom the Government had promised to repatriate.[58]

In 2007, the UNHCR brokered an arrangement by which a group of eight countries offered the refugees resettlement over the course of the next decade. European countries took a comparatively small number of refugees: the Netherlands took 329, the United Kingdom 358, Norway 570, and Denmark 875. New Zealand accepted 1,075 refugees; Australia resettled 6,204. In North America, Canada took 6,773 and the United States of America resettled 92,323 Lhotshampa refugees. By 2016, only two out of seven refugee camps in Nepal remained, with fewer than 12,000 refugees between the two.[59] Resettlement is not the end of the story, of course. While some refugees have thrived in their new homes, others suffer ongoing depression and anxiety. The suicide rate for Bhutanese refugees both in camps in Nepal and after resettlement in the United States is significantly higher than that of the overall US population. More research is needed, but early analyses list unemployment, lack of resettlement services or social support, and family separation as possible causes for suicide in the resettled Lhotshampa community.[60]

UNSPOKEN/UNSPEAKABLE

What remains of the Lhotshampa crisis within Bhutan? In 2011, Jigmi Thinley, the first popularly elected prime minister of Bhutan, described the refugee issue as "the biggest political, social and security challenge for Bhutan,"[61] but according to Karma Phuntsho, the primary cost was to Bhutan's reputation. By 2013, he argued,

> the refugee issue has ceased to be of any significance, apart from the havoc it continues to cause to Bhutan's international projection as a happy country. [. . .]The Lhotshampas, who still make up about twenty-five per cent of the population, have integrated into the northern culture and the ethnic tension is disappearing while the new democratic system also allows for greater multicultural co-existence.[62]

Few external observers seem to agree with Karma Phuntsho's optimistic view of cultural integration (nor would all agree that integration is required or appropriate). Freedom House, an NGO tracking political rights and civil liberties around the globe, notes various forms of discrimination still faced by Nepali-speaking Bhutanese in 2022, including "citizenship rules" that "disenfranchise" many Nepali-speaking people and constrain foreign travel, the presence of 6,000–7,000 Bhutanese refugees remaining in Nepal, a ban on NGOs working on issues related to ethnic Nepalis, reports of employment discrimination and other forms of bias.[63] Despite constitutional protections, Lhotshampa citizens (described by Freedom House as ethnic Nepalis) continue to suffer infringement of their political rights and civil liberties.

Line Christensen, reporting on seven months of fieldwork completed at Sherubtse College between 2013 and 2015, suggests that the expulsion crisis had a larger, more diffuse and largely negative effect on Bhutanese civil society. Bhutan's 1992 National Security Act, established in the wake of Lhotshampa protests, served to codify a "political censorship regime" which hampers freedom of speech. While some of her informants seemed to know nothing about the "conflict of the 1990s," Christensen noted that they did not seek out information to fill the gaps in their knowledge. Instead, these students collaborated "in the silence surrounding the sensitive issues by practising an indifferent style of response when faced with questions about such issues. The fact that they do not seek information is a practice [. . .which] can be seen as an adaptation to power."[64] Christensen also draws attention to the eeriness of Bhutan's broad silencing of past conflict: "nothing is mentioned in the school curricula or museums." [65] The conflict has not been fully erased, but neither has it been resolved. As a result, Bhutan's "democratic project is tainted by wariness, lack of openness and lack of access to information," resulting from the enforced silencing of conflict.[66] Some of her student informants—notably, those with greater political security as Drukpa citizens—argued that Bhutanese people needed to practice opposition more openly in order to strengthen democratic norms on the level of civil society. Christensen's work suggests that removing the taboo on discussing the "conflict of the 1990s" and reducing discrimination against Lhotshampas in Bhutan could benefit not only Lhotshampa but also young Drukpa citizens who find their constitutionally guaranteed freedom of speech and opinion elusive.

My own experiences in Bhutan align with the silences Christensen described, suggesting that unresolved fragments of that thirty-year-old conflict still shape public discourse. When we arrived, jetlagged, in Thimphu, the Immigration Office required me to affirm in writing that I would obey the provisions of the Immigration Act of 2007: I would go only where my permit specified and do only the work specified; neither the College nor I would have any reason for complaint if my work permit were revoked under section eight of the law; I had no claim to residence; the College would repatriate me at the end of my contract or within three years, whichever came first. Later, I looked up section eight and discovered it banned "infractions likely to disrupt the public good"—without defining those infractions. The imprecision suggested that officials would have significant latitude in objecting to a foreign worker, leaving a sense of uncertainty and anxiety about what was safe to say and what might put us or others at risk—and of course I had little at stake compared to my Bhutanese students and colleagues.

Still, like Line Christensen's interview subjects, I found myself not seeking information. I taught Lhotshampa graduate students—and avoided discussing the conflict with them, out of a vague, unarticulated worry about making their lives harder. (It was hard not to notice, however, that the proportion of Lhotshampa graduate students was significantly below the Lhotshampa proportion of the Bhutanese population.) I seldom spoke about the crisis with northern friends, either, out of a sense that it remained taboo. Sometimes, however, a passing comment would draw attention to what we weren't discussing. For instance, when I was asking yet another northern friend about the idea that the fourth King had "given" Bhutan democracy before they even asked for it, the friend corrected me: "Southerners wanted democracy earlier, but the King was not ready." When I asked him to say more, my friend just shook his head: "The southerners made demands, but those demands were not met. They suffered a lot."

Was it true those demands were never met? I wondered. I know of no one who connects the abdication of the fourth King with his vow to abdicate if he could not resolve the Lhotshampa crisis—but his abdication was announced in 2005 and accomplished in 2006, after the failure of the Joint Verification Exercise in 2003 and before the resettlement agreements of 2007. And yet, as discussed in Chapter 3, many people associate that abdication with the installation of democracy in Bhutan—and constitutional democratic monarchy was one of the demands presented by the 1990 marchers.

From southern friends and passing acquaintances, I heard individual stories of discrimination I cannot share publicly for fear of putting people at risk. Bhutan is such a tiny country that anonymity seems impossible. Whenever I tried to anonymously describe anything in Bhutan, the person I was speaking to usually asked, "Who did you hear that from? Was it so-and-so?" The result, from my perspective at least, was that the "troubles" of the 1990s remained largely unspoken and unspeakable in Bhutan as late as 2018.

This eerie silencing made me think of the karamshing, the "curse tree" of eastern Bhutan. My family first encountered a curse tree on one of our daily walks down the farm roads below Sherubtse College, when one of the houses we passed installed an odd structure at the roadside (Figure 4.1).

On a forked stake that stood a little higher than my head, someone had nailed thin miniature planks. From this central structure, nine spiky sticks radiated outward: string had been looped around those spokes to

Figure 4.1. Karamshing, a "curse tree" to turn away malicious speech.

make something that looked a little like a spider web. A phallus protruded from the base of the fork; a scrotum-like sack hung below the phallus, with multiple arrows penetrating the sack. Hanging down beside the sack were a cup, a ladle, a large spoon and a couple of baskets. The mixture of domesticity, phallic imagery, and weaponry was pretty striking to our American eyes. The Yonphula librarian told me it was a karamshing: a structure designed to turn aside curses and/or slander. The forked stake was supposed to be nutgall or Chinese sumac, *Rhus chinensis*, cut down at night; the sack contained nine kinds of grain. Each member of the household was represented by one of the kitchen utensils so that they would be protected from the curse of bad gossip.

"But why would they need protection?" I asked. "What kind of bad gossip would be circulating about a family? And wouldn't building a curse tree just call attention to that bad gossip?"

"No, no!" The logic was so obvious to the librarian that he couldn't find the words to explain it to me—though scholars Sonam Chopel and Karma Phuntsho offer this explanation:

> Bhutanese believe that people's words about someone, when spoken slanderously, have a negative impact on the person talked about. Even positive words, out of envy, are said to have an unpleasant outcome for the person talked about. The words and their results are called *kharam*, which literally means 'ruin by words', or *mikha* (མི་ཁ་), literally, 'words of other people.'[67]

Bad gossip is evidently so harmful that the curse tree's symbolic self-defense is worth invoking. Curse trees are particularly common in eastern Bhutan, but the instinct to avoid "ruin by words" seems to operate also at the national level, as seen in the silences surrounding the Lhotshampa crisis.

In the end, perhaps predictably, disputes over citizenship within Bhutan are being resolved primarily through the King's gift: the practice of granting citizenship as kidu. On May 24, 2016, for instance, the *Kuensel* reported that "individuals seeking citizenship Kidu submit their appeals to His Majesty through the Office of the Gyalpoi Zimpon, which also receives applications through dzongkhag officials in 20 dzongkhags. His Majesty The King personally grants Audience to every recipient of the citizenship Kidu." Those receiving citizenship Kidu swear an oath of loyalty to the Tsa-wa-sum—as the National Assembly had wanted back in 1991. The *Kuensel* also reported that "During Royal Tours across the country, His Majesty has said that granting citizenship Kidu and resolving census issues of the people continues to be a priority." During the first ten years of his reign, the fifth King granted citizenship kidu to "over 9,000" people.[68] By November 2022, the total had risen to 25,000.[69] The process remains ongoing—as does the process of adaptation for resettled Bhutanese refugees.

The next chapter approaches "Gross National Happiness" or GNH, sometimes called "Bhutan's greatest contribution to the global community," with this difficult history still in view. Is Bhutan's GNH just ideological cover for anti-Lhotshampa discrimination? And what, if anything, does GNH have to offer a world facing rapid changes, including environmental catastrophe and political turmoil?

CHAPTER FIVE

THE RISE AND FALL OF GROSS NATIONAL HAPPINESS

"What's so gross about national happiness?" Jeremy asked one day as he and I headed out on our daily afternoon walk. We were following a narrow trail down the mountain, heading toward an unpaved farm road.

"Gross means something different in this context, Jem," I replied. "It means 'big' or 'overall.' When people say gross national happiness, they're talking about how much happiness there is in the country as a whole."

The trail ran between two half-open barns, along a fence line whose posts had been carved into phalluses, red paint highlighting the carved tips. (Bhutan's phallus fixation has become a focus of Western tourism recently, but this aging fence was clearly not aimed at tourists. See Figure 5.1.)

Marijuana grew wild along the fence line; periodically, Sherubtse students would fan out across the countryside near the College to root it up, before it could become an illicit temptation. As the trail turned sharply by the wall of a large house, Jeremy and I scooted around some buckets and ancient pots full of scummy water, presumably left for the cows to drink. Below us, the fields and rice paddies stretched out, offering exuberant colors and expansive space (Figure 5.2)—though the path itself was narrow and slippery with mud.

"Why do people say gross if they don't mean gross?" Jeremy grumbled.

Figure 5.1. Sample phallus carved and painted on the top of aging fence posts.

"What people say and what they mean is often kind of complicated," I said, hedging. Even before coming to Bhutan, I had been interested in Gross National Happiness, insofar as I understood it. I knew the fourth King had suggested the proper goal of government policies should be to increase Gross National Happiness rather than merely increasing Gross National

Figure 5.2. The view from our walks down the farm road below Kanglung, post-monsoon.

Product. I also had a general sense that Bhutanese GNH was an attempt to secularize Vajrayana insights for a more general public, and that Bhutan's diplomatic insistence on promoting happiness as a development goal might have influenced the United Nations' Sustainable Development Goals (SDGs) as well as the Better Life Index (BLI), now tracked by the Organization for Economic Collaboration and Development (OECD).[1] I didn't think this kind of alphabet soup would help Jeremy understand GNH, however.

As the chair of an Environmental Studies program (from 2014–17), I had been pleased that one of the four "pillars" of GNH was "environmental conservation"; as a humanist, I was pleased that GNH also took culture into account (as another of those four pillars, along with "sustainable and equitable socio-economic development" and "good government"). After we arrived in Bhutan, however, I found myself repeatedly frustrated in my desire to learn more about GNH. In 2017, almost every Bhutanese person we met ended up mentioning GNH to us, mostly, I believe, because they thought foreigners would recognize the term and be interested. But conversations on this topic rarely went anywhere. Once the word—and it often seemed a single word, something like jeenaitch—appeared, conversations seemed to falter. Together, we would canvass the four pillars—environment, culture, government, equitable development—and then look around for something else to talk about. When I tried to ask specific questions about any of those pillars, I received only very general answers.

Still, it was clear early on that Bhutanese GNH didn't always operate the way a Westerner might expect. One example came in local disputes over corporal punishment in the schools. My family got caught up in these debates after Jeremy came home one day, shocked at having seen his classmates beaten for not doing their Dzongkha homework.

"She made them line up and hoist up their ghos and kiras so that they would feel it more, and then she hit them with a piece of bamboo. She seems so nice—not like a teacher who would hit you. She saw me looking shocked and she came to explain to me: 'If I don't hit them, they won't do their work. I have to do it.' If I were taking Dzongkha class, I would probably have been beaten too."

"Wait: which teacher?" I asked. "The one with the big glasses and the big smile?" I had given a talk at the primary school earlier that week. That Dzongkha teacher had been present, nodding along at the idea of mastery-based education, the importance of giving students power over their own learning. "There must be some mistake."

"Yeah, I told you: she doesn't seem like a teacher who would hit you. But she hit them. She hit them hard."

Up at Yonphula, about this same time, one of my students was outraged to discover that her six-year-old daughter, at school back in western Bhutan, had been beaten, along with all of her classmates, for making noise when there was no teacher in the room.

"Whose fault is it," my student demanded rhetorically, "if children make noise when no teacher is present? Where was the teacher? Why should my child suffer bruises because the teacher was late?"

Other graduate students, meanwhile, drew on their years of teaching experience to put this kind of moment in context: they told me that parents often insisted that teachers beat their children. "They say, 'If you don't discipline this child, no one will. I can't manage him!'"

Even some of the professors at Sherubtse who seemed to me most "modern" and Westernized spoke approvingly of the effects of corporal punishment. "My son is very lazy," said one parent. "But at least he is focused on getting his Dzongkha homework done, because he is afraid of what will happen if he doesn't."

"Does it help him learn?" I asked.

"He does the work!" my colleague replied.

"Is Dzongkha his best subject?" I asked.

"No, his best subjects are English and math, but he never gets the homework done for those!"

On Mondays after I finished teaching, I sometimes caught a ride down the mountain with a colleague to pick Jeremy up from school. This Bhutanese colleague had earned a Master's degree in Australia, and, as a result, he usually understood both sides of the cultural differences that baffled me. When he asked how the family was doing, I said we had all been a little taken aback to discover that students were still beaten in school.

"Well, of course they are!" said my colleague, carefully guiding the car over dried ruts in the dirt track as we passed the sports field full of grazing cows and horses. "We were all beaten, in my generation! Where would we have been without that discipline and motivation?"

My eyebrows shot up. I had thought he would oppose corporal punishment. "Did you find yourself motivated by being beaten?" I asked.

"Of course! I stopped forgetting to do my homework. I behaved myself in class."

"But were you motivated to learn?"

"I was motivated to learn by the possibility of becoming educated, going to college, getting a job, taking care of my parents."

"Fair enough," I said. I knew that this man had grown up in very constrained circumstances and had used money he earned working in Australia to build a house for his parents. Still, as he swung the car out onto the highway for the long descent to Kanglung, I pushed the discussion one step further. "I just wonder whether beating children really motivates them to learn. And isn't beating the opposite of compassion? What about Vajrayana values? GNH?"

"My Western friends who want to come to Bhutan, I have to warn them not to expect some land of ideal happiness," said my colleague. "Life can be hard here."

"No, I know," I said. "GNH is about trying to manage development pressures, not a proclamation that happiness has been achieved."

"When life is hard, you need to be tough to face it. Our teachers help build that toughness." My friend's certainty, as he sped around the road's sharp turns, seemed emblematic of Bhutanese toughness—a certainty that eluded me, even as I could see that he was right on at least one count: many Westerners associate Bhutan with happiness, but in a mythical sense of Bhutan being "the happiest country in the world." What little I knew about GNH suggested something very different: a kind of governmental hypothesis that commodity culture would not bring happiness, that economic development on its own was socially and environmentally costly and could not answer human beings' most fundamental needs. The GNH hypothesis, as I understood it, was that its four pillars would do a better job of answering those needs.

But how was that hypothesis holding up? By the middle of the year, I still knew so little about what GNH meant in practice, or how its principles had been implemented in Bhutan. It was time to get more serious about research. During the winter break, as Kanglung emptied of students and faculty, my family traveled to Thimphu, and I arranged to interview Karma Ura, a man widely known as the architect of GNH (Figure 5.3).

When time for the interview arrived, however, I couldn't quite work out where to find him. I was nervous about the interview to begin with: Karma Ura is not just the president and former director of the Centre for Bhutan Studies and GNH (often abbreviated CBS), he is also a past member of Bhutan's Ministry of Planning; he helped draft Bhutan's Constitution; and he is renowned as a painter, a poet, a historical novelist, and a translator. In 2010, he was given the honor of Druk Khorlo, the Wheel of the Dragon Kingdom, for his contributions to literature and the fine arts. All of this was on my mind because our students had been reading Karma Ura's *Ballad of Pemi Tshewang Tashi* (1996) and *The Hero with a Thousand Eyes* (1995) with my colleague Chitra.

I tried flagging down a taxi on the main street of Thimphu, but the taxi driver didn't speak much English and he didn't know where to find

Figure 5.3. Karma Ura below a composite portrait of Bhutan's kings, giving an impromptu lecture on his personal collection of thangkas for attendees of a Vajrayana summit in Thimphu, March 2018.

the Centre for Bhutan Studies either. I called Karma Ura's assistant for clarification and the sound of my call coming into her phone was not the standard Bhutanese ring, but Ed Sheeran's *Shape of You*, which promptly wormed its way into my brain. I hadn't expected the lyrics "I'm in love with your body" to be hanging over my meeting with one of the most powerful proponents of Bhutan's cultural traditions. Still, the assistant was very helpful: it turned out that the Centre for Bhutan Studies is contiguous to Karma Ura's house, and both are located just outside the armed patrol at the gates of the ministers' compound. GNH was starting to seem like serious stuff.

Once I had found the building, Karma Ura's assistant led me through a book-lined study to his sitting room, with seating around a low table, underneath windows that looked up into the spreading branches of a still-green tree. Karma Ura's daughter came to chat with me until her father was free; she was busy applying to colleges and universities in Canada and the UK, with a few American schools on her list.

"Kuzozangpola!" Dasho Karma Ura stood in the doorway, wearing a traditional plaid gho, his cuffs gleaming white. Because it was December, after the national monk body had moved to their winter residence, the Dasho (a term of high respect, mostly reserved for ministers and similar high-level officials) was also wearing white thermal long underwear to keep his legs warm under the knee-length gho.

"Kuzozangpohla!" I replied, returning the traditional greeting, with a little lengthening of the "o" to show extra respect. "Thank you so much for seeing me!" We exchanged a few remarks, his daughter said goodbye, and he sat down, announcing that tea was on the way. I was still processing the fact that the daughter of someone I thought of as the prime guardian of traditional Bhutanese culture was planning to study abroad, and so my first question, after asking permission to record our conversation, centered on her plans, or rather his hopes for her.

"That is not an interesting question," Karma Ura informed me, sounding more instructive than irritated. "Of course I want the same things for my daughter that you want for yours. I want her to be a good person, to make some contribution to the world, to be happy. These are universal desires—not distinct or interesting."

Indeed. I had apparently been influenced by my Yonphula students' commitment to communal, universal values, while Karma Ura took on the role I more commonly filled: insisting on attention to particularities and telling details. I let the conversation swerve back to the questions I was there to pursue, even as the question of particular traditions versus universal values lingered at the back of my mind.

"Fair point," I said. "But let's talk about GNH. Maybe we could begin with the four pillars."

"There are no pillars," said Karma Ura, waving his hand to dismiss the idea. "We have nine domains."

Oops. I was starting to feel stupid. "My apologies," I said. "In the east, people refer to the four pillars with some frequency."

"Not just in the east," he replied. "Everywhere they talk about the four pillars of GNH. It's like a public relations campaign. The four pillars were an idea of our previous prime minister—a lovely man, but a little imprecise in his wording."

When I asked him to specify the problems with the pillars, Karma Ura seemed to find the first pillar the most troublesome. "As soon as you say socio-economic development, you include everything. There are no distinctions maintained."

In expanding from pillars to domains, the pillar of "sustainable and equitable socio-economic development" became three domains: living standards, education, and health. "Preservation and promotion of culture" developed into four domains: cultural diversity and resilience, community vitality, time use, and psychological well-being. Only the pillars of environmental conservation and good governance didn't expand in the shift from four pillars to nine domains, and only good governance remained unchanged, since environmental conservation became "ecological diversity."

I wondered—not quite clearly enough to frame a question—whether the revised model (as seen in Table 5.1) meant that people spent less time talking about governance and environment while spending more time talking about things like education, health, living standards, time use, and so on. Did this attempt at greater precision become simultaneously a redirection of attention?

The Dasho's assistant brought tea and then vanished again. The windows of the sitting room were wide open. I felt a little chilly in that cool December afternoon but Karma Ura seemed entirely at ease. Settling into

Table 5.1. GNH Pillars and Domains.[2]

Four Pillars	Nine Domains
Sustainable and equitable socio-economic development	Living standards Education Health
Preservation and promotion of culture	Cultural diversity and resilience Community vitality Time use Psychological well-being
Conservation of environment	Ecological diversity
Good governance	Good governance

conversation in a slightly different way, we spoke in general terms about GNH and the new Yonphula Centenary College. Our conversation turned gradually to engage with tourism as an important sector of the economy, and the possibility that Bhutan's self-presentation as a "living museum" would hollow out the very traditions I thought people like Karma Ura were hoping to sustain. In a recent essay in *The Druk Journal*, for instance, Kinley Dorji had noted that "Bhutan proudly boasts that the kingdom is not a museum presenting itself as a photo opportunity for tourists, but a living culture," but he warned that "if Bhutanese culture does not evolve with the times, Bhutan will become the museum that we claim not to be."[3] What did Karma Ura think of this? I asked.

"Well, to begin with," Karma Ura said briskly, "Bhutan makes very little money from tourism."

"What?" I was again taken aback: every Bhutanese person I knew seemed to see tourism as central to Bhutan's future well-being. Hydropower might be vulnerable to climate change, my friends said, but tourism would keep the economy going.[4]

"Our tourist industry is dominated by luxury hotels. Those hotels are owned by multinational corporations. In a capitalist system, profits rise to the top." Karma Ura looked out the window at the darkening sky, tilted his head, and took a sip of his tea. "I am not saying that there is no money that comes into the country via tourism. People who work in the industry—as guides, in the hotels—earn wages, of course. But the bulk of the money goes to the multinational corporations." He smiled at me, a little grimly. "People who are cautious about capitalism should be wary of inviting capitalists into their country. When tourism is brought from outside, and the companies are multinational, the effects are incalculable. The Bhutanese do not know, because they have not also seen the force wielded behind the billions." He took another sip of tea, seeming to watch as evening shadows gathered. "People forget," said Karma Ura, "that Bhutan is a small country. Many people have come, with the best of intentions, and done real damage, because they forget that we are small, and that any interventions must take our scale into account."

I struggled to reorient my thinking. "If tourism doesn't even bring in money, what development strategy makes sense for Bhutan?"[5] I asked.

"How do you help people get more distance from poverty, from the problems of suffering?"

Karma Ura frowned at me over his tea. "There was no real suffering in Bhutan in past times," he asserted, his tone flat, suggesting no room for disagreement.

I looked at him, finding myself at a loss for words.

"Real suffering," he emphasized. "Not just labor, or the effort of climbing a mountain, where you may work your muscles and perspire, but then you take a break, and there is pleasure to be had from resting in the sun. That is not suffering. Real suffering was not prevalent in Bhutan in previous times."

"But illness—suffering—medicine," I said, incoherently. In Karma Ura's own *The Hero with a Thousand Eyes*, the protagonist suffers from a terrible eye infection and is temporarily paralyzed by typhoid; his mother dies young from a different fever. Surely, these experiences would count as suffering.

"Yes, yes," he replied, a little dismissively. "Western medicine has some benefit for us. But overall health is different from these medical interventions. And you must know that the traditional name for Bhutan was *Men Jong*, the place of medicinal herbs. This land has traditionally supported its people's needs in a very generous and gentle manner."

Karma Ura went on to stress the importance of the village as a unit of social life, to a degree that surprised me.[6] He spoke about the way a given family might obtain prominence and broader cultural assets for a generation or two—"you have an instance of that where you are," he said, peering at me to see whether I followed this allusion to the Yonphula Rinpoche—but then time would move on, and some other family would move into prominence. The government's cap on land ownership, with exceptions for the monarchy and the monk body, put some constraints around this kind of fluid generational changes.

As our conversation drew to a close, Karma Ura asked about my teaching at Yonphula Centenary College and I mentioned some attempts to get my students to engage in critical thinking.

"Oh!" he shook his head in mock dismay, standing to mark the end of the interview. "This generation knows nothing of critical thinking."

I too stood and smiled, noting that the Dasho had found us a point of curmudgeonly agreement about the failings of the younger generation—but I also felt that my own critical thinking had been sorely absent in this interview. Overwhelmed with the demands of teaching and learning more generally about Bhutan, I had not done my homework on GNH properly—but I had a few weeks now in which I could do some deeper background reading.

Over the next week, while Jeremy consumed masses of waffles and cakes in a Western-style café, James had bloodwork done to check on the status of a chronic blood disorder, and Zoë struggled with what turned into strep throat, I belatedly dove into that work. I used the hotel's fast connection to download a series of articles about GNH: articles that had gotten stuck in the ether when I tried to download them in Kanglung. I thought back to Jeremy's question on the farm road. Just how gross was GNH, anyway? I had come to Bhutan with only limited awareness of the Lhotshampa expulsion. It was unexpected but salutary to be learning about the expulsion as a result of researching GNH, by way of international scholars objecting to analyses that didn't take the Lhotshampa expulsion into account.

How intertwined was the GNH Index with the Lhotshampa expulsion anyway? Chronologically, there are striking moments of overlap, even as some degree of separation is maintained, as shown in Table 5.2. I've used roman-font text to show GNH-related developments and italicized text to show refugee-related developments.

The fourth King's definition of happiness in terms of political stability, social harmony, and Bhutanese culture seems darkly ironic, coming as it does the year before the 1988 Census begins to deny citizenship to southern Bhutanese families. A still more biting irony is the fact that tens of thousands of Bhutanese refugees began to be resettled in third-party countries the very same year Bhutan conducted its first GNH Survey. At the height of the crisis, however, there seems to have been little discussion of GNH, though, as discussed in Chapter 3, certain phrases associated with Vajrayana religious practice became political slogans during this time, and some of those phrases/slogans subsequently came to be closely associated with popular understandings of GNH, especially driglam namzha, which encompasses both national dress and behaviors denoting respect to superiors.

One might argue, in any case, that the promotion of cultural preservation by a nation that had expelled tens of thousands of ethnic minority residents should make Bhutan's GNH the poster child of how *not* to pursue public happiness in a pluralistic, multicultural world. In fact, this view seems to have found widespread albeit tacit acceptance. Even as the GNH Index has been credited with influencing the UN's Sustainable

Table 5.2. Chronology showing the development of GNH (plain text) amid the Lhotshampa expulsion crisis (italicized text)

1729	Bhutanese legal code states that 'if the government cannot create happiness (dekidk) for its people, there is no purpose for the government to exist'[1] (quoted by Karma Ura 2010)
1980	The *New York Times* quotes the fourth King on importance of gross national happiness
1980	*Marriage Act (restrictions on Bhutanese marrying non-Bhutanese)*
1985	*Citizenship Act (citizenship available only to offspring of two Bhutanese parents)*
1987	Fourth King describes government's pursuit of public happiness in *Financial Times* in terms of "political stability, social harmony, and the Bhutanese culture and way of life"
1988	*Disputed southern Census begins: new categories of non-citizen residency applied*
1989	*Ngalong-style national dress required at all government offices; end of Nepali-language instruction in public schools*
1990	*Mass protests; violence; economic embargo in the south*
1991-93	*Peak of expulsion/refugee flight to Nepal*
1996-97	National Budget includes first reference to GNH in relation to environmental policy
1997	Eighth Five-Year-Plan subordinates income expansion and commodity production to Gross National Happiness

1 Cited in Karma Ura, "Leadership of the wise: Kings of Bhutan" (Thimphu: Centre for Bhutan Studies, 2010).

(*Continued*)

Table 5.2. (*Continued*)

1999	*Bhutan 2020* planning document links GNH, Bhutan's "central development concept," to the "overarching goal" of "the future independence, sovereignty and security of our nation state."[2]
2003	*Joint Verification Exercise ends without repatriation of any refugees*
2005	Draft Constitution enshrines GNH as a "principle of state policy"
2007	*Third-country resettlement arranged for over 100,000 Lhotshampa refugees*
2008	First GNH Survey conducted and Index published; *Third-country resettlement of refugees begins*
2011	Bhutan proposes a widely embraced United Nations Resolution on Happiness[3]
2012	Bhutan hosts a UN "high level panel discussion" involving UN Secretary Ban Ki Moon and other diplomats and scholars
2012	First World Happiness Report published by Columbia economist Jeffrey Sachs with praise for Bhutan's GNH Index as a model for forthcoming UN Sustainable Development Goals
2014	*First scholarly article challenging global approval of GNH (Pelligrini and Tasciotti, "Bhutan: Between Happiness and Horror")*

2 Planning Commission, *Bhutan 2020: A Vision for Peace, Prosperity and Happiness* (Thimphu: RGOB, 1999), 43, 45, quoted in Lauchlan T. Munro, "Where Did Bhutan's Gross National Happiness Come From? The Origins of an Invented Tradition," *Asian Affairs* 47, no. 1 (2016): 79, https://doi.org/10.1080/03068374.2015.1128681. See also the claim that "Our future sovereignty as a nation state will continue to depend upon the articulation of a cultural imperative that asserts our distinctive Bhutanese identity" (Planning Commission, *Bhutan 2020*), 25.

3 UN Resolution 65/309, entitled "Happiness: towards a holistic approach to development," was introduced by Bhutan, sponsored by a total of 68 member states, and adopted unanimously.

Development Goals and the OECD's Better Life Index, those later models include no reference to culture, as shown in Table 5.3.

But is this the right lesson to have learned? GNH is not just driglam namzha, nor is it the same as "Buddhist values" (though some Bhutanese identify it that way). And attempts to avoid ethnic conflict by ignoring

Table 5.3. Comparison of GNH, BLI, SDGs[7]

Bhutan: 9 GNH domains	**OECD's Better Life Index**	**UN Sustainable Development Goals**
Living standards	Income and wealth Jobs and earnings Housing	SDG 1 (poverty) 2 (food) 8 (decent work and economies) 11 (cities) 7 (energy) 5 (women) 9 (infrastructure)
Education	Education and skills	4 (education)
Health	Health	3 (health)
Ecological diversity	Environmental quality	6 (water) 11 (cities) 12 (sustainable production) 13 (climate) 14 (oceans) 15 (biodiversity)
Cultural diversity and resilience		
Community vitality	Civic and social engagement Social connections	16 (institutions)
Time use	Work-life balance	8 (decent work and economies)
Psychological well-being	Subjective well-being Personal security	16 (institutions)
Good governance	Civic and social engagement	16 (institutions)

culture have not resulted in clean hands. The most widely accepted "beyond-GDP" model is the United Nation's Sustainable Development Goals, sometimes referred to as the 2030 Agenda, and in July 2022, E. Tendayi Achiume, United Nations Special Rapporteur on contemporary forms of racism, racial discrimination, xenophobia, and related intolerance, reported that "the development framework, including the 2030 Agenda, preserves colonial injustice, perpetuates the domination of powerful nations over peoples and territories that were subject to historical colonial extraction and preserves structural racial discrimination within nations."[8] Attempts to remain "culture-neutral" have (not unpredictably) still perpetuated harmful structures of oppression and discrimination.

Meanwhile, a growing number of scientists and economists argue that surviving the climate crisis will require cultural transformations on a global scale. In 2020, for instance, a group of leading climate scientists published an analysis of "Social tipping dynamics for stabilizing Earth's climate by 2050," urging action on the part of multiple actors, from governments at various levels, citizens, investors, and more.[9] Many of the social changes envisioned by the authors involve social support for technological change (decentralized energy generation, carbon-neutral cities), but some are more broadly cultural (moral implications of fossil fuels, and climate education and engagement), though still in service to policies shaped by scientific and technological principles (fossil fuel divestment, removing fossil fuel subsidies, etc.). Critics argue that the paper lacks a robust model of social change—which suggests we still need to learn more about how best to adapt ourselves and our cultures to the climate-driven changes coming at us.

Instead of dismissing cultural considerations as inevitably tainted by ethnic bias, then, we might treat Bhutan's GNH model as experimental data, marking out both valid points of consideration and specific mistakes to avoid. I would argue that the early GNH Survey questionnaire and GNH Index did show instances of ethnic cultural bias—some of which remain even in later versions of the Survey and Index—but that such bias can and should be removed from the Survey questions and the Index. Rather than just cutting categories such as culture resilience or questions that prioritize Ngalong culture, GNH Index administrators might consider adding or revising questions to explicitly value contributions and traditions of various minority groups, including the Lhotshampas. Those of us interested in alternatives to endless GDP-growth might need to think harder about how culture contributes to human thriving.

Taking the GNH Index seriously means grappling with its expansive, even sprawling exploration of Bhutanese lived experience. When you ask thousands of people how they spent their time in ten-minute increments over the course of 24 hours, the resulting data are fascinating, but hard to wrangle. In fact, the data generated by the 2010 survey seem to have proliferated beyond what the research team could manage: data generated had to be pruned back in order to produce a functioning index in 2012.

In working to assess possible cultural bias, I have tried to engage the various levels of GNH, from the four pillars to the nine domains to the 33 indicators to some of the categories of questions asked as a means of assessing those indicators. Table 5.4 lists pillars, domains, and indicators, with shaded blocks noting indicators associated with cultural bias. If we only look at the top layers of the Index, then we might not recognize signs of cultural bias present in the pillar of development or the domain of education. But within that domain of education, under the indicator of Knowledge or Literacy, GNH Survey questions emphasize Ngalong cultural forms like tshechu festivals, traditional song forms, and traditional arts. By contrast, the GNH Pillar of Cultural Preservation (and the closely related Domain of Cultural Resilience and Diversity) is often blamed for ethnic bias, but it leads with an emphasis on maintaining native languages: an unexpected support for cultural pluralism.[10] As you read through the table and the discussion that follows, I encourage you to pay attention to the questions and indicators that surprise you and try to identify the assumptions being challenged in that moment. I will discuss the kinds of bias I see and make suggestions for how the Index could be made more inclusive.

Table 5.4. Exploring possible bias in GNH Pillars, Domain, and Indicators. Shaded blocks indicate parts of the GNH Index associated with cultural bias. Subsequent discussion of these shaded blocks notes some instances of remediation.[11]

GNH Pillar	GNH Domain	Indicators
Sustainable and equitable socio-economic development	Living standards	Assets
		Housing
		Household per capita income
	Health	Mental health
		Self-reported health status
		Healthy days
		Disability
	Education	Literacy
		Educational level
		Knowledge
		Value[s] (included under culture in GNH survey after 2012)
Preservation and promotion of culture	Cultural diversity and resilience	Speak native language
		Cultural participation
		Artistic skills (traditional arts)
		Driglam namzha
	Time Use	Work
		Sleep
	Psychological well-being	Life satisfaction
		Positive emotions
		Negative emotions
		Spirituality
	Community vitality	Donation (time & money)
		Community relationship
		Family
		Safety

Table 5.4. (*Continued*)

GNH Pillar	GNH Domain	Indicators
Good governance	Good governance	Government performance
		Fundamental rights
		Services
		Political participation
Conservation of environment	Ecological diversity and resilience	Ecological issues
		Responsibility toward environment
		Wildlife damage (rural)
		Urbanization issues

REMEDIATING BIAS, ACKNOWLEDGING CULTURAL TENSION

Education: Literacy/Knowledge

The historical literacy section of the questionnaire suggests that Bhutanese history is defined by the institution of the monarchy in 1907, celebrated annually on National Day, and understood through the "historical events of our kings." This monarchical national history takes shape against a timeless context of (implicitly Ngalong) local legends and folktales. Lhotshampa communities obviously have their own local legends and folktales: the impact of this question might depend upon who is asking the question and how it is presented. Indeed, this part of the questionnaire could be easily redesigned to pursue a more multi-ethnic model of historical literacy by asking respondents to give examples of legends or folktales associated with other ethnic groups within Bhutan. Requiring active recall of cultural diversity would raise the bar for historical literacy.

Questions under cultural literacy clearly privilege Ngalong cultural productions: tshechu or religious festivals, and traditional song forms (zhungdra and boedra).[12] The annual repetition of the tshechu, with familiar dances performed with some variation across the country, builds a common cultural repertoire for Drukpa members of the nation as a whole. Some dances, such as the Black Hat Dance, serve to clear the space of obstructive energies—while implicitly shaping audience members as they observe the monk-dancers' precision and harmonious movement. Other dances, such as the Hunter and the Hounds, or the Dance of the Rakshas and the Judgment of the Dead, tell moral tales about virtue and its rewards—or the suffering that comes from harming others. The interweaving of community dances with sacred dances creates its own narrative of interdependence between monastic and lay communities.

Contrasting the "imagined community" created by tshechu dances with that created by Western print culture highlights the different temporalities and emphases of both the imaginations and communities in question. In *Imagined Communities: Reflections on the Origin and Spread of Nationalism*, Benedict Anderson saw newspaper consumption as a "mass ceremony" helping to constitute the nation: "the newspaper reader, observing exact replicas of his own paper being consumed by his subway, barbershop or residential neighbours, is continually reassured that the imagined world is visibly rooted in everyday life."[13] By contrast, Drukpa spectators at annual tshechus can be reassured that daily life is visibly rooted in a spiritual world—but Lhotshampa spectators, with a different understanding of the spiritual world, might not find the spectacle equally reassuring. Even within Buddhist communities, the cultural forms of masked dances and tshechus may become sites of contestation, highlighting differences between the Drukpa of western Bhutan and the Sharchops of eastern Bhutan. Mona Schrempf, for instance, sees the annual tshechu at Gom Kora in eastern Bhutan as a site where local traditions, nation-building, and tourism exist in tension with one another.[14] Again, questions that invite respondents to develop greater familiarity with other groups' and regions' cultural traditions could help keep those traditions alive and authentic in a time of increasing cultural homogeneity.

Questions about "indigenous knowledge literacy" claim indigeneity for the zorig chusum or (Ngalong) traditional arts, though Bhutanese historians suggest that those arts represented a cosmopolitan gathering of cutting-edge artistry in the seventeenth century. Dorjee Tshering and Thinley Wangchuk cite historian Lam Nado to the effect that the Zhabdrung "invited artists from neighboring countries to refine the arts of clay sculpturing, painting, and calligraphy; build the

Punakha, Trashichodzong, and Wangduphodrang dzongs; and set a formal curriculum for monastic studies."[15] During this period of rapid twenty-first-century change, it might be interesting to consider the overlap of tradition and hybridity in Bhutanese art forms. At the same time, explicitly valuing traditional arts beyond the zorig chusum would only strengthen the ability of the GNH Index to reflect and preserve Bhutan's cultural heritage: Nepali crafts could be included along with nettle weaving and other traditions included in Tarayana Foundation's Bhutan Textiles collection or the Loden Foundation's documental of cultural traditions.

Cultural Resilience and Diversity

Questions about "core values" were clearly streamlined and secularized between the first iteration of the GNH Survey and more recent versions. In 2010, six separate questions, elaborated through more than fifty alternative responses, asked about politically loaded terms like tha damtshig, a contrasting list mingling stereotypically Western and traditional Bhutanese values, and a recognizable list of the "Ten Bad Courses of Action," summarizing key elements of Buddhist moral discipline. This list is often broken down into three destructive actions of the body (killing, stealing, sexual misconduct), four destructive actions of speech (lying, divisive speech, harsh speech, idle chitchat), and three destructive actions of mind (covetousness, malice, wrong view), though the GNH questionnaire mixed these categories and uses slightly different terminology. By the 2012 Index and the 2015 questionnaire, all of these core values have been simplified into a question about whether or not any of five "statements" can ever be justified: killing, stealing, lying, creating disharmony in human relations, sexual misconduct. While all of these are included in the Ten Bad Courses of Action, prohibitions on murder, theft, dishonesty, and sexual misconduct are common to many religions and ethical codes.

Cultural participation was similarly reframed after 2010 in ways that reduced the degree of cultural bias shown. In 2010, the use of Dzongkha words highlighted the centrality of Ngalong culture in this indicator: "On average, how many days do you spend in a year attending social and cultural activities, such as community festivals or *choku* of neighbours? How important is it for you to participate in such community festivals and gatherings?" A choku is an annual household ritual in which Buddhist monks or lay monks come to the house to perform rituals associated with well-being over the coming year. Neighbors usually also gather in that household and "feast for a day with good food and alcoholic drinks provided by the host."[16] Other instances of cultural participation similarly presume Ngalong norms: "List the ways by which you observe *duezang* or auspicious days (e.g. by visiting *lhakhangs*)." Vajrayana Buddhism is assumed to shape cultural traditions: "Do you consult the astrologer for matters related to you and your family's well-being? Do you pay homage/propitiate the local deity in your village or community?" Yet some traditions were clearly not faith-based: "During the past 12 months, how often have you played traditional sports (archery, khuru [darts], degor,[[17]] etc.)? During the past 12 months, how often have you played modern games/sports (e.g. football [soccer])?" By 2015, however, these questions had been scaled back strikingly to a single query: "On an average, how many days did you spend in the past 12 months attending social and cultural activities, such as community festivals or *choku* of neighbours?" Adding a reference to a Lhotshampa or other minority community festival would further increase the extent to which the question addresses non-Ngalong citizens.

Community Vitality: Vounteering and Donations

Under the domain of community vitality, questions around volunteering and donations were framed in ways that suggest Vajrayana cultural and political norms, such as laboring on or donating toward different Vajrayana religious structures, rituals, religious figures, as well as house construction or death rituals. We were very impressed to see this kind of volunteerism in action as community members helped build a new convent building, apparently from scratch (Figure 5.4). Still, explicit references to forms of volunteering and donation most likely to prevail in Lhotshampa and other minority communities will make this section of the questionnaire more inclusive.

Figure 5.4. Dudjom Tersar (Nyingma) nuns (in saffron and maroon robes) supervising volunteer community labor in the construction of an addition to the nunnery complex in Radi, Trashigang, October 2017, exemplifying the Vajrayana norm of community labor donations to religious institutions.

Psychological Well-being: Spirituality

Spirituality was originally considered part of Cultural Preservation, but in 2012 it was changed to an indicator of Psychological Well-being. In 2015 and 2022, questions asked respondents to state "how spiritual" they are, how frequently they meditate, pray, visit religious establishments, the extent to which they consider karma in their daily life, and how many days in the past year they had received religious teachings. The *Extensive Analysis* argues that most of these questions "are relevant to Hindu as well as Buddhist practitioners," though it acknowledges that these questions might not encompass the "newer cohort of agnostics or atheists who might experience transcendence through music, art or nature, but might not self-identify as spiritual."[18] While the *Extensive Analysis* reveals some thoughtful discussion around inclusiveness in this area, further refining of these questions in conversation with Lhotshampa spiritual leaders might produce responses more representative of the entire Bhutanese population. “Receiving teachings,” for instance, is a practice more common to Vajrayana than to Hindu traditions. What kind of question would atheists suggest to represent aesthetic transcendence?

Good Governance: Political Participation

While other beyond-GDP indices, such as the Better Life Index, equate political participation with voting, the GNH Survey and Index expect more active engagement in local government, with separate questions asking about attendance and speaking at local government meetings. Again, zomdu is a Dzongkha term highlighting northern Bhutanese organizational norms: village meetings in Lhotshampa and other minority communities might well take different forms. Using language that invites the broadest possible accounts of local political engagement would provide a more accurate account for this indicator.

Even this cursory look at the GNH questions and Index works to disrupt the antinomies of GNH praise and blame. Instead, this reading suggests more modestly that some cultural bias does exist within the Index, that the degree of bias has been reduced somewhat between the launching of the Index and the present day, but that further revision could be beneficial, both to the intellectual integrity of the Index and its stated goal of improving the well-being of the Bhutanese people as a whole. Revision was, after all, built into the original model of GNH: the *Extensive Analysis of GNH Index* (2012) noted a need for “constant review and adaption in the years to come” at least in setting thresholds for different domains, and some changes appeared in the questionnaire and Index presented in 2015.[19]

Meanwhile, non-Bhutanese readers, rather than turning away from culture as a component of human thriving, might use Bhutan’s GNH as a series of challenges to ourselves:

- How do we participate in our own imagined communities?
- What do we know of the cultural traditions of ethnic groups different from our own, with whom we share a national identity?
- What values do we share?

- How do we participate in our local communities? How do others, different from us, participate in their communities?
- How do we contribute to those communities?
- What practices contribute to our psychological well-being?
- How active are we in local politics? Do we go beyond just voting?

What other questions should we be asking, based on your reading of the GNH Index materials?

GNH VERSUS GDP AND HUMAN RIGHTS IN BHUTAN

The fourth King's formulation of gross national happiness explicitly came into being as an alternative to GDP or GNP (gross national product, the slightly different model used before 1991). While Karma Ura argues that the idea of gross national happiness dates back to the legal code of 1729, Karma Phuntsho tells a story that highlights the translated hybridity, the non-native quality, of the term:

> [. . .] there was no terminology for [gross national happiness] in Dzongkha or other Bhutanese languages and the rough equivalent, Gyalyong Gakyi Pelzom, was coined only at the turn of this [twenty-first] century. When this was first introduced, most people had no clue while some thought it was a new government department. It was also confusing because the term sounds like a feminine name. On being asked for his take on it by a radio journalist, a man replied: 'From what I hear, she seems beautiful but I have not yet seen her.'[20]

First conceived in an era of long-serving kings and civil servants, GNH came into its most fully elaborated form amid Bhutan's transition to representative democracy (including a central appearance in the country's 2008 Constitution)—but that new representative democracy has introduced much shorter time horizons, with increasingly rapid policy shifts.

The short time horizon associated with party politics and representative democracy has created new challenges for GNH in Bhutan. Bhutan's first elected prime minister was pro-GNH "policy entrepreneur" Jigmi Thinley, but the second elected prime minister ran on a platform seen as moderately anti-GNH.[21] Once in office, however, Tshering Togbay became a GNH-promoter as well, though his administration struggled to integrate GNH with Bhutan's commitment to sign onto the United Nations Sustainable Development Goals.[22]

In 2023, Lotay Tshering, Bhutan's third elected prime minister, dissolved the GNH Commission that once defined Bhutan's high-level engagement with GNH—and proposed a Five-Year Plan for 2023–28 aiming at 10 percent GDP growth—an outcome almost directly opposed to the fourth King's original proposals for gross national happiness. Indeed, the Concept Note for the thirteenth Five-Year Plan overseen by Lotay Tshering included massive development projects such as "airports, railways, highways, tunnels, digital/IT hubs and infrastructure, special economic zones, multimodal hub, growth centers, smart cities, educational and vocational institutions, hydropower and alternative renewable energy"—a mind-boggling degree of change.[23] Environmental implications are not considered here, and the separation between (and relative priorities of) construction and environmental concerns suggest that environmental conservation will remain something of an afterthought in the plan as a whole.

The return of Tshering Tobgay as prime minister for 2024–29 seems to have slowed the decline of GNH as an influential development model within Bhutan, at least in the short term. Karma Ura noted in a 2024 *Kuensel* interview that "HPM Dasho Tshering Tobgay has extended application of GNH in governance seriously, as he did with GNH Business Certification in his previous tenure." Ura also asserted that "The 13th FYP proudly incorporates many GNH indicators as baselines. The plan is intended to improve the conditions of GNH."[24] Still, some of the primary issues motivating the election season in 2023–24 were high youth unemployment (29 percent), low GDP growth (1.7 percent), and the departure of many educated youth to Australia in search of better pay and living conditions. The so-called "massive" 13th Five-Year-Plan still seeks 10 percent GDP growth.

At the same time, discrimination against ethnic Nepali Bhutanese remains a problem that Bhutan must confront and resolve. Anti-Lhotshampa bias within government policies seems to have remained steady even as GNH has grown progressively weaker in Bhutan's government plans and policy positions. Bhutan's score in the annual report from Freedom House, for instance, held steady at 61/100 in 2022 and 2023: "Ongoing problems include discrimination against Nepali-speaking and non-Buddhist minorities, the use of defamation cases to silence journalists, and media censorship."[25] GNH could potentially aid in this resolution if the Index were made more supportive of Bhutan's true cultural diversity, but GNH alone cannot resolve an issue as historically vexed and politically obscured as Lhotshampa political rights and cultural diversity within Bhutan. Interestingly, the most recent *GNH 2022* report notes that

> People achieved the least sufficiency in the knowledge indicator (14.3%), that measures knowledge on local legends, the constitution, local festivals, and HIV/AIDS. The next lowest sufficiency (31%) was in the Driglam Namzha indicator, which measures people's views on the significance and decline of the traditional etiquette of courtesy.[26]

Inclusion on the GNH Survey does not guarantee cultural resilience for any chosen term.

LESSONS FROM BHUTAN'S EXPLORATIONS OF GROSS NATIONAL HAPPINESS

Western engagement with GNH has not been particularly productive either for Western countries or for Bhutan. Oscillating through uncritical praise, overstated accusations, and silent, strategic disengagement, Western scholars have failed to push for important revisions to the GNH model. Between 2010 and 2022, the Centre for Bhutan Studies and GNH independently modified the GNH Index, in some cases reducing explicit and implied bias—but further revisions, including more explicit outreach to minority communities, are called for. Still, GNH remains one of the only models for measuring human thriving beyond GDP that takes explicit notice of cultural diversity as a resource. At this time of environmental and human catastrophe, we need more such models; in the short term, surely we should be encouraging the work of the GNH Index, demanding important revisions, amplifying its strengths.

While Karma Ura has emphasized that GNH is specific to Bhutan and other countries will have to develop their own models, the fourth King along with the first and second prime ministers all pitched the underlying concept of GNH to the global community. This policy entrepreneurship was happening at the same time that Bhutan was benefiting from high levels of GDP growth (partly driven by demographic changes, partly by hydropower development). Bhutan's promotion of GNH amid GDP growth has meant that the country could (to some extent) have its cake and eat it too, though recent developments suggest that if faced with a forced choice between GNH and GDP, Bhutan, like the rest of the world, will opt for pursuing GDP. Given our vulnerability to environmental catastrophes worsened by this pursuit of economic growth at all costs, it seems worth re-stating, in slightly more argumentative terms, some core ideas promoted by GNH, connecting those ideas with similar work promoted elsewhere:

1. Belief in prosperity through endless economic growth has become a global monoculture, against which some Indigenous communities, small nations like Bhutan, scholars, and a handful of politicians have tried to raise the alarm. In order to live in greater balance (and provide future generations the conditions required for human thriving), we need to restore and maintain at least some cultural forms that acknowledge and support human beings' ecological integration. In addition to Bhutan's investment of research in GNH, South American economists have explored the Indigenous way of life known as sumak kawsay in Ecuador and suma qamana in Bolivia, translated into Spanish as buen vivir or good living. Like GNH, sumak kawsay stresses community aid, generosity, and reciprocity.[27] Raising up such alternatives to assumptions of endless growth helps us to begin charting better paths into the future.
2. Instead of aiming at ever-rising living standards, we should aim for "decent living standards" for all, closing inequality gaps within and across national boundaries. Here, GNH scholarship could usefully partner with other attempts to define what constitutes "decent living standards" as a means of countering existing norms of endless

growth. Merely measuring living standards will not move human societies in the direction of greater equality and human thriving.[28] Instead, a model like DLS (Decent Living Standards), developed by Narasimha Rao, Jihoon Min and others, begins to define a range for more egalitarian conditions. In 2020, Joel Millward-Hopkins, Rao and others argued that DLS could be met globally with a 60 percent reduction in energy needs (including up to a 95 percent reduction in regions using particularly high levels of energy, such as the United States).[29]

3. To replace the material consolations of commodity culture, we need to rebuild our communal capabilities. Here, Bhutan offers an important though imperfect model of promoting participation in communal events, time spent playing with friends and family, volunteer efforts to answer community needs, and support from friends, neighbors, family, etc., when coping with personal and financial difficulties. The loneliness epidemic in the United States as highlighted by Surgeon General Vivek Murthy and the loss of civil society recorded in books like Robert Putnam's *Bowling Alone* suggests the perils of relying on commodity culture to answer human beings' need for connection and meaning.[30] Instead, the GNH domain of community vitality and the communal practices of sumak kawsay may provide healthier paths forward.
4. Good government should be defined not by endless GDP growth ("the economy, stupid"), but by a commitment to citizens' well-being, equal access to government, limits to partisanship, and modes of accountability that do not cede the importance of a vision for communal thriving beyond short-term election cycles. At the same time, GNH should not be used as cover for discrimination or to enable toxic politicization of culture. External (non-Bhutanese) understandings of GNH have tended to equate GNH with driglam namzha; within Bhutan also, GNH seems sometimes to be equated with "Buddhist values." Both of these oversimplifications of GNH threaten to increase religious nationalism—and using cultural dominance as a proxy for national success has been damaging in Bhutan and the Unites States alike. Freedom from discrimination appears in the GNH Index as part of Bhutan's national aspirations;

> the government rather than the Index must make this aspiration a reality. One could say the same of the United States. Without effectively functioning governments, we are unlikely to meet our climate goals, or find ways of responding to environmental catastrophes with humanity and grace.

This summary comes closer to the four pillars than the nine domains. Perhaps all those conversations about four pillars had a deeper effect on me than I realized at the time—or perhaps, if our task is to disentangle human thriving from GDP growth, it remains easier and more effective to limit the number of threads we are teasing out of "the most important number in the world." Pursuit of ecological balance, material sufficiency rather than excess, strengthened communities, and redefined government goals: this may be enough to work on at one time.

Against this kind of systematicity, however, it seems to me that some of the most intriguing aspects of GNH come not from the pillars or domains but rather from observations and implications scattered throughout the questionnaire and Index. For instance, one of the most interesting environmental questions on the 2010 questionnaire appears not under the section of Ecological diversity and resilience, but rather under "Ecological literacy," in the questionnaire's Education section. The second of two questions asks, "Does your community observe ladam and ridam?" –a query that opens onto larger patterns of human relations with their environment. According to Karma Phuntsho,

> Ridam/ladam (རི་བསྡམ་/ལ་བསྡམ་) is a practice of mountain closure which is known in many parts of Bhutan. The entire area or a certain part of the mountain is closed to human entry and use during certain periods, often from spring to autumn. During this period, people are generally not allowed to enter the area for the purpose of collecting natural resources or visiting a place within that area. The restriction is particularly applied to outsiders who are not from the area.[31]

We encountered ladam and ridam when some friends took us on a pilgrimage to a remote ney or place of spiritual power in Trashi Yangtse in May. We waited on the path while one of our friends went to ask a nearby monastery for permission to cross an invisible "gate"; permission was readily granted. Without having read the 2010 GNH questionnaire, I would not have known what was happening. Flexible in implementation, ladam and ridam nonetheless serve to create temporary refugia, spaces where species can shelter, free from human disruption; the common closure period, from spring to autumn, protects a wide range of species during seasons of reproduction. This kind of practice is both clearly a Bhutanese tradition and more broadly interesting as a means of protecting biodiversity during our current human-driven climate-change-intensified mass extinction.

The GNH Index partly works to make such cultural particulars universally legible, but of course Karma Ura, architect of GNH, had pointedly reminded me that universal values are seldom as interesting as cultural particularity. Perhaps the best way to learn from Bhutan, I thought, was not to focus on writings about GNH but rather to keep trying to exist contentedly while living "far from the market" (as the Dean of Yonphula Centenary College had described life in Kanglung), and keeping my eyes open to the cultural forms indexed by GNH. What could I learn from traditional stories, dances, songs, and arts directly, rather than at one remove? Perhaps that was my challenge for the second half of the year.

PART IV

LEARNING FROM BHUTAN

CHAPTER SIX

"ONLY POOR PEOPLE CAN DO THIS WORK"

Stuffed into a borrowed car, stiff in our fine clothes, James, Zoë, Jeremy, and I pulled in beside a white coaster bus, labeled "Institute for Zorig Chusum," and looked across the stark, stone courtyard at a grand Bhutanese building (Figure 6.1). It was a bright morning in late November. Wooden pillars, window frames, joists, and other protruding woodwork were all integrated into the stone walls and painted with stylized repeating patterns. All four of us had put on Bhutanese national dress in an attempt to fit in at this traditional school, but it was hard not to feel daunted by the courtyard and building. Slowly we eased out of the car. We straightened our shoulders, took a deep communal breath, and walked across the courtyard.

The upper panel of the front door was covered in embossed copper, beaten and burnished to a high shine. Pushing it open, we walked into an entryway with a cathedral ceiling. The table in front of the door was draped with an altar cloth of carefully pieced, brightly colored fabric; on top of the fabric stood the seven small bowls of a traditional water offering, alongside a bumpa or container of holy water, all in front of a large framed photograph of the fourth King crowning the fifth King. Behind the table, a massive mural, exquisitely executed, climbed two stories' worth of wall. At the bottom of the painting were two of the four geps, or traditional

Figure 6.1. Main administrative building of the College of Zorig Chusum, Trashi Yangtse, seen from the side rather than straight across the courtyard.

guardian-kings of Bhutan. Above them, a wrathful deity in yab-yum posture glared down on any tiny mortals entering this space.[1] To the right, another mural, starting with the other two guardian-kings, climbed another set of walls. The fabric, the metal-work, and the painting all exemplified the traditional arts taught in this school. Brief documentary videos of the school and its traditional arts can be found on this book's Fulcrum page (https://doi.org/10.3998/mpub.12970479) under the "Resources" section.

The air was still, the space eerily quiet. "Kuzozangpola?" we called: the standard Bhutanese greeting. A member of the school staff eventually came out from behind a curtained door on the left and led us up the stairs, through another cloth-covered doorway, into a large room where again the décor ran riot. This was the principal's office; he would be with us shortly.

We had driven several hours from Kanglung to explore this school as a place where we might find tradition and development brushing shoulders, and where we could learn about the zorig chusum as one of the key indicators of cultural diversity and resilience in Bhutan. We knew from the start that the diversity in question was conceived in relation to global mass culture rather than to the many minority cultures within Bhutan: the traditional arts were central to Drukpa culture, dating back to the Zhabdrung. But we also knew we had a lot to learn about Drukpa culture and the way the tangible biocultural heritage of the zorig chusum contributed to Vajrayana practice on the one hand and biodiversity on the other.

Arranging the trip had required various leaps of faith—moving forward in the hope that elusive logistics would come together for us. The principal hadn't responded to email queries, but one of James's colleagues had tracked down his personal mobile number for me to call. (I still wondered whether the principal had agreed to our visit only because I rang him in the midst of a school assembly and he had wanted to get off the phone quickly.) Next, James had organized travel permits, working with the Sherubtse College president's personal assistant (PA) to fill out forms that were then sent to the immigration office in Thimphu. The immigration office had to send us official permission to travel before we would be allowed through the checkpoint at the Chazam river crossing. Travel permits rarely came through on a first try; the forms had to be corrected multiple times before James and the Sherubtse PA managed to land on a bureaucratically acceptable category and framing for the trip. Then, once we had permission for a specific set of dates (chosen because my students were on study leave for a few days before the first semester's examinations), we had to find transportation. There were no cars to rent in Kanglung or nearby Trashigang (some 50 minutes down the mountain). The whole trip was on the brink of falling through when a colleague and friend said he would loan us his car.

Then, as we drove down the mountain from Kanglung, we came across the inevitable roadblock. (Whenever we left Kanglung, some section of the road was blocked by a landslide or ongoing construction or repairs.) This time, the trunk of a massive tree blocked both lanes, its upper portions extending several meters out over the cliff beyond the road. The road workers, pragmatic as always, had created a packed-earth ramp on either side of the four-foot diameter trunk, so that we and others could drive up and over the obstacle. The pine branches juddered over the cliff's edge as our wheels bounced across the trunk. It all seemed emblematic of the daily obstacles our Bhutanese friends and colleagues had learned to take in stride.

I had wanted to come to the traditional arts school in Trashi Yangtse not just to explore cultural diversity and resilience but also because I wondered whether it might offer a distinct model of education and learning, on the borders of what Karma Phuntsho had described as "two ways of learning in Bhutan."[2] Educated first in Bhutan's monastic system and with a Ph.D. from Oxford University, Phuntsho describes himself as "a bat-like scholar," noting that in Bhutanese folk stories,

> [. . .] the bat would show its teeth to the birds to evade the bird tax, and show its wings to the beasts to evade the beast tax. But come winter, when the food supplies are distributed, the bat would show its wings to the birds and teeth to the beasts to claim its share from both.[3]

Most of Phuntsho's article stresses the difference between a "traditional" system focused on spiritual training for the benefit of all beings and a "modern" system focused on the development of secular and scientific skills for "human development."[4] Phuntsho's analysis seemed to value the spiritual values of "traditional education" on the one hand and the pedagogical strategies of "modern education" on the other, arguing that in the modern system, "All kinds of educational equipment and methods are used for making learning faster, easier and enjoyable," while "the traditional system of education lacks such stimulating and exciting methods and techniques."[5] I was less convinced about this comparative analysis of pedagogical strategies (monk debates struck me as pretty spectacular, while Bhutanese secular education seemed to include a lot of lecturing), but I was intrigued by a remark Phuntsho made "in passing," that "the tradition of thirteen crafts (*bzo rig bcu gsum*), the concept of which is unique to Bhutan, is less associated with religious education and is often practised outside religious institutions."[6] Like Phuntsho and the scholars he cites (Diederik Prakke and Michael Aris), I hoped to see "sparking dialogue between Bhutan's modern and traditional heritage, making the best of both available."[7] Unlike those three scholars, I wondered whether schooling in the traditional arts might be a place where that sparking dialogue might already be happening, where students might be stretching their wings and sharpening their teeth at the same time. The school, presenting a "middle path" approach to Bhutanese education, also seemed an interesting place to explore the blurry, shifting boundary between the GNH categories of cultural diversity and education.

Kinley Penjor, the head of the institute, came bustling into his office full of greetings and offers of tea. Soon he was explaining to us that he himself was not a traditional artist but rather an administrator; in previous posts, he had run what we might think of as a trade school, where students trained to become plumbers, electricians, and so on. I hadn't thought of traditional arts as "trades" in this way, but the connection seemed obvious to Kinley Penjor. Perhaps the College for Zorig Chusum was also a place to see indicators associated with development, such as per capita household income, interwoven with both education and culture.

Secular education has been seen as an engine of development in Bhutan for generations. Accounts of early educational developments differ, but many report that first King Ugyen Wangchuk instructed his chamberlain Ugyen Dorji to open Bhutan's first private secular school in Haa in 1913 or 1914. The following year, another school was begun in Bumthang (and soon moved to Trongsa) in order to educate the Crown Prince and the children of royal attendants. In the late 1940s and early 1950s, a number of schools were started in southern districts as well as in Trashigang in eastern Bhutan. Most sources agree that third King Jigme Dorji Wangchuk launched a far more expansive and inclusive wave of secular school creation. Karma Phuntsho, for instance, asserts that "the introduction of formal school education in 1959 marks a watershed in the modern history of education in Bhutan. Eleven schools were established and a total of four hundred and forty students are recorded to have been enrolled in them."[8] Sherubtse began as a public high school before becoming the country's first college. Teacher training colleges soon followed in Samtse and Paro. The Royal University of Bhutan was founded by kasho or royal decree in 2003 and has continued adding different colleges and campuses in different areas of the country.

Building on this historical blending of education and development, the first administration of Prime Minister Tshering Tobgay, elected in 2013 and re-elected in 2024, had promised to launch three new colleges as accelerators of development in the underdeveloped east. All three colleges were being inaugurated in the fall of 2017, just before the new round of elections in 2018. Yonphula Centenary College, where I taught, was one of the new colleges; Gyalpozhing College of Information Technology, in the nearby district of Mongar, was perhaps the most promising and best resourced of the three promised institutions; Rigney College, here in Trashi Yangtse, was the third. In fact, the "College of Rigney" was designed to connect the "trade school" approach to traditional arts with a more academic approach to Bhutanese culture and traditions.[9] Unfortunately, funding to start three new colleges had not been included in the Five-Year Plan produced by the previous administration and money was tight. New students had been added in Trashi Yangtse without any new space being built to accommodate them. By the end of this academic year, the experiment in extending traditional arts into a broader cultural program would close; the new academically focused students would transfer to the College of Language and Culture Studies (CLCS), located at Taktse in Trongsa, central Bhutan. But a side result of the educational experiment was that the "Institute for Zorig Chusum" here in Trashi Yangtse would remain the "College of Zorig Chusum" going forward. This College of Zorig Chusum, however, represented more than another site of secular education: it represented the preservation of core national traditions, as discussed in chapter five.

Kinley Penjor was generous with his time. After letting us record an interview, he led us on a tour of the school, from classrooms devoted to tailoring and machine embroidery, through separate areas dedicated to wood carving, painting, sculpture, wood turning, and mask carving. Penjor noted with regret that the school had been unable to find instructors for certain traditional arts, such as slate carving. (We saw other traditional arts, such as weaving and bamboo work, practiced in the local community, but they may have been too common, too humble to include in the school curriculum.) Kinley Penjor also gave us permission to return over the next couple of days, to film teachers and students at work and interview anyone willing to discuss their experience of the school. From those later conversations and observations, a few themes emerged. First, traditional arts and development seemed to come together in an entrepreneurial mindset that had helped produce the school and now helped new graduates create and maintain small businesses. The College emphasized problem solving and student-centered education in ways that did indeed seem to blend the strengths of the "two ways of learning in Bhutan." Second, while teachers and students made no explicit claims for ecological benefits of their work, their descriptions of that work frequently involved physical interactions with local landscapes and environments—and the location of the school, near one of Bhutan's more remote wildlife refuges, suggested further connections between traditional arts and environmental practices. Third, within the limits of northern Bhutanese cultural context, the traditional arts as maintained by this institute seemed to build community through the ongoing replication of cultural forms and values. Finally, the larger social contexts invoked in our discussions of these traditional arts stressed the impact of shifting gender and economic norms on the maintenance of cultural traditions.

BUILDING A SCHOOL, A BUSINESS, A MINDSET

Several teachers had been present at the school's founding some 18 years earlier: the woodcarving instructor, the gold-and-silversmithing instructor, and one of the painting instructors had all been students in the first year of the new school; another painting instructor had been one of the few teachers. Clearly, that founding period was a life-changing experience for some. "I was in the first batch from this institute," were some of the first words out of Namgay Wangchuk's mouth. A stocky man full of energy and enthusiasm, Namgay Wangchuk was the wood-carving teacher in Trashi Yangtse, and he clearly identified strongly with the school as a whole. When the school was first founded, he told us, "we were only 21 trainees. We had only two instructors, including our principal." Not only was the school very small to start with, but the physical campus was far from finished. "Everything was [. . .] unturned. We had mostly very heavy work due to a shortage of facilities. We suffered a lot." Namgay Wangchuk's tone made clear that he was pleased by his past contributions: the students may have "suffered a lot," but they had helped to shape the school, of which he was justly proud. In the spring semester at Yonphula, my own students would similarly create basic infrastructure: a college garden, waste management facilities including metal trash receptacles they had to design and commission themselves from a nearby company, a compost bin, and a rainwater harvesting system. Bhutanese students and faculty are used to expectations of "social work"—efforts on behalf of the community that may range from cleaning to construction and beyond.

Thukten Jamtsho, one of the school's painting instructors, also joined the school in the first year. His experience underscored the importance of tradition and artistic apprenticeship at the school. As a teen, Thukten Jamtsho had already engaged in elementary modes of painting—house decoration, an altar box—but the school showed him how much more he had to learn. "My master is still with me," he told us, referring to the sixth-year painting instructor who, along with the original principal, had been one of the two founding instructors. Thukten Jamtsho stressed that his teacher, his master, was the one to determine the images taught to students. "The iconography in our curriculum comes from the texts. Our master, he knows very well the scripts, he knows all the meanings, he designed the curriculum and researched all the other iconography also." By contrast, Thukten Jamtsho consciously limited himself to teaching craft: "I am a skilled man and in my classes, I used to teach them only the skill, not the meaning, because the meaning I don't know." He paused to consider this: "Actually I had the interest to learn the meaning also. Side by side, I used to study the skill and the meaning, but I'm not perfect on the meaning, and that's why I'm not teaching the meanings to my students also." This kind of division between skill and knowledge—with the latter demanding a "perfect" grasp of meaning—struck me as another version of the division between folk religion and elite practices, the way Bhutanese laypeople referred almost all questions about Buddhism to an officially qualified monk.

Finally, Lungten Wangdi, the gold- and silversmithing instructor, had been studying at a junior high school in Khaling, near where we lived in Kanglung, when word came of the new Institute for Zorig Chusum. From his place at the Khaling school, young Lungten Wangdi wrote to the Trashi Yangtse principal who told him he was welcome to join the school. This was in the late 1990s, before cell phones were permitted in Bhutan. Lungten Wangdi took a leap of faith. "I didn't ask my parents," he told us. He had no opportunity to explore the facilities available at the school. "I took my life in my own hands," he said, underscoring the risk he had taken in coming to a brand-new school in this remote town. Lungten

Wangdi arrived hoping to become a painter, but the principal persuaded him that his exposure to chemistry through the school in Khaling made him a better candidate for gold and silver working. Soon after completing the four-year course, Lungten Wangdi became the school's gold- and silversmith instructor.

For the principal, Kinley Penjor, the major difference between the building trades he had worked with before (plumbing, electricity, etc.) and the traditional arts at the school in Trashi Yangtse was that students of traditional arts had much better employment prospects than electricians or plumbers. I found it a little surprising that in the midst of a developing economy, plumbers and electricians might struggle to find work, but traditional painters or woodworkers would do well opening their own shops. "There's a high demand, in Bhutan, for these products," Kinley Penjor explained:

"Like tailoring, there's a big market. Woodworking: also a big market. Then, for instance, painting: everyone requires that. Even while they are undergoing training, the students are doing part-time work. They are earning money, even while they are doing their degree."

One young gold- and silversmithing student put the same idea in his own words a few days later: "The job is all the time knocking to us!" These students don't have to go looking for work; instead, jobs come knocking on their doors. Still, I wondered what sustained demand for these kinds of traditional goods. Did government insistence on maintaining driglam namzha, the code of etiquette including national dress, support not just tailoring but the associated arts? Or were there other factors driving local markets? "Cultural traditions," suggested Kinley Penjor. GNH at work.

As a counterpoint to those cultural traditions, the entrepreneurial vision it had taken to get the school started seemed to extend through the kinds of skills and mindsets fostered by the school, which in turn appeared likely to help young graduates when it came to starting their own small businesses. From his experience of helping to build the new school, for instance, Namgay Wangchuk seemed to have developed great confidence in his ability to solve any technical problem—and he worked hard to impart a similar confidence and ability to his students. In the first year of the two-year wood-carving program, he explained, he would teach the students to make the tools: "How to shaft the tools and how to handle the tools, how to take care of the tools." Students would have to learn not only to make but also to modify "many many tools"—in the first year, they would make from scratch five gouges in different sizes, five different kinds of chisel in different sizes (including straight, bent, and fish tail), as well as five sizes of grouter.

James eventually found the area below the school where students worked on creating their tools. The students began by inserting a piece of tool metal into a rectangle of wood; they would then heat the metal until it was red-hot in the glowing embers of a fire maintained by bellows. After beating and or cutting the heated metal into the appropriate shape, they would douse the tool edge in cold water. After this process of heating, shaping, and cooling, students would use a circular sander (or grinder) to smooth and shape the edges of the tool. Once the metal of the tool was in the form they wanted, the students would take the wood outside and use a classic Bhutanese knife and a short chopping motion to trim the wood down to a size and shape appropriate for a shaft.

Namgay Wangchuk demanded that his students (Figures 6.2 and 6.3) engage in problem-solving on multiple levels:

> A client may want a design worked in a harder wood—not the blue pine we use for training, but hard wood. The tools we have developed here may not be appropriate for that wood: they may not be strong enough. But the students know how to make and modify stronger tools to fit that need. They can solve the problems they encounter in the work: any problem, they can solve it.

BIOCULTURAL HERITAGE

Beyond the grassy lawns of the College for Zorig Chusum, the hills dropped away to reveal the town of Trashi Yangtse below. Having spent almost four months perched on the side of a mountain in Trashigang, the next province over, we greatly appreciated Trashi Yangtse's broad valley, so luxuriously open and spacious. But mountains are never far away in

Figure 6.2. A woodcarving student, working from a photocopied imaged to guide his carving.

Bhutan; here, they rose sharply on the left, across the river, though more gently to the right. The river valley itself led north, toward Bomdeling and the still higher mountains marking the border with China.

As we moved through the school, talking with teachers and students, the backdrop of the mountains was almost always in view. It made me think about Bhutan's biocultural heritage, what the United Nations Convention on Biological Diversity (CBD) defined in 2018 as

> [. . .] the holistic approach of many indigenous peoples and local communities [to their environmental resources]. This holistic and collective conceptual approach also recognizes knowledge as 'heritage', thereby reflecting its custodial and intergenerational character.[10]

I wanted to know more about how people at the school thought about biocultural heritage, but I struggled to find the right way to frame the question.

Figure 6.3. Some woodcarving students working on a phurba or ritual dagger (an extra assignment) on the lawn in front of their classroom.

"How does your work here relate to GNH?" I had asked Kinley Penjor when we first spoke.

"Well," he replied, "one of the pillars of GNH is cultural preservation."

I nodded.

"So this is the institute for cultural preservation."

That was about as far as these conversations about GNH seemed to go.

"Well, what about the other pillars?" I asked. "Aren't they all interconnected?"

Kinley Penjor looked at me, a little puzzled.

"You say the students will find it easy to get work, so that's a contribution to fair and equitable socioeconomic development, right? What about the environment?" I asked. "That's another pillar, isn't it? Does the school help preserve the environment?"

"Perhaps we are not so good on that front." Penjor seemed a little embarrassed:

> We take our wood from the mountains, from the local people, but we are consuming that wood. We import other raw materials from India. But without these materials, we cannot practice these traditional arts. So perhaps we must focus on cultural preservation and let others focus on environmental conservation.

But the practice of these traditional arts beyond the walls of the College told a different story. Yes, the painters relied on imported pigments and the gold- and silversmiths on imported metal—and when we climbed to a lhakhang in the hills above Trashi Yangtse, we could see where the students had dragged blue pine trees and logs down the mountain, creating channels that increased erosion in the long rainy season. But the use of local materials also kept the artists engaged with their local environment. For instance, the "guardian" or caretaker of the lhakhang we visited was weaving a basket out of bamboo strips. His eyes were milky with age; his wife, as far as we could understand her, explained that he was blind and so she would give us a tour of the temple. He, meanwhile, continued to weave, his hands confidently turning the half-made basket, weaving the strips through the structuring outline already created (Figure 6.4). After our hike, as we drove through the lengthening evening shadows, we passed a group of young boys playing on the roadside as their fathers and older brothers wove much larger sections of bamboo into fencing for livestock. The College for Zorig Chusum did not teach bamboo weaving, but clearly this traditional art was still alive and well in the broader area. Thimphu's version of the school for zorig chusum—an institution often known more simply as "the painting school"—is more urban, and thus more separate from local ecosystems, but the Trashi Yangtse school seemed to be maintaining traditional arts on a level close to the traditional practices and environment of this largely undisturbed locale.

We wondered how far these implicit connections between traditional arts and the local environment might extend. In fact, in the afternoon of our first day in Trashi Yangtse, we went off to explore the Bomdeling Wildlife Sanctuary, rushing up a rough road in hopes of catching Sonam Tenzin, a ranger at the sanctuary, before he left on a three-day trip to the sanctuary's northern edge, on the border with China. We found him

Figure 6.4. A blind temple guardian weaving a foraging basket out of bamboo splints.

waiting for us outside his house, alerted to our presence by a WeChat from the sanctuary's central office.

Many of Bhutan's glacial rivers reveal the promise of hydroelectric power at first glance, but in late November, the Khulong Chhu in north-east Trashi Yangtse seemed shallow, barely deep enough to cover the multitude of river rocks time had worn smooth.[11] Sonam led us further up the rutted track by car before steering us on foot across a log bridge over one of the Khulong's tributaries, then further, over fallen trees that let us scramble out to some of the islands formed from river depositions. Across from us on yet another stony island, wild ponies and black-necked cranes grazed together. The cranes, four feet tall, were almost as large as the ponies. As they foraged, heads down, their stocky white bodies looked, from a distance, like grazing sheep. Black heads, necks, and tails, book-ending those white fluffy bodies, faded into the shadowy background. Omnivores, the cranes stepped slowly, on the lookout for roots, frogs, snakes, bugs. Further down the valley, we had seen the birds moving through farm fields, hunting tubers left in the fields. The government had negotiated with farmers growing barley and potatoes to leave some fragment of their crops in the field to support the cranes.

According to the Ramsar Convention on Wetlands, this glacial valley was a rice-producing floodplain "until a series of floods washed away the paddy fields and left it fallow with sandy soil"[12] (Figure 6.5). Along with Phobjikha or Gangtey valleys in western Bhutan, Bomdeling serves as precious habitat for the black-necked crane, officially a vulnerable but not an endangered species. In contrast with Phobjikha, which is at a high

Figure 6.5. The sandy floodplain of Bomdeling, with ponies and black-necked cranes grazing in the distance.

altitude and cold, Bomdeling offers a more temperate climate—perhaps too temperate for the birds. Numbers of black-necked cranes overwintering at Phobjikha are increasing, while the numbers at Bomdeling have been decreasing in recent years. In November 2017, the valley hosted only 70 cranes, but Sonam expected roughly 150 birds to overwinter between November and mid-March. Sonam woke at 4:00 a.m. to get out on the river to count the birds when they first took flight in the morning. "That is the way to be accurate in your counting: to catch them in flight, just taking off," he told us. I thought about how challenging the trail up the valley must be in the dark. On this cloudy afternoon, flowers bloomed vividly at the river's edges, hiding among the meanders, the slippery banks. The hazy light made everything seem at once close and distinct.

Black-necked cranes, known onomatopoeically as thrung-thrung in Dzongkha, symbolize good luck and happiness in Bhutan. In Phobjikha, they are said to circle Gangtey abbey three times upon their arrival into the valley, and again three times as they depart, these circumambulations suggesting that they too are good Buddhists. In Bomdeling, part of the good luck they bring includes protection for other species, including tigers, snow leopards, musk deer and more, not least the "only endemic butterfly in the world," Ludlow's Bhutan swallowtail. UNESCO's tentative listing for Bomdeling includes

> [. . .] a total of 100 species of mammals, 432 species birds, 650 species of plants, 46 species of orchids, 130 species of butterflies, 7 species of fishes, 29 species of dragonflies, 45 species of Herpeto-fauna and other important, endangered, threatened, and endemic species of flora and fauna.[13]

With two colleagues, Sonam was leaving early the next day (3 a.m. instead of 4 a.m.) on a three-day trip north to examine camera traps they were using to try to count current populations of tigers, snow leopards, and other large mammals.

I asked Sonam whether he saw any connection between the wildlife sanctuary and the nearby school for traditional arts, but he shook his head. Mostly, he said, his encounters with residents focused on chasing off people who parked by the river to wash their cars. Given the remoteness of the refuge, this seemed to me to represent both a deep personal commitment to car-cleaning, and a comically banal challenge to wildlife conservation. To meet Sonam, we had had to drive up a deeply rutted dirt track and ford a river where the bridge had washed out. Despite the beauty of the sanctuary, we would not choose to repeat that drive in our borrowed car—certainly not for cosmetic reasons.

On our way back to the town of Trashi Yangtse, we passed a road sign pointing to a traditional paper factory, off the road, beyond a steep driveway plunging down toward the river. James, behind the wheel of the car, shook his head even as I pointed at the sign. The car would not make it down that track and back up again. We had already visited a traditional paper factory in Thimphu in any case. I had just wanted to see whether there were any major differences here in the east.

Bhutanese hand-made paper derives from the daphne "tree" or bush; evidently, the daphne species that grows in eastern Bhutan is far taller than the more bush-like form available in western Bhutan. First, the bark is stripped from the trunk and then soaked for twelve hours. After soaking, the fiber is boiled or "cooked" for another four hours, then rinsed in running water. The remaining material is sorted and cleaned to make sure the fibers remaining are sufficiently fine to produce good quality paper. That material is then pounded and ground into pulp. In a large tank, the pulp is mixed with water along with starch from the hibiscus or abelmoschus plant. The paper-maker dips a wooden frame with a bamboo screen into the tank; he then raises this frame horizontally, covered with pulp, and shakes it from side to side to make the excess water drip off. The resulting sheet of paper is piled upon previously shaped sheets; a weight is placed on top of the pile to help squeeze out additional water. Eventually, individual sheets are placed on a smooth board to dry. In Thimphu, the drying was done on heated metal easels, and the sheets of paper were whisked briskly from the drying pile to the easel to the finished pile by a second paper-maker in the small "factory."

Although not taught at the Institute in Trashi Yangtse, paper-making is one of Bhutan's 13 traditional arts—and the location of the paper-making "factory," part way between Bomdeling Wildlife Refuge and the College for Zorig Chusum, seemed the symbolize the way many of the traditional arts balanced between cultural institutions and the local environment. We would soon learn that this handmade paper was used to reinforce clay sculptures back at the Institute.

Our second day in Trashi Yangtse, we spent some time in the mask-making workshop at the College, noting further connections between cultural values and the environment. The wooden masks carved here would be worn by monks and lay dancers in local tshechus. The masks themselves range from the faces of wrathful deities, crowned with skulls, to animal heads with ritual meanings: pig, rabbit, dog, tiger, bear, vulture-headed garuda, snow lion, and more.

The workshop was located in a small building, set off from the other classrooms. We had to cross the main driveway and duck down some steps to find the open doorway. As in several other classrooms, the cheery yellow paint was peeling from the walls; the electric lights were off, leaving students to rely on natural light from the windows, which seemed to us a little dim. The students sat cross-legged on the floor, laps covered with a work-apron, each in their own little workshop space, covered in wood chips (Figure 6.6).

As we came in, the teacher was sitting cross-legged, facing one of the students in the first-year classroom. He took the student's wooden block, a mask-in-the-making, into his own hands, set it on his lap, and set to with mallet and chisel, quickly cleaning up the lines of the piece, sorting out the carving problem. Cheki Gyeltshin, a quiet and even bashful student, then received the piece back and studied it carefully. Later, he would summarize his education for us in these terms: "The hard part is done by the teacher. And then we just carve as was done by the teacher. They teach us well." The teacher himself noted the difference between doing and teaching: he himself could produce in a day or two most of the masks that the students would spend weeks laboring over.

Like the woodworking students, these students had to learn to care for their tools; we saw them clean and sharpen their tools at every stage in the carving process. But the students also stressed the labor in obtaining the raw material of their work: "At the start of the year, we spend 15 days in the forest, cutting wood," Cheki explained. "We have to measure the wood and cut it in square shapes." That basic square form will be hollowed out to create the mouth and skull cavity of a given animal mask. Lines drawn with something like a Sharpie pen indicated the places

Figure 6.6. Mask-making students in their workshop.

where the wood would need to be shaped or simply removed. In the first year of the curriculum, Cheki Gyeltshin told us, he and his classmates had carved around six or seven masks.

Students worked at different stages of the carving process. One student cradled a half-formed mask in his left arm, using the strength of his right arm to shave wood from the front of what would become the mask's teeth or lips. Another student was shaping large canine teeth at the edges of his mask's mouth opening. In the next room, another student was scraping out the inside of his mask, to reduce the weight the dancer would have to bear while performing at a tshechu. The motion of a curved tool shaving wood from the inside of the mask's mouth and inner skull seemed eerily similar to an animal hide being scraped for drying. Even in the early stages of its creation, the mask seemed almost lifelike, on the edge of sentience. Yet another student was working on the snout of his mask; shifting from one tool to another, he would rest his hands on the mask's snout, sticking a finger up its nostril almost meditatively (presumably to check the width of the opening). The effect was an uncanny intimacy between human, animal shape, and wooden substance. Next to him, another student was busy hammering a chisel into the nose of his mask and then vigorously circling his tool to free it as he simultaneously cleared out the shape of a nostril. This student had already shaped the eyes of his mask, and they were wide open and noble in appearance. The mask seemed to gaze on the violent production of its nostrils with immense patience and fortitude. The masks, once finished, would be worn by dancers in the sacred dances of Bhutan's tshechus, suggesting some connection between northern Bhutan's "spiritual heritage" and its biocultural traditions (Figure 6.7). What these carvers were busy learning and transmitting by touch could be said to complement in important ways the lessons available in Vajrayana religious texts.

There are good reasons to be skeptical about attributing any innate environmentalism to Bhutanese culture. One might remember, for

Figure 6.7. Animal masks worn by dancers at the Yonphula tshechu.

instance, that the "Green" Druk party came in last (well behind the industrializing "Blue" Druk party) during the practice elections of 2006. I have spoken with Western scholars of Vajrayana who tell me that the religious texts of the tradition never explicitly valued the non-human world in its own right, but only as a source of metaphors for what we might call interior experience. More generally, scholar Toni Huber has noted the extent to which Tibetan environmentalism developed as a by-product of global politics. She dates the origin of "Green Tibetans" to the years 1985 and 1986, when fact-finding missions from Dharamsala to Tibet returned with reports of ecological destruction and outsiders may have advised the government in exile that stressing the ecological consequence of China's policies would have useful political effects.[14]

Despite these reasons for skepticism, however, the traditional arts of Bhutan seem to me to maintain traditional forms of ecological knowledge and imaginative engagement with other life-forms—both actual animals like deer, rabbits, tigers, and so on, and also figures imagined somewhere between human existence and forms of death (the skulls surrounding wrathful deity masks). As I watched the mask-makers at work, I thought of Sonam Tenzin on his three-day hike to the border with China, in search of tiger photographs from camera traps. I also remembered hiking past a bull in a field just above the men weaving a livestock fence from bamboo. In Trashi Yangtse, the community's holistic approach to natural resources and traditional arts still made visible a custodial, intergenerational engagement with the local extra-human environment.

CULTURAL SIGHT WORDS AND IMAGINED COMMUNITIES

At the same time, the stylized aesthetic norms governing artistic production at the College underscored the cultural transformation of natural imagery into social and spiritual lessons. The images defining the curriculum of the Institute shaped something like a communal alphabet or perhaps early sight words by which northern Bhutanese citizens could learn to read their culture. The woodworking classroom, for instance, was divided into two rooms; in the first room, closest to the door onto the courtyard, first-year students were hard at work carving a series of bas-relief designs onto flat squares of wood. Hammers tapped chisels into the wood, following lines from a photocopied image glued to the front of the thin block. "What are they carving?" I asked, and the instructor Namgay Wangchuk responded with a wave at a chart on the wall: "Tashi Tagye: eight lucky signs." Many of the designs were familiar: a pair of fish, a lotus flower, a wheel, a conch shell, and so on. But what I kept trying to ask through the noise of the hammering was what made those signs lucky. Why was this the iconography that mattered to Bhutan?

Eight Lucky Signs, Four Harmonious Friends, Four Dignities

The eight lucky signs (Figure 6.8) were part of the first-year curriculum not just for woodcarving but for other arts as well.

These signs, also known as Ashtamangala, are used in Hindu as well as Buddhist rituals and can be seen in India and China as well as Bhutan; they serve to focus people's attention on specific values, or, in the words of Karma Phuntsho, "auspicious topics and enlightened qualities."[15] The parasol, for instance, protects those beneath it from the heat of the sun as Buddhism offers protection from suffering. Two golden fish were originally a Hindu image symbolizing the Ganges and Yamuna rivers, but in Buddhism they offer assurance that practitioners will not drown in an ocean of suffering. The conch shell is blown to awaken those who hear it from their ignorance. The lotus, rooted in mud, but blossoming into purity, symbolizes Buddhists rising into enlightenment out of samsara or suffering. The victory banner registers Buddha's victory over the demon Mara, or the victory of wisdom over ignorance. The vase represents Buddha's teachings, which will never be emptied, no matter how much we draw from that source. The wheel of dharma, each turn of which symbolizes a major teaching, is sometimes pictured with eight spokes representing the eightfold path. The eternal knot symbolizes dependent origination and the interdependence of all things. These eight signs summarize key aspects of Buddhism as a faith and a philosophy.

In the zorig chusum curriculum, the next step up from the eight lucky signs seemed to be a tableau summarizing the story of the four harmonious friends (Figure 6.9). We saw this image first in the machine-embroidering

Figure 6.8. The Eight Lucky Signs (painted). From the top, the parasol, two fish, the vase, the lotus, the conch shell, the eternal knot, the victory banner, the wheel of dharma.

Figure 6.9. Machine embroidery of the Four Harmonious Friends.

class, located between the woodworking and the tailoring classrooms. Here, one male and seven female students bent over their sewing machines, working on a tightly embroidered, complexly colored design. The machine-driven needles churned through fabric at a furious pace, pausing only when the colored thread needed to be changed over for a new section of the design. The sewing machines were moving so rapidly that at first I mistakenly believed the students had programmed those patterns into a computer driving the machine—but the students were just moving their fabric, stretched on a round embroidery frame, with so much speed and confidence that the driving needle acted almost as a thin paint-brush on canvas. Signs on the wall mapped out different colored threads to be used in each part of the design, but variation was included in the process: one student was creating the four friends on a red background, while another had chosen green as the backdrop to the design. The shades used for each animal or the plants and mountains in the background varied with the choice of background color. The use of colors—pale blue or white thread shading the darker blue of a wave or a cloud—effectively recreated the brushwork of students in the painting classes.

The story being driven into the fabric emphasized both respect for the elderly and collaborative efforts for the benefit of all. Different students were at work on different parts of the four friends design, but in each version of the story, an elephant stands beneath a fruit tree with a monkey, a hare, and a bird on his back. The four animals try to determine who among them is the eldest; they establish that the elephant first saw the tree fully grown, the monkey passed it as a sapling, the hare as a seedling, and the bird excreted the seed from which it grew. The Buddha told the story partly as a means of urging respect for his elder disciple Sariputra who had been mocked by some younger members of the community. In some versions of the story, the animals also collaborate to enjoy the fruit of the tree: the bird plants the seed, the hare waters it, the monkey provides manure, and the elephant shelters it. Then they climb on one another to harvest the fruits.

In an upper story of the building across the courtyard, the second-year painting class was working on canvases divided between the four harmonious friends on one side and four dignities on the other. From the front of the classroom, all we could see was a line of easels, with bare knees peeking out from under the gho's visible beneath the bottom of each canvas. Some of the feet wiggled as the artist concentrated; others were perfectly still. Occasionally, one of the students would grasp the top of the canvas as he worked. We moved behind the line of easels to see the young men (and they were all young men, no women in this class) hard at work on their identical paintings. Different brushes were used for subtly different effects. One young artist bit his tongue as he worked; another grinned at us as we leaned in close to watch him shifting from one brush and color to the next, wiping each one clean between his thumb and index finger.

Beyond the eight lucky signs and the four friends, the four dignities (Figure 6.10) offered some additional sight words within this Vajrayana iconography: a set of mythic animals including the tiger, the snow lion, the garuda, and the dragon. The tiger is associated with the wind and the south; the dragon with water and the west; the snow lion with earth and the east; the garuda with fire and the north. Beyond these elemental qualities, however, lie their spiritual associations. Each of these figures, associated specifically with lungta or wind-horse teachings, has a symbolic register as well as its material form. According to Sakyong Mipham, son of Chogyam Trungpa, the Kagyu teacher who popularized Tibetan Buddhism in the United States, the tiger registers "discernment, the virtue of touching

Figure 6.10. A young painter working on a garuda in a painting of the Four Dignities: tiger, snow lion, garuda, dragon.

our feet to the earth of every moment. As we slow down and consider our thoughts, words, and actions [. . .], we become like tigers who carefully observe the landscape before pouncing." The snow lion stands for discipline, which it experiences as joy and "delight, a practical way to uplift the mind of 'me' into the highlands of a bigger view." The garuda ("a mythical bird with human arms that is hatched from space, ready to fly") represents outrageousness, "the confidence of equanimity, an unbiased view." The dragon, emblem of Bhutan as a "dragon kingdom," stands for prajna or deep wisdom; beyond petty grasping, the dragon represents the mind beyond ego, as well as the dynamic qualities of the natural world, with its weather and seasons.[16] While the four harmonious friends seem like a tale designed to draw attention to community values, the four dignities summon the traditional viewer to a focus on different elements of psychological well-being. Grounded discernment, joyous discipline, outrageous equanimity, deep wisdom: the images of these mythic animals offer a kind of shorthand for the qualities Vajrayana practitioners are invited to develop.

Painting and Sculpting Meditation Deities

Meditation deities take this kind of cultural meaning to a much higher level, and producing images or sculptures of those deities involved much more complex technical skills as well. Deity yoga, one of the more advanced Vajrayana practices, involves visualizing and identifying with a particular meditation deity and then dissolving that image into an understanding of "luminous emptiness." The meditation deities must be represented very precisely, whatever the medium of representation (Figure 6.11)

Tashi Phuntsho, the sculpture instructor, stressed the religious meaning behind the figures he taught. The shapes and the details of each sculpture, he noted, were "based on the scriptures of lamas, from their meditations." Vajrayana Buddhism claims to offer skillful methods for achieving direct perception of reality. The meditations of these teachers are written down in detail; their account of these meditational deities are precise because those deities offer a path to enlightenment, to

Figure 6.11. A student in the sixth-year painting class, working on a thangkha of the thousand-armed form of Chenrezig (Avalokiteshvara).

direct perception of reality. The shaping of those deities is not open to individual artistic interpretation by someone who is not a Vajrayana master. "Many lamas have written how to make these statues and how to paint them," Tashi Phuntsho explains. "Still, when we do the work, it's very hard. We have to follow the scripture and follow the ancestors." Tashi Phuntsho explained that the first sculptural figure taught is that of the Buddha, both because he is the founder of Buddhism and because the figure is very simple and unadorned. The simplicity of faith and of the figure seemed to go together.

Meanwhile, down in a classroom on the lower level of the western wing of the school, the second-year class of hand embroidery, which included only female students, was focusing hard on Padmasambhava, considered a second Buddha here in the Himalayas. The young women were recreating the figure of Guru Rinpoche on a background of luscious cream-colored silk, their darting needles marking out with colored silk the different lines of Guru Rinpoche's face and neck and clothing (Figure 6.12).

When I stopped back to talk with them two days later, the bulk of the outline had been finished in a mix of colors: turquoise contrasting with orange to highlight the Buddhist robes around the figure's head, in contrast with the burgundy marking the robes wrapped around his body.

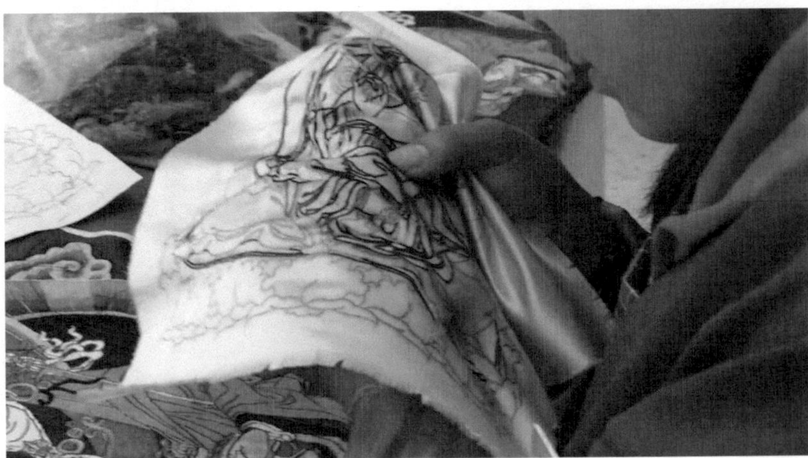

Figure 6.12. Hand embroidery of Guru Rinpoche.

Some of the girls had begun driving their needles through the figure's eyes, nose, and mouth.

I asked the girls how their schooling in zorig chusum compared with their more conventional schooling. "Very different," they said.

"Practice versus theory?" I asked, and they looked at me, baffled. "Some of the teachers at this school have used the word 'theory' for the kind of learning you do with books and lectures and 'practice' for this kind of work with your hands."

"Ah," they nodded.

"Which do you like better?" I asked. "Or are they both the same?"

Not the same. Zorig chusum was much better. But our ability to communicate broke down over the question of why.

Still, as we spoke, they held Guru Rinpoche in their hands, the silk crumpling under the pressure of their hold, their needles sketching, speaking, telling a story they had known all their lives.

Higher-level students in painting and sculpture work on more complex figures. By their second or third year, for instance, sculpture students are constructing the standing figure of Chana Dorje (Sanskrit: Vajrapani, meaning "Vajra [thunderbolt] in his hand"). The day we visited, students had mostly managed to shape the legs and torso of the figure. One student was busy refining the head of a tiger which decorates Chana Dorji's right leg—the tiger skin is his loin cloth, and it trails down behind him to touch the ground (and offer a point of triangulation to stabilize the figure). The clay used for these sculptures is mixed with handmade paper in a workshop down the hill; the combination of clay and paper is pounded with a wooden mallet to integrate the fibers with the clay. This produces a lightweight but sturdy medium; the sculptures will not be fired, but the daphne fibers offer additional structure and stability to the forms produced.

A mid-level sculpture student named Rinchen Wangchuk explained to us that Chana Dorje's legs are filled with nails, to strengthen them and support the upper half of the figure. That upper portion, beginning with Chana Dorje's protruding belly, is left hollow. The sculptors will cut an opening in the back of the figure so that prayers blessed by monks can be inserted into the sculpture. "In this way," Rinchen told us, "that god will be for all time: until the end of the world." In a corner of the classroom, more advanced students seemed to be working on Vajrakilaya: a wrathful meditation deity with three heads, six arms, embracing a female consort. The more finished figures were crowned with many small skulls; sharply edged aluminum wings protruded from the back of the male figure, waiting to be encased in clay (Figure 6.13).

While teachers in other fields had stressed the secular, skill-based aspect of their work, Tashi Phuntsho described a more devotional undercurrent to sculpture work. He explained the advice he had received from lamas and teachers alike. "When we are making the statues, we have to think positively; we call it tsa wa sum," he said. "Tsa wa sum means that we don't look at the money. Whatever the lama requires, we produce that sculpture." (As discussed in Chapter 4, the Dzongka phrase "tsa wa sum" translates into English as the "three main elements," once the guru, the yidam (meditation deity), and the khandro of Vajrayana practice, but now more commonly the King, government, and people of Bhutan. In answering the needs of the Vajrayana teachers, these sculptures also contribute to the nation.) "Our traditional things are very important," said Tashi

Figure 6.13. A sculpture-in-process of Vajrakilaya.

Phuntsho. "I think they are the backbone of our country. I am very happy to be doing this sculpture work."

Tashi Phuntsho's patriotic references reminded me of the extent to which the skills and imagery taught by the school served to maintain and confirm national (northern Bhutanese) cultural norms, tropes, and stories. In his classic work on nationalism, *Imagined Communities*, Benedict Anderson argues that people imagine themselves in "deep, horizontal comradeship" with other members of their national community. For Anderson, the shared experience of reading a newspaper (as one imagines other people simultaneously reading the same paper) helps build the imagined community of the nation.[17] In Bhutan, it seemed to me, a (northern) citizen's repeated encounter with Vajrayana imagery, from the eight lucky signs up to founding figures such as the Buddha and Padmasambhava and a meditational deity like Chana Dorji, might create the same sense of shared experience and horizontal connection.

And yet the tantric aspects of Vajrayana Buddhism still sat oddly with conventional understandings of nationalism. Note, for instance, the differences between nationalistic imagery in the United States and the imagery found in Bhutan. Rather than (increasingly contested) accounts of Founding Fathers such as Washington and Jefferson, Bhutan's imagery presents figures such as Vajrakilaya, the focus of the fifth-year painting class and some of the more advanced sculpture students. A wrathful deity of purification, Vajrakilaya is meant to be scary-looking: he usually has three faces, six hands, and four legs with wide, outstretched wings behind. He is one of the eight famous Herukas, figures known for their embodiment of indivisible bliss and emptiness; despite those apparently happy connotations, the Sanskrit term heruka was translated into both Chinese and Tibetan as "blood drinker." Vajrakilaya's Bhutanese name is Dorje Phurba, and in his two central hands, he holds a phurbu, a "ritual dagger which stabs the obstacles and hostile forces of embodied ignorance, and transmits their consciousness to the Buddha fields." This ritual dagger is meant to be a symbol not of hostility but rather of compassion: "In the often repeated words of the root Kīlaya verses, 'the Vajra Wrath cuts off hatred.'" Vajrakilaya practice is often praised as a path for spiritual development and also a means of resolving social conflicts.[18] But there is a significant gap between the visual impact of the "blood drinker" armed with a dagger and the ideas of spiritual development and conflict resolution. How can such a complex and counter-intuitive figure serve as a unifying national focus? Part of the answer might lie in how the traditional arts function as community connectors above and beyond the specific images they represent.

MAKING A PRAYER WHEEL AND A COMMUNITY

Out on a green field, the air was filled with the high-pitched sound of metal hammers tap-tap-tapping. Groups of four or five students gathered around two metal panels, each panel a couple of feet wide and perhaps six feet long. The students' heads were nearly touching across the panel as they leaned over their hammers and the tools known as liners. At the panel closest to us, the tapping was punctuated by conversational phrases and giggles as people pulled out of their tight focus to start a new line or consider the group's progress.

Occasionally a deeper tone harmonized with the squeaky, fast-pitched staccato drone—the deeper sound produced perhaps by a bigger hammer or an odd angle. The panels were themselves mounted on low wooden tables which had been carried out onto a grassy lawn beside the classroom (Figure 6.14). Even in late November, the sun was warm; the students sat on a cloth or old cushion to keep the cold and damp of the ground at a slight remove while they tapped along the curving lines previously sketched on the metal. Later, an older boy from the workshop helped Jeremy hold a liner or a running punch while he demonstrated the appropriate amount of pressure from the tapping. Everyone else stopped to watch briefly. The apprenticeship approach to teaching seemed to make teachers of them all.

"This will be a prayer wheel for the central school in Rangjung," the gold- and silversmithing teacher Lungten Wangdi told us. Community projects were an important part of the school curriculum: yesterday, we had been shown the fifth-year painting class's community service project, a massive canvas bearing images of meditational deities large and small. In the case of the prayer wheel, the Rangjung community school provided the raw materials, the College for Zorig Chusum provided the labor, and the students learned useful skills as they pulled the project together.

Figure 6.14. Students in the gold- and silver-smithing class work together on a copper panel for a large prayer wheel.

The students who were trying to teach Jeremy exploded in laughter. One of the girls, still laughing, but obviously objecting to something that was said, smacked the boy beside her. A dog shook itself awake and ambled away from the shifting sounds. Behind the two groups of student workers, a prayer wheel gleamed golden in the sun beneath its double pagoda-style roof.

When we had first arrived in Kanglung, a young computer scientist named Namgay had taken us on a walk down some of the farm roads, pointing out his favorite views over the valley, as well as the chorten he had organized people to whitewash the previous year. He also led us in spinning every one of the many prayer wheels we passed on our walk. Some eight prayer wheels in, I asked what the writing on the outside of the prayer wheel said, but our young friend said he didn't know.

"What do you mean, you don't know?" I asked. We couldn't read the writing, of course, but surely the local people could.

"I don't read Chökey," Namgay explained without offense. Chökey is the Bhutanese word for the liturgical, classical Tibetan language learned in monasteries; Dzongkha is often described as a simplified form of Chökey.

"Well, is this symbol the same as what's written on the prayer wheel at the market?"

Namgay shrugged, smiling. I struggled to adjust my thinking: I found it disorienting to be surrounded by writing I couldn't read, but surely this was part of being a foreigner. What did it mean to live in a world of writing intrinsic to one's own culture and still find that writing illegible?

"Don't you care?" I asked. "Doesn't it bother you, not knowing what it says?"

Namgay replied:

"The way a prayer wheel works is that it is filled with prayers. The monks and lamas write out the prayers and wrap them around the axle of the prayer wheel, then they fill the wheel itself with prayers. Each time we spin the wheel, the prayers travel out to bless and protect everyone around and below the trajectory of the spinning wheel."

"Yes, I know," I said. "But don't you want to know *which* prayer you are sending out to bless people? Doesn't that matter?"

Namgay smiled at me again. Clearly it didn't matter to him.

Now, in Trashi Yangtse, I found myself thinking again about the meaning of a prayer wheel. In this case, the material base of the prayer wheel, especially in its construction as a community project, seemed to me to turn the wheel of a circular economy, one with the potential to produce material benefits as well as spiritual enlightenment. The making of the prayer wheel linked the College for Zorig Chusum to the prayer wheel's eventual home: the central school in Rangjung in a separate but nearby province. Within the College, the prayer wheel connected the painting teacher with the gold- and silversmithing teacher and others. The College itself supported a community of people united through their dress, their eating utensils, their decoration—and it supported practices of frugality, reuse, and cultural norms aligned with environmental conservation.

The College for Zorig Chusum may also make visible, if only by contrast, some of the abstract systems of global capitalism that shape modern post-traditional societies like the United States. For sociologist Anthony Giddens, lifestyle choices and habits *appear* to operate within a space of individual autonomy, even though the choices on offer are constrained and defined by much larger abstract systems. Ice cube trays and their shifting design exemplify for Giddens the power of abstract and complex systems in shaping individual lives. We don't choose the specific shape of an ice cube tray—and yet the design of that tiny appliance shapes many moments of individual experience (at least in countries where ice cube trays are used, like the United States). Abstract systems of design and manufacturing intrude into the intimacy of our lived experience; as those abstract systems introduce change, we adjust and readjust our lived practices, shaping our lives to the abstract systems that define us. What goes missing here, Giddens implies, is personal agency; agency and power reside in those larger global systems rather than in the individuals shaped by those systems: "Not just the local community, but intimate features of personal life and the self become intertwined with relations of indefinite time-space extension."[19] This does not necessarily mean that traditional societies allow greater individual agency, but rather that the impression of individual agency in modern societies is illusory.

GENDER AND TRADITIONAL ARTS

We found our interviews and observations at the College both absorbing and exhausting. To restore ourselves, we periodically went back to the wonderful Choki Dorji guesthouse for a meal or a rest, and we stopped by the famous Chorten Kora to join the people circumambulating (Figure 6.15)

The Chorten Kora sits at the bottom of the town of Trashi Yangtse, defining the entire valley. Built in 1740 to subdue a demon afflicting the residents of the valley and interfering with trade, the Chorten Kora is famous throughout Bhutan. As the monument reached completion, the story goes, a dakini or khandro in the form of a young eight-year-old girl from Tawang (across the present border in India) volunteered to be immured—effectively buried alive—within the chorten. Her job was to

Figure 6.15. The Trashi Yangtse Chorten Kora, based on the Boudinath Stupa in Kathmandu.

pray without ceasing for the benefit of all sentient beings.[20] I found the story of the chorten deeply disturbing, but as we walked and spun the many prayer wheels, I enjoyed watching the older women circumambulating, their kiras topped by Western sweatshirts and woolen hats offering winter warmth (Figure 6.16). My favorite was the bright pink "Punk Power" proclaimed in a band over an older woman's deeply lined face, like the "Monster" hat in that figure. We enjoyed the sound of the water turning the prayer wheels at the corners of the courtyard, and the sound of the wheels turning with the old women's surprisingly forceful spinning—punk power, indeed!

Meanwhile, back at the College, among the stories I wanted to learn and share about the zorig chusum, another kind of story kept presenting itself—a story about gender and difficulty in Bhutan. Over the course of our visit to the College, we became increasingly curious about the role of gender in the traditional arts of Bhutan: students in the six-year programs like painting and sculpture were almost entirely male; students in the

Figure 6.16. An older woman circumambulating the Chorten Kora, spinning the many prayer wheels along its sides.

two-year fabric arts programs (like tailoring and embroidery) were mostly female; gold- and silversmithing as a four-year program offered a kind of middle ground (Figure 6.17).

When we asked the painting instructor Thukten Jamtsho about the prevalence of male students in the painting program, for instance, he seemed frustrated about the gender imbalance. He acknowledged that there was only a single woman in the sixth-year painting class, but he felt that this had little to do with innate ability. Thukten Jamtsho thought there should be more women pursuing the art: "Girls are not getting encouraged to learn painting because it is [a course of] long duration." He thought this was a pity in professional terms, however: "Girls can do better than men because girls have soft hands." He thought for a moment and then underscored that (essentializing) assertion with a nod: "They can do better painting than men."

When principal Kinley Penjor took us on a tour of the school, our first stop was the tailoring classroom, similar to yet distinct from the

Figure 6.17. A female gold- and silver-smithing student melts silver onto an in-process bracelet.

machine embroidery class. This space was full of gleaming black sewing machines powered by foot treadles. Together, the whirring sound of the foot treadles and the more pointed noise of needles driving through fabric to pick up the bobbin thread, offered a low accompaniment to the soft babble of voices, as a group of female students worked together to lay out the fabric frame for a thangkha (a devotional painting). Other students were working on the fine piecework involved in making chenzi—the strips of colored chevrons that hang from the ceilings of lhakhangs or decorate other textile pieces. Once sewn, those chevrons had to be turned inside out and ironed flat. A number of students clustered around the ironing table, passing the two irons around so that each could have a turn. Still others remained seated at their machines, their sensible black shoes angling back and forth to push the treadle as if it were an extension of their bodies, hands twisting the fabric around the moving needle, smoothing away wrinkles and possible knots. The room was full of young women; only one young man seemed to be studying in this class.

Kinley Penjor drew our attention to the gender balance. "As you see, most of our tailoring class are girls," he said, leading us toward the next classroom (Figure 6.18).

"Well, that's to be expected, isn't it?" I asked. "Isn't tailoring considered a female art?"

"Not in Bhutan," he replied, a little surprised by my assumption. "In Bhutan, most tailors are men. But these days, many girls are studying the art."

In retrospect, the masculinity of Bhutanese tailoring seems relatively obvious: tailoring and embroidery both developed primarily in the monasteries, as monks designed costumes for rituals and objects for daily use. But now, in a secular context, tailoring allows women an easily accessible field of study.

The tailoring teacher chose not to be interviewed, but a second-year tailoring student Karma Yangki came to represent the class and the curriculum. Karma Yangki thought the school was perfectly designed to meet the needs of people like her and her family. In particular, it provided an attractive option for students who did not manage to obtain government-sponsored higher education. In Bhutan in 2017 and 2018, education was free through tenth grade. At the end of the tenth grade, students took a national examination. Those with the highest scores earned a place in

Figure 6.18. A member of the tailoring class working on one of the chevron strips that hang from the ceilings of many lhakhangs.

eleventh- and twelfth-grade classes. At the end of twelfth grade, another national examination determined who would receive a free place at one of the public campuses of the Royal University of Bhutan.

"My family background is a little bit poor, little bit poor," Karma Yangki told us. When she did not score highly enough on the tenth-grade national examination to earn a place in the eleventh- and twelfth-grade program, her parents suggested that she attend a private high school. Karma Yangki was grateful for her parents' support, but she decided that private high school was a bad idea: not only would it consume scarce family resources, but if her grades in twelfth grade were not high enough to get her into college, those resources would have been wasted.

Nima Tshering's 2014 Brookings Institute paper lays out some of the wider background to Karma Yangki's remarks.[21] As that essay explains, the merit-based cutoff point for publicly funded higher secondary school was calculated using test scores in English, plus "scores of the best of any four subjects from the remaining subjects." Girls performed slightly better in English, Dzongkha (the national language) and computers, but boys outperformed girls in economics, mathematics, science, and history, civics and geography, giving the boys an overall edge on admission to publicly funded eleventh- and twelfth-grade education. This gendered educational inflection point has decreased in recent years: in 2003, there were only 43 girls for every 100 boys in public high schools, but by 2013, this ratio had improved to including 83 girls for every 100 boys. Still, there have been important consequences to this differential. Bhutan's election laws, for instance, require candidates for national elections to have a minimum of a university bachelor's degree, but as of 2012, only 4.3 percent of women in Bhutan had higher secondary or tertiary educational qualifications.[22] As a result, Bhutan ranked 130th out of 142 countries for women's political empowerment in 2014.[23] The good news is that this tenth-grade cut-off of publicly funded higher secondary education was removed in 2019, which means that a Karma Yangki in tenth grade today would not have to make a choice between private high school and tailoring school.

But perhaps, as our conversation with Karma Yangki in 2017 seemed to suggest, tailoring would continue to be a compelling choice anyway. Certainly within the options available to her, becoming a tailor offered Karma Yangki a middle path, something between the high risk of aiming for and possibly failing to earn a place at university (with a further attempt to earn a place in the civil service afterwards) and the low-risk, low-reward strategy of remaining at home. Karma Yangki loved the sense of creativity enabled by the school—the opportunity to design her own work within the larger structure of the tradition: "So far I have learned to make gho, kira, Bhutanese national dress, curtain, money pocket, an altar [cloth] which we call chesham, [. . .] and thangkha." But the most important thing for her was the independence she was earning by learning a trade. "After this December I am also working," she said with great satisfaction: "I think: I will be independent! I am glad that I got into tailoring. When I finish my work and I see what I have made, I feel satisfied that I have done something. If I lived at home without doing anything, I would know nothing, I would have learned nothing." But in the midst of this tale of triumph came a secondary thought, an idea that startled those of us listening. "After two to three years," Karma continued, "I will get married and [. . .] what if my husband beats me? I think now [. . .] I feel happy that I learned something at Zorig Chusum and after next year I will be independent. It feels great." In context, the independence promised by her craft-based employability was also a guarantee of security in a world where domestic violence seemed entirely predictable.

As Nima Tshering noted:

> Bhutan is a country of gender paradoxes. It is a matrilineal society, and thus more women (60 percent) hold land registration titles than anywhere else in South Asia. Yet matrilineal inheritance patterns have increased women's responsibilities to care for aging parents, constraining their social, political and economic choices.[24]

Friends explained the traditional view to us this way: "Daughters inherit property anyway, so they don't need to be educated." But in a world in which economic opportunity is frequently linked to geographic mobility, especially rural-urban migration, matrilineal property norms have ironically contributed to keeping women poor. The Bhutan Labour Force Survey of 2012 showed women overrepresented in the informal economy (marked by unstable and unregulated low-paying jobs such as subsistence farming or domestic work). Only 6.1 percent of the female labor force holds jobs as regular paid employees, compared with 17.8 percent of the male labor force (also a low figure).[25] More tragically, in 2010, 68 percent of women were found to accept and tolerate gender-based domestic violence, such as believing that a man is justified in beating his wife or partner. Most of the women accepting gender-based domestic violence were illiterate.[26] Karma Yangki's education up to tenth grade may have contributed to her refusal to accept a beating at the hands of a future husband, but her training in tailoring was clearly for her the best means of defending herself from that potential for domestic violence.

CLASS, ECONOMICS, AND TRADITIONAL ARTS

We were wrapping up our last interviews at the school when the sculpture teacher Tashi Phuntsho suddenly spoke directly of his concerns about the future: "I worry that in ten or twenty years, these skills will not be learned by young people in Bhutan."

This comment came out of the blue. Everyone else had seemed so positive about the school and the students' subsequent careers. So I objected. "Surely not! This school seems to be thriving."

Tashi Phuntsho's response offered a simple economic analysis: "These skills can only be practiced by poor people in Bhutan. These students are poor. They are here to study because they are poor, because their parents have few resources." I glanced around the sculpture classroom and the students who understood English seemed to be nodding in agreement with their teacher. Tashi Phuntsho saw the entire nation defined in some ways by its lack of material resources: as a small, landlocked, and mountainous country, Bhutan could not develop major industry. The traditional arts (and their high level of development, one might add) were somehow intrinsically related to the difficulty of industrial development in this small mountainous land.

But Tashi Phuntsho saw that development or modernization had nonetheless arrived, and with it, a discounting of Bhutan's cultural traditions. Tashi Phuntsho acknowledged that "many dashos" might stress the importance of "preserving culture," but he noted that their actions contradicted this stated goal. ("Dasho" is an official honorific in Bhutan, but the term is also used more generally to encompass the most powerful members of Bhutanese society.) "They send their children to study abroad, in places like India, Australia. Maybe after going there, the younger generation won't feel our traditions; they may be interested in other cultures instead." In short, the fact that wealthier members of Bhutanese society now send their children to be educated abroad "can be harmful to our traditions." Shifting tastes based on interest in other cultures might disrupt the bond between production and consumption of traditional arts, a connection still—perhaps barely—keeping Bhutanese tradition alive.

We said our farewells the next morning and drove back to Kanglung along the dusty dirt road, past the old dzong-turned-monastery we could see peeking out at us through the trees, on the far ridge beyond the valley cut by the Khulong river. We stopped to watch a troop of langur monkeys moving among the trees on the right of the road; just a little further on to the left of the road, a tall and slender waterfall cast rainbow light on the surrounding vegetation. At times, basking in the warm light at odds with our expectation of late November weather, we felt as if we were traveling through a beyul, a kind of magic hidden valley, a place of power. At other times, it took all our energy to look past the environmental damages caused by the construction of a massive dam in this deep remote valley. Still, we marveled at the slender road with endless tight switchbacks down which the heavy construction equipment had to drive to get down to the river and the hydropower plant.

As we drove, I thought about Karma Phuntsho's essay on the "cultural construction of Bhutan," and another essay by Karma Dorji, entitled "The Story of Bhutanese Culture," both published in 2015, and included in the Yonphula Centenary College curriculum. Karma Phuntsho had raised issues related to Tashi Phuentsho's closing concerns: he warned that "in the current global context, the survival of cultures is also tied to their economic expedience." Karma Phuntsho argued for "shunning unethical commercialization of cultural traditions," while also asserting that "Bhutan's cultures will have to become economically viable."[27] He noted that "an increasing number of people" had begun to "drop their traditional rituals or even convert to other faiths due to the economic burden some cultural practices entail," though he offered no concrete examples of economically motivated conversion. Where the sculptor Tashi Phuentsho was focused on the tangible culture of the traditional arts, Karma Phuntsho seemed to be thinking more about performance and intangible cultural heritage. Still, both Phuntsos seemed to see only one future for Bhutan: "As people avidly seek prosperity, Bhutan will increasingly see the economisation of its cultures, and the marriage between economy and culture would determine their mutual sustainability and progress."[28] This essay seemed to outline the parameters of a pressing problem without presenting any detailed solution: what would distinguish "unethical commercialization" from a beneficial "marriage" of economy and culture? What kinds of criteria would let artisans and citizens find the resources necessary to continue valuable cultural practices? And how do we determine which practices are most valuable or beneficial in any case?

Like Karma Phuntsho, Kinley Dorji's essay also focused on the need for financing, specifically of contemporary arts, but the threat he raised was that of cultural stagnation. He considered the founding intention of the Royal Academy of Performing Arts—"to train and promote these artistic traditions in all dzongkhags, maintaining their indigenous features, so that the rural communities preserve them"—in contrast with the existing "commercialised environment with a growing number of private companies competing." Dorji noted that "sacred dances like the Durda [are] being performed in hotel restaurants as dining entertainment for tourists. Meanwhile the visual arts and crafts are co-opted at hotels to portray 'culture' for tourists." All of this seems to fall under Karma Phuntsho's category of "unethical commercialization," making a beneficial mingling of culture and commerce seem all the more elusive. Dorji acknowledged a "niche demand" for "exquisite Bhutanese handicrafts," but complained that "more than 90 percent of the handicrafts on sale in Bhutanese bazaars and handicraft shops are mass produced items from India and Nepal." This importation of handicrafts from other nations was "embarrassing." Dorji's main point, however, was the social value of the arts:

> We do not just promote art for the sake of art, literature for the sake of literature, or culture for the sake of culture. The culturalist raises critical topics for discussion. The very function of culture must be to create this space for the broad discussion of social, political, and economic issues.[29]

I had been impressed by the way traditional arts in Trashi Yangtse presented familiar cultural sight words, creating and maintaining space for cultural re-creation and shared re-collection. But what artistic forms were vibrant enough to frame the cultural sight words of today? What discussions would artists choose or be able to open?

Visiting the College for Zorig Chusum had let us explore some of the connections among the four "pillars" of Bhutan's Gross National Happiness: the way cultural preservation could support "equitable and sustainable socio-economic development" at a government-supported school helping students develop a livelihood distinct from both the (highly desired) government's civil service and the subsistence-level farming that their parents would have relied on. Development, culture, and governance all seemed mutually supportive here—though entrepreneurial development opportunities seemed to work against some gendered constraints in the larger culture, a change I wanted to applaud. It was a little more difficult to assess the extent to which the biocultural heritage of the traditional arts supported ecological diversity in Trashi Yangtse, given the remoteness of the location and the relative poverty of the student population and the surrounding community; either the remoteness or the relative poverty could have a more powerful ecologically protective effect than the arts themselves.

I also thought I could see some larger, more diffuse effects of the school. Considering the role of "good governance" in relation to the zorig chusum, for instance, emphasized the way that preservation of traditional crafts served to maintain not only the technical skills of carving or embroidery or painting, but also the cultural sight words that provided visual continuity and unity to the "imagined community" of the Bhutanese nation. At the same time, the extended community created and maintained by the zorig chusum offered possibilities for reduced consumption and environmental impact. This extended community was created not only by larger class projects such as the prayer wheel for a school in the next district, or a large and detailed painting for a temple wall, but also by the cultural patterns of re-use and conservation encouraged by apparently idiosyncratic design decisions, such as the way the "world's largest pocket" in ghos and kiras enabled people to carry small turned cups and bowls instead of using disposable items. In the end, while we had come to Trashi Yangtse to explore the tangible cultural heritage of these traditional arts, what we discovered was the inevitable interaction of tangible and intangible cultural heritage: craft objects encouraged certain patterns of behavior that in turn gave those objects meaning. I was eager to learn more about those intangible patterns.

CHAPTER SEVEN

DEMONS AND EXISTENTIAL ANXIETY

> *[To claim our] entanglement, [the condition of being both more and less than one], one would have to give up [. . .] a normative conception of subjecthood and citizenship. Or another way to put it is: you'd probably have to give up the idea of home. There are a whole range of modes of security that you would be required to relinquish in order to make this claim. [. . .] I'm not talking about relinquishing a self that you have, I'm talking about relinquishing a fantasy of self, a fantasy of fullness. It's not losing something that you have, it's disavowing or relinquishing the desire for that thing.*
>
> —poet and theorist Fred Moten, speaking at Muzeum Sztuki Nowoczesne[1]

A few days after we returned from Trashi Yangtse, I sat shivering beside the space heater in my chilly Yonphula office, shaking my head in bewilderment. There it was: the exact same phrase in yet another exam paper! In fact [. . .] I set three different exams side by side on my desk. Yes: again! The same *paragraph* in all three exams, with only minor word changes. I was sure they hadn't copied from one another; I had proctored an exam for one of my colleague Chitra's classes, so I knew how carefully the desks had been separated and how closely the students had been overseen. Flipping through exam after exam, I tried to pin down the meaning of the pattern. Groups of four to six exams hewed closely to the same sentences, in some cases to the very same paragraphs. The repetition was especially clear in the work of the weakest students. I sat back and rubbed my eyes. Finally, I understood how my students, or at least a number of them, had approached this challenging semester. They saw their job as the production of academic writing in an exam setting. They had worked in groups to create communal essays, and then the weaker students had memorized those essays in order to reproduce them on the day of the exam. No wonder they had ignored my efforts to get them to practice timed writing! If you're reproducing a memorized essay, the only timing limit is the speed of your handwriting.

In Trashi Yangtse, at the College for Zorig Chusum, I had been focusing on Bhutan's tangible (bio)cultural heritage, but the habits that define us most deeply are often intangible: habits shaping how we move through the world, which procedures we agree to and which we alter to match our own mental models and expectations. In responding to the "modern" expectations of this Master's program in English literature, for instance, my graduate students were drawing on cultural norms of collaborative work and the memorization skills fostered by a culture strong in oral traditions.

The United Nations' Convention on Safeguarding Intangible Cultural Heritage keeps lists of intangible culture worthy of protection or safeguarding. In order to be included on such a list, the intangible cultural heritage in question must

(1) be recognized by communities, groups and, in some cases, individuals as part of their cultural heritage,
(2) be transmitted from generation to generation and be constantly recreated by communities and groups in response to their environment, their interaction with nature and their history, and
(3) provide them with a sense of identity and continuity, thus promoting respect for cultural diversity and human creativity.[2]

My students' cultural adaptation to the stress of timed writing would not count as intangible cultural heritage, because the adaptation is not recognizable as heritage, nor does it provide a sense of continuity. But my students were nonetheless doing something interesting, it seemed to me: they were adapting to large-scale societal changes—the kinds of broad cultural changes that all of us may confront in the climate-altered years ahead. Societies around the world face questions about the kinds of intangible cultural practices they will work to retain, the kinds they will adapt, the kinds they will leave behind. The criteria listed above privilege (1) recognizance, (2) re-creation and responsiveness, and (3) identity and continuity. The tension between responsiveness and continuity in particular marks what seems to me a narrow path into future human thriving.

Sociologists and scholars of international relations often discuss the kind of continuity valued by the UN Convention on intangible cultural heritage in terms of "ontological security," a term invented by psychologist R. D. Laing, translated into sociology by Anthony Giddens, and more recently revised by scholars of international relations (IR). In *The Constitution of Society* (1984), Giddens first defined ontological security as "confidence or trust that the natural and social worlds are as they appear to be, including the basic existential parameters of self and social identity."[3] By 1991, in *Modernity and Self-Identity*, Giddens had expanded on the source and implications of this existential confidence. Infants, he argued, learn that they can trust their original caregivers and by extension, the world around them. Ontological security presents an emotional commitment to others and to the world, a commitment that weaves together trust, hope, and courage to exemplify and enable creativity's leap of faith.[4] But anxiety also underlies that mode of creativity: Giddens quotes Kierkegaard's description of anxiety as "the possibility of freedom" (47),[5] and describes human motives as "born of anxiety, coupled with the learning process whereby a sense of ontological security is engendered."[6] Finding the right balance between anxiety and confidence enables human beings to act efficaciously in pursuit of their own needs and pleasures. For Giddens, "the maintaining of habits and routines is a crucial bulwark against threatening anxieties," even though such routines can be "tensionful phenomen[a]" themselves.[7] In a world of unsettling changes, existential anxieties may exceed the social and individual confidence that enables creative adaptation.

Scholars of international relations have found Giddens' work helpful not only for thinking about individuals in society, but also as a framework for understanding the identity of and relationship among nation-states, and Bhutan's cultural engagements are particularly interesting here. Nation-states can be seen as providing ontological security to their citizens, or they can be understood as individuals-writ-large, seeking to maintain their own ontological security in relation to other nation-states. In the latter context, ontological security has been used to explain policy choices that seem irrational from a strictly realist perspective. Jennifer Mitzen, for instance, notes that

> [. . .] even a harmful or self-defeating relationship can provide ontological security, which means states can become attached to conflict. That is, states might actually come to prefer their ongoing, certain conflict to the unsettling condition of deep uncertainty as to the other's and one's own identity.[8]

One might say the same of internal conflicts: Bhutan's insistence on the link between national identity and national sovereignty invites an ontological security interpretation. As the Lhotshampa expulsion and the GNH Index both show, Bhutan has been deeply invested in maintaining ontological security through the preservation of national culture—but it has defined that national culture in terms of a specifically Vajrayana Buddhist tradition—and Vajrayana Buddhism rejects the illusion of a whole, continuous, stable identity, in order to stress instead the impermanence of both the world and the self.

Giddens' account of ontological security sounds oddly similar to certain Vajrayana teachings, at least as framed by US Vajrayana teachers. Giddens notes, for instance, that in daily life, most "actors take for granted existential parameters of their activity that are sustained, but in no way 'grounded' by the interactional conventions they observe."[9] Chögyam Trungpa, one of the Tibetan lamas most influential in bringing Vajrayana Buddhism to the United Kingdom and the United States, famously described his sense of Vajrayana's "crazy wisdom" as groundlessness: "The bad news is you're falling through the air, nothing to hang on to, no parachute. The good news is, there's no ground." Pema Chödrön, one of Chögyam Trungpa's best-known American students, more clearly acknowledged the difficulty of accepting this kind of groundlessness. In Pema Chödrön's teaching, groundlessness creates an existential restlessness, the angst or suffering summed up in the Buddha's first noble truth;

she suggests that the best response to groundlessness is to refrain from action we think will bring relief from that suffering. Pema Chödrön suggests we are always turning away from groundlessness, trying to avoid it through various kleshas or harmful mental states. Where Giddens observes that human beings hold anxiety at bay by maintaining a largely unconscious faith in the basic parameters of existence, Pema Chödrön invites us to confront more directly the groundlessness creating our existential anxiety.[10]

What could Bhutan teach us about ontological security in a world of impermanence, I wondered?

SPECTATORSHIP AND ENLIGHTENMENT

A few days after my grading marathon, James and I attended the local Yonphu tshechu with my colleague Chitra, the director of the M.A. program. From Kanglung, Chitra led us up the road, turning off to climb a long, steep set of cement stairs built into the hillside, leading all the way up to the stone courtyard at Yonphu, a small but ancient temple perched on the mountainside. We followed other Kanglung neighbors around the corner of the temple and tried to follow them through an open doorway, but Chitra, ahead of me, found herself blocked: women are not allowed in the Gyenkhang or inner sanctum of Vajrayana temples. Instead, the three of us turned at the edge of the courtyard, joining the queue to receive a blessing of holy water in front of the thongdrel, a massive religious appliqué hanging from the roof down the temple wall. Many of our neighbors, dressed in beautiful ghos and kiras, were gathered on the grassy slope above the courtyard, with brightly colored prayer flags flapping in the breeze behind them. At the edge of the courtyard, the mountain fell away into space; across the valley carved by the Drangme river, we could see the famous Drametse monastery standing on its promontory like a distant promise.

A young man, sitting on a blanket with his family, waved us over to him. This was one of Jeremy's teachers: a friendly, enthusiastic person who nonetheless, according to Jeremy, had picked up and thrown the class bully across the room, and who had threatened to beat the entire class unless someone confessed to stealing a student's money. (Jeremy, relying on his foreign status, had told the teacher that he would have to beat Jeremy first, and the teacher had backed down—in the aftermath of this episode, we had decided to try homeschooling for the spring semester.) Clearly there were no hard feelings; I sat down next to the teacher, on the edge of the family blanket, and he tried to give me a preview of the dances scheduled for the day. The next dance, he told me eagerly, promised to bring enlightenment to all spectators; it would show us the demons that appear in the bardo, the period between death and rebirth, which seemed to be a swirl of energy full of frightening and seductive visions. When we mistake (demonic) appearances for reality, we find ourselves trapped in a negative rebirth. This tshechu dance would help us to recognize the demons so that we could see them in the bardo without fear and panic.

We had arrived in the middle of an extended Black Hat dance. Sixteen gomchen—lay monks—in blue and red brocade wore aprons with images of demonic-looking protector deities. They circled and spun in a synchronized rhythm, swooping forward toward the ground and straightening up again as they turned, first clockwise and then counterclockwise, beating on large handheld green drums with ornately painted rims. During various pauses in the performance, three atsaras—jester-like figures—would plunge into the center of the circle and perform slapstick comedy, pretending to be drunk, knocking one another down. One wore a mask with a large red phallus growing out of its forehead; others wore loose black trousers and ghos, suggestively patched at groin and rear. In contrast, the spectacle of the Black Hat dance was beautiful, especially against the brilliant red and gold embroidery of the thongdrel, but I struggled to connect with the ritual. How did the gomchens' swinging motion work to dispel obstructive energies and facilitate enlightenment? And did the ritual connect somehow with the setting, or was Vajrayana indifferent to the environment? "Ask a monk," Jeremy's teacher told me when I asked him. But the gomchen were all busy dancing.

At the lunch break, Chitra, James, and I explored the tshechu market, sharing tea and momos in a café with walls and a roof built out of blue tarpaulins. The place was a sun trap, toasty at midday. The space filled and emptied as if the café itself were breathing warm blue air. For a brief time, I felt as if I were part of a communal body, breathing in, breathing out, along with the café and the villagers gathered for the annual ritual. As we returned to the courtyard, the young atsara with the red phallus on his forehead was strutting around amid the strains of a popular song, entertaining the gathered children until the formal dances began again (Figure 7.1)

The dance of demons from the bardo never appeared. Instead, the afternoon's performances offered a narrative of struggle and celebration. First came "The Lords of the Charnel Grounds," performed by a set of four skeleton dancers. We had seen a different version of this dance at a nearby Karma Kagyu monastery in Barshong; there, the skeleton dancers had been young boy monks who turned somersaults and tossed glittering dust into the air. Here at Yonphu, the four adult skeleton dancers brought out a small black box and placed it in the center of the courtyard. Once the skeletons had left, the three atsaras clustered around the box, eventually giving into their curiosity and prying it open, only to flee with dramatically flapping arms once the lid lay on the ground. Their exaggerated fears

Figure 7.1. One of the more striking atsaras or jester-figures at the Yonphu tshechu. December 2017.

seemed to suggest that the box had held dangerous forces—obstructive energies that their curiosity had let loose into the world.

This Bhutanese Pandora's box set up the three dances that followed: dances associated with Pema Lingpa and the monastery at Drametse, and included in the UN list of Intangible Cultural Heritage in 2008. In the first, known as the stick dance or "Gings with sticks," some twelve gomchen, wearing a set of peaceful animal masks, point out the forces of obstruction to all ten directions, then use their sticks to beat those forces (supposedly with the "power of compassion") to drive them back into the box. The idea of compassionate beating made me think again about corporal punishment in schools and what compassion really meant in Bhutan. In the sword dance, gomchen wearing wrathful red masks slice up the effigy of evil and scatter the pieces in the four directions. Then they lay down their swords. Finally, in the drum dance, dancers in dark blue masks (of protector deities) swing hand drums to proclaim the victory of Buddhism over obstructive forces. In this final dance of the day, a line of leaping bare-chested men in fiercely fanged masks moved in concert against the advancing shadows. The light and shadows, the visual extravagance of the masks and the primary-colored costumes, the bare chests and feet on the cold stones, the sounds of the drums and cymbals and chanting, seemed to me both eloquent and elusive. These dancers had practiced for months to embody the wisdom of bodhisattvas and Vajrayana adepts. Their moving meditation—this gestural story of overcoming obstructions through bodily and spiritual devotion—was especially powerful, given the beauty of the light cutting across the stones, the commitment embodied in every leap and stamp, the spectators huddling close for warmth as the sun dipped below the peaks of far-off Trashi Yangtse and Arunachal Pradesh (Figure 7.2).

A handful of honored guests had been sitting in a raised room with a plate-glass window facing the dancing and the temple proper. One of the guests paused on his way out of the special viewing room to welcome me and James. "Four hundred and forty-three years!" he said. "That is how long these dances have been performed here." That was a lot of cultural continuity, for sure.

The United Nations category of Intangible Cultural Heritage acknowledges that cultural heritage includes not only intangible

Figure 7.2. Yonphu dancers performing the Drum Dance of Drametse, December 2017.

"practices, representations, expressions, knowledge, and skills," but also "the instruments, objects, artifacts and cultural spaces associated therewith." In the case of the masked dances, this means the combination of elaborate choreography with robes and masks and props such as sticks and daggers, and even the courtyard and its relationship to the mountain's steep descent to the Drangme river or the view of the far side of the steep glacial valley. But what about the market that helps pay for the tshechu festival? What about the Bhutanese tax structures that include expectations of community labor, such as woola, that bring women of the community together to perform dances as the monastery's masked dancers take a brief rest or change their costumes? These are also components of the masked dance as intangible cultural heritage, but components that tend not to be emphasized in national submissions to UNESCO cultural judges.

In February, the man who told us how old the Yonphu tshechu was came as the honored guest for the Sherubtse College celebration of the fifth King's birthday, and James and I joined the College president and the honored guest for lunch. Some friends later told us this honored guest was a local gep, something like a mayor, and also the uncle of the queen; others said he was the previous head cook at Sherubtse. He could of course have been all of these things—and in any case he was very charming. "There is nothing like this Sherubtse dal," the honored guest asserted, as we dug into our food. "The secret is that it is boiled over a wood fire for 24 hours. No pressure cookers, no skimping on the time. *This* is Sherubtse dal!" (You see, our friends said later: we told you he was the cook!) But what intrigued me most was the intangible cultural heritage of the 24-hour wood fire defining Sherubtse dal. Would Sherubtse dal someday attain the status of cultural heritage, not at a UN level, but at a local level? I wondered. Or was even local ICH restricted to high cultural forms?

Over lunch, I mentioned now how much we had enjoyed the December tshechu, and the honored guest described how excited he had been as a child, to come to that Yonphu tshechu, how he would be climbing the mountain with his family, and when they heard the horns, the dungchen announcing the start of the tshechu, his heart would leap with joy at their near arrival. His enthusiasm for the festival, decades later, was contagious.

"But here's what I don't understand," I said:

"The embroidered imagery of the thongdrel, that massive fabric portrait, and the dances: how are we supposed to become enlightened just by seeing them if we don't understand what the images mean? We kept asking people what things meant but no one could or would tell us. Is there some book where these things are explained?"

The honored guest shook his head, smiling at my simplicity. "Some things," he said, "you cannot learn from books. You must open your heart. Find new ways of learning."

This was how my students often spoke too; I was never quite sure how to take such oracular pronouncements.

DEMONS RECOGNIZED AND UNRECOGNIZABLE

"We met a man with a demon today," Jeremy said as I tipped a pile of minced onions into sizzling oil.

"What?" I said, assuming I had misheard.

"A man with a demon," he repeated.

"Not a demon," James said. "An autistic man."

"But the monks told him he had a demon inside of him." Jeremy stuck out his jaw, holding his ground.

"Really? The monks?" I felt a twinge of dismay at this monastic diagnosis. My brother Lobsang used to joke about the similarities and differences between Western and Tibetan approaches to mental health, but he had been trained in both traditions. And I didn't think Lobsang had ever told anyone they had a demon inside—though of course that diagnosis would sound different in New York than it did in Kanglung.

"He was spinning and spinning the prayer wheels. You know: on the little bridge by the college entrance. Spinning and spinning. Hard, like he couldn't stop."

"I think the physical action gave him some relief," James added.

"Stimming," I said.

"What's stimming?" Jeremy asked.

"What Dad said," Zoë answered, bringing me a pile of chopped eggplant to add to the now-burnt onions. "Self-stimulation. For relief."

After years as a social worker in New York City helping homeless men who often suffered from schizophrenia and drug addiction, Lobsang used to say that the DSM (The Diagnostic and Statistical Manual of Mental Disorders) listed 410 diagnoses, but Buddhist traditions of 52 mental factors with wholesome and unwholesome variations offered 84,000 possible diagnoses—or, from a more traditional Buddhist perspective, 84,000 paths to enlightenment. But even in Kanglung, I wondered, how would "you have a demon inside you" compare to being told you have depression or anxiety or autism or OCD? I was also intrigued by the challenge of discerning what was and was not a demon.

Vajrayana Buddhists sometimes talk about "skillful means," the idea that the Buddha adapted his teaching to the capacities of very different kinds of people. In Kanglung, some friends had tried to explain demons to me as an example of skillful means, but I found this baffling.

"What does a demon have to do with skillful means?" I demanded of Sonam one afternoon. Other days, he had fielded Vajrayana questions while watering the vegetables he grew outside the shop, or chatting with college students, or working on Dechen's mobile banking business. Today when I came to get chickpeas from Dechen's shop, I had found Sonam working on arrows near the shop door—positioning an arrow shaft in a vise as if to straighten it. Archery was the national sport and a local obsession, Sonam an expert fletcher. I didn't think he'd mind a brief interruption of the arrow work: "How do demons—or protector deities draped in skulls—serve as an example of skillful means?"

Sonam finished sighting down another arrow shaft, set it in a pile of others to repair, and then smiled at me. "Well, imagine you are someone who experiences the world very concretely," Sonam said:

> You might need and appreciate the boundaries set by protector deities. Very scary. You are motivated by rules, and by fear of breaking those rules. You need that clarity. Another person—let's say James—is committed to self-discipline. He likes to structure his life, but he sees the dharma in terms of psychological or moral development. You need outer structure, he seeks inner structure.

Outer/inner: I had heard these categories before as part of a three-part division of teachings and interpretations, in which principles of moderation and monastic discipline (often associated with Sravakayana or Theravada Buddhism) were seen as external teachings; the path of the bodhisattva associated with Mahayana Buddhism was seen as internal teachings, and Vajrayana's esoteric tantric methods were seen as secret teachings. Within Vajrayana itself, though, different teachings or imagery were sometimes described as having separate outer, inner, and secret meanings. I started to ask about the secret meaning of demons, but a group of college students arrived, and Sonam went off to help them manage a series of mobile bank transactions.

Another day, Zoë and I were walking down the farm road, chatting and looking out over the terraced rice fields, a whitewashed chorten draped in prayer flags in primary colors, the river far below, the slopes of the mountain on the far side of the valley. Somewhat more ominously, the cornfield just above the road contained a pole from which a doll hung, a rope around its neck, bouncing in the wind. I hoped the doll was there to scare off monkeys, like the stuffed tiger toys we had seen on the other side of the hill (Figure 7.3), rather than as a figure in some scary Bon ritual. Glancing at the road ahead, further down the slope of the mountain, I noticed two small girls, presumably sisters or close friends, about three or four years old. They stood absolutely still, staring at us.

I smiled at the little girls, hoping to put them at ease. But they remained stiff, frozen in place. As we came closer, their eyes grew wider and they clutched each other. They looked terrified, ready to bolt.

I nudged Zoë. We slowed our steps. Together we smiled broadly, trying to seem harmless and friendly.

Faces blank and pale, the girls stepped back off the road, clutching each other. Then the slightly larger girl reached out for the smaller one's hand, and they scuttled sideways, moving up the slope past us, keeping

Figure 7.3. A stuffed tiger serving as a "scare monkey" (like a scarecrow).

their eyes on us until they were well clear, at which point they ran for safety, moving at high speed past the turn in the road that hid us from their sight.

"What was that about?" asked Zoë. We were wearing Western clothes—hiking boots, jeans, fleece jackets—which usually placed us in the category of harmless foreigners, but perhaps these particular girls had never seen any Westerners. Ever.

"I think they thought we were demons," I said, as we turned together to climb the road back toward the guesthouse. Maybe to those girls our pale skin was as eerie as the blue skin of Mahakala or Chana Dorje, my straw-colored hair and Zoë's bright golden-red hair additional signs of the supernatural.

In 2008, Kunzang Choden published an in-depth account of some strategies used to manage "malevolent spirits" in the Tang valley of central Bhutan.[11] Choden's account contrasted the shi'dre, a malevolent spirit of the dead, with the gson'dre, a malevolent spirit of the living, and the rgyal po, or a haughty or kingly spirit. A shi'dre might be produced if the officiant conducting death rites lacked the learning or the power to help the conscious principle make the transition to the next bardo. Gson'dre, by contrast, refers to an evil spirit housed within the body of a living person—that living person is seen as "highly ambitious, blatantly envious and fiercely competitive."

According to Choden, diviners in the Tang valley could identify the presence of a malevolent spirit using prayer beads or dice, or the folding of a man's gho. Once a spirit had been identified and categorized, it could be placated, often by offering food, but only after midday, since feeding a spirit in the morning would increase its powers. Tea and alcohol were usually included in the offering, but other foods would depend on the desires of a particular spirit. Some spirits were to be honored and treated with great formality; others were to be scolded and treated harshly.

Once food was prepared, an appropriate seating arrangement would be made (to align with the degree of respect required), and the food would be served using appropriate utensils. Then the food would be taken out of the house and scattered. The person feeding the spirits would say, "Whoever you are and where ever you have come from, eat, eat, and drink and drink." If dogs and ravens came to take the food, that was a sign that the appropriate spirits had appeared. But all the spirits in the valley might arrive to consume the food, so an experienced feeder of demons would say: "Those who are responsible, come forward, those who are not responsible move backwards." After the feeding, the person who scattered the food then had to spit three times onto the ground to ensure that the spirits did not follow them back into the house. Sometimes a feeding would have to be repeated before a patient experienced significant relief; sometimes no amount of feeding would bring improvement, and then it would be decided that more than one malevolent spirit was involved and the food didn't reach the right spirits. Stronger action—a ritual dedicated to the ruler of spirits—would be required.

The attribution of demons to a household or a person usually came from outside that household or person. Instead of announcing "I have a demon afflicting me," people would more commonly assert something like "A demon from your household is causing us problems." People would scatter food for the demons attached to other households. Sometimes the demon-ridden person or household would joke about this, but sometimes they would be angry and tell the food scatterers that they should give the family the food directly. The ritual of feeding the demons seems designed to make visible the cost to others of a given household's demonic (aggressively competitive, haughty) behavior. Apparently, we don't recognize the demons of our own household, only those from elsewhere.

Perhaps it is unsurprising, then, that this kind of food-based exorcism ritual seems to have played a part in the Lhotshampa expulsion. Rosalind Evans, interviewing Lhotshampa residents of a camp on the Nepali border, spoke to one young boy who described what happened when the first family left his village: "the army came and used roti flour and banged gongs to force the family out. The Drukpas use the same method to chase away evil spirits."[12] The villagers were not the demons who needed to be driven out with roti flour and gongs—but they were the ones left stationary and defenseless against military exorcism. Being a stranger, a demon, could be dangerous in Bhutan.

And yet, to our unpracticed eyes, Vajrayana protector-deities looked a lot like demons, too. This might be where the secret meaning of demons came in, I thought.

In the middle of the fall, we had gone to Rangjung, a town about an hour away, to visit a Nyingma monastery and monastic school where an English-speaking monk offered to give us a tour of the temple and all its imagery. The monk, named Karma, spoke very quickly and many of the explanations went by a little too fast for us to follow, but as we moved around the temple, we paused briefly to discuss the figure of Vajrakilaya, which we would soon see portrayed at the College of Zorig Chusum. Vajrakilaya is a figure with four legs, six arms, three heads, and wings. In the image we were looking at, all three heads sported a third eye and a headpiece of three small skulls above their foreheads. Vajrakilaya was also pictured in yab-yum posture, which is to say, holding his consort Vajrakumara, during what a formal description would call "sexual congress"—her legs wrapped around his waist, mid-intercourse. Vajrakumara had her own skull head-dress, and ten more heads were hung, apparently as trophies, either from the tiger skin around her lower half or peeking out from between the arms of the embracing figures. One of the lower heads seemed to be weeping blood as its eyes fell out of their sockets (Figure 7.4)

"In reality, nothing is there!" Karma said, cheerfully. This had been something of a refrain. Karma kept showing us gruesome images and

Figure 7.4. An image of Vajrakilaya on the walls of the Rangjung Woesel Choeling Lhakang.

then telling us that nothing was there. Perhaps this was the effect aimed at by the dance displaying demons in the bardo.

But obviously the image *was* there, I thought stubbornly; metaphors carry excess meaning, and they demand that we grapple with that meaning. Eyeballs dripping blood meant something or the artist wouldn't bother to paint them.

James started to ask a question about the Vajrakilaya figure: "What is it about this demon in particular—?"

Karma interrupted. "We have a prophecy, actually. We say that gods—our meditation deities—and demons are different, but they are the same. According to our needs, they come in different forms. Sometimes they come as deities, sometimes as teachers, sometimes as demons."

Perhaps the demonic appearance was the outer reality; the teacherly presence the inner reality; the deity the secret meaning. I wondered whether demonic foreigners, like ourselves or the exiled Lhotshampa, could also appear as teachers rather than demons—or what particular frame of reference would allow us to be seen that way. How much insecurity could the average Bhutanese citizen withstand, in this time of many changes?

CHANGE AS A THREAT TO ONTOLOGICAL SECURITY

Soon after our arrival in Kanglung, Zoë had pointed out that Bhutanese national dress established a rigid gender opposition: "Men wear ghos and women wear kiras. But what would a gender-fluid person wear?" Western clothing, it appeared. Over the next months, we saw various Sherubtse students on the streets of Kanglung developing a more mixed aesthetic: young men wearing t-shirts and jeans along with eye makeup and fingernail polish; young women wearing sweatshirts and sweatpants without makeup or polish. Since these students had to wear national dress to their classes, we imagined quick before- and after-class changes occurring in dorm rooms (hostels, as they were called in Bhutan) all over Kanglung. One more point in favor of modernity over tradition, as far as my kids were concerned—but how did this kind of fluidity relate to ontological security in Bhutan? Considering that gay sex was decriminalized in Bhutan only in December of 2020, the wearing or not wearing of national dress shaded into some weighty questions about legal status and social norms.

Karma Phuntsho in his 2015 essay on "The Cultural Construction of Bhutan" raises other concerns, noting that only a minority of Bhutanese men wear a gho most of the time now. "Would wearing a gho once a month," Phuntsho asks, "suffice for someone to be considered a Bhutanese in his dress culture?" He then turns to Bhutanese women's relationship to the kira, wondering not about the percentage of wearing time but rather how much of the garment must persist for it to retain its essential kira-nature. Phuntsho notes:

> [. . .] the term kira has become synonymous with half-kira, which resembles an Indian lungi or a Thai sarong in size. Just as the top half of kira has been truncated, what would it be like if the bottom quarter is curtailed? Would it be a kira or a skirt? When will it stop being a kira and its essence of being a Bhutanese costume cease?

This question is accompanied by an illustration apparently sketched by Karma Phuntsho himself, in which the woman's appearance and posture changes along with her garment. The woman wearing the full kira looks pleased and powerful and uninterested in the viewer; the woman in the half-kira, looking directly at the viewer, seems more tentative; the woman in the quarter-kira, like a Western skirt, looks still less happy, and the figure in the mini-kira gazes at the ground in apparent dejection or possibly even shame (Figure 7.5).

Why did the essay break out of words to offer this particular implied narrative about women, national dress, and (un)happiness, I wondered. Given that a man's gho only comes to the knee, why emphasize the amount of coverage a kira provides? At the time Karma Phuntsho's essay was published, the half-kira seemed stable enough as a form. Outside this essay, I never saw a knee-length "kira-skirt" in Bhutan, though I did see plenty of women wearing Western-style jeans or sweatpants in contexts where a kira was not required. The mini-kira pictured here seemed to say more about a man's imaginings than it did about contemporary female practices.

Figure 7.5. The kira evolution: When will the kira stop and skirt begin? Reproduced from Karma Phuntsho, "The cultural construction of Bhutan: An unfinished story," *Druk Journal* 1, no. 1 (2015).

Beyond gender norms, we might remember that Buddhist dharma traditionally insists on the emptiness of form and on the idea of non-identity or dependent arising. No quality exists independently of any other quality. A cloud, for instance, cannot exist without a mix of air/wind and moisture and the sun whose heat creates the cycle of evapotranspiration. How does this idea of interdependence apply to cultural or national identity? Karma Phuntsho nods to "the Buddhist idea of non-self or absence of self-existence," but slides from that idea to "contemporary theories of cultural identity as combination of various cultural identifiers" to assert that a "single factor or an identifier such as citizenship, religious faith or political allegiance do[es] not define the cultural identity of a Bhutanese person." But Phuntsho's application of this principal of "no self" to national identity paradoxically circles back to the traditional, often material, cultural practices that visibly define (western) Bhutanese cultural identity: "What ultimately will define the Bhutanese identity if Bhutanese stop wearing the traditional dress, eating Bhutanese cuisine, speaking Bhutanese languages, reading and writing Bhutanese literature and observing traditional social events and customs?" Instead of arguing that material props and immaterial traditions are irrelevant for an enlightened understanding of existence, Karma Phuntsho seems to accept the primacy of Bhutanese cultural identity, arguing that "the cultural facets of a person form the bedrock of personal identity" and that "cultural ideas and practices serve as the social cement to hold societies together." Words like "bedrock" and "cement" make cultural identity seem powerfully fixed and determinate. But surely Buddhism's broader insistence on impermanence suggests that Bhutanese national identity might itself be a part of the impermanent phenomenological world. Against this philosophical embrace of impermanence, however, there remain our existing investments in fixed norms of gender, sexuality, and national identity.

During my meeting with Karma Ura in Thimphu, the dasho kindly agreed to share with me a copy of a book chapter he had written for an American audience that I couldn't easily access from Bhutan. This "Dialog on the Destiny of Nations" (2013) stages a highly stylized conversation among six imaginary figures walking the Snowman trail in northern Bhutan, one of the most challenging treks in the country.[13] The dialog is not a level playing field—none of the speakers are women or Lhotshampa, and of the six speakers, one in particular (Tantric Lama) gets most of the good lines—but it does allow for some occasionally comic or whimsical back and forth. At one point in the conversation, Skeptic Youth complains:

> Tantric Lama talks glibly about self-afflictions and dissolving the self. What are they? Do you mean all the particularities that make me what I am in terms of gender, communal affinity, cultural heritage, political leanings, biographic memories, and emotional patterns should be dissolved, and I should transcend them? How can I? They are the basis of me.

Skeptic Youth here summarizes one significant challenge blocking a broader embrace of Buddhist philosophy, both for individuals and for a broader sense of national identity.[14]

Tantric Lama acknowledges the basic difficulty. "You are right," he tells Skeptic Youth: "Dissolving the self, without being nihilistic, may entail transcending the particularities that give you your identity.

Personal identity is vital at an ordinary level, but should be increasingly abandoned as we try to achieve a state of enlightenment." Tantric Lama urges his companions to consider "shedding constituents of ordinary personal identity and acquiring another perspective. It should be a perspective from nobody's points of view, yet a composite of everybody's point of view. That is what I meant by ethics." He suggests to Skeptic Youth in particular that "a life guided and led by such a composite viewpoint ultimately brings happiness to all, including yourself." This composite view created by shedding the attribute of personal identity is presented as a Buddhist ideal—something more fluid than the reliance on fixed "Bhutanese" cultural referents described by Karma Phuntsho. Still, the absence of even stylized figures of women or minority community members undercuts Tantric Lama's implicit claim to be able to hold or articulate the composite vision to which he aspires—the view of a "hero with a thousand eyes." I found myself wondering what a female tantric lama might bring to the Snowman dialogue.

VAJRAYANA TRANSFORMATIONS AND FEMALE ADEPTS

On Christmas Day 2018, our friend Chimi Dorji took us to climb up to Bhutan's most famous monastery: Taktsang or Tiger's Nest, the name encapsulating the story of Guru Rinpoche landing on the cliff while riding on the back of a tiger, a form adopted by his female student and consort Yeshe Tshogyel for the purpose of their journey. The trailhead to Taktsang was on the road north from Paro toward Jomolhari, further out of town than we had anticipated. As we drew close to the turning point for Taktsang, Chimi pointed out the school he had attended as a boy, and he told us the story of Taktsang burning, the fire probably started by a butter lamp, back in 1998.

"We could see the fire from the school," Chimi told us. "Actually, you could see the fire from most places in the valley. But they released us all from our classes so that we could go and join the bucket brigade."

"How long did it take to get water up that mountain?" I asked.

"Oh, it was hopeless," said Chimi. "I didn't join—I just was glad to be let out of class. Some of my classmates joined, but Taktsang was already in flames: there was no way that we would have been able to stop the fire."

The massive parking lot at the trailhead underscored the number of people traveling the path each year, but we were off season, and the trail was not crowded. Mule trains carried the faint of heart or body up the first part of the trail, but we were eager for the hike. The dry, packed earth of the path wound around various boulders; the pines lining the way opened up periodically onto views across the valley floor far below. Often, the angle of the mountain ridges blocked the houses and smallholdings of Paro from view, so it seemed as if we were looking down on uninhabited wilderness.

As we climbed the mountain, I thought about female Vajrayana masters, like Yeshe Tshogyel, of "Tiger's Nest" fame. But I also found myself thinking about more subtle Vajrayana transformations: emotional or cognitive shifts rather than body shifting from woman to tiger.

In Trongsa, in the Royal Heritage Museum, I had been struck by an exhibit of the five Tathagata Buddha families. The exhibit, consisting of different colored Buddhas with explanatory labels, offered a method for transforming harmful mental states or delusions into corresponding strengths. A blue Buddha, for instance, represented the Vajra family of Buddhas: he was associated with the east and with the klesha (the poison or harmful mental state) of anger. In Sanskrit, vajra means diamond or lightning; in this context, it seemed to register anger's hardness and force. The antidote to anger was patience, which was supposed to transform anger into "mirror-like wisdom," with the mirror exposing the non-inherent-existence of all phenomena, including anger. Tempered by the antidote of patience, anger offers us the gift of clarity.

A yellow Buddha (from the Ratna family, meaning jewel or precious gem) was associated with the south, with earth, and with the klesha of pride. The antidote to greed or prideful excess was equanimity: seeing the commonality of all phenomena was supposed to create the wisdom of equality. A red Buddha (from the Padma or Lotus family) was associated with fire, the west, and the klesha of desire, attachment, or selfishness. The antidote to red desire was compassion or, in some texts, inquisitiveness. Desire or grasping could be transformed through compassion and curiosity into a discriminating wisdom that perceives the uniqueness of all phenomena. A green Buddha symbolized the Karma family, associated with the north, with air or wind, and with the klesha of jealousy. Karma means work or action as well as the effects of actions (and their associated intentions). Here, the promise was that jealousy could be transformed by joy into "all-accomplishing wisdom." A white Buddha was associated with space and the klesha of ignorance. The antidote to ignorance is teaching the dharma, symbolized by the wheel of dharma, and the result of that teaching (and learning) is an all-accommodating or all-pervasive wisdom, sometimes described as bare, non-conceptualizing awareness, the base of all other wisdom.

These promises of transformation are hard to hold onto, even pared down to their bare components:

- anger plus patience equals clarity;
- pride plus equanimity produces a recognition of equality;
- (selfish) desire plus compassionate curiosity highlights the uniqueness of all;
- jealousy plus joy leads to accomplishment;
- ignorance plus dharma creates awareness.

By the time we reached the gates of Taktsang, I had decided transformation was more than I could manage.

Beyond the gate and up a narrow set of stone steps, I found the actual monastery of Taktsang disorienting. We had heard so many stories of this place, but it was hard to get properly positioned in the cavernous dark. Which was the cave where Padmasambhava and Yeshe Tshogyel had first landed? Which was the cave where Guru Rinpoche spent three years meditating? Where was the statue that had spoken to the first Yonphula Rinpoche? It was supposedly the only thing to have survived multiple fires that had razed Taktsang over the years. Which was the cave holding scripture written in gold dust combined with a lama's powdered bones? The chill seeping up through my socks made me think of Vajrayana masters generating their own heat, with precious little body or food to keep them alive.

On the way up the mountain, I had been thinking of Bhutan's early adepts—not just Guru Rinpoche and Yeshe Tsogyel, but also Milarepa, the crazy poet, Machig Labdrön, creator of the first widespread teaching to emerge from Tibet (rather than traveling from India into Tibet) and others—but now I found myself thinking about the later builders of the temple complex: the people who shaped the spaces we were now moving through. Sonam Gyeltshen, a Nyingma lama from Tibet built the first sanctuary here in the fourteenth century, but the main temple was constructed by Tenzin Rabgye, an early successor to the Zhabdrung. For his part, the Zhabdrung had visited Taktsang during the midst of many battles against (other) invading Tibetan forces. He came to call on Padmasambhava and other Vajrayana deities for their help in dispelling Tibetan invaders from Bhutan. Was Taktsang more meaningful as a place of Vajrayana practice or of nation-building?

Chilled and unsettled, I struggled to understand the logic of the temple complex. Its most obvious feature was that the more important spiritual sites lay on the inner side of the temple, against the cold cliff face. By contrast, a shrine to a deity of good fortune faced outward, its windows offering an amazing view out over Paro valley (Figure 7.6). From this angle, distant buildings on the floor of the Paro river valley looked

Figure 7.6. Taktsang or Tiger's Nest Monastery, at an angle emphasizing its location among Paro's pine forests. Structures on the valley bottom are just out of sight.

like grains of rice scattered on the folds of a piece of dark cloth. The dark green of the forests lightened into cultivated fields at the river bottoms and darkened into purples and blues on the upper sides of the distant mountains. Climbing the mountain, I had wanted to connect with Bhutan's spiritual masters, but now that we had arrived, all I longed for was the warm beauty of that outer-facing shrine.

Soon, the rest of the family was ready to go. As we left the main temple and started across the bridge over the canyon, I stopped to visit a small building commemorating Yeshe Tsogyel's meditation cave (Figure 7.7). The building stood beside a slender waterfall that leapt from the cliff at the path's final turn. Many damp and mossy steps led up to the shrine; the others were too tired for the brief ascent, so I went alone. The inside of the small building was dark; rough boards shaped a crude altar with a single candle flickering before a framed image of Yeshe Tsogyel. Even colder than Taktsang, this tiny space encapsulated Yeshe Tsogyel's place in the story of Taktsang—a site as extreme as Guru Rinpoche's lonely meditation cave, but less admired, less visited.

In most versions of the story, Yeshe Tsogyel is the one who turned herself into a tiger to fly Guru Rinpoche to this cliff. I thought the Tiger's Nest should be, by its very name, her place. And yet the story is all about the Guru; she appears only as a kind of accessory. I touched a small ngultrum bill to my forehead, imbuing it with a prayer of thanksgiving for Vajrayana women's learning and teaching, and laid it on the altar. Mindful of my family and Chimi waiting below, I didn't linger, except briefly at the top of the steps outside the door to the building. I was happy to have that moment to myself; Yeshe Tsogyel's place might be icy cold, but perched above Taktsang itself, it provided an amazing sense of space and depth. Like the half-frozen waterfall beside it, this meditation site seemed to generate both rainbows and ice patterns, beauty and bitter cold.

On the way down the mountain, I turned over in my mind what I knew about Yeshe Tsogyel and her later incarnation, Machig Labdrön. (Padmasambhava supposedly predicted Yeshe Tsogyel would be reborn as Machig Labdrön, making Machig's teachings an extension of Yeshe Tsogyel's spiritual development.) While Yeshe Tsogyel gave the Tiger's Nest its name in the ninth century, Machig Labdrön came to live and teach on this same cliff in the eleventh and twelfth centuries.

Figure 7.7. Yeshe Tshogyel's "Lion cave," to the side of Taktsang.

According to the stories, Machig's family recognized her as a dakini, a female figure of enlightened energy, from birth, and they supported her early spiritual education. By the age of eight, Machig was able to recite all 100,000 lines of the long-form Heart Sutra. But when the young savant was about twenty, a teacher challenged her to go beyond reciting and explaining the Heart Sutra, to internalize it. In meditating upon a chapter on demons, Machig suddenly grasped the deeper meaning of the sutra. She started wearing beggar's clothing, associating with lepers, living in charnel grounds, detached from her society.

One day, in a state of deep meditation, Machig floated through some temple walls and into a tree at the edge of a lake that belonged to a naga, a demon. In response to her intrusion, the naga attacked her with the gathered forces of many demons. Instead of responding with fight or flight, Machig offered her body as a feast to the host of nagas, in a gesture which was codified as the practice of Chöd. The full ritual involves drums, wind instruments made from human femurs, and an imagined feast in which practitioners visualize their bodies being cut up, cooked by internal combustion, expanding like the biblical meal of loaves and fishes, until an unending soup of blood and human flesh satisfies the hunger of all the gathered ghouls.[15] Quite a striking practice.

Some years after her big moment of insight, Machig retreated to a cave known as Zangri Khangmar or the Red House of Copper Mountain, Copper Mountain being another name for the cliffside where we were walking. Her reputation spread widely, and the teaching of Chöd became accepted as the first Buddhist teaching to come out of Tibet to India, instead of traveling from India to Tibet.

Machig seems important to me not just as an early female Vajrayana adept, but because her practice of feeding demons flips the script on human defensiveness and ontological security. Her radical generosity in the face of territorial battles at once underscores pre-existing Buddhist norms and extends that Buddhist model to a whole new level of engagement. Demons or devils are, after all, almost as common in Buddhist tradition as in Bhutanese culture. In traditional accounts of the Buddha's life, for instance, demons appear just before his moment of enlightenment; a demon called Mara tried to distract Siddhartha as he was on the brink of enlightenment under the bodhi tree. But when Mara's soldiers shoot arrows at Siddhartha, Siddhartha turns those arrows into flowers. In some versions of the story, Mara sends daughters rather than arrows against Siddhartha, but the daughters' attempts to seduce Siddhartha go astray as well. Daughters or arrows, Mara's weapons of distraction traditionally include the three main kleshas: desire (or pleasure-seeking), aversion (avoidance or aggression), and ignorance (or maintaining the status quo). Mara himself is often understood as the fear of death.

Machig Labdrön's teaching is almost the antithesis of the kind of ritual practiced in the Tang valley. Unlike the villagers who aim to feed a particular malevolent spirit in order to drive it away (making sure no other spirits come and take the food instead), Machig calls all hungering hordes to come and feast on her body, which will never run short of material to ease their hunger. And unlike the soldiers driving Lhotshampa villagers away in defense of a fixed sense of national identity, Machig Labdrön reframed the "devil" not as the other, but rather as the "fixation to a self." Against more conventional understandings of the conflict between Siddhartha and Mara, Machig argued that a devil

> [. . .] is not some actual great big black thing that scares and petrifies whomever sees it. A devil is anything that obstructs the achievement of freedom [. . .] Most of all, there is no greater devil than this fixation to a self. So until this ego-fixation is cut off, all the devils wait with open mouths.[16]

No greater devil than the fixation to a self: scholars of ontological security should all be required to read Machig Labdrön, I thought, wondering how she would have responded to Karma Ura's "Skeptic Youth." Given a choice between the monumental nationalism of Taktsang and Machig's radical humility and generosity, I at least would follow Machig every time. Or I would like to believe I would—though I doubted I would last very long in charnel grounds and other haunted spaces.

One story of Padmasambhava describes King Indrabhuti of Oddiyana not only as the Guru's adoptive father, but also his first, somewhat fussy student. Instead of following the dharma where it led, the King wanted a path to enlightenment that didn't involve giving up too much of his existing life. And who could blame him? Abandoning our familiar ways cuts against our longing for continuity and ontological security.

Still, Vajrayana as a philosophical system insists on impermanence, and ontological insecurity seems an unavoidable logical consequence of impermanence. If we take seriously the notion of change and impermanence as underlying features of our lives, the challenge becomes finding or developing better ways to manage our own resistance to uncertainty. Vajrayana offers multiple strategies for managing our existential anxieties and insecurities, strategies ranging from what Western psychologists might call exposure therapy (encountering demonic figures through imagery and ritual dance in order to be able to see them without fear), through conceptual transformation (the Tathagata transformation of mental poisons, difficult emotions, into wisdom) and allegorical resolution (as in the dance of the Gings with sticks, with knives, and with drums, in which dancers identify obstructive energies, cut them to pieces and send them to the place they belong, then celebrate their victory—or as in the Tang valley feeding of demons, where literal food is consumed by wild dogs and other animals embodying demonic energies); to the correction of cognitive errors (as when Machig Labdrön taught that demons do not exist independently, but only as an outgrowth of human failure to cut off our egotistical self-defense). Recognizing these strategies, however, is far easier than putting them into practice. Our time in Bhutan was speeding by and we still had so much more to learn and to practice.

CHAPTER EIGHT

FOREIGNER, IMMIGRANT, LOCAL DEITY

Back in Kanglung in early March, I scuffed my feet into my hiking boots and swilled down my last sip of instant coffee; I looped the always-knotted laces around the hooks at my ankles. Already out the door, I called back to Jeremy to hurry; he wanted to walk up to Yonphula with me for the day, but I had to get there in time to teach.

I eased up the Sherubtse College road, watching over my shoulder for Jeremy to appear. On the right, the College president's family was extending their veggie patch. Someone in the Director of Academic Affair's household had dyed yarn and hung it to dry in the yard. Someone was spinning the large prayer wheel at the College temple; I could hear the deep interior bell tolling as the wheel completed each rotation. On my right, the Biology professor was burning cypress branches on her raised platform for morning incense. I waved to her and she waved back; when we had met out on the hills the week before, she had tried to explain to me the different plants she gathered for healing and ritual purposes.

Jeremy caught up with me as I crossed the national highway, here just a thin ribbon of tarmac. Together, we walked toward "the boys' hostels"—dorms for male college students. The tarmac ran out as the road switchbacked behind the boys' dorms, cutting between the two archery stands of the college archery field. When an archery match was in session, I tended to run inelegantly up or down the road: Bhutanese archers are highly skilled, but also prone to shooting while drunk. Just above the roofed archery pavilion, where archers gathered to share food and drink during a long day's competition, we turned off the road, up onto a path you wouldn't notice if you didn't already know it was there. Now we were really on the "short cut" up to Yonphula Centenary College.

Jeremy and I agreed to time the commute by the chortens, the Buddhist monuments we passed. Chortens, symbolizing the presence of the Buddha and commemorating major moments in his life, still baffled me: why build monuments to materialize the Buddha's spiritual presence, when so much of Vajrayana Buddhism seems to push toward a freedom from material constraints? Regardless of this kind of paradox, the first, best-maintained set of chortens on our path were just 15 minutes from the guesthouse, and they served as a potent reminder of the power of Bhutanese piety: dozens of community members working together to keep these chortens whitewashed and gilded, prayer flags replaced as they decayed in the wind (Figure 8.1)

I pushed Jeremy to move faster as we climbed from the first chorten to the second through a different microclimate: a dark woodland, with ferns growing five feet tall, groves of trees full of birds I tentatively identified as white-crested laughing thrushes, a creek where jungle fowl, gaudy ancestors of the domesticated chicken, sometimes lingered in their red, green and blue iridescence. Here the trees were thick-trunked and old, with epiphytes—non-parasitic plants—growing on their large horizontal

Figure 8.1. Partial view of triple chorten above Kanglung, close to Sherubtse College boys' hostels, facing down the mountain on a stormy day.

Figure 8.2. A sample of the microclimate between the first and second chortens on the shortcut to Yonphula.

limbs, some quite low to the ground (Figure 8.2). I had seen barking deer in these woods, though I heard them more often than I saw them, with a sound closer to what I think of as a crow's call than anything I would associate with either a deer or a bark. This was Jeremy's favorite part of the hike, this semi-tropical microclimate.

I checked the time anxiously as we took a bread and water break at the second chorten. Thirty minutes in. Jeremy and I were both sweating from the climb, so we dropped our backpacks and sat on the spongy turf. This chorten hadn't seen a coat of whitewash for a long time; its stones were starting to fall, especially on the western side. I always thought it should be vaguely melancholy, this visible decay of faith, and yet I still experienced it as a quiet refuge, the small clearing gradually taking back the stone of the chorten (Figure 8.3).

For a couple of weeks in the winter, I had passed a family cutting wood here, on the edge of the chorten's clearing. The children swung on the low limbs of the trees while the mother sawed wood and loaded up a basket with small logs to carry home. Part of me felt like I should offer to

Figure 8.3. The second chorten on the shortcut to Yonphula, pictured in August, during the monsoon.

help carry the firewood; part of me wanted to object to the whole project. Didn't this family know, as I knew from reading scholarly American papers, that they weren't supposed to be cutting wood near a sacred site?[1]

The sacred site was supposed to be an ecological *refugium*: religious faith protecting a multitude of other species from human encroachment.

Of course foreign scholars are not facing the challenge of keeping their family warm, and this chorten is clearly suffering from human inattention—which may signal to local residents that its sacred power has waned.

Jeremy could have used a longer rest, but the clock was ticking. "What do you think we'll see ahead?" I asked, coaxing him back to his feet. Between the second and third chortens, I had occasionally seen a Himalayan fox, or a giant flying squirrel, 90 percent tail, vanishing into the underbrush. Maybe even a red panda, though again, not with enough clarity to be certain. A field of bracken fern provided food and shelter for barking deer and birds of many kinds: flycatchers, forktails, lots of species I couldn't identify.

"Hoophoe!" said Jeremy, pointing to the bird with the striped crest, a species that visited the guesthouse too. "And look at all the butterflies!"

The path took a 90-degree turn between two farms; Jeremy and I paused beside the worn grey wood of an old manidhar—a tall post with a long white prayer flag erected to mark the first anniversary of someone's death—to look back over the valley. We could see for miles down the side of the mountain to the Drangme Chuu, the longest-running river in Bhutan. Today skies were clear enough to see the snowy peaks of the Indian Himalayas over the next mountain range.

The last chorten, 45 minutes from home, was a mani wall, an older style monument (Figure 8.4). Ferns and grasses grew close around its base and out of its crumbling upper stones. Flat stones that once held mantras gleamed blankly in the sun. Both the existence and the gradual decay of the three chortens suggested that this shortcut up the mountain had once been a significant footpath, though it was now less traveled. Most people now drove from Kanglung to Yonphula on a stretch of the paved national highway. But this last, most neglected chorten was also close to a farm road—a dirt road cutting horizontally across the mountain—reminding us about the impact of roads and economic development on Bhutanese society. New roads had enabled many modern conveniences: in this case, the construction of a new school for differently-abled students and a cistern to ensure a more reliable supply of clean water during the disruptive monsoon season. But of course new Bhutanese roads were also associated with air pollution, a more sedentary lifestyle, a shift away from cultural

Figure 8.4. The mani wall on the shortcut from Kanglung to Yonphula.

traditions toward Western consumables, and new kinds of mental and physical health challenges.

Crossing the farm road ahead of me, Jeremy opened the gate onto a path between spiky fig fence lines. "There it is," he said a few minutes later, pointing to the sign in the window of the next farmhouse: "Biology lab." Presumably the sign had come from Sherubtse College. Jeremy and I had laughed when we first saw it, but over time I had come to see these farm fields, this mountain, as the best kind of biology lab. A short distance up the hill, someone had gathered leaves into piles and held them in place with branches; the leaves would be mixed with cow dung to make compost piles then used to fertilize fields of maize and potatoes. Yesterday I had happened upon a Bhutanese friend from the Kanglung temple here; she came periodically to inspect a field of hazelnuts being grown as part of a development project. Apparently there were now millions of hazelnut trees in Bhutan. I had yet to meet a Bhutanese person who would contemplate eating hazelnuts. The goal seemed to be producing oil for export: Yonphula, meet global capitalism!

Now Jeremy and I were both panting hard, shirts damp against our backs, foreheads slick with sweat. One hour in, 15 minutes to go: our last major trail marker was not a chorten but a cluster of manidhar marking a set of metal steps over the fence that defined the grounds of Yonphula Centenary College—a fence built when this was still a Bhutanese military base (Figure 8.5). I had started to think of our ten months in Bhutan as their own kind of manidhar, a way of marking and commemorating the deaths of my mother and Lobsang, as well as a search for resilience in the face of impermanence—specifically, the impermanence of our existing cultures and expectations in the face of the climate crisis.

Over the fence, we launched into the final stretch; the path here was steep, eroding with use and heavy rains, until we popped up onto a mostly level field, currently full of horses. On our way back down the mountain, Jeremy and I would take turns pretending to be Maria in *The Sound of Music* here, spinning in circles and singing about hills coming to life (Figure 8.6). For now we had to keep rushing, the college finally in view.

Figure 8.5. The cluster of manidhar near the fence around the old Bhutanese military base, then Yonphula Centenary College.

Figure 8.6. View from the road in front of Yonphula Centenary College, with the cluster of manidhar visible on the right and the Drangme Chhu a sliver at the bottom center of the valley.

The rusted roof was part of the Bhutanese military base that preceded the College. Locals let their horses and cattle graze across the grounds of the College. My students spent many hours gathering loose trash from the grounds.

Five minutes until the start of class. Jeremy sat to unlace his shoes just inside the door of the main academic building. I dropped my walking sticks and boots beside him, mentally revisiting our landmarks, which felt like a list of reasons to love this corner of the planet. Chorten 1: the mysteries of Vajrayana Buddhism; Chorten 2: Bhutan's rich biocultural heritage; Chorten 3: new roads offering developmental opportunities and contradictions, including more humane access to basic services like education and water. Cluster of manidhar: coming to grips with mortality. And what about the mountain itself? Wasn't it teaching me, changing me, through the physical connections of this daily commute—shaping my muscles, strengthening my bones, deepening my breaths?

"Can I have the iPad?" asked Jeremy.

Right: time to refocus. I handed him the iPad and the key to my office. Please, I thought, pulling kira and wangju out of my backpack as I crossed the College lobby with its green-felt-over-cement flooring, please let there be running water today.

Watching Zoë and Jeremy as we all eased into a new way of being in Kanglung, I noticed that when they didn't have to brave the threats of bullying, loneliness, linguistic alienation, and corporal punishment, their desire for hollow treats and empty calories also subsided. Time and habit were also on our side here, of course, but now none of us could quite remember or understand why we had felt so desperate in the fall about the lack of chocolate or pecorino cheese or other comfort foods. Instead of grumpily expecting ourselves to accept deprivation more gracefully, I thought now, we could have focused on easing the demands we faced. That strategy seemed relevant to our lives back in the United States as well. As we had all participated in the ubiquitous brinkmanship of academic and adolescent life—all of us overscheduled, overworked, underslept—we had taken high-consumption shortcuts to keep enabling our unhealthy choices. Maybe this year in Bhutan would help us make healthier choices back home.

Tim Jackson uses the image of the "iron cage of consumerism" to talk about the ways people in the West have constrained themselves through the same kinds of high-consumption choices my family was used to making. Jackson's image of consumerism-as-cage is modified from Max Weber's influential analysis of *The Protestant Work Ethic and Spirit of Capitalism* (1905). Weber argued that the ideological mantle of earlier Protestants had become a burden: "the Puritan wanted to work in a calling; we are forced to do so." But Weber also argued that a monkish "asceticism" had played a major role

> [. . .] in building the tremendous cosmos of the modern economic order. This order is now bound to the technical and economic conditions of machine production which to-day determine the lives of all the individuals who are born into this mechanism [. . .] with irresistible force. Perhaps it will so determine them until the last ton of fossilized coal is burnt.

Weber's linking of fossil fuels and the spirit of capitalism echoes eerily today. But Weber's conclusion is especially important to Tim Jackson's analysis of modern malaise: "In Baxter's view the care for external goods should only lie on the shoulders of the 'saint like a light cloak, which can be thrown aside at any moment'. But fate decreed that the cloak should become an iron cage."[2]

Jackson takes Weber's image of the iron cage and reframes it as the "iron cage of consumerism," arguing that human beings use objects to defend against existential anxieties. For Jackson, drawing on the work of sociologists such as Zygmunt Baumann, Russell Belk, and Colin Campbell as well as Giddens, "confidence in our place in the social world hangs or falls on our ability to participate in consumerism."[3] As Mary Douglas put it, "An individual's main objective in consumption is to help create the social world and to find a credible place in it."[4] But Jackson argues that human beings in their object-based world-building paradoxically ramp up the anxiety, the ontological insecurity, they are trying to resolve:

> Individuals are at the mercy of social comparison. Firms must innovate or die. Institutions are skewed towards the pursuit of a materialistic consumerism. The economy itself is dependent on consumption growth for its

very stability. Governments who preside over instability soon find themselves out of office. The 'iron cage of consumerism' is a system in which no one is free.[5]

But how exactly did we come to be so unfree in this cage we seem to have built for ourselves?[6]

Tim Jackson suggests that the only way out of the iron cage of consumerism is to find modes of world-building and consolation outside of market structures. "If consumption plays such a vital role in the construction and maintenance of our social world," he notes, "then asking people to give up material commodities is asking them to risk a kind of social suicide. People will rightly resist threats to identity. They will resist threats to meaning."[7] Certainly global society at present seem to be resisting any reduction in commodity consumption, despite the clear and present dangers of climate catastrophe. Jackson believes the best alternative to social affirmation through consumption is to build "meaning structures, communities of meaning, that lie outside the realm of the market; and that offer credible answers to the deep foundational questions that continue to haunt us."[8] Faith and culture are both associated with such "meaning structures" and "deep foundational questions," so it is perhaps unsurprising that Jackson and others have explored linkages between (Christian) religion and socially conscious and frugal behaviors, albeit without clear results.[9]

One might argue more broadly that the twenty-first-century resurgence of Christian nationalism, Buddhist nationalism, and Islamism all demonstrate efforts to rebuild meaning structures outside the realm of the market. But while all three modes of religious nationalism pose some claim to universal validity, all three have also been associated with violence and oppression.[10] In the United States, people may be prone to attributing political violence to Islamic extremism, but Christian nationalism has been a far more common source of violence. Whitehead and colleagues note, for instance, that "for the substantial proportion of American society who are Christian nationalists, gun rights are God given and sacred."[11] Armaly and colleagues look more closely at "the relationship between Christian nationalism and support for political violence," stressing that this connection "is sharply conditioned by white identity, perceived victimhood, and support for the QAnon movement."[12] In South East and Central Asia, meanwhile, Buddhist nationalism has given rise to anti-Muslim violence, as seen in Myanmar and Sri Lanka; Bhutan's Lhotshampa expulsion could be framed in part as anti-Hindu violence, though select Hindu rituals are accepted by many Bhutanese Buddhists.[13] If we look to religion (or, more broadly, culture) to open the door of consumerism's iron cage, we must be prepared to counter the increasingly violent forms of religious nationalism that seem to be growing in power around the world. Here again, as with discussions of corporal punishment or the GNH Index, the challenge may be to retain only those practices and ideas that increase wisdom and loving kindness—to get better at distinguishing the kinds of values and practices that can contribute to greater human thriving and those that are likely to contribute to conflict and violence.

THE ROAD TO SAKTENG

The end of April brought us into the domain of Aum Jomo, another powerful female figure in the Bhutanese imagination. My family joined a Yonphula Centenary College field trip designed to compare ecological practices in the remote Brokpa villages of Merak and Sakteng (villages under the aegis of the yulha or local deity known as Aum Jomo) with ecological practices in other parts of Bhutan.

The Brokpa community's oral history traces its migration to Bhutan from Tibet back to 1347; the community's isolation in this remote corner of the country has meant that its distinctive culture has survived somewhat more intact than more centrally located minority cultures. The Sakteng conservation area, encompassing both villages, was closed to outsiders from 1995 to 2010 to support Brokpa culture and traditions; the challenges that Yonphula student and staff organizers had had to overcome in order to acquire travel permits showed that the community, officially open to travel, was still seen as vulnerable. But my students didn't seem especially worried about cultural protection or the prohibitions on our visit during an election year. "*Officially*," they kept saying. "We can't speak to them *officially*, but of course we will be speaking with them as people."

Helping Jeremy put one foot on a tire lug, then another on the top of the tire, and then swing himself over the side of the open-backed construction truck, James noted that our family had expanded our travel repertoire: from Hilux to shared jeep-taxi to public bus, we had now graduated to an open truck. Baburaj and Chitra, the two other Yonphula faculty members, rode in the cab with the driver; my family piled in the back with the students (Figure 8.7).

The drive from Rangjung to the Sakteng trail-head would take two to three hours. As we drove along the paved roads in Rangjung proper, half of the students were still standing in the truck bed, slathering themselves with sunscreen and pulling out scarves against the dust we all knew was coming. While the truck slowly growled its way up the hill on the far side of Rangjung, the students were singing—one was even dancing. But the dance came to a rapid halt as we left the paved road; the truck bed lurched underneath their feet and the cliff dropped away beside us.

Figure 8.7. The truck taking us from Rangjung to the trailhead to Sakteng. It was acceptable to dress informally for hiking on this trip, though we were expected to wear national dress for visits to lhakhangs and so on.

Soon we were all braced hard against the jouncing of the truck, sitting, swaying, leaning on one another as the truck braked and accelerated around bends and bumps. Both as respected professors (James and I) and as feeble chilips (the whole family), we had been given comfy spots at the back of the truck, where we could lean back on our packs and the bags of supplies. The ride was still uncomfortable, the truck bed hard and unforgiving.

Then three of the women students began to sing. One of the men picked up their challenge, and soon, over the roar of the truck engine, amid the swirling dust from the road, a singing contest was taking place. On some of our bus journeys, the students had tried to explain to me the Bhutanese cultural form of tsangmo, a singing competition made up of two couplets: the first couplet makes a statement or describes a situation; the second responds to the first. My students told me that *their* students would sing tsangmo in the school yard, to express either love or ridicule. It was very much a living form, with ideas communicated through metaphors and symbols, and singers improvising and modifying familiar melodies that carry strong associations. On the truck, the women sang vigorously, an East-Asian-style vocal twang marking their rising pitches and the concluding melodic fall. They leaned forward in unison, gesturing together, one waving an empty plastic water bottle for extra emphasis. Every time they completed a verse, they would laugh and lean into one another in triumphant delight. I laughed too, sharing their delight, even though I couldn't understand the verses. Another woman took the role of judge, pointing to the debaters in turn. She kept trying to get other men to join the one man holding up the men's side of the challenge, but only one other man threw in a few verses. The three women seemed particularly strong at pulling out appropriate lines, but our solo male student had his moments of triumph, as when he adapted a traditional set of verses in the persona of a frantic mobile phone user.

Tsangmo, like the similarly improvisational form of lozey, was one of the practices highlighted under "cultural literacy" in the GNH Questionnaire of 2010, but references to both forms vanished from the 2012 Index and later publications. The GNH report struggled to articulate the social and cultural benefits of "cultural resilience and promotion" in anything more than the most general terms, but on the back of the truck, I could see how these improvisational traditions train people to listen closely to their opponents while also thinking rapidly about how to cap and/or undercut those verses. The competitive aspect of the game encourages creativity, leading participants to combine known verses and tropes with modern ideas and memes, creating new forms. The practice as a whole seemed to facilitate mental dexterity, creative recombinations, and community.

Eventually the singers paused, coughing from the dust. The woods deepened as we drove further into the mountains. The bridge over a river had washed out and our truck driver carefully forded the river just above the ruined bridge. Finally we arrived at the trail head, with mule carriers waiting to haul our heavy bags of potatoes and other stores up to Sakteng.

The landscape we entered is hard to convey. I hadn't realized that the government was in the early, explosive stages of building a road through the forest. If I had been alone with my family, I might have balked at walking through what looked like an ongoing landslide. From the back of the group, I watched the students wander under what seemed like a skyscraper-sized tree that had slid down the scree slope above the trail, pausing with its immense branches towering over the heads of our puny hiking team (Figure 8.8).

We didn't see the warning sign on the way in. It was mid-afternoon and we had been walking for about half an hour along a beautiful forested hillside, with a brook spilling noisily over rocks hundreds of feet below. I was bringing up the rear to be sure we didn't lose anyone along the way.

Just ahead, one of my students had stopped to chat to a man standing beside a mighty digger. Smiling at the two men's animated conversation, I tripped over my own feet, and when I looked down, I saw a tell-tale pink wire snaking through the white chalky sand of the path. I had been thinking of Percy Shelley's "Mont Blanc," a poem which imagines the human mind as a "feeble brook" overwhelmed by "a vast river" of reality, which "over its rocks ceaselessly bursts and raves." What, I was wondering, is a path when over its rocks a mighty road bursts and raves? Now, looking at the pink fuse, I realized we were hiking over a hillside already set with dynamite, ready to be blown up to make way for the new road. The question was less abstract than I had thought.

Figure 8.8. The trail to Sakteng, April 2018.

My student finished his conversation. "They will be blasting ahead also," he warned me, and he and a couple of the other male students hung back to urge me through areas where they thought the blast might send boulders plummeting down on our heads. We tried to shout over the noise of the brook, but our voices didn't break through and the sound of a few mid-sized stones bouncing on the upper hillside chased us on. When we arrived at safer ground, we found some of the stronger students pulling my weary Indian colleagues up the next rise. One student, a small woman who all along had doubted her ability to do this hike, rested on a rock. "Leave me, madam, please" she said. "I need to rest. At midnight, I will finish the climb. I will see you at 3 a.m., madam." I laughed at first, but she seemed completely serious. I gave her my walking sticks—my knees were holding up well enough—and on we went.

At the next rest stop, some of the students handed me a large brown lump of something. I looked at it dubiously, then looked back at them. One of the women, modeling what to do, tore off a small piece of what turned out to be dough and ate it. I gingerly followed suit. It was mildly sweet, but oddly flavored—at least to my palate.

"What is it?" I asked.

"For the altitude sickness, ma'am," the students said.

"But what is it?"

"Flour, oil, arra [. . .]" The other ingredients, with unfamiliar names, went by too quickly for me to grasp.

"What makes it good against altitude sickness?" I asked.

"The arra, of course!" exclaimed one of the men, and everybody laughed.

As we walked further from the blast sites, the way seemed calmer. Where the path passed under a massive overhanging rock, people had painted prayers on the rock and some of my students pointed out a meditation cave used by some famous mystic. Bright red and pure white rhododendron blossoms punctuated the greenery draping the hillsides down to the river. We met several freight trains—which is to say donkeys and horses wearing light packs and driven mostly by young Brokpa women—heading for the trail head. Heading out, the donkeys and horses carried no baggage; presumably they were heading down to gather goods and bring them up to Sakteng. At one point, we were overtaken by a few men carrying building materials on their shoulders or strapped to their backs; they were coming from the trailhead *en route* to Sakteng. Some of the roofing panels they carried were very wide, and the trail was very narrow. As a result, these men with their heavy loads would have to ascend and descend rough portions of the trail walking sideways, crossing one

Figure 8.9. The outskirts of Sakteng, with yaks grazing.

leg over the other. And yet they still moved more quickly than we did through the landscape.

After miles of winding through rhododendron and pine forest, the path suddenly opened onto a gentle valley, full of gentle streams and grazing yaks (Figure 8.9). We caught up with a group of Brokpa men, some of whom had carted our food supplies in on their ponies, and some who had passed us on the trail. My students, posing for the inevitable group photos, seemed both giddy and rapt. "Madam," said one woman, "This is like a golden dream for us. We could only dream of coming here; but you have made it possible for us!"

My primary contribution: being foreign, not understanding the difficulties, not knowing what I was proposing, or how much work it would require from others.

On the other hand, the trip had taught me more than I expected about the ways a group of Bhutanese travelers shared the burdens and the pleasures inherent in a challenging trip to a remote village.

OVERLAPPING STORIES AND HISTORIES

The villages of Merak and Sakteng are defined by their local deity, Aum Jomo. Stories about Aum Jomo vary in many ways, but the general outline goes something like this. Some villagers in Central Tibet were suffering under an unjust ruler. This local king had complained that his palace, overshadowed by the peak of a nearby mountain, was always dark. He ordered the villagers to cut off the peak of the mountain so that it would no longer block his sun. There was grumbling, of course, but the villagers were forced to comply; in addition to their daily labor for food, shelter, and clothing, they now had to break rock and carry the rock in pieces down the mountain. One day the villagers heard a young woman talking to a baby strapped to her back as she passed them in their labor: "It would be easier to cut off the head of the king than to cut off the top of the mountain." That young woman was Aum Jomo, who took on this form as the most appropriate way to convey her radical idea.

The villagers took the message to heart. They feasted the king, got him drunk, and assassinated him. But then they must have realized that retribution would come from whoever arrived to fill the vacuum left by the king's death. They asked their lama to help them resettle in some far place. He sought guidance from (a perhaps now disembodied) Aum Jomo; she suggested they move to a village near Tawang in present-day Arunachal Pradesh, but that area proved inhospitable and the group eventually traveled to Bhutan. Many of the travelers settled in Sakteng, the plain (teng) of dwarf bamboo (sak); others traveled further, over a mountain pass to Merak. I wondered how this community, defined by a historical regicide, was seen in a country so committed to its kings.

Aum Jomo herself seemed to strike fear into the hearts of many. Before venturing to Sakteng, our group had spent one night in the higher Brokpa village of Merak. Two of the women had spent the evening with an uncle, the director of the Sakteng wildlife refuge, listening to his tales of Aum Jomo's power. That night, they couldn't sleep. Lying terrified by random noises in the cold night, they had finally begged two of the men, assigned a different sleeping area, to come and protect them from Aum Jomo's wrath.

"But why would Aum Jomo be angry with you?" I asked them, but they looked a sideways warning at Jeremy and shook their heads at me. Maybe they had been too playful with Jeremy, letting him make cartoons of them on a plateau outside of town. Certainly, the climate and conditions seemed forbidding, even if the town is now accessible by road (Figure 8.10).

Figure 8.10. Merak, Trashigang, in April 2018.

Like many places in Bhutan, Sakteng's storied landscape features competing stories overlaid and sometimes peeking through one another. On our one full day in Sakteng, we toured two lhakhangs on the hills above the town. Both lhakhangs had stunning views over the valley (Figure 8.11); both had female caretakers, unusually for Bhutan, who had accumulated a variety of stories, many of which are now jumbled in my mind. One story pointed back to Kanglung; my students told me that the Kanglung Palas storekeeper was the granddaughter of a lama revered as a god in Sakteng. Whenever this woman and her mother came to visit family in Sakteng, my students said, the women were greeted and feted like royalty—or like gods. How do you know this? I asked, but the answer

Figure 8.11. A view from the path to the two lhakhangs above Sakteng.

was simply that everyone knew. The Palas store sells clothing, fabric, dried goods; the shop is small and far from grand. It was hard for me to understand a deified shopkeeper. Maybe in England, I thought, a fragment from Byron about that "nation of shopkeepers" popping up in my mind. But in Bhutan?

Another story: once there was a single lhakhang above Sakteng. Its lama lived simply, with one servant to cook for him. One day, the servant was chopping up turnips, and one of the turnips began to bleed. The servant continued cooking, undeterred, eventually serving his master a stew containing that bloody turnip. The master ate a few bites and immediately achieved enlightenment. He flew up into the air and circled the lhakhang. The servant ran after him, crying "Master, master! Take me with you!" The master looked down and asked, "Is there any left?" The servant ran to the bowl, found one final piece of bleeding turnip, and ate it. He too achieved enlightenment and rose into the air, flying after his master, fully equal at last. The second temple was built in his honor—perhaps a fitting rebuke to my snobby doubts about deified shopkeepers.

The last story was more "modern." The master of the first lhakhang had a very illustrious student who built the second lhakhang on the hillside across from his master's temple in order to remain close to him. Once the temple was built, however, he perceived to his horror that he was looking down on his master's temple. He immediately went to the master and offered him the new lhakhang: "You are my master: it is only fitting that your temple should be above mine. Let us trade."

But the master rejected this offer. "No, no!" he said. "You are the incarnation of my own master, which is to say that you are my master. You must be in the higher lhakhang." They argued this point back and forth again over the years, never quite settling the issue of precedence. Finally, geologists working in the broader region arrived in Sakteng with precision altimeters and announced that the two lhakhangs were built at the exact same elevation; the sense that one was higher than the other was a visual illusion.

These stories and counter-stories seemed to me to echo the structure of the lozey or tsangmo; using repetition and variation, the combination of stories provided a complex, nuanced mixture of accounts from which the hearer could choose their own preferred elements.

BOUNDARY CONTROL

After our climb to the two lhakhangs, we all felt very lazy. We cooked and ate a late lunch, and then our host wanted us to visit "Aum Jomo's place," but no one was willing to move.

"It's very close!" he urged us.

That was what we had been told about the two lhakhangs. We were evidently very slow hill-walkers. A communal yawn swept through the room. "Tomorrow," one of the students suggested. "We can go tomorrow, as we get ready to leave for home."

No sooner had our host agreed to this plan than a massive hailstorm swept over the school. The dense percussion of the hailstones on the metal rooftops was overwhelming; the dogs came to shelter in the doorway from the pebbles dancing in the courtyard. Now, really, no one wanted to leave the building. The more violent the storm, the more intimate and cosy our inner gathering.

"You see," said our host, standing by the door, "when strangers enter the town, they bring bad weather. They may be met with a drizzle or with a hailstorm such as this. Or on the night after their departure, snow falls." (That remark was directed at our group. We had already been told we had been the cause of snowfall in Merak.)

"This is pretty dramatic," I said, as Zoë and I joined him in the doorway to watch the stones pound down.

"So is the impact of strangers," said one student, coming to watch the hail with us.

Another came to poke his head through the now-crowded doorway too. "Yes, we believe that strangers entering will disturb an entire ecosystem."

"Disturb it how?" I asked.

"They make noise," said our host.

"They throw stones," added the first student.

"They pick leaves," said the second.

"Okay, okay," I said, "We get the point. Not that we've thrown stones or picked leaves. But we have definitely been noisy. Is there anything that we can do to propitiate or compensate for this disruption?"

Our Bhutanese friends looked at one another for a long moment, and then shrugged. "No," they told me. "We mostly try not to enter new places."

I remembered one of my students waiting for me at the crest of the hill, just as we were about to enter the wide open plain of Sakteng. He stood beside a pile of stones and leaves. "Here, madam," he said. "You must give a gift before entering. Put a stone or leaf on this pile." The crowd of us had scoured the area quite bare; I had to go back down the path several yards to find a pebble to contribute to the pile. We do disrupt ecosystems, even when arriving by foot, in relatively small parties.

Through the late afternoon and evening, we chatted, clustered around the bokhari or in small groups around the communal room. Jeremy, having worn out the card-playing stamina of several groups of students, was nudging in close to the warmth and nibbling on an extra tea biscuit. The door to the bokhari was left open, for extra heat, and when the fire sparked and spit out burning embers, two of the women would pick the embers up in their bare fingers and fling them back into the fire.

"Doesn't that burn you?"

"Oh, it is no problem! We are used to it—we do this all the time."

We talked about the coming road; the students were persuaded that Sakteng would lose its charms once people could arrive in motored vehicles. Our host said that "we" (by which I think he meant the people of Sakteng with whom he identified) had opposed the building of the road, but that they had been overruled by the government. It wasn't clear to me at what level this local desire had been expressed or this governmental overruling had occurred, but I could see that road-building was a topic which, once raised, would be difficult to resolve to the happiness of all involved. Yes, the village would be subject to far more pressures of modernization and globalization once a road was built, but what about those men, stepping sideways on the path, with roofing panels tied to their backs? Was it really true that they didn't want a road? Was it right for us as tourists (this Yonphula Centenary College group) to desire that the people of Sakteng retain their inconvenient beauty and isolation? But, conversely, had anyone ever gotten rid of a road and its impact once the road was built?

THE LOST BOYS

There is another origin story for Sakteng, a sadder story, predating Aum Jomo by several centuries. Trisong Detsen, known as the second Dharma King of Tibet, was the man responsible for inviting Guru Rinpoche to Tibet to translate Sanskrit Buddhist texts into classical Tibetan. That King also undertook other projects for the ritual defense of his realm. In one such project, his astrologer selected hundreds of teenaged boys to participate in a ritual dance to protect Tibet from natural calamities and disease. The boys, serving as national scapegoats, were stripped naked and paraded through Lhasa, along with an enormous altar. People cursed them, spat at them, flung flour and ash at them. The boys and the altar, carrying the community's collective misfortunes with them, were then taken to a place far south of the capital, where the altar was thrown into an enormous bonfire. The boys were feasted like kings, then exiled forever. (Natural calamities aside, one might suspect the royal astrologer was trying to reduce aggression within the kingdom by scaling back the population of young restless males.) The young exiles kept moving south, eventually forming the settlements of Khaling, Merak, and Sakteng.

The tercham dance, evoking this history, is held every third year in Sakteng.[14] The tercham dancers are twelve men between sixteen and sixty years of age; they are mostly chosen from yak herders, though at least one schoolteacher has served as a dancer. The family, parents, and relatives of present-day dancers are assured protection from all forms of adversity for the next three years. Dancers swear an oath of secrecy; their identities are supposed to be concealed even among themselves. (But since the community is so small, their identities seem an open secret.) The naked dancers wear only a wooden mask, an amulet, and a kata or prayer scarf (Figure 8.12).[15] After several hours of dancing in the temple courtyard, the naked masked men visit every house in the village, where they are feasted with millet beer, draught beer, and fermented rice soup. Those household offerings are supposed to "quell" misfortunes, sickness, and untimely death in the coming three years.

If, as the legend says, the dance reenacts the experience of the exiled boys who settled in Sakteng long ago, it also inverts and transforms the terms and the meaning of that experience. No longer exiled scapegoats, the male dancers are now pillars of the community. They may still fulfill a ritual role, one that requires their nominal absence from the community's daily life—an absence achieved by the masks that cover their faces, the ritual secrecy about their participation—but instead of being driven out of the community, they shelter in place, as we say nowadays. Instead of being abused by the community, they are feasted in each and every home. I fell asleep wondering whether there were other rituals that could help us transform migrants into community pillars during the climate migrations that are coming.

Figure 8.12. The wooden mask of the tercham dancers, hung beneath a photo of the fifth King (wearing his raven crown) in a temple below Sakteng.

FROM IMMIGRANT TO LOCAL DEITY

Of course Aum Jomo was herself once a migrant. Instead of emanating out of the land forms of this place, Aum Jomo traveled here from Tibet, and yet she still became a force of the land. She is not a mountain herself, but she inhabits the mountain Jomo Kulkhar. And she is understood to control the weather, which certainly seems to be a superpower associated with local deities. After our trip, for their ethnographic work on "Green Bhutanese Writing," my students gathered from Khaling a story about the relationship between Aum Jomo and her brother Dangling: Meme Dangling is the yulha or local deity for Khaling and the sacred lake Dangling Tsho is found above Khaling. In this area, two days' hike from Merak, the two siblings are understood to have committed incest. Their illicit union is part of what bound them to the land, what made it impossible for them to advance toward enlightenment. This story of incest, by offering an explanation for what turned Aum Jomo into a local deity, emphasized (for me, at least) what makes Aum Jomo different from other kinds of yulha, many of whom seem to be local spirits of mountains or lakes. Transgression—political, geographical, sexual—brought her to this corner of Bhutan; perhaps blurring the lines between human and natural forces was a logical extension of those other transgressions. Still, I wondered, was there a way in which Aum Jomo might model a different understanding of migration in this time when so many people are displaced by environmental disaster or political conflicts? Perhaps her story offered a model for becoming native to a place—by demanding that others respect the boundaries and the needs of the place, by maintaining visible consequences for actions that bring physical or moral pollution to disrupt the generous and generative functioning of ecosystems. But the fear she inspired also gave me pause. I'm looking for an Aum Jomo who could welcome other migrants, other political refugees, rather than bolting the gate behind her. How do we offer respect to fellow travelers as well as demanding respect from them?

AUM JOMO'S CATTLE

Aum Jomo's place was, as promised, ridiculously close to the school. The next morning, we wandered through the village, pausing as a villager released a large herd of sheep from their pen and they went galloping down the road, weaving around those of us at the back of the group. As we reached the outskirts of the village, one of the students said something to me that made no sense.

"There are Aum Jomo's cattle."

We were on the edge of an empty field close-cropped by some kind of grazing livestock. "You mean this is where she kept her cattle," I said, trying to clarify the statement.

"No, those are her cattle." The student waved his hand toward the right side of the field.

I was so baffled that I stopped walking. "I don't understand."

Our host, the Sakteng teacher, dropped back to see what was holding us up. I started walking toward him. "Look out!" he called, and I stopped again. "You mustn't step on Aum Jomo's cattle," he said.

I looked down at the ground and back up at him. Under my feet: grass, dirt. Ahead of me: grass, dirt, stones. "I am so confused," I said.

"There!" he said, pointing to the white stones I was standing among. They stuck up out of the ground slightly and I had indeed been just about to use them as stepping stones amid the slightly muddy ground.

"I beg your pardon?"

"Aum Jomo's cattle!" he said.

"The stones?"

"Yes, of course. She left them here when she went on." And with that, he went to catch up with those at the head of our straggling pack, to guide them to the place where Aum Jomo's yak was tied under the tree just outside the wall of the lhakhang.

I looked at my student, bemused. "The stones?!"

He nodded, amused at my bafflement.

"I'll catch up with you," I said, waving him on. The temple itself was within sight; it wouldn't matter if I lagged behind a little.

The sun was struggling through the watery clouds. I bent down to look more closely at the stones, thinking about what was implied by seeing these stones as Aum Jomo's cattle (Figure 8.13). Biology to geology, time congealing into stone. Bhutan's holy places demand a perspective attuned to the longue durée rather than a short election cycle—and yet we seem to be hurtling into a new geologic era as human actions alter

Figure 8.13. Aum Jomo's cattle: these, unlike the stones in the meadow, are marked by being "tied" outside her temple on the outskirts of Sakteng.

both the climate and the face of the earth. Of course Aum Jomo and her places, her cattle, have already seen far more change than any short-lived human being alive today has seen. Aum Jomo's cattle themselves might represent a geologic era, a time of migration so distant from us, so apparently slow moving, that we can't even see its motion. If we *could* see stones as moving cattle—as black-haired yaks, perhaps, their long coats swaying as they sashay across the meadow—what else might we see in that moment of altered vision?

Later, as we jounced and rattled our way back to Rangjung, in the truck's open back, in the chilly rain, I thought about Sakteng as one particular pinch point for the intersection of development and environmental conservation. Our host had described to us the challenges faced by families where the parents were up on the hills with their herds, and children as young as three were left in village houses run by other children so that all could attend school. They faced a forced choice between the traditional ecological knowledge of past generations and the access to lives of greater ease promised by modern education. And the coming of the road would further alter both the ecology and the society of Sakteng.

Himalayan communities are no strangers to existential challenges. While Vajrayana nationalism seems as violent and problematic as other forms of religious nationalism, Vajrayana dharma engages intensively with the cognitive-emotional challenges of impermanence and the sense of ontological insecurity that often results. In Sakteng, for instance, the tercham dance that remembers and recreates exiled scapegoats as pillars of a new community uses masks to emphasize community-building roles over potentially conflictual identities. The care extended to Aum Jomo's stone cattle similarly reminds us of a much larger-than-human geological frame of reference. Perhaps there are lessons here for communities around the world, struggling to cope with the radical changes brought by our new climate extremities—floods, droughts, massive storms, heatwaves, polar vortices, shifting monsoons, and more—as well as with the ontological insecurities we confront now, beyond our fantasies of stability and safety.

As the rain cleared and I watched Jeremy lead the students in a spirited card game (proper Bhutanese public servants enthusiastically calling out BS!), I realized that we ourselves had become more tightly interwoven as a community, an extended family, through the process of sharing this adventure. Perhaps this too was a gift from Aum Jomo: in doing something hard together, traveling this road together, we deepen our commitment to one another—and that deeper commitment may help carry us where we need to go.

EPILOGUE: DRINKING FROM A SKULL

Figure 9.1. The Black Hat Dance with Drums, clearing the ground of obstructive energies at Yonphula tshechu, April 2018.

"Mom just drank out of a skull," said Jeremy, as he and I returned to our place in the crowd around the stone plaza.

"I did not," I said reflexively, straightening my kira over my crossed legs as I sat down next to Zoë.

Another masked dance was just beginning. At the entrance to the temple, at the top of a flight of stairs on the south of the square, monks were clanging cymbals, blowing on six-foot-long horns, chanting. Dancers with wooden animal masks tied to their heads were entering the dance floor from a curtained doorway at the east (Figure 9.2). Soon their individualized spinning and circling from the waist would give way to communal stamping and leaping.

"That bright red bowl?" said Jeremy insistently.

I froze. He could be right. A man had ladled arra into my hand as part of the blessing, but his long-handled silver spoon had drawn the arra from an oddly shaped bowl, its inside painted a lurid red. I had thought the liquid was water. Jeremy had refused to accept any, and I was beginning to see why.

"A fake skull?" I suggested half-heartedly.

Jeremy turned to my husband James. "It was a skull, Dad. For real: a skull. How could you not realize you were drinking out of a skull, Mom?"

Figure 9.2. Dancers wearing animal head masks enter from a curtained doorway, watched over by a member of the monastic community.

What could I say? I hadn't exactly put the skull to my lips, but clearly I could have been paying closer attention. Jeremy grinned, suddenly less perturbed by the skull than gratified at having caught me out.

Yonphula monastery was looking appropriately fine, the doors covered by curtains, colored draperies on every roof edge waving in the wind. Jeremy was wearing jeans and a hoody, but the rest of us were in our best Bhutanese clothes. And all around us, my students and many others were wearing luscious silk brocade in honor of the occasion.

As explained in Chapter 2, tshechus like this—religious festivals held on the tenth day of a given month in the Bhutanese lunar calendar—celebrate the birth of or miraculous events associated with Padmasambhava, perhaps the most famous figure of Vajrayana "crazy wisdom" (yeshe cholwa). The phrase in Tibetan combines yeshe (pre-existing wisdom) with cholwa (wild or uncontainable), which to me evoked the wisdom of that wide-open sky above the dancers. A skull bowl—open to the elements, filled with liquor that devout Buddhists might ordinarily shun—similarly embodies crazy wisdom. In fact, some of the masked dancers carried small disks identified as skull bowls in their hands as they danced.

During the next set of community dances—an opportunity for the masked dancers to change their outfits and rest—a group of us from Yonphula Centenary College watched my student Yangchen's daughter dance with her classmates. The dance itself had been choreographed by one of the fifth-graders, and the choreographer was easy to spot—her energy and precision made every dance move pop. We were particularly amused by the combination of traditional music and more modern moves, such as a sassy nae-nae. On the edge of the courtyard, the chief atsara—a stocky man wearing a costume patched with fabric phalluses, plus a mask featuring a wispy beard—stepped through the moves, following the fifth-graders even to the extent of performing the nae-nae. Cultural construction: an unfinished story.

Yangchen's daughter ran over to sit with us as the masked dancers again emerged, one by one, from the curtained door at the east of the square. Some of my students who hailed from Paro in the west shouted to the atsaras, the jester-figures, to pick up a piece of fabric that had fallen and might trip one of the dancers. "These are very lazy atsaras," my students complained. "Not like the atsaras in the west." As we had learned over the course of the year, atsaras are traditionally master-dancers themselves and the most senior often serve as a master of ceremonies at a tshechu. Atsaras collect donations from spectators; they help adjust the costume of a dancer as needed, even in the middle of a dance; they keep the dance floor clear; they lead some dances and generally ensure that the events go according to plan.

But atsaras are also a different manifestation of crazy wisdom, a form closer to Bhutan's "divine madman" Drukpa Kunley, famous for defeating demons and seducing women by wielding his penis as a thunderbolt and thereby generating the phallus-worship that's been getting a lot of Western attention lately. These Yonphula atsaras, for instance, had been busy distributing condoms to the gathered multitudes; they had also attached a condom to the mouth of a plastic bottle, so that when they squeezed the bottle, the condom would inflate. That inflated condom was then thrust into various spectators' faces, to the amusement of everyone around the hapless target. I had come on my own a day early, to watch the formal dress rehearsal of the dances (Figure 9.3) and had received an overly enthusiastic welcome from one of the atsaras (Figure 9.4).

During the lunch break, my family left the temple grounds to meet up with Sonam and his wife Dechen, who had invited us to join their family for a picnic lunch. We stepped through the temple gate into the chaos of the marketplace, a sprawling mass of temporary stalls, roofed with blue tarps,

Figure 9.3. Dress rehearsal for the masked dances: the gomchen are wearing special robes, designed specifically for such a dress rehearsal.

Figure 9.4. This enthusiastic atsara ran towards me at speed before sliding into this position. I found it more alarming than amusing, I have to confess, in part because I was alone—but he clearly wanted a photo taken, so I obliged.

serving food and drink, selling clothing, dishes, toys, and other novelties, or offering various opportunities to gamble on the turn of a wheel or the throw of the dice. As we had seen before, the market was the counterpart to the tshechu dances: part of the economic engine supporting the religious rituals that reconstruct the community of monastics and supportive lay people every year. But the tshechu market produces its own contradictions. To our foreign eyes, these contradictions were most striking in the sight of children with toy machine guns at the edges of the masked dances, or the piles of plastic waste around the edges of the monastery.

The crowd flowed down the dirt road toward the fenced-in whitewashed stupas, but Sonam led us away from the crowd, weaving through the stalls, down across the multipurpose field where the College inauguration had been held, where the Indian Army had offered the community a free lunch to celebrate the birth of the first great Sikh guru, where my students and the monks and villagers liked to play soccer, where horses and cattle graze, and where children were currently chasing each other with their machine guns and other toys. Sonam's big truck was parked on the road below the field; he climbed into the back and handed out cases and woven bamboo mats. My family's concept of a picnic is a loaf of bread to keep hunger at bay. Clearly, Sonam and Dechen had a different approach.

It took time to find the best picnic spot, away from cow and horse dung, with the right mix of sun and shade and quiet. We laid out the mats, and Dechen and her children opened multiple containers of food: momos plus ezay (relish), Bhutanese red rice, white rice, ema datse (spicy chili curry), kewa datse (mild potato curry), shewa datse (mushroom curry), and more. In the meantime, Sonam offered us arra. For himself, he pulled out his aunt's antique silver-lined cup that he always carried in the "Bhutanese pocket" at the front of his gho. Before drinking, Sonam once again dipped his ring finger into the cup, turned his hand so the palm faced upward, and then used his thumb to flick the liquid from his ring finger as a kind of offering to the gods. James and I each accepted one cupful of arra, but we tried to resist a second helping. Patient as ever, Sonam persevered in his attempt to teach us the local rules of hospitality, warning us that a refusal would put us at enmity; we must accept at least a second tiny sip. So I did. James, confident in his friendship with Sonam, just smiled and tried to engage the older children in conversation.

I asked about Sonam's father, who had been to Nepal for eye treatment back in the fall. He was doing well, Sonam told us. Sonam himself had been to Thimphu, to visit the country's main hospital, the referral hospital, with the power to send patients for government-paid medical care abroad. Sonam had been having headaches so he went for a scan, which found nothing wrong.

"But after that," Sonam said, with the pleasure of a born storyteller who has a good tale to share:

"I took the family for a picnic at a holy site on the outskirts of the city. I saw an older man walking toward us, and something about him caught my attention. I can't tell you what it was, exactly, but as he walked up to us, I recognized him. The fourth King! He greeted us and I introduced my family and explained how we were having a picnic, that we were in Thimphu so that I could have a scan to be sure the headaches were not a problem. The King told me that I had done just right, that we Bhutanese don't do enough preventive care, so that when we come to the hospital it is already a crisis and that costs the state a great deal of money."

"The fourth King!" I said, marveling. "We saw him from a distance back when we first arrived, but we were told he stayed mostly in retreat. That must have been incredible, to be having a conversation with him."

"And he told me," Sonam went on, the story not yet complete, "he told me that I should have my stomach checked as well while I was in Thimphu, so I went back to the hospital the next day to have my stomach checked, and they found I had an ulcer!"

"An ulcer!" I said. "That must be painful. What do you think made the King think you should have your stomach checked?"

Sonam spread his arms and eyes wide, shaking his head as if to say who knew what sources of knowledge were available to the King of destiny?

"Do you remember when you came to the shop and we were busy?" Sonam asked me.

I did remember. I was stopping by to pick up some chickpeas, but mostly to say hello, when I realized that the family was all standing together, near a red-robed lama who seemed to be leading some kind of ritual:

"We decided to have a ritual, too, to help my spirit heal. What gave me the ulcer, you know? Perhaps it was some arra that was a little dirty or something else. We don't know. But the purification has helped me improve significantly. And now Dechen doesn't let me drink arra."

I laughed, looking pointedly between Dechen and Sonam's hand-turned, silver-lined cup full of arra. Dechen laughed also, and Sonam grinned, having set up the joke. "Just a little sip between friends—not enough to do any harm."

We had barely finished eating when the horns from the temple sounded again. Jeremy and Zoë ran off to try to catch The Lords of the Charnel Grounds: our family's favorite skeleton dance (Figure 9.5).

Moving a little more slowly, I left James chatting with Sonam and climbed back to the monastery grounds by a side path, avoiding the main drag of the marketplace. I stepped around a Zero Waste Monastery sign that my students had brought back from a field trip to a Zero Waste monastery, the Chökyï Gyatso Institute, in Dewathang. But walking the path beside the sign involved tiptoeing through a mass of garbage, a mixture of plastic and rotting food—the inevitable by-product of the market in

Figure 9.5. One of the four skeleton dancers in The Lords of the Charnel Grounds masked dance.

its current form. Grappling with waste from the tshechu market would clearly take additional thought and effort.

The crowd at the tshechu had watched the dancing through several days of heat and cold. We had been burnt by the midday sun, only to shiver in the late afternoon cold. Now, by mid-afternoon of the third day, as individual droplets built to a steady rain, many of us tried to cluster under a bit of roofing. I found myself beside two young friends of an atsara, soon to appear as a dancer in the pawo or hero dance. As the rain lightened and gradually stopped, Zoë and I moved out to sit beside another female student as one of the senior atsaras, accompanied by a small masked figure, came to gather contributions. My student, very devout, was predictably also very generous. She told me she planned to become a nun after retirement, some decades from now. Talk of retirement brought up a lurking question: "Do you mind if I ask how old you are, madam?"

"I don't mind at all. I am 55."

"But so active, madam!"

This had been a repeated refrain over the past few months. I had to ask: "Everyone keeps saying I'm so active! What does it mean when you say that?"

"The retirement age here is 58, madam. Mostly at this time we sit in a corner and think about death."

Well that certainly put things in perspective. Life expectancy in Bhutan was then about 70, up from somewhere in the 60s less than a decade previously. But perhaps "sitting" meant meditation: retirement as time to come to grips with human mortality.

As the rain cleared, I found myself thinking back to the skull. Jeremy and I had gone to see the new thongdrel—a huge embroidered tapestry hung from the roof of the monastery (Figure 9.6). The word thongdrel means "liberated through sight," the idea being that a person can be enlightened just by laying eyes upon the religious tapestry. Until now, the process had always been relatively low-key; we would follow a friend to the thongdrel, make an offering of 10 or 20 ngultrum, and a monk would pour blessed water from a holy vase into our cupped hands. As in a temple, to receive the blessing, you drink the water from your hand (ideally, imagining bad karma being washed away as you swallow) and then

Figure 9.6. The new thongdrel. The Yonphula Rinpoche is visible in the foreground, slightly to the left of the hanging banners.

you wipe any remaining moisture over your head, to purify not only your speech but your body. I can't say that I had ever felt especially enlightened through seeing a thongdrel—I always wanted someone to explain the images to me, underscoring my own belief in liberation through rational explanation—but I was happy to keep trying.

Our experience this morning had been a little more intense. Jeremy and I had lined up with hundreds of our Bhutanese neighbors and others who had come to the tshechu from much further away. We had struggled to stay together as three lines of aspirants merged into one at the corner of the building giving access to the thongdrel. Officials stood between the thongdrel and those in the line, blocking people from touching the fabric, but people would gaze up and reach out toward the thongdrel, even while moving steadily forward, impelled from behind by the press of those wanting their turn.

At the end of passing by the thongdrel, after the money offering, we were given a small brown and red lump of something that might have been a pill or an object to take home and put on your altar. I was puzzling over what to do with that object when I was offered liquid out of a bright red bowl, conveyed to my hand by a long-handled silver spoon. Sipping from my cupped hand, I was surprised by the arra. Evidently, I should have been more surprised by the skull. But I think I was mostly concerned with working out where I was supposed to put the clay-like ball: in my mouth or my pocket? In the end, I carried it over to one of my students to ask. It was to be ingested, as I should have guessed: a blend of flour and oil and arra, roughly the same as the dough my students had made to ward off altitude sickness on our last field trip.

PRECIOUS BREATHS

In the days and weeks after the tshechu, I kept thinking about drinking from the skull I hadn't fully seen. I thought too about the model of Machig Labdrön and the extremity of her teaching. Just as there aren't many Christians willing to sell all they have and give it to the poor, there aren't many Buddhists willing to spend their time in charnel grounds and other haunted sites, offering their bodies up for demons to feast upon. Most of us are more like King Indrabhuti of Oddiyana, Guru Rinpoche's adoptive father and first student: if we were to discover a miraculous being in the heart of a lotus, we would ask that teacher for a path to enlightenment that didn't involve giving up too much of our existing life.

But all the evidence suggests that we are already, unwittingly, in the charnel ground, along with our loved ones. In 1949, in his eloquent *Sand County Almanac*, Aldo Leopold wrote that

> [. . .] one of the penalties of an ecological education is that one lives alone in a world of wounds. Much of the damage inflicted on land is quite invisible to laymen. An ecologist must either harden his shell and make believe that the consequences of science are none of his business, or he must be the doctor who sees the marks of death in a community that believes itself well and does not want to be told otherwise.[1]

I had come to Bhutan to learn from its crazy wisdom strategies ideas that might help the diverse communities of my own nation better cope with the coming climate catastrophes. But I had also come to Bhutan still mourning my dead, and unwilling to acknowledge the presence of death all around me.

By the end of the year, I was struggling to synthesize what I had learned from and about Bhutan that could possibly be relevant to my communities back home. Some ten days after the tshechu, I joined a multi-week fast begun by a handful of my colleagues back in Swarthmore: we were asking the Swarthmore College Board of Managers to divest the College's billion-dollar endowment from fossil fuels. One of my students joined the fast for a day, mostly (she said) out of curiosity. "We Bhutanese people like our food," my students kept telling me. "We could not possibly fast that way." But some Bhutanese people do fast for spiritual purposes, and Chador made it through her day of fasting without a whimper. I loved the feeling we were learning from each other and acting together.

In the middle of that fasting week, some of my students arranged for a visiting lecture from one of the monks at the monastic school in Kanglung. He spoke about the importance of water in Buddhism as part of our ecocriticism class. Then, at the end of class, he led us through a brief meditation called "Ten Precious Breaths." The meditation seemed to me to offer a historical summary of Mahayana Buddhism. Its steps were simple:

1. Breathing in a long breath, I know I am breathing in a long breath. Breathing out a long breath, I know I am breathing out a long breath.
2. Breathing in a short breath, I know I am breathing in a short breath. Breathing out a short breath, I know I am breathing out a short breath.
3. Breathing in, I am aware of my whole body. Breathing out, I am aware of my whole body.
4. Breathing in, I am calming my body. Breathing out, I am calming my body.
5. Breathing in, I am aware of my mind. Breathing out, I am aware of my mind.
6. Breathing in, I am calming my mind. Breathing out, I am calming my mind.
7. Breathing in, I am aware of the impermanence of all phenomena. Breathing out, I am aware of the impermanence of all phenomena.
8. Breathing in, I am feeling joyful. Breathing out, I am feeling joyful.
9. Breathing in, I am observing letting go off. Breathing out, I am observing letting go off.
10. Breathing in, I feel liberated. Breathing out, I am sharing happiness with all beings.

The meditation moves from an awareness of breathing to a calming of both body and mind, each very broadly defined. For breaths three and four, the lopen or teacher invited us to "touch all the parts of our body with our breath, including the parts we normally forget." In describing the mind, he included not only our immediate thoughts but also the perception of thinking itself, the awareness of the thinking self. But it was his discussion of the later breaths that was the most interesting to me. In describing the seventh breath, the teacher emphasized

> [. . .] one of Buddhism's most fundamental teachings: impermanence. Everything changes, but our resistance to change creates suffering. We need to recognize the impermanence of all phenomena, from massive and apparently permanent things like mountains and rivers to the basic elements of human existence—the truth that we will all someday die—to

the constant changing of our own experience, the fluidity of our thoughts and feelings. Thoughts and feelings rise and subside again, like a wave on the shore.

With our next breath, we feel joy. If you have done all of the previous breaths as described, you really will feel this sentiment. Even in prison, the people I have worked with: they feel the joy.

But all phenomena are impermanent, no? We cannot cling to that experience of joy or we will once again be increasing our own suffering. Letting go of pleasing emotional states is also an important part of reducing suffering. Now we practice releasing joy.

With our final breath, we touch a state of enlightenment. What do we do with that enlightenment, that liberation? The very last step of the process represents the innovation of Mahayana Buddhism: to reach for happiness not for one's own sake only, but in order to share that happiness with all sentient beings.

I loved this mini-enactment of Buddhist principles and practice: physical and mental preparation for an acceptance of impermanence, then joy, letting go, and liberation. Chogyam Trungpa had taught that crazy wisdom required us to give up hope. The counterpart to that claim, I thought now, was that crazy wisdom rejects despair. Our guest teacher this afternoon had insisted—rightly—that a deep, full-throated, full-chested acceptance of impermanence paradoxically leads, in the very next breath, to joy. One of the things I had always admired about both my brother Lobsang and the Dalai Lama was their capacity for laughter and jokes despite the loss of homeland, sovereign identity, even physical security. Still, this seemed a steep order: to accept the impermanence of our world and find joy in that impermanence, without ignoring the reality of human suffering and societal change on an almost unimaginable scale.

LESSONS TO BRING HOME

So what had I learned from this year in Bhutan that could be help ease suffering and manage the coming changes? In trying to understand what it meant to think of Bhutan as the "last Vajrayana state," I had found not only some of the animating stories of national identity, but also some of the tensions between 1) Vajrayana's radical insistence on emptiness and discontinuity, as seen in the eight manifestations of Padmasambhava, and 2) a desire for a national identity conceived of in terms of continuity over time, as seen in the powerful figure of the Zhabdrung. These tensions pointed to Bhutan's ongoing desire for ontological security, or what I had come to see as its varied strategies for managing ontological anxiety. At the same time, in looking more closely at Bhutan's transition from religious rule to absolute monarchy to constitutional democratic monarchy, I had been reminded that democracy is more varied than we tend to remember in the United States, and that local government provides crucial connections between communities and a larger sense of communal agency, and that the most intransigent forms of patriotism often emerge in response to perceived threats (real or invented).

In struggling to understand the core questions of the Lhotshampa expulsion—especially how, why, and who—I found myself tracing a kind of recipe for humanitarian disaster, mingling fears about the integrity of territorial boundaries, the rise of new figures of authority with indeterminate sources of power, demonization of minorities, and abuse of bureaucratic procedures. In Bhutan, the (not-well-aligned but emotionally potent) model of Sikkim's fall from independent nation to Indian state, combined with the Gorkhaland movement in nearby Indian regions raised fears about territorial integrity. At the same time, as the fourth King's new in-laws rose to positions such as Home Minister and Foreign Minister, Bhutan's internal politics shifted in ways that remain difficult to parse. Bureaucratic procedures such as the census, the implementation of mandatory national dress, and most importantly "voluntary leaving certificates" were all weaponized against a minority population perceived as a threat to national integrity. The same (or similar) features contribute to humanitarian crises elsewhere: in the United States, for instance, abusive procedures at the southern border separated children from their parents in an attempt to create disincentives for asylum seekers, at roughly the same time civil servants were being replaced by party loyalists, shifting government norms.

In grappling with the rise and fall of GNH within Bhutan, I found myself disagreeing with those who blamed the Lhotshampa crisis on the concept of GNH, while still finding evidence of anti-Lhotshampa bias within the Index. GNH's fall from influence even in Bhutan emphasizes the difficulty of holding onto any genuine alternative to GDP for more than a moment in time—but the similar inefficacy of other "beyond GDP" models suggests the importance of engaging culture in trying to develop less destructive understandings of human thriving than that provided by GDP growth assumptions. Still, in order to articulate cultural components of national thriving while minimizing bias against minority groups, we need to develop different procedures for discursive debate over values and cultural literacy—an experiment that has already been undertaken (though not maintained) in the United States.[2]

While Bhutan doesn't offer a model for open debate over cultural values, it does exemplify the persistence of certain traditional arts and crafts. Our visit to the College of Zorig Chusum allowed us to explore some of the ways those arts have contributed to community building, waste reduction, and ecological resilience. But our visit also highlighted the extent to which material arts are always interwoven with intangible cultural heritage, inviting a closer look at how Bhutan's intangible culture provides continuity and/or grapples with the challenges of radical change, ontological insecurity. Bhutan's tshechu dances, for instance, offer spectators a chance to confront communally imagined demons, or to construct narratives of allegorical resolution in which obstructive energies are dismantled and returned to their proper homes. Other Vajrayana traditions propose to transform negative mental states such as anger and jealousy into different modes of wisdom such as clarity and accomplishment. Perhaps most radically, Machig Labdrön's Chöd teaching aims to cut through our very desire for ontological security, to cut off our fixation on a stable sense of identity.

Over the course of the year, my family's emotional struggle to adapt to a lower-carbon lifestyle highlighted the extent to which Americans and Westerners more generally use commodity culture as a means of managing our existential anxieties, our desire for ontological security—but our eventual adaptation suggested that we can find our way out of what Tim Jackson called the "iron cage of consumerism." I thought this hope for greater cultural fluidity and resilience might apply to national boundaries as well. Our visit to the remote villages of Merak and Sakteng helped us see the extent to which Bhutan had experienced multiple waves of immigration and naturalization—even if Bhutan's recent insistence on national identity and national sovereignty produces a concomitant hostility toward immigration. The case of Aum Jomo leading the Brokpa people to settle in Sakteng and Merak—and related stories of adolescent male scapegoats being driven out of Tibet and settling in Khaling, Merak, and Sakteng—suggests an unexpectedly inclusive approach to immigration and naturalization, as seen through the model of Aum Jomo transforming herself from a leader of migrants into a local deity.

RETURNING HOME

I would like to say that we went to Bhutan and learned to live in harmony with one another and our Bhutanese friends and neighbors and with the more-than-human world, and that we came home and lived happily ever after. But of course it didn't work out quite that way. We came home and I at least had to learn many of the same lessons all over again.

Our house felt insanely oversized when we first returned and I spent months looking for opportunities to downsize with no success. Some member of the family was unhappy about every possible housing option. This little house was moldy, that one was tacky, a condo apartment was obviously not right for a family—and what about our garden, Mum? I gave up on the time-consuming, unsuccessful house hunt.

Our tenants had let our aging hand-me-down furniture get moldy. I found some beat-up Arts and Crafts-style armchairs on Craigslist to replace the stuff that was making us wheeze. James and I rented a truck to go pick up the furniture one sunny autumn afternoon, and suddenly we were just another oversized vehicle filling ten lanes of a highway going nowhere very special. After a year away, it was hard to take. The richest nation in the history of the world, its wealth based on the profligate burning of fossil fuels, and this was what we had built: rivers of tar coating the earth so thousands of people at a time could burn more fossil fuels in search of junk, material to consume and throw away in short order. This was drinking from a skull with a vengeance, it seemed to me, but no one seemed to see the death streaming in all directions.

In trying to grapple with my sudden, stark vision of mortality, I found myself remembering the moment at the Yonphula tshechu just before Jeremy called me out: the red-painted skull bowl, the unexpected bite of the arra on my tongue, the red-dyed pill that puzzled me. I am not a scholar of Vajrayana practice, but it seems to me that swallowing a red-painted ball of clay-like substance while drinking arra that has been held in a human skull are both strategies for breaking the taboo that maintains reverence for the human body through a fear of death. As certain masked dances teach their audiences not to fear what they will see after death, in what Vajrayana Buddhism calls the bardo of becoming, so it seemed to me that the blessing of the skull offered a lesson in fearlessness, in seeing beyond the physical aftermath of death. Emptiness (shunyata) is wisdom; the hollow skull, open to the sky, invites us to turn our understanding of the world inside-out.

This all seems relatively consistent with what one can read about Vajrayana in any number of books today. But here's what I think I learned from sitting at the tshechu among friends and colleagues, with no books or texts to consult. Vajrayana rituals take the evidence of human mortality—the skull bowl, the human femur flute—and turn that mortal residue into art: objects that make music or hold a ritual drink, promising to open the doors of perception. And whether the religious texts discuss ecological knowledge or not, the place-based rituals contain and repeatedly reconstruct an ecology as (well as) a community. Those rituals themselves contain a fundamental teaching. We are wood (in mask form), we are animals, we are stone, we are sun, and rain, and motion in space. We are open to the sky even when and where we seem most closed.

The night before we left Bhutan, our visas expiring, I asked a Drukpa Kagyu monk about the proper mental attitude for a spectator of a masked dance. The question pleased him. We should come to a tshechu, he replied, as if we were arriving at the zangtopelri, the paradise of Guru Rinpoche, the precious teacher who brought Buddhism to the Himalayas. Surely this was more than metaphor, I thought. Padmasambhava's paradise was visible here, in Kanglung and Yonphula: in the space formed of sky and stone, sun and rain, the community constructed and sanctified by the dances communally performed, by the prayers carried on the winds and the waters, even by the dragonflies circling the burning cedar near the corner of the wall where Jeremy had perched with friends both new and old. Like the dragonflies, we had circled the communities of Kanglung and Yonphula, had been welcomed to rites that intrigued and puzzled and fed us as we struggled, and still struggle, to make sense of the underlying connections between impermanence and joy.

Notes

TIMELINE OF KEY EVENTS IN BHUTANESE HISTORY

1 S. Wangmo, "The Brokpas: A semi-nomadic people in eastern Bhutan." In *Himalayan Environment and Culture*, eds. N. K. Rustomji and C. Ramble (Shimla: Indian Institute of Advanced Study, 1990), 141–158.

PROLOGUE

2 This division between supporters and critics is of course an oversimplification, and many scholars are now working to bring the two perspectives closer together. Scholars writing from a positive perception of Bhutan include, for instance, William J. Long, *Tantric State: A Buddhist Approach to Democracy and Development in Bhutan* (New York: Oxford University Press, 2019); Ritu Verma, "The Eight Manifestations of GNH: Multiple Meanings of a Development Alternative," *Journal of Bhutan Studies* 41 (Winter 2019): 1–33, https://www.bhutanstudies.org.bt/jbs-41-winter-2019/, and Katsu Masaki, "Exploring the 'Partial Connections' between Growth and Degrowth Debates: Bhutan's Policy of Gross National Happiness," *Journal of Interdisciplinary Economics* 34, no. 1 (January 2022): 86–103, https://doi.org/10.1177/02601079211032103. Critical perspectives can be found in various articles linking GNH to the Lhotshampa expulsion of the early 1990s, including multiple pieces of varying quality included in Johannes Dragsbaek Schmidt, ed., *Development Challenges in Bhutan: Perspectives on Inequality and Gross National Happiness* (Cham: Springer, 2017).

3 For its part, Bhutan has diplomatic relations with 54 of the United Nation's 193 member states, including the European Union. Limiting diplomatic relations has been part of the country's policy of gradual opening. A 1949 friendship treaty with India agreed that Bhutan would accept Indian guidance on foreign affairs, without giving India diplomatic authority for Bhutan. A revision of that treaty in 2007 strengthened the idea of reciprocal cooperation between India and Bhutan in relation to the sovereignty and territorial integrity of each.

4 Outside sources reported Bhutanese concerns over threats to national sovereignty from the actions of both China and India. See for instance, Steven Lee Myers, "Squeezed by an India-China Standoff, Bhutan Holds Its Breath," *New York Times*, August 15, 2017, https://www.nytimes.com/2017/08/15/world/asia/squeezed-by-an-india-china-standoff-bhutan-holds-its-breath.html. Tensions over India's attempts to control Bhutan's relationship with China have only intensified over the past few years, especially around Chinese-Bhutanese diplomacy around disputed border issues.

5 I later learned that this image echoes King Prithvi Narayan Shah's description of Nepal as a yam between two boulders. See for instance, Manish Jung Pulami, "Discursive Analysis of 'Yam Theory': Mapping King Prithvi Narayan Shah's Essence to Contemporary Geopolitics," *Unity Journal* 3, no. 1 (2022): 1–12.

6 See for instance, figures cited by Johannes Dragsbaek Schmidt, "Donor-Assisted Ethno-Nationalism and Education Policy in Bhutan," in *Development Challenges in Bhutan: Perspectives on Inequality and Gross National Happiness*, ed. Johannes Dragsbaek Schmidt (Cham: Springer, 2017), 29–46; Jaquelyn Poussot, "Indian Labourers, the Invisible Class of Bhutan," *South Asia@ LSE* (blog), January 31, 2018, https://blogs.lse.ac.uk/southasia/2018/01/31/indian-labourers-the-invisible-class-of-bhutan/; Damber Singh Kharka, "Dependence of Bhutanese Economy on India: Empirical Analysis of Inflation Dependency," *Journal of International Economics* 4, no. 2 (July–December 2013): 4–20; Udisha Saklani and Cecilia Tortajada, "India's Development Cooperation in Bhutan's Hydropower Sector: Concerns and Public Perceptions," *Water Alternatives* 12, no. 2 (June 2019): 734–759, https://www.water-alternatives.org/index.php/alldoc/articles/vol12/v12issue3/525-a12-2-8.

7 Religion scholar Elizabeth Allison has argued that "deity citadels" in Bhutan provide this kind of ecological refuge. See Elizabeth Allison, "Deity Citadels: Sacred Sites of Bio-Cultural Resistance and Resilience in Bhutan," *Religions* 10, no. 4 (April 2019), https://doi.org/10.3390/rel10040268

8 This is an oversimplification and some scholars dismiss this framing as orientalist, but Bhutanese friends and neighbors repeatedly responded to questions about Buddhism by telling me to ask a monk. Occasionally, people would explain that their answer might introduce error or confusion about the dharma, which is a serious matter within Buddhism. Some discussion of the popular/elite division in understandings of Vajrayana Buddhism can be found in Claire Villarreal, "Shaman, Lama, Buddha: "Occult Techniques" and the Popularization of Tantric Ritual in Tibet," *Magic, Ritual, and Witchcraft* 9, no. 1 (Summer 2014): 62–84, https://doi.org/10.1353/mrw.2014.0007.

9 Leo Rose memorably remarked in 1977 that Bhutan was "about as 'data free' as it is possible for a polity of over three hundred years old to be." Leo E. Rose, *The Politics of Bhutan* (Ithaca, NY: Cornell University Press, 1977), 11. Drawing on figures provided by Leo Rose, Michael Hutt offers one 1969 example of official population figures being off by 10 percent (and officially corrected) because "quite simply, someone got their sums wrong" (Michael Hutt, *Unbecoming Citizens: Culture, Nationhood, and the Flight of Refugees from Bhutan* (New Delhi: Oxford University Press, 2003), 151, https://doi.org/10.1093/acprof:oso/9780195670608.001.0001). Hutt also notes that "in 1990, King Jigme Singye announced in an interview given to a Kolkata magazine that the total population of Bhutan was not over one million and growing steadily, as had been stated, assumed and asserted in all official literature since the early 1970s, but was actually only 600,000 (Hutt, *Unbecoming Citizens*, 159).

10 The fourth King's mother, Kesang Choden, was the daughter of Sonam Tobgay Dorji and Mayum Choyin Wangmo, princess of Sikkim.

11 For external concerns about ethnic discrimination, see for instance, Bhutan's country profile in "Bhutan: Freedom in the World 2022 Country Report," Freedom House, accessed January 15, 2024, https://freedomhouse.org/country/bhutan/freedom-world/2022.

12 See Karma Phuntsho correcting Richard Whitecross and Karma Ura. Karma Phuntsho, "Echoes of Ancient Ethos: Reflections on Some Popular Bhutanese Social Themes," in *The Spider and the Piglet: Proceedings of the First International Seminar on Bhutan Studies*, eds. Karma Ura and Sonam Kinga (Thimphu: Centre for Bhutan Studies, 2004), 564–579, https://www.bhutanstudies.org.bt/the-spider-and-the-piglet/.

13 The College began classes in the summer of 2017 and closed in July 2022.

14 For discussions of the imperial presidency, see for instance, Peter Irons, *War Powers: How the Imperial Presidency Hijacked the Constitution* (New York: Henry Holt, 2005); Ryan C. Hendrickson, *Obama at War: Congress*

and the Imperial Presidency (Lexington: University Press of Kentucky, 2015). For a discussion of rising authoritarian populism in relationship to environmental concerns, see James McCarthy, "Authoritarianism, Populism, and the Environment: Comparative Experiences, Insights, and Perspectives," *Annals of the American Association of Geographers* 109, no. 2 (2019): 301–313, https://doi.org/10.1080/24694452.2018.1554393.

CHAPTER ONE

1 Bhutan Department of Urban Development and Housing, *Traditional Architecture Guidelines* (Thimphu: Department of Urban Development and Housing, [1993–?]), 39–40.
2 See Sonam Tobgye, "Guru Padmasambhava and Jurisprudence in Bhutan: Golden Yoke and Silken Knot," *Journal of Bhutan Studies* 34 (Summer 2016): 9–19, https://www.bhutanstudies.org.bt/journal-of-bhutan-studies-volume-34-summer-2016/
3 Rostow did not identify modernization with cultural instability per se, but the linearity of his model suggests that cultural stability associated with tradition may be left behind in the process of development. See Walt Whitman Rostow, *The Stages of Economic Growth: A non-Communist Manifesto* (New York: Cambridge University Press, 1960).
4 Rabah Arezki et al., "Testing the Prebisch-Singer Hypothesis since 1650: Evidence from Panel Techniques That Allow for Multiple Breaks," (working paper, IMF Working Papers, no. 2013/180, August 15, 2013), https://www.imf.org/en/Publications/WP/Issues/2016/12/31/Testing-the-Prebisch-Singer-Hypothesis-since-1650-Evidence-from-Panel-Techniques-that-Allow-40880.
5 See for instance, Walter Rodney, "How Europe Underdeveloped Africa," in *Beyond Borders: Thinking Critically about Global Issues*, ed. Paula S. Rothenberg (New York: Worth Publishers, 2006), 107–125. Aid dependency, in which a less developed country relies on foreign donors for more than 15–20 percent of government spending, is often discussed as a particular category of dependency; in this context, it's worth noting that international public finance supplied 15.8 percent of Bhutan's total financing in 2010–11, but that percentage had dropped to 12.2 by 2020–21. See Tandin Wangchuk, "Resource Mobilization for Sustainable LDC Graduation of Bhutan in the Context of Emerging Challenges to Development Financing" (working paper, South and South-West Asia Development Papers, no. 22-02, February 2022), https://hdl.handle.net/20.500.12870/4430.

6 Joseph Nathan Cohen and Miguel Angel Centeno, "Neoliberalism and Patterns of Economic Performance, 1980–2000," *Annals of the American Academy of Political and Social Science* 606, no. 1 (July 2006): 32–67, https://doi.org/10.1177/0002716206288751. Cohen and Centeno do acknowledge an exception in Asian developing markets.

7 See for instance, Majid Rahnema and Victoria Bawtree, *The Post-Development Reader* (Atlantic Highlands, NJ: Zed Books, 1997). See also Arturo Escobar, *Encountering Development: The Making and Unmaking of the Third World* (Princeton, NJ: Princeton University Press, 1995).

8 According to Elise Klein and Carlos Morreo, for instance, "Postdevelopment in practice begins with the insistence that an enduring diversity of socialities, a multiplicity of southern knowledges and nature/culture assemblages, and postcolonial political economies reveals already existing alternatives" to earlier Rostovian understandings of development. See Elise Klein and Carlos Eduardo Morreo, eds., *Postdevelopment in Practice: Alternatives, Economies, Ontologies* (Abingdon: Taylor & Francis, 2019).

9 Anthony Giddens, "Living in a Post-traditional Society," in *Reflexive Modernization: Politics, Tradition and Aesthetics in the Modern Social Order*, eds. Ulrich Beck, Anthony Giddens, and Scott Lash (Stanford, CA: Stanford University Press, 1994), 56.

10 Giddens, "Living in a Post-traditional Society," 84.

11 For work on placemaking, see for instance, Derek Thomas, *Placemaking: An Urban Design Methodology* (London: Taylor & Francis, 2016); Wessel Strydom, Karen Puren, and Ernst Drewes, "Exploring Theoretical Trends in Placemaking: Towards New Perspectives in Spatial Planning," *Journal of Place Management and Development* 11, no. 2 (2018): 165–180, https://doi.org/10.1108/JPMD-11-2017-0113; Andrew Zitcer, "Making Up Creative Placemaking," *Journal of Planning Education and Research* 40, no. 3 (September 2020): 278–288, https://doi.org/10.1177/0739456X18773424.

12 Giddens, "Living in a Post-traditional Society," 85.

13 See Sarina Theys and Katharina Rietig, "The Influence of Small States: How Bhutan Succeeds in Influencing Global Sustainability Governance," *International Affairs* 9, no. 6 (November 2020): 1603–1622, https://doi.org/10.1093/ia/iiaa157.

14 "GNH Happiness Index," GNH Centre Bhutan, accessed January 15, 2024, https://www.gnhcentrebhutan.org/gnh-happiness-index/.

15 See for instance, GNH Centre Bhutan, accessed January 15, 2024, https://www.gnhcentrebhutan.org/.

16 Kinley Dorji, "Drafting the Constitution: A Profound Task," *Kuensel*, April 12, 2002, quoted in Sonam Kinga, *Democratic Transition in Bhutan: Political Contests as Moral Battles* (Oxon: Taylor & Francis, 2020), 39.

17 Jigme Singye Wangchuk, "His Majesty the King's National Day Address on December 17, 2005," *RAOnline*, December 17, 2005, https://www.raonline.ch/pages/bt/rfam/bt_royalfam01b1.html.

18 Dorji Penjore, "Causes and Conditions of Bhutan's Democratic Transition," *Journal of Bhutan Studies* 37 (Winter 2017): 100, https://www.bhutanstudies.org.bt/jbs-37/.

19 Sonam Kinga, *Democratic Transition in Bhutan: Political Contests as Moral Battles* (Oxon: Taylor & Francis, 2020), 37.

20 Somini Sengupta, "Bhutan Reluctantly Embraces Democracy," *New York Times*, April 23, 2007, https://www.nytimes.com/2007/04/23/world/asia/23iht-web0423-bhutan.5402558.html.

21 "Bhutan Goes to Polls to End Absolute Monarchy," *New York Times*, March 24, 2008, https://www.nytimes.com/2008/03/24/world/asia/24iht-bhutan.1.11366582.html.

22 Jennifer Billock, "The 250-Mile Trans Bhutan Trail Will Reopen after 60 Years," *Smithsonian Magazine*, September 14, 2022, https://www.smithsonianmag.com/travel/ancient-trans-bhutan-trail-will-reopen-after-60-years-180980740/.

23 See J. S. Mehta's wonderful account of this trip in Jagat S. Mehta, "Catalysing Graduated Modernisation through Diplomacy: Nehru's Visit to Bhutan—1958," *World Affairs: The Journal of International Issues* 6, no. 2 (April–June 2002): 84–103, https://www.jstor.org/stable/45064894.

24 "Bhutan Life Expectancy 1950–2024," Macrotrends, accessed January 15, 2024, https://www.macrotrends.net/countries/BTN/bhutan/life-expectancy.

25 Andrea Matles Savada, ed., *Nepal and Bhutan: Country Studies*, 3rd ed. (Washington, D.C.: Federal Research Division, Library of Congress, 1993), http://hdl.loc.gov/loc.gdc/cntrystd.bt.

26 "Dechenphug Lhakhang, Thimphu, Bhutan," *Asian Historical Architecture*, accessed January 15, 2024, https://www.orientalarchitecture.com/sid/1546/bhutan/thimphu/dechenphug-lhakhang.

27 Kunzang Choden, *The Circle of Karma* (New Delhi: Zubaan, 2014). Rpt. 101.

28 Michael Hutt, "Coming Closer to the King," in *Unbecoming Citizens: Culture, Nationhood, and the Flight of Refugees from Bhutan* (New Delhi: Oxford University Press, 2003), 141, https://doi.org/10.1093/acprof:oso/9780195670608.003.0009.

29 Kanak Mani Dixit, "The Dragon Bites its Tail," *Himal* 5, no. 4 (July/August 1992): 18.

30 Jessica Vincent, "Hiking the Newly Restored Trans Bhutan Trail Is the Best Way to Experience the Country," *Condé Nast Traveler*, October 17, 2022, https://www.cntraveler.com/story/hiking-the-newly-restored-trans-bhutan-trail-is-the-best-way-to-experience-the-country. See also Heather Richardson, "I Hiked the Ancient Trans-Bhutan Trail When It Reopened after 60 Years—Here's What It Was Like," *Travel + Leisure*, November 28, 2022, https://www.travelandleisure.com/trans-bhutan-trail-hike-6830191.

31 "Mobile Cellular Subscriptions, per 100 People—Bhutan," World Bank, accessed January 15, 2024, https://data.worldbank.org/indicator/IT.CEL.SETS.P2?locations=BT.

32 Bhutan Media Foundation, *Social Media Landscape in Bhutan*, n.d., http://www.bmf.bt/resources/bmf-publications-reports/. Based on my own limited experiences with social media, I suspect Instagram has begun to overtake Facebook.

33 Bhutanese objections to enforcement of the tobacco ban were covered in international news outlets, including Kencho Wangdi, "Do Bhutan's Anti-smoking Laws Go Too Far?" *Time*, April 12, 2011, https://content.time.com/time/world/article/0,8599,2057774,00.html; Henry Foy, "Bhutan Police Raid Homes to Stub Out Smoking Habit," *Reuters*, January 11, 2011, https://www.reuters.com/article/us-bhutan-smoking/bhutan-police-raid-homes-to-stub-out-smoking-habit-idUSTRE70A2HP20110111, and "If You Smoke, Don't Vacation in This Kingdom," *New York Times*, January 15, 2011, https://www.nytimes.com/2011/01/16/weekinreview/16grist.html. Perhaps appropriately, in 2021, *Bhutan Today* announced the repeal of bans on selling, distributing, buying, possessing, and transporting tobacco within Bhutan on its Facebook page: *Bhutan Today*, "National Assembly deliberates on the Tobacco Control (Amendment) Bill of Bhutan 2021. The Chairperson of the Legislative Committee, Tshewang Lhamo presented on The Tobacco Control (Amendment) Bill of Bhutan 2021," Facebook, June 24, 2021, https://www.facebook.com/bhutantoday/posts/4108396299226002/.

34 See Deki Choden, "The Role of Facebook in an Election within an Emerging Democracy: A Case Study of the 2018 Election in Bhutan" (Master's thesis, Murdoch University, 2019), https://researchportal.murdoch.edu.au/esploro/outputs/graduate/The-role-of-Facebook-in-an/991005541023407891.

35 Chencho Dema, "Rapidly Rising Suicide Rates Become the Second Biggest Killer after Road Accidents in Bhutan," *The Bhutanese*, November 1, 2013,

https://web.archive.org/web/20131103202047/http://www.thebhutanese.bt/rapidly-rising-suicide-rates-become-the-second-biggest-killer-after-road-accidents-in-bhutan/. Claims about "leading cause of death" should be taken with a grain of salt, however; according to the Institute for Health Metrics and Evaluation, for instance, the leading cause of death in Bhutan from 2009 to 2019 was ischemic heart disease, followed by chronic obstructive pulmonary disease, neonatal disorders, and stroke. Meanwhile the *Kuensel*, in 2019, and *Business Bhutan*, in 2022, both reported that Alcoholic Liver Damage or ALD continued to be the leading cause of death in Bhutan. See "Bhutan," Institute for Health Metrics and Evaluation, accessed January 15, 2024, https://www.healthdata.org/bhutan#:~:text=The%20top%20cause%20of%20death,49%20percent%20to%2049%20percent; "ALD Continues to Be the Top Cause of Death," *Kuensel*, July 8, 2019, https://web.archive.org/web/20190802071235/https://kuenselonline.com/ald-continues-to-be-the-top-cause-of-death/, and Tshering Pelden, "ALD Continues to Be Major Cause of Death in the Country," *Business Bhutan*, March 24, 2022, https://businessbhutan.bt/ald-continues-to-be-major-cause-of-death-in-the-country/. Analysis of reported suicides from 2009 to 2013 can be found in Kuenzang Lhadon, "Suicide Trends in Bhutan from 2009 to 2013," *Journal of Bhutan Studies* 30 (Summer 2014): 30–56, https://www.bhutanstudies.org.bt/journal-of-bhutan-studies-vol-30-summer-2014/.

36 Quoted in Madeline Drexler, "500 Lifetimes: Notes on Suicide in Bhutan," *Virginia Quarterly Review* 93, no. 4 (Fall 2017): 184–196, https://www.jstor.org/stable/26434895.

37 Sonam Pelden, "Making Sense of Suicides by School Students in Bhutan: Documenting a Societal Dialogue" (Ph.D. thesis, Curtin University, 2016), 273, https://espace.curtin.edu.au/handle/20.500.11937/2393.

CHAPTER TWO

1 At the Vajrayana summit of 2018, for instance, then-Prime Minister Tshering Tobgay used the formulation of Bhutan as "the last Vajrayana state" to call for the founding of an international Vajrayana center in Bhutan. He used the same framing in an essay published in the *Journal of Bhutan Studies* that year. See Tshering Tobgay, "Buddhist Contributions to Human Development," *Journal of Bhutan Studies* 38, (Summer 2018): 1–14, https://www.bhutanstudies.org.bt/jbs-38/. This framing has been of interest to Western tourists, as seen in this Google-led expedition and the advertising for a resort in Phobjikha: "Bhutan—Lhakhan Thangbi," *Google Arts & Culture*, accessed

January 15, 2024, https://artsandculture.google.com/story/bhutan-thangbi-lhakhang/DwXBsOEonkT_gA?hl=en; "The World's Last Remaining Vajrayana Buddhist Kingdom," *Gangtey Lodge* (blog), December 2022, https://gangteylodge.com/blog/the-worlds-last-remaining-vajrayana-buddhist-kingdom/.

2 Karma Phuntsho, "The Cultural Construction of Bhutan: An Unfinished Story," *Druk Journal* 1, no. 1 (Spring 2015): 66–75, http://drukjournal.bt/the-cultural-construction-of-bhutan-an-unfinished-story/.

3 Jessica Locke, "Buddhist Modernism Underway in Bhutan: Gross National Happiness and Buddhist Political Theory," Religions 11, no. 6 (June 2020): 297. https://doi.org/10.3390/rel11060297.

4 See article 3.1 ("Buddhism is the spiritual heritage of Bhutan") and 3.3 ("It shall be the responsibility of religious institutions and personalities to promote the spiritual heritage of the country while also ensuring that religion remains separate from politics in Bhutan."). See also article 2.2: "The Chhoe-sid-nyi of Bhutan shall be unified in the person of the Druk Gyalpo who, as a Buddhist, shall be the upholder of the Chhoe-sid." The Chhoe-sid is the dual system of governance, discussed in relation to the Zhabdrung, below. Constitution of Bhutan, July 18, 2008, art. 3 § 1; id. art. 3 § 3; *idem* art 2 § 2 (Constitute, Comparative Constitutions Project), https://www.constituteproject.org/constitution/Bhutan_2008.

5 See Christopher D. Wallis, *Tantra Illuminated: The Philosophy, History, and Practice of a Timeless Tradition* (Petaluma, CA: Mattamayūra Press, 2013), 26.

6 Kezang Namgay, *Sacred Dances of Bhutan* (Thimphu: printed by the author, 2014), and Khenpo Phuntsok Tashi, *Invoking Happiness: Guide to the Sacred Festivals of Bhutan & Gross National Happiness* (Thimphu: 2011).

7 For more background on Vajrayana's tantric practices, see Christian K. Wedemeyer, *Making Sense of Tantric Buddhism: History, Semiology, and Transgression in the Indian Traditions* (New York: Columbia University Press, 2013).

8 While aristocratic families continued to practice pre-existing shamanistic rituals retroactively considered Bön (a belief system that became more unified under Buddhist influences), Buddhism thrived within the royal court through the reign of King Rälpachän (r. 817–36). But Rälpachän was assassinated by his brother Langdarma, who is said to have ordered the closing of Tibet's Buddhist monasteries and the disrobing of monks. Langdarma is said to have been assassinated in turn by a student of Padmasambhava, and after his death, the Tibetan empire collapsed into civil war and the rise of regional

warlords, many of them associated with different monasteries and schools of Vajrayana Buddhism.

9 Thirteen centuries seems like a long lifespan for a tree, but the point, of course, is that the landscape retains the signs of the Guru's passing.

10 See Mona Schrempf, "From Popular Pilgrimage Festival to State Monastic Performance—The Politics of Cultural Production at Gomphu Kora, East Bhutan," in *Approaching the Sacred: Pilgrimage in Historical and Intercultural Perspective*, ed. Ute Luig (Berlin: Edition Topoi, 2018), 323–359.

11 They were actually codified after his death, during the reign of the 4th Temporal Ruler (Desi), Tenzin Rabgye (1680–94).

12 See "Sakya History," Sakya Monastery of Tibetan Buddhism, accessed January 15, 2024, https://www.sakya.org/about/sakya-history/.

13 In the Sakya line, for instance, the direct line of transmission disappeared just two generations down from the founder of the line, when the only male heir died prematurely. The Sakyas solved this problem by broadening the pool of those who could preserve genetic continuity to any male family member in the appropriate generation.

14 Karma Phuntsho, *The History of Bhutan* (London: Haus Publishing, 2013), 165.

15 Phuntsho, *The History of Bhutan*, 165

16 See Phuntsho, *The History of Bhutan*, 219–223.

17 See Richard W. Whitecross, "The Zhabdrung's Legacy: Buddhism and Constitutional Transformation in Bhutan," in *Buddhism and Comparative Constitutional Law*, eds. Tom Ginsburg and Benjamin Schonthal (Cambridge: Cambridge University Press, 2023), 73–98. https://doi.org/10.1017/9781009286022.007.

18 Sonam Tobgye, "Guru Padmasambhava and Jurisprudence in Bhutan: Golden Yoke and Silken Knot," *Journal of Bhutan Studies* 34 (Summer 2016): 9–19, https://www.bhutanstudies.org.bt/journal-of-bhutan-studies-volume-34-summer-2016/.

19 As Whitecross notes, Tibet also used a dual system of government, but Tibetan secular administrators were usually laymen, while in Bhutan under Zhabdrung, most administrators were also monks (Whitecross, "The Zhabdrung's Legacy," 76).

20 Adapted from https://gisgeography.com/bhutan-map/#Physical-Map. Used by permission.

21 Phuntsho, *The History of Bhutan*, 259.

22 So too the death of the fifth Dalai Lama (1682) was concealed by his regent or Prime Minister Sangye Gyatso for 15 years, both to prevent neighboring countries from taking advantage of the transition in leadership and to enable the completion of the Potala. As with the Zhabdrung, people were told that the

Dalai Lama was continuing a long retreat. In each case, concealment seems to have created new problems, however; in Tibet, the sixth Dalai Lama was a rebel, resisting his spiritual vows, and known for his appreciation of wine, women, and song.

23 David Jackson, "Portrayals of Zhabdrung Ngawang Namgyal in Bhutanese Painting: Iconography and Common Groupings of the Great Unifier of Bhutan," in *The Dragon's Gift: The Sacred Arts of Bhutan*, eds. Terese Tse Bartholomew and John Johnston (Chicago, IL: Serindia, 2008), 78–87.

24 Sonam Kinga, *Democratic Transition in Bhutan: Political Contests as Moral Battles* (Oxon: Taylor & Francis, 2020), 4.

25 Phuntsho,*The History of Bhutan*, 342.

26 Sangay Dorji, "*'brug gi sde srid khri rabs rim byon gyi mdzad rnam deb ther dpyod ldan dgyes pa'i do shal*" (Thimphu: The Centre for Bhutan Studies and GNH, 2017), quoted in Kinga, *Democratic Transition in Bhutan*, 4.

27 According to Karma Phuntsho, "By the end of the third war, most followers of the Lhapa, Nenyingpa, Shingtapa and Barawa schools had left Bhutan while some, such as the followers of Chagzampa school, were stripped of their power and forced into submission to the Drukpa authority. It must, however, be remembered that many other lamas who cooperated with the Zhabdrung and accepted his political supremacy continued to thrive under Zhabdrung's rule. Among them were the lamas of the Sakyapa school and the followers of many different forms of Nyingma school." Phuntsho, *The History of Bhutan*, 236.

28 After Van Driem 1993, "Dzongkha." https://commons.wikimedia.org/wiki/File:Languages_of_Bhutan_with_labels.svg. Creative Commons license.

29 Phuntsho, *The History of Bhutan*, 254.

30 After Van Driem 1993, "Dzongkha."

31 This may reflect negatively on the Chogyal of Sikkim Palden Thondup Namgyal's second marriage, to US citizen Hope Cooke, whose public statements did not help Sikkim's attempts to maintain independence from India. This provision, if retroactively applied, would also have banned any marriage between, say, the third King and his Tibetan consort Yangki.

32 See Whitecross, "The Zhabdrung's Legacy." I wrote to Whitecross to ask for more details about this "brief challenge." He replied: "The reference is from a note of the constitutional drafting committee meetings which were for a time available online but were then taken down. I heard various things from Bhutanese but it is something that they have chosen to elide and there is not anything that I have seen that discusses it. It is one of those tantalising references that I suspect people have chosen to 'forget'": Richard Whitecross, email message to author, May 22, 2023.

33 "Chronology for Lhotshampas in Bhutan," Minorities at Risk Project, 2004, https://www.refworld.org/docid/469f386a1e.html.

34 National Assembly of Bhutan, *Translation of the Proceedings and Resolutions of the 73rd Session of the National Assembly of Bhutan Held from 10th August to 2nd September, 1995*, 74, https://web.archive.org/web/20211203050709/https://www.nab.gov.bt/assets/uploads/docs/resolution/2014/73rd_Session.pdf.

35 This specific objection was raised by the people's representatives of Trashigang, Mongar, Trashiyangtsi, Pemagatshel, Lhuntsi, and Zhemgang: National Assembly of Bhutan, *Translation of the Proceedings and Resolutions of the 73rd Session* [. . .], 38–39, https://web.archive.org/web/20211203050709/https://www.nab.gov.bt/assets/uploads/docs/resolution/2014/73rd_Session.pdf.

CHAPTER THREE

1 See Phuntsho, *The History of Bhutan*, 522. Jigme Tenzin was formally installed as the sixth speech incarnation in 1923, but he was never recognized by the King, and he remained out of the political spotlight until his death in 1949 at age 30.

2 Quoted in Phuntsho, *The History of Bhutan*, 555.

3 See Buddhism Bhutan, "10th Mind Incarnation of Zhabdrung Happy 17th birthday your Holiness la. Today (3-11-2020) is the 17th Birth Anniversary of His Holiness the 10th mind," Facebook, April 22, 2021, https://www.facebook.com/147962355782812/posts/10th-mind-incarnation-of-zhabdrunghappy-17th-birthday-your-holiness-latoday-3-11/878488219396885/, and Dordang Dordang, "HH Zhabdrung Ngawang Namgyal's Yangsi," February 6, 2022, https://www.youtube.com/watch?v=Nxs-nw4lWH4.

4 Phuntsho, *The History of Bhutan*, 558. None of our Bhutanese friends or colleagues ever mentioned this, for instance, though the fourth King and the Zhabdrung both came up in conversation.

5 Bhutanese names may be particularly confusing here, since so many of the names are shared across the two families: Ugyen Wangchuk was the first King; Ugyen Dorji his Chamberlain. Jigme Dorji Wangchuk was the third King; Jigme Palden Dorji his Chamberlain and then his Prime Minister.

6 Karma Phuntsho makes no mention of the British inviting Ugyen Dorji to take up the mantle of kingship himself but does wonder "what inspired Ugyen Dorji to put forth this bold proposal": Phuntsho, *The History of Bhutan*, 518.

7 See Nari Rustomji, *Bhutan: The Dragon Kingdom in Crisis* (New York: Oxford University Press, 1978), 53–65.

8 "Bhutan's Royalty Refutes 'Coup' Claims in Rasgotra Book," *The Hindu*, August 20, 2016, https://www.thehindu.com/news/international/Bhutan%E2%80%99s-Royalty-refutes-%E2%80%9Ccoup%E2%80%9D-claims-in-Rasgotra-book/article14581915.ece.

9 Phuntsho, *The History of Bhutan*, 433.

10 Yab Ugyen Dorji and Ashi Dorji Wangmo Wangchuck, *Of Rainbows and Clouds: The Life of Yab Ugyen Dorji as Told to His Daughter* (London: Serindia, 1999).

11 Kanak Mani Dixit, "The Dragon Bites its Tail," *Himal* 5, no. 4 (July/August 1992): 15.

12 Karma Ura, *Leadership of the Wise: Kings of Bhutan* (Thimphu: Centre for Bhutan Studies, 2010), 2.

13 Locke, "Buddhist Modernism Underway."

14 Kinga, *Democratic Transition in Bhutan*, 6.

15 Constitution of Bhutan, July 18, 2008, art. 2; *idem* art. 3 (Constitute, Comparative Constitutions Project), https://www.constituteproject.org/constitution/Bhutan_2008.

16 "The Reality of Kidu," *Kuensel*, May 1, 2021, https://kuenselonline.com/the-reality-of-kidu/.

17 Kinga, *Democratic Transition in Bhutan*, 6.

18 "Direct Democracy," Federal Department of Foreign Affairs, Swiss Confederation, updated July 14, 2021, https://www.eda.admin.ch/aboutswitzerland/en/home/politik-geschichte/politisches-system/direkte-demokratie.html.

19 Tashi Wangchuk, "The Middle Path to Democracy in the Kingdom of Bhutan," *Asian Survey* 44, no. 6 (November/December 2004): 836, https://doi.org/10.1525/as.2004.44.6.836.

20 Leo E. Rose, *The Politics of Bhutan* (Ithaca, NY: Cornell University Press, 1977), quoted in Tashi Wangchuk, "The Middle Path to Democracy in the Kingdom of Bhutan," *Asian Survey* 44, no. 6 (November/December 2004), 836.

21 James C. Scott, *Weapons of the Weak: Everyday Forms of Peasant Resistance* (New Haven, CT: Yale University Press, 1987).

22 Wangchuk, "The Middle Path," 841.

23 See for instance, Manu Sharma and Dupthup Zangmo, "The Participation of Women in Local Government in Bhutan: A Study of Sarpang District," *International Journal of Economic Research* 14, no. 20 (2017): 673–679,

https://serialsjournals.com/index.php?route=product/product/volume article&issue_id=276&product_id=364. See also World Bank, "Proportion of Seats Held by Women in National Parliaments in Bhutan from 2012 to 2022," chart, February 21, 2024, Statista, accessed February 29, 2024, https://www.statista.com/statistics/730576/bhutan-proportion-of-seats-held-by-women-in-national-parliament.

24 See Robert A. Dahl, *After the Revolution? Authority in a Good Society*, rev. ed. (New Haven, CT: Yale University Press, 1990), quoted in Wangchuk, "The Middle Path,": 842, https://doi.org/10.1525/as.2004.44.6.836, and Robert D. Putnam, *Making Democracy Work: Civic Traditions in Modern Italy* (Princeton, NJ: Princeton University Press, 1993), 171, quoted in Wangchuk, "The Middle Path," : 842, https://doi.org/10.1525/as.2004.44.6.836.

25 Wangchuk, "The Middle Path," 842.

26 A. C. Sinha, *Bhutan: Ethnic Identity and National Dilemma* (New Delhi: Reliance Publishing House, 1991), quoted in Michael Hutt, *Unbecoming Citizens: Culture, Nationhood, and the Flight of Refugees from Bhutan* (New Delhi: Oxford University Press, 2003), 131, https://doi.org/10.1093/acprof:oso/9780195670608.001.0001.

27 Hutt, *Unbecoming Citizens*, 131.

28 Rose, *The Politics of Bhutan*, quoted in Hutt, *Unbecoming Citizens*, 131, https://doi.org/10.1093/acprof:oso/9780195670608.001.0001.

29 Om Dhungel and James Button. *Bhutan to Blacktown: Losing everything and finding Australia* (Sydney: NewSouth Books, 2023), 56.

30 According to Karma Phuntsho, these development committees "included many more village elders and community leaders in the deciding the needs and implementing the programmes of development at the level of a county": Phuntsho, *The History of Bhutan*, 427.

31 In 2002, a new chathrim or law shifted the political make-up and impact of these intermediate bodies, changing the DYT from a Tshogchung (committee) to a Tshogdu (council), and providing for a new elected chair, a thrizin, to replace the appointed dzongda or district governor, who had previously served as chair of the DT. This created some confusion and competition over relative authority, especially between the (appointed) dzongda and the (elected) thrizin, given the fact that thrizin or chair must rely on the dzongda to access the resources necessary to implement the council's plans. For more details, see Dorji Penjore, "Who Should Bow to Whom? Power and Politics between Dzongda and Thrizin," *A Bowl of Suja* (blog), December 15, 2022, https://dorjipenjore.wordpress.com/2022/12/15/who-should-bow-to-whom-power-and-politics-between-the-dzongda-and-the-thrizin/.

32 Karma Phuntsho, "Echoes of Ancient Ethos: Reflections on Some Popular Bhutanese Social Themes," in *The Spider and the Piglet: Proceedings of the First International Seminar on Bhutan Studies*, eds. Karma Ura and Sonam Kinga (Thimphu: Centre for Bhutan Studies, 2004), 565. Phuntsho also engages other terms such as le judre and tha damtshig, but I will focus here on Tsawasum and driglam namzha.

33 Phuntsho, "Echoes of Ancient Ethos," 572.

34 Phuntsho, "Echoes of Ancient Ethos," 572.

35 Winnie Bothe, "The Monarch's Gift: Critical Notes on the Constitutional Process in Bhutan," *European Bulletin of Himalayan Research*, no. 40 (Spring–Summer 2012): 33, http://www.digitalhimalaya.com/collections/journals/ebhr/index.php?selection=40.

36 Phuntsho, "Echoes of Ancient Ethos," 571–572. As Phuntsho had pointed out, "*Drig* (*sgrigs*) denotes order, conformity and uniformity. Thus *driglam* literally means the way or path (*lam*) having order and uniformity." Phuntsho notes that others who have translated *driglam namzha* as "the way of conscious harmony" seem to have "confounded *namzha* – concept or system – with *rnam shes* – consciousness."

37 Bothe, "The Monarch's Gift," : 27–58.

38 See Norbert Elias et al., *The Civilizing Process: Sociogenetic and Psychogenetic Investigations*, rev. ed. (Oxford: Blackwell Publishers, 2000), and Pierre Bourdieu, "Structures, *Habitus*, Practices" in *The Logic of Practice*, trans. Richard Nice (Stanford, CA: Stanford University Press, 1990), 52–65.

39 Yonten Dargey, *An Introduction to Values Education* (Thimphu: National Library, 2005), 36, quoted in Bothe, "The Monarch's Gift," 36.

40 Bothe, "The Monarch's Gift," 36.

41 Dargey, "An Introduction to Values," quoted in Bothe, "The Monarch's Gift," 34.

42 Phuntsho, "Echoes of Ancient Ethos," 576.

43 Highlighting the doctrinal paradox of using Tsawasum and slogans like 'One Nation, One People' to arouse "a fervent sense of nationalism," Phuntsho points out that the "value of nationalism itself is ambiguous [. . .]. Looking from a Buddhist perspective, sentient beings have the inborn inclination to love oneself and what is one's own. This attachment, of all negative impulses, is the main cause of problems in the world and the root of the cycle of existence." Still, the religious incoherence of a patriotic devotion to Tsawasum appeared irrelevant in Bhutan's time of trouble: Phuntsho, "Echoes of Ancient Ethos," 577.

44 Phuntsho, "Echoes of Ancient Ethos," 576.

45 Phuntsho, "Echoes of Ancient Ethos," 564.

46 National Assembly of Bhutan, *Proceedings and Resolutions of the 70th Session of the National Assembly of Bhutan*, 1, https://web.archive.org/web/20211203043457/https://www.nab.gov.bt/assets/uploads/docs/resolution/2014/70th_Session.pdf.

47 National Assembly of Bhutan, *Proceedings and Resolutions of the 70th Session* [. . .], 78–79.

48 National Assembly of Bhutan, *Proceedings and Resolutions of the 70th Session* [. . .], 80.

49 National Assembly of Bhutan, *Proceedings and Resolutions of the 70th Session* [. . .], 84.

50 National Assembly of Bhutan, *Proceedings and Resolutions of the 70th Session* [. . .], 4.

51 Later, the Kasho seems to suggest that secret ballot elections for the Council of Ministers will hold the "the divisive forces of regionalism and communalism" at bay, though the specific mechanism of checks and balances within the election remain unclear: National Assembly of Bhutan, *Translation of the Proceedings and Resolutions of the 76th Session of the National Assembly of Bhutan Held from the Fifth Day of the Fifth Month to the Seventh Day of the Sixth Month Of The Male Earth Tiger Year (June 29th to July 30th, 1998)*, 5–6, https://web.archive.org/web/20200527212358/https://www.nab.gov.bt/assets/uploads/docs/resolution/2014/76th_Session.pdf.

52 National Assembly of Bhutan, *Translation of the Proceedings and Resolutions of the 76th Session* [. . .], 10.

53 National Assembly of Bhutan, *Translation of the Proceedings and Resolutions of the 76th Session* [. . .], 10.

54 National Assembly of Bhutan, *Translation of the Proceedings and Resolutions of the 76th Session* [. . .], 8–12.

55 National Assembly of Bhutan, *Translation of the Proceedings and Resolutions of the 76th Session* [. . .], 9.

56 National Assembly of Bhutan, *Translation of the Proceedings and Resolutions of the 76th Session* [. . .], 8.

57 National Assembly of Bhutan, *Translation of the Proceedings and Resolutions of the 76th Session* [. . .], 15.

58 At least one suggestion that would have deepened or extended democratic processes while also causing delay was dismissed. Some representatives explicitly worried about their constituents' possible response to the proposed political changes; two members (from Paro and Bumthang districts)

argued that "it will be better if His Majesty the King's Kasho, proposing that cabinet ministers should be elected by the National Assembly through secret ballot, is first explained by the Chimis to the people in their respective constituencies and the views of the people are then submitted during the next session of the National Assembly." This proposal, despite its commitment to the ideals of representative democracy, fell flat—presumably because it would have delayed implementation of the King's commandment by another year: National Assembly of Bhutan, *Translation of the Proceedings and Resolutions of the 76th Session* [. . .], 13.

59 National Assembly of Bhutan, *Translation of the Proceedings and Resolutions of the 76th Session* [. . .], 17–18.

60 Lyonpo Sonam Tobgye (personal communication, December 28, 2018), quoted in Kinga, *Democratic Transition in Bhutan*, 40.

61 Jigme Singye Wangchuk, "His Majesty the King's National Day Speech in Samtse 2002," 2002, *RAOnline*, transcript, https://www.raonline.ch/pages/story/bt/btbg08.html.

62 Jigme Singye Wangchuk, "King of Bhutan's National Day Address," December 20, 2004, South Asian Terrorism Portal, transcript, https://www.satp.org/document/paper-acts-and-oridinances/king-of-bhutan-s-national-day-address. Worth noting here is the length of time between the first creation of the DYT (1981) and GYT (1991) and the moment when they were granted administrative, policy-making and financial powers (2002–04)—as well as the fact that the GYT were established in the midst of the Lhotshampa crisis.

63 Recent instances of royal gifts/social support include firewood for those keeping watch during cold nights in the pandemic, as well as supplemental medicines, laptops for researchers, programming tools for children, and more: Ugyen Tshering, "An Honour of Delivering His Majesty's 'Soelra,'" *My Own Thoughts* (blog), February 25, 2021, https://ugentshering.blogspot.com/2021/02/delivering-kings-firewood-soelra-to.html; Dechen Dolkar, "Supplement Medicine Soelra Saves Countless Lives," *Kuensel*, February 21, 2023, https://kuenselonline.com/supplement-medicine-soelra-saves-countless-lives/; "His Majesty the King Grants a Laptop to Soelra to Researchers," *Zhichenkhar Center For Bhutan & GNH Studies,* November *2021*, https://dziseldra.com/seldra/9494#/; "His Majesty the King Grants Soelra for Children to Learn Coding," *Kuensel*, July 21, 2021, https://kuenselonline.com/his-majesty-the-king-grants-soelra-for-children-to-learn-coding/.

64 Bothe, "The Monarch's Gift," 28.

65 Bothe, "The Monarch's Gift," 41.

66 Bothe, "The Monarch's Gift," 41.

67 Kinga, *Democratic Transition in Bhutan*, 40. Kinga also describes the gift of the Constitution being "re-sanctified" by being signed into law by the fifth King, parliamentarians, and the chief justice—after a day of monastic prayer. (Kinga also discusses the King's ongoing use of kidu later in the book.)

68 For an account of confusion at the District Development Councils, see for instance, Penjore, "Who Should Bow to Whom?"

CHAPTER FOUR

1 Jamie Zeppa, *Beyond the Sky and the Earth: A Journey into Bhutan* (New York: Penguin Group, 2000).

2 *The Southern Bhutan Problem: Threat to a Nation's Survival* (Thimphu: Ministry of Home Affairs, 1993), 4, http://dspace.cus.ac.in/jspui/handle/1/4327.

3 *The Southern Bhutan Problem*, 4.

4 See the Dangerous Speech Project at https://www.dangerousspeech.org/.

5 As mentioned in the Preface, Jessica Locke notes that "Sikkim, Spiti, Lahul and Ladakh have been absorbed by India; Dolpo, Mustang, Solu-Khumbu and Walung are now Nepalese districts, and of course, Tibet has been colonized and systematically Sinicized by China." Locke, "Buddhist Modernism Underway," 297.

6 For a description of pressures applied to the political process in Sikkim as "a political trick and debauchery," see for instance Nar Bahadur Khatiawara et al., "Sikkim's Merger—A Brief Resume" (unpublished manuscript, July 31, 1977), quoted in Andrew Duff, *Sikkim: Requiem for a Himalayan Kingdom* (Edinburgh: Birlinn Limited, 2015), 224, 308.

7 Other princely states had previously been forcibly annexed by India: Hyderabad and Goa both suffered violent annexations in the years immediately after the British withdrawal.

8 Dago Tshering, quoted in Kanak Mani Dixit, "The Dragon Bites its Tail," *Himal* 5, no. 4 (July/August 1992): 9. Tshering made similar statements in 1991 during the National Assembly debates. *Proceedings and Resolutions of the 70th Session of the National Assembly of Bhutan* (n.p.: n.p., 1991), quoted in Michael Hutt, *Unbecoming Citizens: Culture, Nationhood, and the Flight of Refugees from Bhutan* (New Delhi: Oxford University Press, 2003), 197, https://doi.org/10.1093/acprof:oso/9780195670608.001.0001.

9 Evidently the King also told Reuters that Bhutan was facing "the greatest threat to its survival since the seventh century"—though as Dixit noted, Bhutan was not unified as a nation until the seventeenth century (Dixit,

"The Dragon Bites its Tail," 9). The odd comment to Reuters could potentially have been the result of a typo transforming the "17th" century into the "7th" century.

10 Hutt, *Unbecoming Citizens*, 129.

11 In 1991, for instance, the home minister argued that there was no need for development activities in the south, rhetorically demanding "where all the industries were located, where all the lucrative cardamom and orange gardens were located, and which part of the country had the maximum number of schools and hospitals": National Assembly of Bhutan, *Proceedings and Resolutions of the 70th Session of the National Assembly of Bhutan* (n.p.: National Assembly of Bhutan, 1991), https://web.archive.org/web/20230329132127/nab.gov.bt/assets/uploads/docs/resolution/2014/70th_Session.pdf, 75.

12 Dixit, "The Dragon Bites its Tail," 17. For a much more detailed account, see Michael Hutt, "The Settlement and Administration of the South," in Hutt, *Unbecoming Citizens*.

13 Dixit, "The Dragon Bites its Tail," 17.

14 Dixit, "The Dragon Bites its Tail," 13.

15 Hutt, *Unbecoming Citizens*, 174–175. Dixit reported that the "penalty for going without a gho is a week's labour or Nu 150, of which the apprehending officer is allowed to pocket half" (Dixit, "The Dragon Bites its Tail," 18). Hutt's informants also spoke of being "harrassed, assaulted, imprisoned, or fined for wearing traditional Nepali costume for occasions on which it had previously been customary, such as weddings and funerals."

16 My own experience teaching experienced public school teachers in a graduate degree program suggests that English as a language of instruction would have been heavily supplemented by local languages: my students repeatedly translated my instructions into Dzongkha or Sharchops for those who still struggled with English.

17 Hutt emphasizes that citizenship was sometimes revoked over the course of repeated censuses: a Lhotshampa identified as F1 in the 1988 census might later be reclassified as F7.

18 Omair Ahmad, "The Forgotten 'NRC' in Bhutan," *The Wire*, September 25, 2019, https://thewire.in/rights/the-forgotten-nrc-in-bhutan. This reference to the United States is misleading, given Bhutan's rejection of the US norm of "birthright citizenship," guaranteed by the Fourteenth Amendment. Still, years later, Danish scholar Line Christensen interviewed Lhotshampa students at Sherubtse College who as non-national Bhutanese residents were able to access government scholarships to Sherubtse but not abroad,

suggesting the general validity of the minister's claim. See Line Kikkenborg Christensen, "Piecing Together Past and Present in Bhutan: Narration, Silence and Forgetting in Conflict," *International Journal of Conflict and Violence* 12 (2018): 7, https://doi.org/10.4119/ijcv-3108.

19 From *Bhutan: Human Rights Violations against the Nepali-speaking Population in the South* (London: Amnesty International, 1992), as reproduced in Hutt, *Unbecoming Citizens*, 154.

20 *U.S. Department of State Country Report on Human Rights Practices 1993—Bhutan* (n.p.: United States Department of State, 1994), https://www.refworld.org/docid/3ae6aa4d4.html.

21 Bhutan became a UN member nation in 1971—a status which affirms global recognition of national sovereignty. Sikkim never achieved UN member status, leaving it more vulnerable to annexation.

22 Michael Hutt, drawing on figures provided by Leo Rose, notes that the main difference in the revised figures comes from the fact that "the grand total given in the 1969 report is exactly 100,000 greater than the sum total of district populations as listed. Quite simply, someone got their sums wrong." See Hutt, *Unbecoming Citizens*, 150–151 and Leo E. Rose,"The Politics of Bhutan" (Ithaca, NY: Cornell University Press, 1977), 40–41.

23 Tabulated from data in Dixit, "The Dragon Bites Its Tail," in combination with results from the 1969 Census. Dixit also states that an international agency estimated the percentage of Nepali speakers at 45 percent, between the claims of the government and those of Lhotshampa leaders: Dixit, "The Dragon Bites its Tail," 17.

24 Dinesh Dhakal noted the impact on GDP calculations: "In June 1991, Bhutan's per capita Gross National Product (GNP) jumped from US $190 to US $425 [. . .] due not to a sudden spurt in national productivity, but because of a drastic official reduction of the population estimate from 1.4 million to 0.6 million. This was done on the pretext of correcting a mistake the Government says it made when it joined the UN," D. N. S. Dhakal, "Economic Blueprint for a South Asian Dragon," *Himal* 5, no. 4 (July/August 1992), 34.

25 Dixit, "The Dragon Bites its Tail," 30.

26 Michael Hutt, "The Bhutanese Refugees: Between Verification, Repatriation and Royal Realpolitik," *Peace and Democracy in South Asia* 1, no. 1 (January 2005): 47, http://www.digitalhimalaya.com/collections/journals/pdsa/. Dixit quotes Bhutanese refugees speculating that the crisis would cease once 100,000 Lhotshampa had been expelled from Bhutan. Dixit, "The Dragon Bites its Tail," 30.

27 *Bhutan: Human Rights Violations Against the Nepali-Speaking Population in the South* ([London]: Amnesty International, 1992), 8, quoted in Hutt, *Unbecoming Citizens*, 199.

28 For number of pamphlet-writers arrested, see *Bhutan: Human Rights Violations Against the Nepali-Speaking Population in the South*, 8. Hutt reports that "In 1986, while working for the Royal Audit Commission, [Rizal] uncovered a number of cases in which well-connected senior officials had embezzled government funds. A fellow political prisoner later wrote that the harsh nature of the response to the petition and the 'scapegoating' of Rizal were primarily the consequence of resentment against him for his work for the Audit Commission." See Bhakti Prasad Bhandari, "Hostage in Thimphu," *Himal* (March/April 1994), 31–34, cited in Hutt, *Unbecoming Citizens*, 200.

29 Royal Government of Bhutan, *Anti-National Activities in Southern Bhutan: A Terrorist Movement* (Thimphu: Department of Information, 1991), 37, quoted in Hutt, *Unbecoming Citizens*, 203.

30 Royal Government of Bhutan, *The Southern Bhutan Problem: Threat to a Nation's Survival* (Thimphu: Ministry of Home Affairs, 1993), 57, quoted in Hutt, *Unbecoming Citizens*, 217, https://doi.org/10.1093/acprof:oso/9780195670608.001.0001.

31 The US State Department report noted that "in 1993 growing numbers of refugees reported their citizenship was revoked under this provision," *U.S. Department of State Country Report on Human Rights Practices 1993—Bhutan*, https://www.refworld.org/docid/3ae6aa4d4.html.

32 Rosalind Evans, "The Perils of Being a Borderland People: On the Lhotshampas of Bhutan," *Contemporary South Asia* 18, no. 1 (2010): 33–34.

33 Evans, "The Perils of Being a Borderland People," 33.

34 Hutt, *Unbecoming Citizens*, 209.

35 Om Dhungel and James Button, *Bhutan to Blacktown: Losing Everything and Finding Australia* (Sydney: NewSouth, 2023), 84–85.

36 Dixit, "The Dragon Bites its Tail," 17.

37 *U.S. Department of State Country Report on Human Rights Practices 1993—Bhutan*, https://www.refworld.org/docid/3ae6aa4d4.html. For additional evidence of torture used against Lhotshampa refugees, see Nirakar Man Shrestha et al., "Impact of Torture on Refugees Displaced within the Developing World: Symptomatology among Bhutanese Refugees in Nepal," *JAMA* 280, no. 5 (1998): 443–448, https://doi.org/10.1001/jama.280.5.443 quoted in Hutt, *Unbecoming Citizens*, 215.

38 Interview with a Refugee Woman, December 17, 2007, quoted in Evans, "The Perils of Being a Borderland People," 34, https://doi.org/10.1080/09584930903561598

39 Dixit, "The Dragon Bites its Tail," 19. Dhungel similarly asserts that compensation was roughly 10 percent of the value of properties left behind.

40 National Assembly of Bhutan, *Proceedings and Resolutions*, 23.

41 National Assembly of Bhutan, *Proceedings and Resolutions*, 65. The King had also exempted the Lhotshampas from rural taxes in 1991, in consideration of the difficulties suffered by the population as a whole: "Chronology for Lhotshampas in Bhutan," Minorities at Risk Project, The United Nations Refugees Agency, archived May 18, 2023, https://webarchive.archive.unhcr.org/20230519012329/https://www.refworld.org/docid/469f386a1e.html.

42 National Assembly of Bhutan, *Proceedings and Resolutions*, 70.

43 National Assembly of Bhutan, *Proceedings and Resolutions*, 71–72.

44 Quoted in "Chronology for Lhotshampas"; for efforts to have the pledge removed from the official record, see National Assembly of Bhutan, *Proceedings and Resolutions*.

45 National Assembly of Bhutan, *Proceedings and Resolutions*, 75–76.

46 National Assembly of Bhutan, *Proceedings and Resolutions*, 76.

47 See the definition at the Dangerous Speech Project, founded by Susan Benesch: https://www.dangerousspeech.org/dangerous-speech.

48 See Dixit, "The Dragon Bites its Tail."

49 "His Majesty Appeals to Lhotshampa Migrants Not to Leave Their Country," *Kuensel*, July 18, 1992, quoted in Hutt, *Unbecoming Citizens*, 224.

50 Kinley Dorji, "Hoping for a Gentler Judgement," *Himal Southasian*, July/August 1992, 39.

51 See the Minorities at Risk Project, "Chronology for Lhotshampas."

52 Phuntsho, "The History of Bhutan," 581.

53 Phuntsho, "The History of Bhutan," 581.

54 Hutt, "The Bhutanese Refugees."

55 *Last Hope: The Need for Durable Solutions for Bhutanese Refugees in Nepal and India* (n.p.: Human Rights Watch, 2007), https://www.refworld.org/reference/countryrep/hrw/2007/en/43088.

56 According to Michael Hutt, some individuals who had come from Bhutan as minors and thus had no citizenship papers were classified as non-nationals despite their parents being classified as bonafide Bhutanese or emigrants. Other children were classified as criminals because their fathers were classified as such.

57 Phuntsho, "The History of Bhutan," 581; Hutt, "The Bhutanese Refugees," 50.

58 Hutt, "The Bhutanese Refugees," 50–51.

59 Keshav P. Koirala, "Where in US, Elsewhere Bhutanese Refugees from Nepal Resettled To," *Himalayan Times*, February 6, 2017, https://thehimalayantimes.com/nepal/where-in-earth-have-been-bhutanese-refugees-from-nepal-resettled; *UNHCR Statistical Yearbook 2016* (Geneva: United Nations High Commissioner for Refugees, 2017), https://www.unhcr.org/statistics/country/5a8ee0387/unhcr-statistical-yearbook-2016-16th-edition.html.

60 See Ashley K. Hagaman et al., "An Investigation into Suicides among Bhutanese Refugees Resettled in the United States between 2008 and 2011," *Journal of Immigrant Minority Health* 18, no. 4 (August 2016): 819–827, https://doi.org/10.1007/s10903-015-0326-6 and Laura A. Vonnahme et al.,"Factors Associated with Symptoms of Depression among Bhutanese Refugees in the United States," *Journal of Immigrant Minority Health* 17, no. 6 (December 2015): 1705–1714, https://doi.org/10.1007/s10903-014-0120-x.

61 Jigmi Y. Thinley, "Gross National Happiness: A Holistic Paradigm for Sustainable Development," *APFA News*, December 23, 2011, https://www.apfanews.com/commentary/gross-national-happiness-a-holistic-paradigm-for-sustainable-development.html.

62 Phuntsho, "The History of Bhutan," 436.

63 "Bhutan: Freedom in the World 2023 Country Report," Freedom House, accessed January 15, 2024, https://freedomhouse.org/country/bhutan/freedom-world/2023.

64 Line Kikkenborg Christensen, "Freedom of Speech and Silent Youth Protest in Bhutan: 'Plz Delete it from Your Inbox,'" *South Asia Research* 37, no. 1 (February 2017): 105, https://doi.org/10.1177/0262728016675523.

65 Line Kikkenborg Christensen, "Piecing Together Past and Present in Bhutan: Narration, Silence and Forgetting in Conflict," *International Journal of Conflict and Violence* 12 (2018): 6, https://doi.org/10.4119/ijcv-3108.

66 Christensen, "Piecing Together," 10.

67 See Sonam Chophel and Karma Phuntsho, "Kharamshing: A Structure to Ward off the Effects of Gossip," Bhutan Cultural Library, The University of Virginia, 2017, https://texts.mandala.library.virginia.edu/text/kharamshing-structure-ward-effects-gossip.

68 https://kuenselonline.com/his-majesty-the-king-grants-citizenship-to-163/

69 https://kuenselonline.com/picture-story-1238/

CHAPTER FIVE

1 For discussion of SDGs in relation to GNH, see John Helliwell, Richard Layard, and Jeffrey Sachs, *World Happiness Report* (New York: UN Sustainable Development Solutions Network, 2012), https://worldhappiness.report/ed/2012/. Actual influence is harder to trace, especially between GNH and BLI, though the two measures are not infrequently considered together, and the first GNH surveys (2008, 2010) preceded the launch of the BLI in 2011.

2 Drawn from Sriram Balasubramanian and Paul Cashin. *Gross National Happiness and Macroeconomic Indicators in the Kingdom of Bhutan*, International Monetary Fund, 2019.

3 Kinley Dorji, "The Story of Bhutanese Culture," *Druk Journal* 1, no. 2 (Winter 2015): 63, http://drukjournal.bt/the-bhutanese-state-and-its-institute/.

4 Tourism is indeed a major source of income for Bhutan: in 2018, for instance, 274,097 tourists visited Bhutan, bringing in revenues estimated at US$85.4 million, second only to hydroelectric revenues of approximately US$180 million in the same year. Tourism revenues drawn from *Bhutan Tourism Monitor 2018* (Thimphu: Tourism Council of Bhutan, 2018), 6–7, https://www.tourism.gov.bt/uploads/attachment_files/tcb_xx8r_BTM%202018%20_final.pdf.

Hydroelectric revenues drawn from *Annual Report 2018* (Thimphu: Druk Green Power Corporation Limited, 2018), 7 https://www.drukgreen.bt/en/annual-reports/. Average exchange rate BTN to USD in 2018 was 0.0147.) Bhutan's hydroelectric production has already suffered from inconsistency in river flows, as noted in the Druk Green Power Annual Report 2018, but in Bhutan's case, the loss of glacial ice may be compensated at least in part by increased monsoon rains.

5 The recent post-pandemic increase in Bhutan's "Sustainable Development Fee" from $65 to $200 offers one answer to the question of how to pull tourism dollars away from multinational corporations and into funding human needs, but that fee was halved in September 2023 to try to boost a tourism industry that had not yet rebounded from Covid restrictions.

6 Other voices similarly praise the traditional value of village communities. Anthony Giddens, for instance, describes the moment of high modernity in terms of the "evacuation of local contexts," arguing that the "disembedding consequences of abstract systems" ties globalization to "the excavations of traditional contexts of action." Giddens' link between globalizing modernity, and the excavation of local contexts set Karma Ura's idealizing of village life in a different context for me. Later in the year, a Japanese scholar visiting

Sherubtse College talked about the social costs (in Japan) of rural-urban migration. Karma Ura had also conducted earlier research into small communities' collective approach to food security and land rights. According to "The Nomads' Gamble: Pastoralists of Northern Bhutan," for instance, "a household's diversification of its livestock holding includes several species of cattle, and also equines and pigs," as well as "a wide range of crops and vegetables, [. . .] exploiting various agronomic skills, ecological niches and institutional frameworks." The goal of this diversification was to "reduce risk between seasons, and between and within households and communities, through well-defined access to and entitlements over numerous micro-environments." In the same essay, Karma Ura stressed the use of different protocols to support consensus decision-making about the assigning of summer and winter pastures for yak herders in Haa and cattle herders in Ura, as well as norms of community labor in clearing and maintaining pastures and forest tracks. Karma Ura's praise of small communities might seem nostalgic from a distance, but he argues that "the persistence of pasture distributive rules for centuries without damaging the forest calls for greater faith in the system" (97). Karma Ura, like Nobel economist Elinor Ostrom, was focused on communities' collective capacity to manage their shared resources. See Karma Ura, "The Nomads' Gamble: Pastoralists of Northern Bhutan," *South Asia Research* 13, no. 2 (September 1993): 81–100, https://doi.org/10.1177/026272809301300201, and Elinor Ostrom, *Governing the Commons: The Evolution of Institutions for Collective Action* (Cambridge: Cambridge University Press, 1990), 90, 91–102.

7 Compiled from the *Extensive Analysis*, p. 26, the OECD Better Life Index (https://www.oecdbetterlifeindex.org), and the United Nations Sustainable Development Goals (https://unstats.un.org/sdgs/indicators/Global%20Indicator%20Framework%20after%202023%20refinement_Eng.pdf). The alignment of comparable domains or indicators is my own; others might suggest slightly different arrangements. SDG 2 (End hunger), for instance, could be considered part of health instead of living standards. Still, the major point here is that none of the major beyond-GDP measures engage cultural diversity and resilience—and examples of beyond-GDP measures includes not just the SDGs and the BLI but also the Human Development Index, the Sustainable Development Index, the Genuine Progress Index, the Happy Planet Index, and others. This disregard for culture remains even as climate scientists increasingly call for greater public, cultural engagement in reversing ongoing growth in carbon emissions.

8 https://documents-dds-ny.un.org/doc/UNDOC/GEN/G22/383/75/PDF/G2238375.pdf?OpenElement

9 Ilona M. Otto et al. "Social tipping dynamics for stabilizing Earth's climate by 2050," *Proceedings of the National Academy of Sciences* 117.5 (2020): 2354–2365. The article works to provide a counterpoint to the physical climate's tipping points—where small changes trigger irreversible system shifts—by articulating social tipping points that might lead to more effective climate action.

10 Celebration of Bhutan's linguistic diversity should be noted and supported: Indigenous languages are often repositories of Traditional Ecological Knowledge (TEK) and loss of languages is correlated with loss of biodiversity. See L. J. Gorenflo et al., "Co-occurrence of Linguistic and Biological Diversity in Biodiversity Hotspots and High Biodiversity Wilderness Areas," *Proceedings of the National Academy of Sciences* 109, no. 21 (May 22, 2012): 8032–8037, https://doi.org/10.1073/pnas.1117511109.

11 Drawn from *The Second Gross National Happiness Survey Questionnaire* (April 2010), the *Extensive Analysis* (2012), and *A Compass Toward a Just and Harmonious Society* (2015). The 2022 report suggests the same questions were used in 2022 and in 2015.

12 As with local legends and folktales, the GNH questionnaire could broaden its definition of cultural literacy to include dance and song forms important to various ethnic groups within the country. Similarly, defining cultural literacy as knowledge of more than one group's cultural traditions could strengthen national unity beyond the identity of a single ethnic group.

13 Benedict Anderson, *Imagined Communities: Reflections on the Origin and Spread of Nationalism*, 2nd edition (New York: Verso, 2006), 36.

14 Mona Schrempf, "From Popular Pilgrimage Festival to State Monastic Performance—The Politics of Cultural Production at Gomphu Kora, East Bhutan," in *Approaching the Sacre: Pilgrimage in Historical and Intercultural Perspective*, edited by. Ute Luig (Berlin: Edition Topoi, 2018) 323–359, http://doi.org/10.17169/refubium-490.

15 Dorjee Tshering and Thinley Wangchuk, "Zorig Chusum: Bhutan's Living Arts and Crafts," *Smithsonian Folklife Festival on the National Mall, Washington, D.C.: [Program]* (2008): 30–33, https://festival.si.edu/articles/2008/zorig-chusum-bhutan-s-living-arts-and-crafts.

16 Kuenga Namgay et al., "Transhumant Agro-Pastoralism in Bhutan: Exploring Contemporary Practices and Socio-Cultural Traditions," *Pastoralism: Research, Policy and Practice*, 3 (June 13, 2013): 13, https://doi.org/10.1186/2041-7136-3-13.

17 Degor is played “with a pair of round flat stones, which are thrown in the direction of two wooden targets placed on the ground roughly 20 meters apart. The only required equipment is a pair of flat round stones for each player. The size and weight of the stones vary, depending on player’s strength and preferences”: “Digor or Degor (Bhutan),” *Traditional Sports*, accessed January 15, 2024, https://www.traditionalsports.org/traditional-sports/asia/digor-or-degor-bhutan.html.

18 Ura et al., *An Extensive Analysis*, 133.

19 Ura et al., *An Extensive Analysis*, 122.

20 Phuntsho, *The History of Bhutan*, 447.

21 Gardiner Harris, “Index of Happiness? Bhutan’s New Leader Prefers More Concrete Goals,” *New York Times*, October 4, 2013, https://www.nytimes.com/2013/10/05/world/asia/index-of-happiness-bhutans-new-leader-prefers-more-concrete-goals.html.

22 See for instance, Tshering Tobgay, “This Country Isn’t Just Carbon Neutral—It’s Carbon Negative,” February 2016, TED Video, 18:45, https://www.ted.com/talks/tshering_tobgay_this_country_isn_t_just_carbon_neutral_it_s_carbon_negative. The talk promotes GNH and Bhutanese traditions, including national dress.

23 Draft Concept Note for the 13th Five Year Plan (FYP 2024–29). Posted on the GNH Commission website before its decommissioning. https://web.archive.org/web/20220928130011/https:/www.gnhc.gov.bt/en/wp-content/uploads/2022/05/Draft-Concept-Note-for-the-13FYP-for-Feedback.pdf. Elements of this Draft Concept Note can still be seen in the published 13th Five-Year Plan: https://www.pmo.gov.bt/wp-content/uploads/2019/09/13-FYP.pdf.

24 https://kuenselonline.com/sovereignty-is-the-only-thing-worth-fetishising/.

25 “Bhutan: Freedom in the World 2023 Country Report,” Freedom House, accessed January 15, 2024, https://freedomhouse.org/country/bhutan/freedom-world/2023.

26 Karma Ura et al., *GNH 2022* (Thimphu: Centre for Bhutan and GNH Studies, 2023), 22, https://ophi.org.uk/bhutan-gnh-2022/.

27 See for instance, Juan M. Ramírez-Cendrero, Santiago García, and Alejandro Santillán, “Sumak Kawsay in Ecuador: The Role of Communitarian Economy and the Experience of the Rural Communities in Sarayaku (Ecuadorian Amazonia),” *Journal of Rural Studies* 53 (July 2017): 111–121, https://doi.org/10.1016/j.jrurstud.2017.05.018. Ramírez-Cendrero argues, “the economic relations within the SK are based on three alternative principles to the capitalist rationale: community aid (yanapana by means of the minga), generosity

(kuna by way of gift), and reciprocity (kunakuna by exchange of products over time, without commercial or monetary relations)," 117.

28 In the Better Life Index, for instance, OECD "wealth" far exceeds the accumulation of "assets" a Bhutanese family might achieve. The Bhutanese sufficiency level for annual household income in 2012 was set at Nu 14,200 (US$266.96 in 2012), while the Better Life Index's figure for household net adjusted disposable income in 2013, the first year available, was US$23,047, almost ten times more. Noting the discrepancy does not automatically reduce the gap.The early GNH Index defined housing sufficiency as two persons per room, while in the OECD, the average home contains 1.7 rooms per person—almost four times more spacious. (See "Housing," OECD Better Life Index, accessed January 15, 2024, https://www.oecdbetterlifeindex.org/topics/housing/. and Ura et al., *An Extensive Analysis*, 174.) Where the BLI asks about disposable income, multiple GNH questions look into financial shortfalls and food insecurity. Noting these discrepancies does not automatically reduce the gap in living standards. Still other questions further detail differences in living standard assumptions between OECD citizens and citizens of least developed nations. The GNH questionnaire asks whether a respondent's roof is made of concrete/stone, metal, mud, wood, straw/leaves, bamboo, slate, or other. Is the floor permanent? Uncovered concrete? Wood directly on earth? Clay, plastic, or mud on an earthen base? Dirt? How many rooms? Is piped water available, or does the family have to go to a village tap or a stream or pond? Is there a flush toilet or a pit latrine or no toilet facilities at all? Bhutan's largely agricultural economy is further underscored by the list of equipment a household might be expected to own: tractors top the list, mobile phones appear at #9, a personal computer at #11, and a refrigerator at #12.

29 Joel Millward-Hopkins et al. "Providing Decent Living with Minimum Energy: A Global Scenario," *Global Environmental Change* 65 (November 2020): 102168, https://doi.org/10.1016/j.gloenvcha.2020.102168. See also Joel Millward-Hopkins, "Inequality Can Double the Energy Required to Secure Universal Decent Living," *Nature Communications* 13 (August 26, 2022): 5028, https://doi.org/10.1038/s41467-022-32729-8.

30 See for instance, Robert D. Putnam, *Bowling Alone: The Collapse and Revival of American Community* (New York: Simon and Schuster, 2000), Vivek H. Murthy, *Together: Loneliness, Health and What Happens When We Find Connection* (London: Profile Books, 2021), and Susan Mettes, *The Loneliness Epidemic: Why So Many of Us Feel Alone—and How Leaders Can Respond* (Grand Rapids, MI: Baker Publishing Group, 2021).

31 Karma Phuntsho, "Ridam/Ladam: Closing Mountains to Human Activity," Bhutan Cultural Library, The University of Virginia, 2018, https://texts.mandala.library.virginia.edu/text/ridamladam-closing-mountains-human-activity.

CHAPTER SIX

1 Yab-yum posture shows a male meditational deity in "sexual congress" with his female consort. Yab is Tibetan for father; yum means mother.
2 Karma Phuntsho, "On the Two Ways of Learning in Bhutan," *Journal of Bhutan Studies* 2, no. 2 (Winter 2000): 96–126, https://www.bhutanstudies.org.bt/journal-of-bhutan-studies-vol-2-no-2/.
3 Phuntsho, "On the Two Ways," 96.
4 Phuntsho, "On the Two Ways," 100.
5 Phuntsho, "On the Two Ways," 103.
6 Phuntsho, "On the Two Ways," 101.
7 Diederik Prakke, "Development with Sparks: Placing the Hamburger in the Mandala," in *Gross National Happiness: A Set of Discussion Papers*, eds. Sonam Kinga et al. (Thimphu: The Centre for Bhutan Studies, 1999), 66, 90.
8 Phuntsho cites Planning Commission, "Bhutan 2020: A Vision for Peace, Prosperity and Happiness" (Thimphu: Planning Commission Secretariat, 1999), 30, https://www.fao.org/faolex/results/details/en/c/LEX-FAOC151334/, and Mahbub ul Haq, *Human Development in South Asia 1997* (Karachi: Oxford University Press, 1997), 65–66. See "Education System In Bhutan," *Chhundu Enterprises ECPF, Global Reach* (blog), July 30, 2021, https://web.archive.org/web/20210916180929/https://globalreach.bt/education-system-in-bhutan/ for slightly different dates and figures.
9 In fact, a new Rigney School for the east had been proposed in Bhutan's National Assembly as early as 1995: see National Assembly of Bhutan, *Translation of the Proceedings and Resolutions of the 73rd Session of the National Assembly of Bhutan Held From 10th August to 2nd September, 1995*, 23, https://web.archive.org/web/20211203050709/https://www.nab.gov.bt/assets/uploads/docs/resolution/2014/73rd_Session.pdf.
10 Peter Bridgewater and Ian D. Rotherham, "A Critical Perspective on the Concept of Biocultural Diversity and Its Emerging Role in Nature and Heritage Conservation," *People and Nature* 1, no. 1 (September 2019): 291–304, https://doi.org/10.1002/pan3.10040.
11 Some 35 kilometers further south, the river speeds and deepens enough to support the Khulong hydropower project.

12 "Bumdeling," Ramsar Sites Information Service, May 7, 2012, https://rsis.ramsar.org/ris/2032.

13 "Bumdeling Wildlife Sanctuary," UNESCO World Heritage Convention, August 3, 2012, https://whc.unesco.org/en/tentativelists/5700/.

14 Toni Huber, "Green Tibetans: A Brief Social History," in *Tibetan Culture in the Diaspora: Papers Presented at a Panel of the 7th Seminar of the International Association for Tibetan Studies, Graz 1995*, ed. Frank J. Korom (Wien: Verlag der Österreichischen Akademie der Wissenschaften, 1997), 103–119.

Emily Yeh's work traces the complex politics of landscape ecology in Tibet with implications for the larger Himalayan region. See Emily T. Yeh and Chris Coggins, eds., *Mapping Shangrila: Contested Landscapes in the Sino-Tibetan Borderlands* (Seattle: University of Washington Press, 2014), and Emily T. Yeh, *Taming Tibet: Landscape Transformation and the Gift of Chinese Development* (Ithaca, NY: Cornell University Press, 2013).

15 Karma Phuntsho, "Tasha Tagye: The Eight Auspicious Signs," *Kuensel*, April 23, 2017, https://web.archive.org/web/20170511152343/https://kuenselonline.com/tasha-tagye-the-eight-auspicious-signs/.

16 Sakyong Mipham, "Four Dignities That Bring Confidence into Everyday Life," *Lotus Happiness* (blog), December 24, 2017, https://www.lotus-happiness.com/four-dignities-bring-confidence-everyday-life/.

17 Anderson, *Imagined Communities*.

18 See Khye'u-chung Lotsawa, "The Namchak Putri, or the Meteoric Iron Razor Teachings on Vajrakīlaya," Pema Yoedling, 2009, https://web.archive.org/web/20110427233609/http://pemayoedling.org/Vajrakilaya.htm.

19 Anthony Giddens, "Living in a Post-Traditional Society," in *Reflexive Modernization: Politics, Tradition and Aesthetics in the Modern Social Order*, by Ulrich Beck, Anthony Giddens, and Scott Lash, 56–109 (Stanford, CA: Stanford University Press, 1994), 59.

20 Some people believe this was an instance of child sacrifice in keeping with earlier Bon traditions, that other religious monuments in eastern Bhutan have been found to contain the bones of children. Others say that it is a mistake to think that a human child was involved in this voluntary self-sacrifice. Some say the chorten kora tips toward Tawang in the east, as the dakini-child reaches out toward her people's home.

21 Nima Tshering, "Informing the Blueprint: Bhutan's Strategy for Girls' High-Quality Learning Outcomes," Working Papers from the 2014 Echidna Global Scholars, Center for Universal Education at Brookings, December 16, 2014,

https://www.brookings.edu/articles/informing-the-blueprint-bhutans-strategy-for-girls-high-quality-learning-outcomes/.

22 National Statistics Bureau of Bhutan and Asian Development Bank, *Bhutan Living Standards Survey 2012 Report* (Thimphu: National Statistics Bureau, Bhutan and Asian Development Bank, 2013), 12, https://www.adb.org/publications/bhutan-living-standards-survey-2012.

23 World Economic Forum, *The Global Gender Gap Report 2014* (Geneva: World Economic Forum, 2014), https://www.weforum.org/publications/global-gender-gap-report-2014/.

24 Tshering, "Informing the Blueprint," 6.

25 Ministry of Labour and Human Resources, Bhutan Labour Force Survey 2012 (Thimphu: Ministry of Labour and Human Resources, 2012), 21, quoted in Tshering, "Informing the Blueprint," 6.

26 National Statistics Bureau, *Bhutan Multiple Indicator Survey 2010* (Thimphu: National Statistics Bureau, 2010), quoted in Tshering, "Informing the Blueprint," 7.

27 Karma Phuntsho, "The Cultural Construction of Bhutan: An Unfinished Story," *Druk Journal* 1, no. 1 (Spring 2015), 74, http://drukjournal.bt/the-cultural-construction-of-bhutan-an-unfinished-story/.

28 Phuntsho, "The Cultural Construction," 74–75.

29 Kinley Dorji, "The Story of Bhutanese Culture," *Druk Journal* 1, no. 2 (Winter 2015): 62, https://drukjournal.bt/the-story-of-bhutanese-culture/.

CHAPTER SEVEN

1 Fred Moten, "Performans i, czarność,'" June 26, 2014, Muzeum Sztuki Nowoczesnej w Warszawie, video, 1:36:49, https://artmuseum.pl/pl/doc/video-performans-i-czarnosc.

2 UNESCO Intangible Heritage Section, Division of Cultural Heritage, *Report of the Expert Meeting on Criteria for Inscription on the Lists Established by the 2003 Convention for the Safeguarding of the Intangible Cultural Heritage* (Paris: UNESCO, 2005), https://ich.unesco.org/doc/src/00035-EN.pdf.

3 Anthony Giddens, *The Constitution of Society: Outline of the Theory of Structuration* (Berkeley: University of California Press, 1984), 375.

4 Anthony Giddens, *Modernity and self-identity: self and society in the late modern age* (Stanford, CA: Stanford University Press, 1991), 40–41.

5 Giddens, *Modernity and self-identity*, 47.

6 Giddens, *Modernity and self-identity*, 64.

7 Giddens, *Modernity and self-identity*, 39.

8 Jennifer Mitzen, "Ontological Security in World Politics: State Identity and the Security Dilemma," *European Journal of International Relations* 12, no. 3 (September 2006): 342, https://doi.org/10.1177/1354066106067346.

9 Anthony Giddens, *Modernity and Self-Identity: Self and Society in the Late Modern Age* (Stanford, CA: Stanford University Press, 1991), 37.

10 Pema Chodron, *When Things Fall Apart: Heart Advice for Difficult Times* (Boston, MA: Shambhala Publications, 1997).

11 Kunzang Choden, "The Malevolent Spirits of sTang Valley (Bumthang)—A Bhutanese Account," *Revue d'Etudes Tibétaines*, no. 15 (November 2008): 313–330, https://www.digitalhimalaya.com/collections/journals/ret/index.php?selection=54.

12 Rosalind Evans, "The Perils of Being a Borderland People: On the Lhotshampas of Bhutan," *Contemporary South Asia* 18, no. 1 (2010): 36, https://doi.org/10.1080/09584930903561598.

13 Karma Ura, "Dialog on the Destiny of Nations," in *Learning from the World: New Ideas to Redevelop America*, eds. Joe Colombano and Aniket Shah (Basingstoke: Macmillan, 2014), 277–288. The six figures participating in the dialog are a "Tantric Lama" who provides "psychological and spiritual backdrop to the dialogs" without being "antimodern"; a "Skeptic Youth," full of "self doubt and existential riddles" but lacking the appetite for "hardship, humility, and self-sacrifice" that would help him find contentment; a "Bhutanese peasant" steeped in indigenous knowledge, myth, and folklore; an "Anglo-Saxon Historian" whose historical views are limited by their uncritical acceptance of international norms; a "Techno Utopist" who is blind to ecological contexts, and a "General Mankiller" who has to "wage unjust campaigns" and unfortunately does it "brilliantly."

14 Of course Skeptic Youth goes on to weaken his argument by linking the difficulty of transcendence to a kind of underlying selfishness: "It would be immensely difficult to practice altruism and to practice compassion if giving [these particularities] up are conditions of an enlightened mind and behavior."

15 According to Heather Stoddard, for instance,

> it is well known that the *gcod* ritual is a symbolic offering of one's own body to all the demonic forces in the universe, to get rid of fear, attachment and ego-clinging. The practitioner imagines his or her body being cut up and offered fresh or cooked by internal combustion and exponentially increased until the bounteous flow of greasy soup, blood, and flesh, manages to satisfy all the

ghoulish hosts of the trichiliocosm who are invited to the feast. Furthermore, the powerful and enchantingly beautiful ritual recalls in many ways the cutting up of the ordinary human body and its offering to vultures and other wild creatures in Tibet.

Stoddard is particularly interested in the way *gcod* (Chöd) intervened in Tibetan burial rituals as the culture shifted from earth burial to sky burial, "the stripping of the flesh and the crushing of the bones and the offering of everything (except those parts that are of special value such as skulls for ritual use or organs that can be used to diagnose the reason for death) to vultures and other wild creatures." See Heather Stoddard, "Eat It up or Throw It to the Dogs? Dge 'Dun Chos' Phel (1903–1951), Ma Cig Lab Sgron (1055–1153) and Pha Dam Pa Sangs Rgyas (D. 1117): A Ramble through the Burial Grounds of Ordinary and 'Holy' Beings in Tibet," in *Buddhism beyond the Monastery: Tantric Practices and Their Performers in Tibet and the Himalayas*, eds. Sarah Jacoby and Antonio Terrone (Leiden: Brill, 2010), 22, https://doi.org/10.1163/ej.9789004176003.i-202.5.

16 Sarah Harding, trans., ed., *Machik's Complete Explanation: Clarifying the Meaning of Chöd*, expanded ed. (Boston, MA: Snow Lion, 2013), 117.

CHAPTER EIGHT

1 See Elizabeth Allison, "Deity Citadels: Sacred Sites of Bio-Cultural Resistance and Resilience in Bhutan," *Religions* 10, no. 4 (April 2019), https://doi.org/10.3390/rel10040268.

2 Max Weber, *The Protestant Ethic and the Spirit of Capitalism* (London: Routledge, 2001), 123.

3 Tim Jackson, "Angst Essen Seele Auf—Escaping the 'Iron Cage' of Consumerism," in *Economy of Sufficiency: Essays on Wealth in Diversity, Enjoyable Limits and Creating Commons*, eds. Uwe Schneidewind, Tilman Santarius, and Anja Humburg (Wuppertal: Wuppertal Institute for Climate, Environment and Energy, 2013): 66, https://epub.wupperinst.org/frontdoor/index/index/docId/5191. For some of the scholars of consumerism mentioned by Jackson, see Mihaly Csikszentmihalyi and Eugene Rochberg-Halton, *The Meaning of Things: Domestic Symbols and the Self* (Cambridge: Cambridge University Press, 1981); Colin Campbell, *The Romantic Ethic and the Spirit of Modern Consumerism* (Oxford: Basil Blackwell, 1987); Russell W. Belk, Melanie Wallendorf, and John F. Sherry, Jr., "The Sacred and the Profane in Consumer Behavior: Theodicy on the Odyssey," *Journal of Consumer*

Research 16, no. 1 (June 1989): 1–38, https://doi.org/10.1086/209191; Anthony Giddens, *Modernity and Self-Identity: Self and Society in the Late Modern Age* (Stanford: Stanford University Press, 1991); Zygmunt Bauman, *Work, Consumerism and the New Poor* (Buckingham: Open University Press, 1998).

4 Mary Douglas, "Relative Poverty, Relative Communication," in *Traditions of Social Policy: Essays in Honour of Violet Butler*, ed. A. H. Halsey (Oxford: Basil Blackwell, 1976), 207.

5 Jackson, "Angst Essen Seele Auf," 54

6 Giorgos Kallis and colleagues ask a similar question, calling for additional research into how the growth paradigm "infiltrated everyday practices and became popular commonsense." In response, Kallis and colleagues turn to Anthony Giddens' structuration theory, which spells out how cultural norms provide ontological security. Giddens argues that structures like conventions, laws, GDP, and economic growth are not just pre-existing entities but are continually re-constructed by human action: GDP and national statistical accounts, for instance, are constructed through the gathering, analyzing, and codifying of particular kinds of statistical data. At the same time, however, Giddens noted that people "obey" or act in accordance with these social structures because they are constrained by the structures *in the moment they are acting*, leading to a situation in which human beings themselves reproduce the structures that constrain them: Giorgos Kallis, Vasilis Kostakis, Steffen Lange, Barbara Muraca, Susan Paulson, and Matthias Schmelzer, "Research on Degrowth," *Annual Review of Environment and Resources* 43 (2018): 291–316, https://doi.org/10.1146/annurev-environ-102017-025941.

7 Jackson, "Angst Essen Seele Auf," 66.

8 Jackson, "Angst Essen Seele Auf," 66.

9 Miriam Pepper, Tim Jackson, and David Uzzell, "An Examination of Christianity and Socially Conscious and Frugal Consumer Behaviors," *Environment and Behavior* 43, no. 2 (March 2011): 274–290, https://doi.org/10.1177/0013916510361573.

10 Jonathan Fox uses cross-national data to argue that religious nationalism is increasingly associated with political violence, while also arguing that religious nationalism's influence should be thought of as contingent on broader political dynamics in a given country. See Jonathan Fox, "The Rise of Religious Nationalism and Conflict: Ethnic Conflict and Revolutionary Wars, 1945–2001," *Journal of Peace Research* 41, no. 6 (November 2004): 715–731, https://doi.org/10.1177/0022343304047434.

11 Andrew L. Whitehead, Landon Schnabel, and Samuel L. Perry, "Gun Control in the Crosshairs: Christian Nationalism and Opposition to Stricter Gun

Laws," *Socius: Sociological Research for a Dynamic World*, 4 (January–December 2018), https://doi.org/10.1177/2378023118790189.

12 Miles T. Armaly, David T. Buckley, and Adam M. Enders, "Christian Nationalism and Political Violence: Victimhood, Racial Identity, Conspiracy, and Support for the Capitol Attacks," *Political Behavior* 44, no. 2, (June 2022): 937–960, https://doi.org/10.1007/s11109-021-09758-y.

13 See Mikael Gravers, "Anti-Muslim Buddhist Nationalism in Burma and Sri Lanka: Religious Violence and Globalized Imaginaries of Endangered Identities," *Contemporary Buddhism* 16, no. 1, (2015): 1–27, https://doi.org/10.1080/14639947.2015.1008090; Niklas Foxeus, "The Buddha Was a Devoted Nationalist: Buddhist Nationalism, Ressentiment, and Defending Buddhism in Myanmar," *Religion* 49, no. 4 (2019): 661–690, https://doi.org/10.1080/0048721X.2019.1610810. Acceptance of Hindu ritual: we saw Sharchop and Drukpa neighbors participating in Ayudha Puja, or the festival of tools, for instance, while we lived in Kanglung, and Hindu and Buddhist rituals have many points of convergence.

14 Sonam Chophel, "Tercham: A Sacred Dance of Sakteng," Bhutan Cultural Library, University of Virginia, 2018, https://texts.shanti.virginia.edu/content/tercham-sacred-dance-sakteng.

15 Evidently at the start of the new millennium, the local ruler of Sakteng called for an end to the naked dance, asking the dancers to wear short trousers for the sake of modesty. The shorts were carefully stored in the same box as the ritual scarves. Three years later, when the box was opened, the clothing had been eaten up by moths. The festival went back to its original form. By contrast, the Yonphu tshechu used to include a naked dance, but at some point in time, the "bashful" surrounding villagers refused to attend until dancers put on shorts.

EPILOGUE

1 Aldo Leopold, *A Sand County Almanac* (New York: Ballantine Books, 1970), 197.

2 See Eric Liu, "What every American should know: Defining common cultural literacy for an increasingly diverse nation," *The Atlantic*, July 3, 2015. https://www.theatlantic.com/politics/archive/2015/07/what-every-american-should-know/397334/. See also the conversation "What Every American Should Know," a conversation among Viet Thanh Nguyen, Laila Lalami, Tommy Orange, and Eric Liu. https://www.aspeninstitute.org/videos/what-every-american-should-know-2/.

Bibliography

Admin, "His Majesty the King Grants a Laptop to Soelra to Researchers." *Zhichenkhar Center For Bhutan & GNH Studies*, November 2021. https://dziseldra.com/seldra/9494#/.

Ahmad, Omair. "The Forgotten 'NRC' in Bhutan." *The Wire*, September 25, 2019. https://thewire.in/rights/the-forgotten-nrc-in-bhutan.

Allison, Elizabeth. "Deity Citadels: Sacred Sites of Bio-Cultural Resistance and Resilience in Bhutan." *Religions* 10, no. 4 (April 2019). https://doi.org/10.3390/rel10040268.

Arezki, Rabah, Kaddour Hadri, Prakash Loungani, and Yao Rao. "Testing the Prebisch-Singer Hypothesis since 1650: Evidence from Panel Techniques That Allow for Multiple Breaks." Working paper, IMF Working Papers, no. 2013/180, August 15, 2013. https://www.imf.org/en/Publications/WP/Issues/2016/12/31/Testing-the-Prebisch-Singer-Hypothesis-since-1650-Evidence-from-Panel-Techniques-that-Allow-40880.

Asian Historical Architecture. "Dechenphug Lhakhang, Thimphu, Bhutan." Accessed January 15, 2024. https://www.orientalarchitecture.com/sid/1546/bhutan/thimphu/dechenphug-lhakhang.

Bell, Charles A. "Report on Area in Bhutan West of the Ammo Chu." Confidential to the Chief Secretary to the Government of Bengal, dated Gangtok, 21 July 1904, (OIOC Mss Eur F80/159b, p. 2). Quoted in Michael Hutt, *Unbecoming Citizens: Culture, Nationhood, and the Flight of Refugees from Bhutan* (New Delhi: Oxford University Press, 2003), https://doi.org/10.1093/acprof:oso/9780195670608.001.0001.

Bhandari, Bhakti Prasad. "Hostage in Thimphu." *Himal* (March–April 1994), 31–34. Cited in Michael Hutt, *Unbecoming Citizens: Culture, Nationhood, and the Flight of Refugees from Bhutan* (New Delhi: Oxford University Press, 2003), https://doi.org/10.1093/acprof:oso/9780195670608.001.0001.

"Bhutan." In *The Statesman's Yearbook 2021*, 197–200. London: Springer Nature, 2021. https://doi.org/10.1057/978-1-349-95972-3_30.

Bhutan Department of Urban Development and Housing. *Traditional Architecture Guidelines*. Thimphu: Department of Urban Development and Housing, [199–?].

Bhutan: Human Rights Violations against the Nepali-Speaking Population in the South. [London]: Amnesty International, 1992. https://www.amnesty.org/en/documents/asa14/004/1992/en/.

Bhutan Media Foundation. *Social Media Landscape in Bhutan*. n.d. http://www.bmf.bt/resources/bmf-publications-reports/.

Bhutan Today. "National Assembly deliberates on the Tobacco Control (Amendment) Bill of Bhutan 2021. The Chairperson of the Legislative Committee, Tshewang Lhamo presented" Facebook, June 24, 2021. https://www.facebook.com/bhutantoday/posts/4108396299226002/.

Billock, Jennifer. "The 250-Mile Trans Bhutan Trail Will Reopen after 60 Years." *Smithsonian Magazine*, September 14, 2022. https://www.smithsonianmag.com/travel/ancient-trans-bhutan-trail-will-reopen-after-60-years-180980740/.

Bothe, Winnie. "The Monarch's Gift: Critical Notes on the Constitutional Process in Bhutan." *European Bulletin of Himalayan Research*, no. 40 (Spring–Summer 2012): 27–58. http://www.digitalhimalaya.com/collections/journals/ebhr/index.php?selection=40.

Bourdieu, Pierre. "Structures, *Habitus*, Practices." In *The Logic of Practice*, trans. Richard Nice, 52–65. Stanford, CA: Stanford University Press, 1990.

Buddhism Bhutan. "10th Mind Incarnation of Zhabdrung 🎉Happy 17th birthday your Holiness la🎉🍂Today, (3-11-2020)is the 17th Birth Anniversary of His Holiness the 10th mind." Facebook, April 22, 2021. https://www.facebook.com/147962355782812/posts/10th-mind-incarnation-of-zhabdrunghappy-17th-birthday-your-holiness-latoday-3-11/878488219396885/.

Choden, Deki. "The Role of Facebook in an Election within an Emerging Democracy: A Case Study of the 2018 Election in Bhutan." Master's thesis, Murdoch University, 2019. https://researchportal.murdoch.edu.au/esploro/outputs/graduate/The-role-of-Facebook-in-an/991005541023407891.

Choden, Kunzang. "The Malevolent Spirits of sTang Valley (Bumthang)—A Bhutanese Account." *Revue d'Etudes Tibétaines*, no. 15 (November

2008): 313–330. https://www.digitalhimalaya.com/collections/journals/ret/index.php?selection=54.

Chodron, Pema. *When Things Fall Apart: Heart Advice for Difficult Times*. Boston, MA: Shambhala Publications, 1997.

Chophel, Sonam and Karma Phuntsho. "Kharamshing: A Structure to Ward off the Effects of Gossip." Bhutan Cultural Library, The University of Virginia, 2017. https://texts.mandala.library.virginia.edu/text/kharamshing-structure-ward-effects-gossip.

Christensen, Line Kikkenborg. "Driglam Namzha and Silenced Ethnicity in Bhutan's Monarchical Democracy." *Social Identities* 27, no. 6 (2021): 644–659. https://doi.org/10.1080/13504630.2021.1899909.

Christensen, Line Kikkenborg. "Freedom of Speech and Silent Youth Protest in Bhutan: 'Plz Delete it from Your Inbox.'" *South Asia Research* 37, no. 1 (February 2017): 93–108, https://doi.org/10.1177/0262728016675523.

Christensen, Line Kikkenborg. "Piecing Together past and Present in Bhutan: Narration, Silence and Forgetting in Conflict." *International Journal of Conflict and Violence* 12 (2018): 629. https://doi.org/10.4119/ijcv-3108.

Cohen, Joseph Nathan and Miguel Angel Centeno. "Neoliberalism and Patterns of Economic Performance, 1980–2000." *ANNALS of the American Academy of Political and Social Science* 606, no. 1 (July 2006): 32–67. https://doi.org/10.1177/0002716206288751.

Constitution of Bhutan July 18, 2008. Constitute, Comparative Constitutions Project. https://www.constituteproject.org/constitution/Bhutan_2008.

Dahl, Robert A. *After the Revolution? Authority in a Good Society*. Rev. ed. New Haven, CT: Yale University Press, 1990. Quoted in Tashi Wangchuk, "The Middle Path to Democracy in the Kingdom of Bhutan," *Asian Survey* 44, no. 6 (November–December 2004): 836–855, https://doi.org/10.1525/as.2004.44.6.836.

Dargey, Yonten. *An Introduction to Values Education*. Thimphu: National Library, 2005. Quoted in Winnie Bothe, "The Monarch's Gift: Critical Notes on the Constitutional Process in Bhutan," *European Bulletin of Himalayan Research*, no. 40 (Spring–Summer 2012): 27–58. http://www.digitalhimalaya.com/collections/journals/ebhr/index.php?selection=40.

Dema, Chencho. "Rapidly Rising Suicide Rates Become the Second Biggest Killer after Road Accidents in Bhutan." *The Bhutanese*. November 1, 2013. https://web.archive.org/web/20131103202047/http://www.thebhutanese.bt/rapidly-rising-suicide-rates-become-the-second-biggest-killer-after-road-accidents-in-bhutan/.

Dhakal, D. N. S. "Economic Blueprint for a South Asian Dragon." *Himal* 5, no. 4 (July/August 1992): 31–34.

Dhungel, Om with James Button. *Bhutan to Blacktown: Losing Everything and Finding Australia*. Sydney: NewSouth, 2023.

Dixit, Kanak Mani. "The Dragon Bites its Tail." *Himal* 5, no. 4 (July/August 1992): 7–30.

Dolkar, Dechen. "Supplement Medicine Soelra Saves Countless Lives." *Kuensel*. February 21, 2023. https://kuenselonline.com/supplement-medicine-soelra-saves-countless-lives/.

Dordang, Dordang. "HH Zhabdrung Ngawang Namgyal's Yangsi." February 6, 2022. https://www.youtube.com/watch?v=Nxs-nw4lWH4.

Dorji, Kinley. "Drafting the Constitution: A Profound Task." *Kuensel*. April 12, 2002. Quoted in Sonam Kinga, *Democratic Transition in Bhutan: Political Contests as Moral Battles* (Oxon: Taylor & Francis, 2020).

Dorji, Kinley. "The Story of Bhutanese Culture." *Druk Journal* 1, no. 2 (Winter 2015): 58–66. http://drukjournal.bt/the-bhutanese-state-and-its-institute/.

Dorji, Kinley. "The View from Thimphu: Hoping for a Gentler Judgement." *Himal* 5, no. 4 (July/August 1992), 39.

Dorji, Sangay. *'brug gi sde srid khri rabs rim byon gyi mdzad rnam deb ther dpyod ldan dgyes pa'i do shal*. Thimphu: The Centre for Bhutan Studies and GNH, 2017. Quoted in Sonam Kinga, Democratic Transition in Bhutan: Political Contests as Moral Battles (Oxon: Taylor & Francis, 2020).

Dorji, Yab Ugyen and Ashi Dorji Wangmo Wangchuck. *Of Rainbows and Clouds: The Life of Yab Ugyen Dorji as Told to His Daughter*. London: Serindia, 1999.

Drexler, Madeline. "500 Lifetimes: Notes on Suicide in Bhutan." *Virginia Quarterly Review* 93, no. 4 (Fall 2017): 184–196. https://www.jstor.org/stable/26434895.

Druk Green Power Corporation Limited. *Annual Report 2018*. Thimphu: 2018. https://www.drukgreen.bt/en/annual-reports/.

Duff, Andrew. *Sikkim: Requiem for a Himalayan Kingdom*. Edinburgh: Birlinn Limited, 2015.

Elias, Norbert, Eric Dunning, Johan Goudsblom, and Stephen Mennell. *The Civilizing Process: Sociogenetic and Psychogenetic Investigations*. Rev. ed. Oxford: Blackwell Publishers, 2000.

Elliott, John. "The Modern Path to Enlightenment." *Financial Times*, May 2, 1987.

Escobar, Arturo. *Encountering Development: The Making and Unmaking of the Third World*. Princeton, NJ: Princeton University Press, 1995.

Evans, Rosalind. "Cultural Expression as Political Rhetoric: Young Bhutanese Refugees' Collective Action for Social Change." *Contemporary South Asia* 18, no. 3 (2010): 305–317. https://doi.org/10.1080/09584935.2010.501101.

Evans, Rosalind. "The Perils of Being a Borderland People: On the Lhotshampas of Bhutan." *Contemporary South Asia* 18, no. 1 (2010): 25–42. https://doi.org/10.1080/09584930903561598.

Evans, Rosalind. "The Two Faces of Empowerment in Conflict." *Research in Comparative and International Education* 3, no. 1 (March 2008): 50–64. https://doi.org/10.2304/rcie.2008.3.1.50.

Foy, Henry. "Bhutan Police Raid Homes to Stub Out Smoking Habit." *Reuters*, January 11, 2011. https://www.reuters.com/article/us-bhutan-smoking/bhutan-police-raid-homes-to-stub-out-smoking-habit-idUSTRE70A2HP20110111.

Freedom House. "Bhutan: Freedom in the World 2022 Country Report." Accessed January 15, 2024. https://freedomhouse.org/country/bhutan/freedom-world/2022.

Freedom House. "Bhutan: Freedom in the World 2023 Country Report." Accessed January 15, 2024. https://freedomhouse.org/country/bhutan/freedom-world/2023.

Gangtey Lodge (blog). "The World's Last Remaining Vajrayana Buddhist Kingdom." December 2022. https://gangteylodge.com/blog/the-worlds-last-remaining-vajrayana-buddhist-kingdom/.

Giddens, Anthony. "Living in a Post-traditional Society." In *Reflexive Modernization: Politics, Tradition and Aesthetics in the Modern Social Order*, edited by Ulrich Beck, Anthony Giddens, and Scott Lash, 56–109. Stanford, CA: Stanford University Press, 1994.

Giddens, Anthony. *The Constitution of Society: Outline of the Theory of Structuration*. Berkeley: University of California Press, 1984.

Giddens, Anthony. *Modernity and Self-Identity: Self and Society in the Late Modern Age*. Stanford, CA: Stanford University Press, 1991.

GNH Centre Bhutan. "GNH Happiness Index." Accessed January 15, 2024. https://www.gnhcentrebhutan.org/gnh-happiness-index/.

GNH Centre Bhutan. Accessed January 15, 2024. https://www.gnhcentrebhutan.org/.

Google Arts & Culture. "Bhutan-Thangbi Lhakhang." Accessed January 15, 2024. https://artsandculture.google.com/story/bhutan-thangbi-lhakhang/DwXBsOEonkT_gA?hl=en.

Gorenflo, L. J., Suzanne Romaine, Russell A. Mittermeier, and Kristen Walker-Painemilla. "Co-occurrence of Linguistic and Biological Diversity in Biodiversity Hotspots and High Biodiversity Wilderness Areas." *Proceedings of the National Academy of Sciences* 109, no. 21 (May 22, 2012): 8032–8037. https://doi.org/10.1073/pnas.1117511109.

Hagaman, Ashley K., Teresa I. Sivilli, Trong Ao, Curtis Blanton, Heidi Ellis, Barbara Lopes Cardozo, and Sharmila Shetty. "An Investigation into Suicides among Bhutanese Refugees Resettled in the United States between 2008 and

2011." *Journal of Immigrant Minority Health* 18, no. 4 (August 2016): 819–827. https://doi.org/10.1007/s10903-015-0326-6.

Harding, Sarah, trans., ed. *Machik's Complete Explanation: Clarifying the Meaning of Chöd*. Expanded edition. Boston, MA: Snow Lion, 2013.

Harris, Gardiner. "Index of Happiness? Bhutan's New Leader Prefers More Concrete Goals." *New York Times*, October 4, 2013. https://www.nytimes.com/2013/10/05/world/asia/index-of-happiness-bhutans-new-leader-prefers-more-concrete-goals.html.

Helliwell, John, Richard Layard, and Jeffrey Sachs, eds. *World Happiness Report*. New York: UN Sustainable Development Solutions Network, 2012. https://worldhappiness.report/ed/2012/.

Hendrickson, Ryan C. *Obama at War: Congress and the Imperial Presidency*. Lexington: University Press of Kentucky, 2015.

"His Majesty Appeals to Lhotshampa Migrants Not to Leave Their Country." *Kuensel*. July 18, 1992. Quoted in Michael Hutt, *Unbecoming Citizens: Culture, Nationhood, and the Flight of Refugees from Bhutan* (New Delhi: Oxford University Press, 2003), https://doi.org/10.1093/acprof:oso/9780195670608.001.0001.

Human Rights Watch. *Last Hope: The Need for Durable Solutions for Bhutanese Refugees in Nepal and India*. n.p.: Human Rights Watch, 2007. https://www.refworld.org/reference/countryrep/hrw/2007/en/43088.

Hutt, Michael. "Coming Closer to the King." In idem, *Unbecoming Citizens: Culture, Nationhood, and the Flight of Refugees from Bhutan*, 127–146. New Delhi: Oxford University Press, 2003. https://doi.org/10.1093/acprof:oso/9780195670608.003.0009.

Hutt, Michael. "Sociocultural and Political Change in Bhutan since the 1980s: Reflections from a Distance." In *Development Challenges in Bhutan: Perspectives on Inequality and Gross National Happiness*, edited by Johannes Dragsbæk Schmidt, 19–27. Cham: Springer, 2017. https://doi.org/10.1007/978-3-319-47925-5_2.

Hutt, Michael. "The Bhutanese Refugees: Between Verification, Repatriation and Royal Realpolitik." *Peace and Democracy in South Asia* 1, no. 1 (January 2005): 44–56. http://www.digitalhimalaya.com/collections/journals/pdsa/.

Hutt, Michael. "The Changing Bases of Subjecthood." In *Unbecoming Citizens: Culture, Nationhood, and the Flight of Refugees from Bhutan*. New Delhi: Oxford University Press, 2003. https://doi.org/10.1093/acprof:oso/9780195670608.003.0006.

Hutt, Michael. *Unbecoming Citizens: Culture, Nationhood, and the Flight of Refugees from Bhutan*. New Delhi: Oxford University Press, 2003. https://doi.org/10.1093/acprof:oso/9780195670608.001.0001.

Institute for Health Metrics and Evaluation. "Bhutan." Accessed January 15, 2024. https://www.healthdata.org/bhutan#:~:text=The%20top%20cause%20of%20death,49%20percent%20to%2049%20percent.

Irons, Peter. *War Powers: How the Imperial Presidency Hijacked the Constitution.* New York: Henry Holt, 2005.

Jackson, David. "Portrayals of Zhabdrung Ngawang Namgyal in Bhutanese Painting: Iconography and Common Groupings of the Great Unifier of Bhutan." In *The Dragon's Gift: The Sacred Arts of Bhutan*, edited by Terese Tse Bartholomew and John Johnston, 78–87. Chicago, IL: Serindia Publications, 2008.

Kaufman, Michael T. "Basketball Is Big in Bhutan but Traditions Too Are Prized." *New York Times*, April 29, 1980.

Kharka, Damber Singh. "Dependence of Bhutanese Economy on India: Empirical Analysis of Inflation Dependency." *Journal of International Economics* 4, no. 2 (July–December 2013): 4–20.

Kinga, Sonam. *Democratic Transition in Bhutan: Political Contests as Moral Battles.* Oxon: Taylor & Francis, 2020.

Kinga, Sonam. "The Attributes and Values of Folk and Popular Songs." *Journal of Bhutan Studies* 3, no. 1(Summer 2001), 132–170. https://www.bhutanstudies.org.bt/journal-of-bhutan-studies-vol-3-no-1/.

Klein, Elise and Carlos Eduardo Morreo, eds. *Postdevelopment in Practice: Alternatives, Economies, Ontologies.* Abingdon: Taylor & Francis, 2019.

Koirala, Keshav P. "Where in US, Elsewhere Bhutanese Refugees from Nepal Resettled To." *Himalayan Times*. February 6, 2017. https://thehimalayantimes.com/nepal/where-in-earth-have-been-bhutanese-refugees-from-nepal-resettled

Kuensel. "ALD Continues to Be the Top Cause of Death." July 8, 2019. https://web.archive.org/web/20190802071235/https://kuenselonline.com/ald-continues-to-be-the-top-cause-of-death/.

Kuensel. "His Majesty the King Grants Soelra for Children to Learn Coding." July 21, 2021. https://kuenselonline.com/his-majesty-the-king-grants-soelra-for-children-to-learn-coding/.

Kuensel. "The Reality of Kidu." May 1, 2021. https://kuenselonline.com/the-reality-of-kidu/.

Lhadon, Kuenzang. "Suicide Trends in Bhutan from 2009 to 2013." *Journal of Bhutan Studies* 30 (Summer 2014): 30–56. https://www.bhutanstudies.org.bt/journal-of-bhutan-studies-vol-30-summer-2014/.

Locke, Jessica. "Buddhist Modernism Underway in Bhutan: Gross National Happiness and Buddhist Political Theory." *Religions* 11, no. 6 (June 2020): 297. https://doi.org/10.3390/rel11060297.

Long, William J. *Tantric State: A Buddhist Approach to Democracy and Development in Bhutan*. New York: Oxford University Press, 2019.

Macrotrends. "Bhutan Life Expectancy 1950–2024." Accessed January 15, 2024. https://www.macrotrends.net/countries/BTN/bhutan/life-expectancy.

Masaki, Katsu. "Exploring the 'Partial Connections' between Growth and Degrowth Debates: Bhutan's Policy of Gross National Happiness." *Journal of Interdisciplinary Economics* 34, no. 1 (January 2022): 86–103. https://doi.org/10.1177/02601079211032103.

McCarthy, James. "Authoritarianism, Populism, and the Environment: Comparative Experiences, Insights, and Perspectives." *Annals of the American Association of Geographers* 109, no. 2 (2019): 301–313. https://doi.org/10.1080/24694452.2018.1554393.

Mehta, Jagat S. "Catalysing Graduated Modernisation through Diplomacy: Nehru's Visit to Bhutan—1958." *World Affairs: The Journal of International Issues* 6, no. 2 (April–June 2002): 84–103. https://www.jstor.org/stable/45064894.

Mettes, Susan. *The Loneliness Epidemic: Why So Many of Us Feel Alone—and How Leaders Can Respond*. Grand Rapids, MI: Baker Publishing Group, 2021.

Millward-Hopkins, Joel. "Inequality Can Double the Energy Required to Secure Universal Decent Living." *Nature Communications* 13 (August 26, 2022): 5028. https://doi.org/10.1038/s41467-022-32729-8.

Millward-Hopkins, Joel, Julia K. Steinberger, Narasimha D. Rao, Yannick Oswald. "Providing Decent Living with Minimum Energy: A Global Scenario." *Global Environmental Change* 65 (November 2020): 102168. https://doi.org/10.1016/j.gloenvcha.2020.102168.

Minorities at Risk Project. "Chronology for Lhotshampas in Bhutan." The United Nations Refugees Agency. Archived May 18, 2023. https://webarchive.archive.unhcr.org/20230519012329/https://www.refworld.org/docid/469f386a1e.html.

Mitzen, Jennifer. "Ontological Security in World Politics: State Identity and the Security Dilemma." *European Journal of International Relations* 12, no. 3 (September 2006): 341–370. https://doi.org/10.1177/1354066106067346.

Mørch, Maximillian. "Bhutan's Dark Secret: The Lhotshampa Expulsion." *The Diplomat*, September 21, 2016. https://thediplomat.com/2016/09/bhutans-dark-secret-the-lhotshampa-expulsion/.

Muni, S. D. "Bhutan in the Throes of Ethnic Conflict." *India International Centre Quarterly* (Spring 1991), 145–154. Quoted in Michael Hutt, *Unbecoming Citizens: Culture, Nationhood, and the Flight of Refugees from Bhutan* (New Delhi: Oxford University Press, 2003), https://doi.org/10.1093/acprof:oso/9780195670608.001.0001.

Munro, Lauchlan T. "Where Did Bhutan's Gross National Happiness Come From? The Origins of an Invented Tradition." *Asian Affairs* 47, no. 1 (2016): 71–92. https://doi.org/10.1080/03068374.2015.1128681.

Murthy, Vivek H. *Together: Loneliness, Health and What Happens When We Find Connection*. London: Profile Books, 2021.

Myers, Steven Lee. "Squeezed by an India-China Standoff, Bhutan Holds Its Breath." *New York Times*. August 15, 2017. https://www.nytimes.com/2017/08/15/world/asia/squeezed-by-an-india-china-standoff-bhutan-holds-its-breath.html.

Namgay, Kezang. *Sacred Dances of Bhutan*. Thimphu: printed by the author, 2014.

Namgay, Kuenga, Joanne Millar, Rosemary Black, and Tashi Samdup. "Transhumant Agro-Pastoralism in Bhutan: Exploring Contemporary Practices and Socio-Cultural Traditions." *Pastoralism: Research, Policy and Practice* 3 (June 13, 2013): 13. https://doi.org/10.1186/2041-7136-3-13.

National Assembly of Bhutan. *Proceedings and Resolutions of the 70th Session of the National Assembly of Bhutan*. https://web.archive.org/web/20211203043457/https://www.nab.gov.bt/assets/uploads/docs/resolution/2014/70th_Session.pdf.

National Assembly of Bhutan. *Translation of the Proceedings and Resolutions of the 73rd Session of the National Assembly of Bhutan Held from 10th August to 2nd September, 1995*. https://web.archive.org/web/20211203050709/https://www.nab.gov.bt/assets/uploads/docs/resolution/2014/73rd_Session.pdf.

National Assembly of Bhutan. *Translation of the Proceedings and Resolutions of the 76th Session of the National Assembly of Bhutan Held from the Fifth Day of the Fifth Month to the Seventh Day of the Sixth Month Of The Male Earth Tiger Year (June 29th to July 30th, 1998)*. https://web.archive.org/web/20200527212358/https://www.nab.gov.bt/assets/uploads/docs/resolution/2014/76th_Session.pdf.

"Nepal Raises Conflict Death Toll." *BBC News*. Updated September 22, 2009. http://news.bbc.co.uk/1/hi/8268651.stm.

New York Times. "Bhutan Goes to Polls to End Absolute Monarchy." March 24, 2008. https://www.nytimes.com/2008/03/24/world/asia/24iht-bhutan.1.11366582.html.

New York Times. "If You Smoke, Don't Vacation in This Kingdom." January 15, 2011. https://www.nytimes.com/2011/01/16/weekinreview/16grist.html.

OECD Better Life Index. "Housing." Accessed January 15, 2024. https://www.oecdbetterlifeindex.org/topics/housing/.

Ostrom, Elinor. *Governing the Commons: The Evolution of Institutions for Collective Action*. Cambridge: Cambridge University Press, 1990.

Otto, Ilona M., Jonathan F. Donges, Roger Cremades, Avit Bhowmik, Richard J. Hewitt, Wolfgang Lucht, Johan Rockström, Franziska Allerberger, Mark McCaffrey, Sylvanus S. P. Doe, Alex Lenferna, Nerea Morán, Detlef P. van Vuuren, and Hans Joachim Schellnhuber. "Social Tipping Dynamics for Stabilizing Earth's Climate by 2050." *Proceedings of the National Academy of Sciences* 117, no. 5 (February 4, 2020): 2354–2365. https://doi.org/10.1073/pnas.1900577117.

Pelden, Sonam. "Making Sense of Suicides by School Students in Bhutan: Documenting a Societal Dialogue." Ph.D. thesis, Curtin University, 2016. https://espace.curtin.edu.au/handle/20.500.11937/2393.

Pelden, Tshering. "ALD Continues to Be Major Cause of Death in the Country." *Business Bhutan*, March 24, 2022. https://businessbhutan.bt/ald-continues-to-be-major-cause-of-death-in-the-country/.

Pellegrini, Lorenzo and Luca Tasciotti. "Bhutan: Between Happiness and Horror." *Capitalism Nature Socialism* 25, no. 3 (2014): 103–109. https://doi.org/10.1080/10455752.2014.898673.

Penjore, Dorji. "Causes and Conditions of Bhutan's Democratic Transition." *Journal of Bhutan Studies* 37 (Winter 2017): 92–108. https://www.bhutanstudies.org.bt/jbs-37/.

Penjore, Dorji. "Who Should Bow to Whom? Power and Politics between Dzongda and Thrizin." *A Bowl of Suja* (blog). December 15, 2022. https://dorjipenjore.wordpress.com/2022/12/15/who-should-bow-to-whom-power-and-politics-between-the-dzongda-and-the-thrizin/.

Phuntsho, Karma. "Echoes of Ancient Ethos: Reflections on Some Popular Bhutanese Social Themes." In *The Spider and the Piglet: Proceedings of the First International Seminar on Bhutan Studies*, edited by Karma Ura and Sonam Kinga, 564–579. Thimphu: Centre for Bhutan Studies, 2004. https://www.bhutanstudies.org.bt/the-spider-and-the-piglet/.

Phuntsho, Karma. "On the Two Ways of Learning in Bhutan." *Journal of Bhutan Studies* 2, no. 2 (Winter 2000): 96–126. https://www.bhutanstudies.org.bt/journal-of-bhutan-studies-vol-2-no-2/.

Phuntsho, Karma. "Ridam/Ladam: Closing Mountains to Human Activity." Bhutan Cultural Library, The University of Virginia, 2018. https://texts.mandala.library.virginia.edu/text/ridamladam-closing-mountains-human-activity.

Phuntsho, Karma. "The Cultural Construction of Bhutan: An Unfinished Story." *Druk Journal* 1, no. 1 (Spring 2015): 66–75. http://drukjournal.bt/the-cultural-construction-of-bhutan-an-unfinished-story/.

Phuntsho, Karma. *The History of Bhutan*. London: Haus Publishing, 2013.

Phunstho, Karma. "Zorig Chusum." *Kuensel*, May 16, 2022. https://kuenselonline.com/zorig-chusum/.

Planning Commission. *Bhutan 2020: A Vision for Peace, Prosperity and Happiness.* Thimphu: RGOB, 1999. Quoted in Lauchlan T. Munro, "Where Did Bhutan's Gross National Happiness Come From? The Origins of an Invented Tradition," *Asian Affairs* 47, no. 1 (2016): 71–92, https://doi.org/10.1080/03068374.2015.1128681.

Poussot, Jaquelyn. "Indian Labourers, the Invisible Class of Bhutan." *South Asia@LSE* (blog). January 31, 2018. https://blogs.lse.ac.uk/southasia/2018/01/31/indian-labourers-the-invisible-class-of-bhutan/.

Pradhan, Alina. "Politics of Separation: The Case of the Gorkhaland Movement." *Indian Journal of Political Science* 73, no. 4 (October–December 2012): 683–690. https://www.jstor.org/stable/41858876.

Proceedings and Resolutions of the 70th Session of the National Assembly of Bhutan. n.p.: n.p., 1991. Quoted in Michael Hutt, *Unbecoming Citizens: Culture, Nationhood, and the Flight of Refugees from Bhutan* (New Delhi: Oxford University Press, 2003), https://doi.org/10.1093/acprof:oso/9780195670608.001.0001.

Putnam, Robert D. *Bowling Alone: The Collapse and Revival of American Community.* New York: Simon and Schuster, 2000.

Putnam, Robert D. *Making Democracy Work: Civic Traditions in Modern Italy.* With Robert Leonardi and Raffaella Y. Nonetti. Princeton, NJ: Princeton University Press, 1993. Quoted in Tashi Wangchuk, "The Middle Path to Democracy in the Kingdom of Bhutan," *Asian Survey* 44, no. 6 (November/December 2004): 836–855, https://doi.org/10.1525/as.2004.44.6.836.

Rahnema, Majid and Victoria Bawtree. *The Post-Development Reader.* Atlantic Highlands, NJ: Zed Books, 1997.

Ramírez-Cendrero, Juan M., Santiago García, and Alejandro Santillán. "Sumak Kawsay in Ecuador: The Role of Communitarian Economy and the Experience of the Rural Communities in Sarayaku (Ecuadorian Amazonia)." *Journal of Rural Studies* 53 (July 2017): 111–121. https://doi.org/10.1016/j.jrurstud.2017.05.018.

Richardson, Heather. "I Hiked the Ancient Trans-Bhutan Trail When It Reopened after 60 Years—Here's What It Was Like." *Travel + Leisure*, November 28, 2022. https://www.travelandleisure.com/trans-bhutan-trail-hike-6830191.

Rodney, Walter. "How Europe Underdeveloped Africa." In *Beyond Borders: Thinking Critically about Global Issues*, edited by Paula S. Rothenberg, 107–125. New York: Worth Publishers, 2006.

Rose, Leo E. *The Politics of Bhutan.* Ithaca, NY: Cornell University Press, 1977.

Royal Government of Bhutan. Anti-National Activities in Southern Bhutan: A Terrorist Movement. Thimphu: Department of Information, 1991. Quoted in Michael Hutt, *Unbecoming Citizens: Culture, Nationhood, and the Flight of Refugees from Bhutan* (New Delhi: Oxford University Press, 2003), https://doi.org/10.1093/acprof:oso/9780195670608.001.0001.

Royal Government of Bhutan. *Bhutan Civics*. Thimphu: n.p., 1999. Cited in Richard Whitecross, ""Virtuous Beings": The Concept of Tha Damtshing and Being a Moral Person in Contemporary Bhutanese Society," *Himalaya: The Journal of the Association for Nepal and Himalayan Studies* 28, no. 1–2 (2008): 71, https://digitalcommons.macalester.edu/himalaya/vol28/iss1/6/.

Royal Government of Bhutan. *Eighth Five-Year Plan 1997–2002*. Thimphu: Planning Commission, 1997. https://web.archive.org/web/20160304190503/http://www.gnhc.gov.bt/wp-content/uploads/2011/04/08fyp.pdf.

Royal Government of Bhutan. *The Southern Bhutan Problem: Threat to a Nation's Survival*. Thimphu: Ministry of Home Affairs, 1993. Quoted in Michael Hutt, *Unbecoming Citizens: Culture, Nationhood, and the Flight of Refugees from Bhutan* (New Delhi: Oxford University Press, 2003), https://doi.org/10.1093/acprof:oso/9780195670608.001.0001.

Rustomji, Nari. *Bhutan: The Dragon Kingdom in Crisis*. New York: Oxford University Press, 1978.

Saklani, Udisha and Cecilia Tortajada. "India's Development Cooperation in Bhutan's Hydropower Sector: Concerns and Public Perceptions." *Water Alternatives* 12, no. 2 (June 2019): 734–759. https://www.water-alternatives.org/index.php/alldoc/articles/vol12/v12issue3/525-a12-2-8.

Sakya Monastery of Tibetan Buddhism. "Sakya History." Accessed January 15, 2024. https://www.sakya.org/about/sakya-history/.

Savada, Andrea Matles, ed. *Nepal and Bhutan: Country Studies*, 3rd ed. Washington, D.C.: Federal Research Division, Library of Congress, 1993. http://hdl.loc.gov/loc.gdc/cntrystd.bt.

Schmidt, Johannes Dragsbaek, ed. *Development Challenges in Bhutan: Perspectives on Inequality and Gross National Happiness*. Cham: Springer, 2017.

Schmidt, Johannes Dragsbaek. "Donor-Assisted Ethno-Nationalism and Education Policy in Bhutan." In *Development Challenges in Bhutan: Perspectives on Inequality and Gross National Happiness*, edited by Johannes Dragsbaek Schmidt, 29–46. Cham: Springer, 2017.

Schrempf, Mona. "From Popular Pilgrimage Festival to State Monastic Performance—The Politics of Cultural Production at Gomphu Kora, East Bhutan." In *Approaching the Sacred: Pilgrimage in Historical and Intercultural*

Perspective, edited by Ute Luig, 323–359. Berlin: Edition Topoi, 2018. http://doi.org/10.17169/refubium-490.

Scott, James C. *Weapons of the Weak: Everyday Forms of Peasant Resistance*. New Haven, CT: Yale University Press, 1987.

See, Helena. "The Two Faces of Gross National Happiness: Can Bhutan's Nation-Building Strategy Also Be a Sustainable Alternative Development Paradigm?" *Journal of Contemporary Asia* 52, no. 3 (2022): 452–470. https://doi.org/10.1080/00472336.2021.1933139.

Sengupta, Somini. "Bhutan Reluctantly Embraces Democracy." *New York Times*, April 23, 2007. https://www.nytimes.com/2007/04/23/world/asia/23iht-web0423-bhutan.5402558.html.

Shaw, Brian C. "Aspects of the "Southern Problem" and Nation-Building in Bhutan." In *Bhutan: Perspectives on Conflict and Dissent*. Edited by Michael Hutt, 141–164. Gartmore: Kiscadale Publications, 1994. Quoted in Michael Hutt, *Unbecoming Citizens: Culture, Nationhood, and the Flight of Refugees from Bhutan* (New Delhi: Oxford University Press, 2003), 200–201, https://doi.org/10.1093/acprof:oso/9780195670608.001.0001.

Shrestha, Nirakar Man, Bhogendra Sharma, Mark Van Ommeren, Shyam Regmi, Ramesh Makaju, Ivan Komproe, Ganesh B. Shrestha, Joop T. V. M. de Jong. "Impact of Torture on Refugees Displaced within the Developing World: Symptomatology among Bhutanese Refugees in Nepal." *JAMA* 280, no. 5 (1998): 443–448. https://doi.org/10.1001/jama.280.5.443. Quoted in Michael Hutt, *Unbecoming Citizens: Culture, Nationhood, and the Flight of Refugees from Bhutan* (New Delhi: Oxford University Press, 2003), https://doi.org/10.1093/acprof:oso/9780195670608.001.0001.

Sinha, A. C. *Bhutan: Ethnic Identity and National Dilemma*. New Delhi: Reliance Publishing House, 1991. Quoted in Michael Hutt, *Unbecoming Citizens: Culture, Nationhood, and the Flight of Refugees from Bhutan* (New Delhi: Oxford University Press, 2003), 131, https://doi.org/10.1093/acprof:oso/9780195670608.001.0001.

Stiglitz, Joseph E., Jean-Paul Fitoussi, and Martine Durand. *Measuring What Counts: The Global Movement for Well-Being*. New York: New Press, 2019.

Stoddard, Heather. "Eat It up or Throw It to the Dogs? Dge 'Dun Chos' Phel (1903–1951), Ma Cig Lab Sgron (1055–1153) and Pha Dam Pa Sangs Rgyas (D. 1117): A Ramble through the Burial Grounds of Ordinary and 'Holy' Beings in Tibet." In *Buddhism beyond the Monastery: Tantric Practices and Their Performers in Tibet and the Himalayas*, edited by Sarah Jacoby and Antonio Terrone, 9–36. Leiden: Brill, 2010. https://doi.org/10.1163/ej.9789004176003.i-202.5.

Strydom, Wessel, Karen Puren, and Ernst Drewes. "Exploring Theoretical Trends in Placemaking: Towards New Perspectives in Spatial Planning." *Journal of Place Management and Development* 11, no. 2 (2018): 165–180. https://doi.org/10.1108/JPMD-11-2017-0113.

Swiss Confederation. "Direct Democracy." Federal Department of Foreign Affairs. Updated July 14, 2021. https://www.eda.admin.ch/aboutswitzerland/en/home/politik-geschichte/politisches-system/direkte-demokratie.html.

"The Gurkhaland." *Strategic Studies* 9, no. 4 (Summer 1986): 7–10. https://www.jstor.org/stable/45182435.

The Hindu. "Bhutan's Royalty Refutes "Coup" Claims in Rasgotra Book." August 20, 2016. https://www.thehindu.com/news/international/Bhutan%E2%80%99s-Royalty-refutes-%E2%80%9Ccoup%E2%80%9D-claims-in-Rasgotra-book/article14581915.ece.

The Southern Bhutan Problem: Threat to a Nation's Survival. Thimphu: Ministry of Home Affairs, 1993. http://dspace.cus.ac.in/jspui/handle/1/4327.

Theys, Sarina and Katharina Rietig. "The Influence of Small States: How Bhutan Succeeds in Influencing Global Sustainability Governance." *International Affairs* 9, no. 6 (November 2020): 1603–1622. https://doi.org/10.1093/ia/iiaa157.

Thinley, Jigmi Y. "Gross National Happiness: A Holistic Paradigm for Sustainable Development." *APFA News*. December 23, 2011. https://www.apfanews.com/commentary/gross-national-happiness-a-holistic-paradigm-for-sustainable-development.html.

Thomas, Derek. *Placemaking: An Urban Design Methodology*. London: Taylor & Francis, 2016.

Thronson, David. "Cultural Cleansing in Bhutan." *Bhutanese Refugees.* October 2009. https://www.oocities.org/bhutaneserefugees/cultural_cleansing.html

Tobgay, Tshering. "Buddhist Contributions to Human Development." *Journal of Bhutan Studies* 38 (Summer 2018): 1–14. https://www.bhutanstudies.org.bt/jbs-38/.

Tobgay, Tshering. "This Country Isn't Just Carbon Neutral—It's Carbon Negative." February 2016, TED Video, 18:45. https://www.ted.com/talks/tshering_tobgay_this_country_isn_t_just_carbon_neutral_it_s_carbon_negative.

Tobgye, Sonam. "Guru Padmasambhava and Jurisprudence in Bhutan: Golden Yoke and Silken Knot." *Journal of Bhutan Studies* 34 (Summer 2016): 9–19. https://www.bhutanstudies.org.bt/journal-of-bhutan-studies-volume-34-summer-2016/.

Tourism Council of Bhutan. *Bhutan Tourism Monitor 2018* (Thimphu: 2018). https://www.tourism.gov.bt/uploads/attachment_files/tcb_xx8r_BTM%202018%20_final.pdf.

Traditional Sports. "Digor or Degor (Bhutan)." Accessed January 15, 2024. https://www.traditionalsports.org/traditional-sports/asia/digor-or-degor-bhutan.html.

Tshering, Dorjee and Thinley Wangchuk. "Zorig Chusum: Bhutan's Living Arts and Crafts." *Smithsonian Folklife Festival on the National Mall, Washington, D.C.: [Program]* (2008): 30–33. https://festival.si.edu/articles/2008/zorig-chusum-bhutan-s-living-arts-and-crafts.

Tshering, Ugyen. "An Honour of Delivering His Majesty's 'Soelra.'" *My Own Thoughts* (blog). February 25, 2021. https://ugentshering.blogspot.com/2021/02/delivering-kings-firewood-soelra-to.html.

UNESCO Intangible Heritage Section, Division of Cultural Heritage. *Report of the Expert Meeting on Criteria for Inscription on the Lists Established by the 2003 Convention for the Safeguarding of the Intangible Cultural Heritage.* Paris: UNESCO, 2005. https://ich.unesco.org/doc/src/00035-EN.pdf.

UNHCR Statistical Yearbook 2016. Geneva: United Nations High Commissioner for Refugees, 2017. https://www.unhcr.org/statistics/country/5a8ee0387/unhcr-statistical-yearbook-2016-16th-edition.html.

Ura, Karma, Sabina Alkire, Tshoki Zangmo, and Karma Wangdi. *An Extensive Analysis of GNH Index*. Thimphu: Centre for Bhutan Studies, 2012. https://ophi.org.uk/extensive-analysis-of-gnh-index/.

Ura, Karma. "Dialog on the Destiny of Nations." In *Learning from the World: New Ideas to Redevelop America*, edited by Joe Colombano and Aniket Shah, 277–288. Basingstoke: Macmillan, 2014.

Ura, Karma, Sabina Alkire, Karma Wangdi, and Tshoki Zangmo.. *GNH 2022*. Thimphu: Centre for Bhutan and GNH Studies, 2023. https://ophi.org.uk/bhutan-gnh-2022/.

Ura, Karma. *Leadership of the Wise: Kings of Bhutan.* Thimphu: Centre for Bhutan Studies, 2010.

Ura, Karma. "The Nomads' Gamble: Pastoralists of Northern Bhutan." *South Asia Research* 13, no. 2 (September 1993): 81–100. https://doi.org/10.1177/026272809301300201.

U.S. Department of State Country Report on Human Rights Practices 1993—Bhutan. n.p.: United States Department of State, 1994. https://www.refworld.org/docid/3ae6aa4d4.html.

Verma, Ritu. "The Eight Manifestations of GNH: Multiple Meanings of a Development Alternative." *Journal of Bhutan Studies* 41 (Winter 2019): 1–33. https://www.bhutanstudies.org.bt/jbs-41-winter-2019/.

Villarreal, Claire. "Shaman, Lama, Buddha: "Occult Techniques" and the Popularization of Tantric Ritual in Tibet." *Magic, Ritual, and Witchcraft* 9, no. 1 (Summer 2014): 62–84. https://doi.org/10.1353/mrw.2014.0007.

Vincent, Jessica. "Hiking the Newly Restored Trans Bhutan Trail Is the Best Way to Experience the Country." *Condé Nast Traveler*, October 17, 2022. https://www.cntraveler.com/story/hiking-the-newly-restored-trans-bhutan-trail-is-the-best-way-to-experience-the-country.

Vonnahme, Laura A., Emily W. Lankau, Trong Ao, Sharmila Shetty, and Barbara Lopes Cardozo. "Factors Associated with Symptoms of Depression among Bhutanese Refugees in the United States." *Journal of Immigrant Minority Health* 17, no. 6 (December 2015): 1705–1714. https://doi.org/10.1007/s10903-014-0120-x.

Wallis, Christopher D. *Tantra Illuminated: The Philosophy, History, and Practice of a Timeless Tradition*. Petaluma, CA: Mattamayūra Press, 2013.

Wangchuk, Jigme Singye. "His Majesty the King's National Day Address on December 17, 2005." *RAOnline*, December 17, 2005. https://www.raonline.ch/pages/bt/rfam/bt_royalfam01b1.html.

Wangchuk, Jigme Singye. "His Majesty the King's National Day Speech in Samtse 2002." *RAOnline*, 2002. Transcript, https://www.raonline.ch/pages/story/bt/btbg08.html.

Wangchuk, Jigme Singye. "King of Bhutan's National Day Address." South Asian Terrorism Portal. December 20, 2004. https://www.satp.org/document/paper-acts-and-oridinances/king-of-bhutan-s-national-day-address.

Wangchuk, Tandin. "Resource Mobilization for Sustainable LDC Graduation of Bhutan in the Context of Emerging Challenges to Development Financing." Working paper, South and South-West Asia Development Papers, no. 22-02, February 2022. https://hdl.handle.net/20.500.12870/4430.

Wangchuk, Tashi. "The Middle Path to Democracy in the Kingdom of Bhutan." *Asian Survey* 44, no. 6 (November/December 2004): 836–855. https://doi.org/10.1525/as.2004.44.6.836.

Wangdi, Kencho. "Do Bhutan's Anti-smoking Laws Go Too Far?" *Time*, April 12, 2011. https://content.time.com/time/world/article/0,8599,2057774,00.html.

Weber, Max. *The Protestant Ethic and the Spirit of Capitalism*. London: Routledge, 2001.

Wedemeyer, Christian K. *Making Sense of Tantric Buddhism: History, Semiology, and Transgression in the Indian Traditions*. New York: Columbia University Press, 2013.

West Asia Development Papers, no. 22-02, February 2022. https://hdl.handle.net/20.500.12870/4430.

Whitecross, Richard W. "The Zhabdrung's Legacy: Buddhism and Constitutional Transformation in Bhutan." In *Buddhism and Comparative Constitutional Law*, eds. Tom Ginsburg and Benjamin Schonthal, 73–98. Cambridge: Cambridge University Press, 2023. https://doi.org/10.1017/9781009286022.007.

Whitecross, Richard. ""Virtuous Beings": The Concept of Tha Damtshing and Being a Moral Person in Contemporary Bhutanese Society." *Himalaya: The Journal of the Association for Nepal and Himalayan Studies* 28, no. 1–2 (2008): 71–82. https://digitalcommons.macalester.edu/himalaya/vol28/iss1/6/.

World Bank. "Mobile Cellular Subscriptions, per 100 People—Bhutan." Accessed January 15, 2024. https://data.worldbank.org/indicator/IT.CEL.SETS.P2?locations=BT.

World Bank. "Proportion of seats held by women in national parliaments in Bhutan from 2012 to 2022." Chart. February 21, 2024. Statista. Accessed February 29, 2024. https://www.statista.com/statistics/730576/bhutan-proportion-of-seats-held-by-women-in-national-parliament/

Zeppa, Jamie. *Beyond the Sky and the Earth: A Journey into Bhutan*. New York: Penguin Group, 2000.

Zitcer, Andrew. "Making up Creative Placemaking." *Journal of Planning Education and Research* 40, no. 3 (September 2020): 278–288. https://doi.org/10.1177/0739456X18773424.

Acknowledgments

This book is the result of a Fulbright grant to Bhutan in 2017–18. Fulbright grants are supported by US taxpayers. As both a taxpayer and a grantee, I would like to express my appreciation for a program dedicated to improving cross-cultural understanding around the world.

I learned so much from the "first batch" of Yonphula Centenary College students: Bal Bahadur Thapa, Chador Wangmo, Cheki, Chime Wangmo, Chimi Dema, Choki Gyeltshen, Dechen Tshomo, Dechhen Dolma, Gyeltshen, Ishor Kumar Bhandari, Lekey, Namgay Tashi, Pema Gyelpo, Pema Tenzin, Pema Wangmo, Pemba, Phub Dema, Rakesh Subba, Sang Tenzin, Shacha, Shedrup Zinjay, Sherub Wangchuk, Sonam Norbu, Sonam Tobgay, Tashi Wangchuk, Thinley Tobgay, Tika Devi Chauhan, Tshering Dorji, Tshewang Eden, Tshoki Dorji, Yangchen Lham, and Yeshey Dorji. These experienced teachers and civil servants taught me persistence and grit, generosity, creativity around obstacles, grace under pressure, and the importance of community.

S. Chitra, director of the English literature M.A. program, was an inspiring model of professionalism and dedication. I also learned a great deal from syllabi and lectures prepared by our fellow instructors. YCC Staff and community members kept the College functioning amid daunting challenges. Tshering Thinley, dean of Yonphula Centenary College, kindly loaned my family furniture to help us organize ourselves in the small Sherubtse guest-house. Like Tshering Wangdi, president of

Sherubtse College, he welcomed us—in all our complexity—with grace and generosity.

We remain deeply grateful to our Kanglung and Sherubtse friends, neighbors, and colleagues, particularly Sonam and Dechen and their family, Phub Namgay, Chencho Dema and Chimi Dorji, Karma and Mr. Pant, our neighbor in the Sherubtse guesthouse. Leyla Rahimi gave us a wonderful introduction to Kanglung when we first arrived, and was a kind and generous presence throughout our stay.

J. P. Das, Fulbright point person in the US Delhi embassy, was a great support when times were particularly challenging, and the Indian Fulbright Commission as a whole put together an amazing and inspiring conference that buoyed our spirits in the early spring.

Swarthmore College generously supports faculty sabbaticals that make it possible to serve as a Fulbright Scholar or work on extended projects such as this book. I am grateful to the College for recognizing and supporting the interdependence of research and teaching.

Rachel Pastan—wonderful novelist, teacher, and friend—demonstrated extreme patience as she helped me wrestle with earlier versions of the story, when it was framed as a memoir (often in search of a narrative arc). Among others, Catherine Kapphahn and Veena Siddharth were particularly helpful in reading and offering useful comments and encouragement.

Sean Guynes of Lever Press was the ideal editor for this project, reading multiple drafts and offering astute commentary that helped shape the shifting material. When I felt stuck in my own rigid definition of an "academic" book, Sean offered models of rigorous texts that remain accessible to a general reader. I am deeply grateful for Sean's intellectual generosity and vision.

Anonymous reviewers engaged by Lever Press offered helpful questions and useful suggestions.

Maria Aghazarian and her cadre of library students—Nicole Barmasai, Brenda Mondragon, and Kayla Nicholas—took on the labor of checking and reformatting footnotes and bibliographic citations, providing alt-text for images, and (maybe) creating transcripts for videos.

James, Zoë, and Jeremy were the best "Fulbright team" I could have had.